Supplement for Vol. 5

CALIFORNIA

PROCEDURE

Second Edition

by B. E. WITKIN
of the San Francisco Bar

Assisted by members of the Publisher's Editorial Staff

1983 SUPPLEMENT
ISSUED IN MAY, 1983

See Supplement
Table of Cases
Table of Code Citations
Index
In Supplement for
Vol. 6 Part II

BANCROFT-WHITNEY CO.
301 Brannan Street
San Francisco, California 94107

BℬW

CALIFORNIA PROCEDURE

Second Edition

1983 SUPPLEMENT

VOLUME FIVE

___

Chapter X

ENFORCEMENT OF JUDGMENT

Sections added in this Supplement:

[3]

EXPLANATORY NOTE: The Execution of Judgment statute (C.C.P. 681 et seq.) was repealed in 1982, effective July 1, 1983, and replaced with a new Enforcement of Judgments Law (C.C.P. 680.010 et seq.). (See Supp., infra, §227A et seq.)

A. [§1] Variety of Methods of Enforcement.

New Law: For the new Enforcement of Judgments law, see Supp., infra, §227A et seq.

See C.E.B., Debt Collection Manual.

B. [§2] Execution on Property.

New Law: For the new Enforcement of Judgments law, see Supp., infra, §227A et seq.

See C.E.B., Debt Collection Manual, Chap. 8.

C. [§3] Other Proceedings.

New Law: For the new Enforcement of Judgments law, see Supp., infra, §227A et seq.

See C.E.B., Debt Collection Manual, Chaps. 9, 13.

(4) *Proceedings against debtor's estate.* In 1980 C.C.P. 686 was repealed and replaced by C.C.P. 686.010, 686.020. Under C.C.P. 686.020, judgments against the decedent must be enforced as provided in the Probate Code. Former Prob.C. 730 was repealed, and a new Prob.C. 730 enacted. The new section collects the various provisions relating to the enforcement of judgments after death; the substance of that portion of former C.C.P. 686 cited in the text is continued in

new Prob.C. 730(d). Clarifying amendments were also made in Prob.C. 716.

p. 3390:

(7) *(New) Application for payment of judgment out of real estate recovery fund:* A special fund has been established to satisfy uncollectible judgments against licensed real estate brokers and salesmen for fraud, misrepresentation, deceit, or conversion of trust funds arising out of a transaction for which the license was required. (B. & P.C. 10470 et seq.; see 1 *Summary, Agency and Employment, §243.*)

Cross-References: 6 *Summary, Parent and Child, §46 et seq.;* 6 *Summary, Husband and Wife, §212;* 7 *Summary, Wills and Probate,* §416 et seq.

D. [§4] Collection Practice.

New Law: For the new Enforcement of Judgments law, see Supp., infra, §227A et seq.

See 17 Santa Clara L. Rev. 685 [Proposals for Limiting Collection Practices].

(2) *Bankruptcy Practice.* See 4 U.C. Davis L. Rev. 301 [wage earner plans]; C.E.B., Debt Collection Manual, Chap. 11.

(3) *Collection Agency Practices.* See C.E.B., Debt Collection Manual, Chap. 1.

(4) *Collections by Individual Attorney.* See C.E.B., Debt Collection Manual, Chaps. 2, 3.

(6) *Enforcement Methods in General.* See C.E.B., Debt Collection Manual, Chaps. 8 et seq.

(8) *Exemptions.* See C.E.B., Debt Collection Manual, Chap. 10.

(11) *Priorities.* See C.E.B., Debt Collection Manual, §12.19 et seq.

p. 1391:

(12) *Third Party Claims.* See C.E.B., Debt Collection Manual, §12.1 et seq.

Cross-References: 1 *Summary, Contracts, §§729, 160, 157, 159.*

E. (New) Fair Debt Collection Practices Act.

1. [§4A] (New) Nature and Scope.

New Law: For the new Enforcement of Judgments law, see Supp., infra, §227A et seq.

The Robbins-Rosenthal Fair Debt Collection Practices Act (C.C. 1788 et seq.), enacted in 1977, regulates the collection of *consumer debts* (C.C. 1788.2(b)). The Act applies to persons and entities engaged in the *debt collection business,* or who compose and sell *form letters* and other *collection media,* but excludes attorneys. (C.C.

1788.2(c)(g).) Consumer debts are those incurred by natural persons to acquire property, services or money for personal, family, or household use. (C.C. 1788.2(e)(f)(h).)

The Act prohibits unfair and deceptive practices (Supp., infra, §4B) and provides cumulative remedies for violations (Supp., infra, §4C). Contemporaneous amendments to the collection agency licensing statute (B. & P.C. 6850 et seq.) (a) empower the Director of Consumer Affairs to establish and enforce regulations implementing the Act's application to licensed agencies, and (b) make violations of the Act grounds for license revocation or other discipline. (B. & P.C. 6863, 6947(b).)

See 9 Pacific L. J. 409.

See generally, C.E.B., Debt Collection Manual, Appendix F [comparison chart of California Fair Debt Collection Act, California Collection Agency Act, and Federal Fair Debt Collection Practices Act].

On the federal Act, see 13 U. S. F. L. Rev. 575; on other state acts, see 87 A.L.R.3d 786.

2. [§4B] (New) Prohibited Practices.

New Law: For the new Enforcement of Judgments law, see Supp., infra, §227A et seq.

Forbidden means of collecting consumer debts fall under the following general categories:

(a) Threats of violence, defamation, or false criminal charges, or of various enforcement measures if the collector does not intend to, or could not legally, carry them out. (C.C. 1788.10.)

(b) Direct harassment by obscene or profane language, abuse of the telephone, or unreasonably frequent communication with the debtor. (C.C. 1788.11.)

(c) Disclosures to third parties by unnecessary communication about a debt with the debtor's employer or family, dissemination of "deadbeat lists" or other advertising naming the debtor, or embarrassing writings addressed to the debtor but intended to be read by others. (C.C. 1788.12.)

(d) False representations of the collector's identity or authority, of the debtor's liability for collection charges, or of intended legal proceedings or assignment for collection. (C.C. 1788.13.)

(e) Overreaching by fraudulently obtaining the debtor's affirmation of a discharged debt, attempting to collect illegal charges, or disregarding a request to address communications to the debtor's attorney (C.C. 1788.14), or by prosecuting judicial proceedings without service of process essential to jurisdiction, or in a county other than that in which the debt was incurred or the debtor then resided or currently resides (C.C. 1788.15).

3. [§4C] (New) Remedies.

New Law: For the new Enforcement of Judgments Law, see Supp., infra, §227A et seq.

(a) *Collector's Liability.* A collector violating the Act is liable for the debtor's actual damages unless the collector shows that the violation occurred unintentionally despite reasonable preventive procedures, or unless a curable violation is corrected within 15 days after its discovery. (C.C. 1788.30(a)(d)(e).) For a wilful, knowing violation, the debtor may also recover a penalty of $100 to $1,000. (C.C. 1788.30(b).)

(b) *Debtor's Conduct as a Defense.* The act forbids credit applications by debtors who knowingly lack ability or intent to pay or who submit fraudulent statements. (C.C. 1788.20.) On written request, the debtor must notify the creditor of changes of address or employment (C.C. 1788.21), refrain from using expired or suspended credit privileges, and notify the creditor of the loss of a credit card (C.C. 1788.22). A creditor may raise the debtor's intentional violation of these provisions as a defense to an action under the Act. (C.C. 1788.30(g).)

(c) *Nature of Action.* To enforce the collector's liability, the debtor may sue *in an individual capacity only* within *one year* of the violation. (C.C. 1788.30(f).) The prevailing party is entitled to costs; a prevailing debtor is also entitled to attorney's fees; and a prevailing creditor may be awarded attorney's fees on a finding of the debtor's lack of good faith. (C.C. 1788.30(c).) The action is cumulative to other remedies. (C.C. 1788.32; see B. & P.C. 6947(b), 6947.1 [collection agency's liability for violating Act].)

1. [§5] In General.

New Law: For the new Enforcement of Judgments law, see Supp., infra, §227A et seq.

See *In Re Marriage of Utigard* (1981) 126 C.A.3d 133, 178 C.R. 546.

(1) [§8] Alternative Method of Enforcement.

New Law: For the new Enforcement of Judgments law, see Supp., infra, §227A et seq.

Under C.C. 4383(a), operative July 1, 1983, support payments not more than 10 years overdue may be enforced by execution without prior court approval. C.C. 4383(b) requires that the application for writ of execution be accompanied by an affidavit stating the total amount not more than 10 years overdue and, if interest is sought, the amount thereof and the amount and due date of each unpaid installment. A copy of the affidavit must be served on the judgment debtor when the writ is first served.

Under C.C. 4385, operative July 1, 1983, any support judgment made, entered, or enforceable in California is enforceable under C.C. 4380 et seq.

Cross-Reference: 6 *Summary, Husband and Wife,* §172.

(2) [§9] Issuance Discretionary.

New Law: For the new Enforcement of Judgments law, see Supp., infra, §227A et seq.

(a) *Rule and Theory.* See *Jackson v. Jackson* (1975) 51 C.A.3d 363, 367, 124 C.R. 101; *Wyshak v. Wyshak* (1977) 70 C.A.4d 384, 394, 138 C.R. 811, citing the text.

C.C. 4384, operative July 1, 1983, requires the court to consider "lack of diligence for more than 10 years in seeking enforcement" of a support judgment, but does not preclude enforcement even if lack of diligence is shown.

p. 3394:

(b) *Procedure.* Execution on an *ex parte* application does not violate the *Sniadach* rule of due process (see 5 *Summary, Constitutional Law,* §296). (*Wyshak v. Wyshak,* supra.) In *Wyshak* the court said: "[R]espondent did have a postjudgment execution hearing, a hearing on noticed motion to recall the writ of execution and to quash the writ and levy, and order for appearance of judgment debtor; he had an opportunity to present any defenses he may have had to the issuance of the writ and the levy made by petitioner." (70 C.A.3d 394.)

See C.E.B., Debt Collection Manual, §8.52 et seq.

p. 3395:

(d) *Execution Denied.* In *Jackson v. Jackson,* supra, plaintiff wife and defendant husband were divorced, and custody of their 16-year-old daughter was awarded to plaintiff. Thereafter, with the consent of the wife, the daughter went to live with her father, and he supported her by expending amounts well in excess of the court-ordered support payments of $750 per month. More than 2 years later, after the husband had succeeded in modifying the decree to eliminate support payments, plaintiff had a writ of execution issued for the arrearages during 22 months. The lower court denied a motion to quash the writ on the ground that it was an attempt to obtain a retroactive modification of the support order. *Held,* reversed. A support order may not be retroactively modified, and accrued arrearages are treated as a judgment for money; but the court has discretion to deny enforcement on equitable grounds. (51 C.A.3d 367.) Here the equitable circumstances were clear: The purpose of the support order had been fulfilled, and it should not be used as a weapon by the former wife against the former husband. (51 C.A.3d 368, 369.)

In *Szamocki v. Szamocki* (1975) 47 C.A.3d 812, 121 C.R. 231, the wife took the child out of the state, remarried, concealed her whereabouts, and had the child adopted by her new husband. *Held,* the husband was justified in assuming that she wanted no further contact or support payments. (47 C.A.3d 819, 820.)

Cross-Reference: 6 Summary, Parent and Child, §124.

(a) [§11] In General.

New Law: For the new Enforcement of Judgments law, see Supp., infra, §227A et seq.

C.C.P. 688 was amended and subdivided, effective January 1, 1976, to bring it into conformity with the new attachment law. (See *Provisional Remedies,* Supp., §§311A, 312A.) New C.C.P. 688(a) continues the wording quoted in the text except that "subject to execution" is substituted for "liable to execution."

(b) [§12] Intangibles.

New Law: For the new Enforcement of Judgments law, see Supp., infra, §227A et seq.

C.C.P. 688 should be C.C.P. 688(a), effective January 1, 1976. (See Supp., supra, §11.) A new subsection (f) was added to C.C.P. 688, effective January 1, 1977, to continue the authority of former C.C.P. 542(6) (see *Provisional Remedies,* §165) to permit attachment of checks, drafts, etc., which come into the possession of the levying officer (see *Provisional Remedies,* Supp., §354A). C.C.P. 688(f) was relettered C.C.P. 688(g) in 1977.

(a) [§13] In General.

New Law: For the new Enforcement of Judgments law, see Supp., infra, §227A et seq.

Cross-References: 3 Summary, Real Property, §222; 6 Summary, Corporations, §38.

(b) [§14] Equitable Interests.

New Law: For the new Enforcement of Judgments Law, see Supp., infra, §227A et seq.

Cross-Reference: 7 Summary, Trusts, §94 et seq.

(a) [§16] Contingent Interests.

New Law: For the new Enforcement of Judgments law, see Supp., infra, §227A et seq.

(New) Cash surrender value of life insurance policy: Unless and until the insured exercises his option to surrender the policy for its cash surrender value, the insurance company does not owe a definite sum. Hence the cash surrender value is not property of the insured but an expectancy which is not subject to execution by his judgment creditor. (*Equico Lessors v. Metropolitan Life Ins. Co.* (1978) 88 C.A.3d Supp. 6, 8, 151 C.R. 618, citing the text.)

Cross-References: 1 *Summary, Contracts,* §739; 3 *Summary, Real Property,* §285.

(b) [§17] Privileges and Licenses.

New Law: For the new Enforcement of Judgments law, see Supp., infra, §227A et seq.

p. 3400:

(2) *State Business or Professional License.* C.C.P. 688 should be C.C.P. 688(f), effective January 1, 1978. (See Supp., supra, §11; Supp., infra, §73A.)

(c) [§18] Other Rights and Interests.

New Law: For the new Enforcement of Judgments law, see Supp., infra, §227A et seq.

p. 3401:

(3) *Choses in action not represented by writing.* The provision of C.C.P. 688, that "no cause of action nor judgment as such" is subject to execution, is continued in C.C.P. 688(f), effective January 1, 1978. (See Supp., supra, §11; Supp., infra, § 73.)

On the enforcement of state tax liens, despite the provisions of C.C.P. 688(f), see 5 *Summary, Taxation,* Supp., §95B.

Cross-Reference: 3 *Summary, Real Property,* §412.

(b) [§20] Cemetery Lots and Pews.

New Law: For the new Enforcement of Judgments law, see Supp., infra, §227A et seq.

(1) *Cemetery lots and improvements.* C.C.P. 690.24 was amended, effective January 1, 1974, to delete reference to attachment, to bring it into conformity with the new attachment law. (See *Provisional Remedies,* Supp., §312A.)

(1) [§21] In General.

New Law: For the new Enforcement of Judgments law, see Supp., infra, §227A et seq.

Error: Page 3403, line 8, 1 A.L.R.2d 936 should be 1 A.L.R.3d 936.

(a) [§25] Nature of Exemption Statutes.

New Law: For the new Enforcement of Judgments law, see Supp., infra, §227A et seq.

See C.E.B., Debt Collection Manual, Chap. 10.

(1) *Exemption of Property and Exemptions of Debtor.* A Uniform Exemptions Act was adopted by the Commissioners in 1976. (See 13 U.L.A. (Master Ed. 365.)

On exemptions under the Employees' Earnings Protection Law, see Supp., infra, §133K et seq.

For a criticism of existing exemption laws as applied to farmers, see 11 U. C. Davis L. Rev. 573.

(New) No exemption for professional corporations: The exemption statutes are for the personal benefit of the debtor as an individual, i.e., as a natural person. (*Canal-Randolph Anaheim v. Wilkoski* (1980) 103 C.A.3d 282, 291, 292, 163 C.R. 30, quoting the text.) In the *Wilkoski* case plaintiff lessor obtained a judgment for unpaid rent against defendant Wilkoski, a professional law corporation, and levied on the corporation's law office equipment and books. Wilkoski filed a claim of exemption on behalf of the corporation under C.C.P. 690.4 (text, §54). *Held,* the claim was properly denied. The language of C.C.P. 690.4, and the history of exemption statutes, make it clear that the Legislature intended only to protect the individual debtor and his family, not a partnership or corporation. (103 C.A.3d 290, 291, 292.) Professional corporations are not entitled to different treatment; they enjoy the commercial benefits of other corporate entities. (103 C.A.3d 292, 293). Hence, as the Supreme Court indicated in an early partnership case, one who desires to form a partnership or corporation must retain exclusive ownership of his tools and implements or he will lose his statutory exemption as to that property. (103 C.A.3d 293.)

p. 3406:

(3) *Liberal Construction.* On constitutionality of *retroactive application* of exemption statutes, see 9 Pacific L. J. 889.

(4) *Revision of 1970.*

p. 3407:

(b) C.C.P. 710 was amended in 1976 to delete the special procedure for reaching wages of public employees. (See Supp., infra, §134.)

(c) C.C.P. 690.18 was amended in 1980 to except from the exemption provided by that section court-ordered child and spousal support payments under specified conditions (see Supp., infra, §58), and conforming amendments were made in Educ.C. 22005 (former Educ.C. 13808) and Govt.C. 21201.

(6) *(New) Alternative Exemptions Available to Individual General Assignor for Benefit of Creditors.* C.C.P. 690.60, added in 1979, deals with individuals who execute general assignments for the benefit of creditors. They may claim (a) the exemptions under C.C.P. 690 et seq., and the homestead exemption under C.C. 1237 et seq., or (b) the exemptions set forth in C.C.P. 690.60. (See 11 Pacific L. J. 339.)

Cross-Reference: 7 *Summary, Wills and Probate,* §517 et seq.

(c) [§27] Alimony and Support Claims.

New Law: For the new Enforcement of Judgments law, see Supp., infra, §227A et seq.

C.C.P. 674.5 was amended in 1976 to provide for enforcement of judgments for "spousal or child support."

C.C.P. 690.6 has been repealed. (See Supp., infra, §60.)

(d) [§28] No Exemption: Judgment for Price or Foreclosure.

New Law: For the new Enforcement of Judgments law, see Supp., infra, §227A et seq.

C.C.P. 690.52 was amended, effective July 1, 1975, to state that its provisions do not prevail over new C.C.P. 690.235. The amendment was repealed as of July 1, 1977, when C.C.P. 690.235 itself was repealed and replaced by new C.C.P. 690.31. (See Supp., infra, §49A.)

(a) [§29] Nature.

New Law: For the new Enforcement of Judgments law, see Supp., infra, §227A et seq.

See 9 Pacific L. J. 723 [Homestead Legislation in California; study prepared for California Law Revision Commission]; C.E.B., Debt Collection Manual, §10.29 et seq.

On the policy of the law, see *Katsivalis v. Serrano Reconveyance Co.* (1977) 70 C.A.3d 200, 212, 138 C.R. 620.

C.C. 1260 was subsectioned and amended in 1980. The citation in the text should now be to C.C. 1260(a)(1); as amended the limit is now $45,000.

Cross-Reference: 7 *Summary, Wills and Probate,* §514 et seq.

[§29A] (New) Necessity of Declaration.

New Law: For the new Enforcement of Judgments law, see Supp., infra, §227A et seq.

In *Taylor v. Madigan* (1975) 53 C.A.3d 943, 126 C.R. 376, plaintiffs, in a class action, attacked the statutes requiring a timely claim of the homestead exemption, contending that execution on a money judgment without notice and an opportunity to claim the exemption was a violation of the debtor's constitutional rights. *Held,* the statutes were not subject to any of the constitutional challenges made.

(1) Plaintiffs first argued that Cal. Const., Art. XVII, §1 (text, §37), stating that "The Legislature shall protect, by law, from forced sale a certain portion of the homestead and other property of all heads of families," is self-executing, and creates the exemption free from any restrictions placed on it by the Legislature. The court, citing authorities on the test of self-executing provisions (53 C.A.3d 950; see 5 *Summary, Constitutional Law,* §38), and decisions on the homestead laws, concluded that the constitutional provision is not operative without legislation. (53 C.A.3d 955, 960): "[T]he Constitution does not require that the homes of all homeowning families in California be exempted from forced sale to satisfy judgment debts. . . . This constitutional mandate gave to the Legislature a vast discretion and control and the right to impose *reasonable* requirements and regulations as to the manner and method of perfecting the claim of exemption, and the right to exempt the homesteads exists only upon compliance with such requirements." (53 C.A.3d 960.)

(2) Plaintiffs' second challenge, based on the *Sniadach* line of cases (see *Provisional Remedies,* §224 and Supp., §118A), was likewise found untenable. The cases invoked dealt with prejudgment proceedings taking a debtor's property without any notice and opportunity to be heard; here the debtors received ample notice in the process served and had the opportunity for a hearing on the merits in the action. And due process does not require either (a) an original notice informing the defendant of the necessity of claiming the exemption, or (b) a second notice of this right at the time of levy of exemption. (53 C.A.3d 963, 964.)

(3) Plaintiffs' third attack, on equal protection grounds, pointed to differences in treatment of probate homesteads and mobilehomes (53 C.A.3d 967); the court found no unconstitutional discrimination in the classifications. (53 C.A.3d 972.)

See 9 Pacific L. J. 724.

(1) [§30] Who May Select.

New Law: For the new Enforcement of Judgments law, see Supp., infra, §227A et seq.

C.C. 1260 was subsectioned in 1980.

(a) *Head of a Family.*

p. 3410:

C.C. 1260(a)(1) was amended in 1976, 1978, and 1980. The limit is now $45,000.

C.C. 1261(1) was amended in 1976 to cover wives as well as husbands when the claimant is married; and C.C. 1260(2)(e) was amended to cover unmarried brothers as well as sisters.

C.C. 1262 was amended in 1976 to permit either spouse to execute the declaration.

(b) *Person 65 Years of Age.* C.C. 1260(a)(2) was amended in 1976, 1978, and 1980. The limit is now $45,000.

(c) *Any Other Person.* C.C. 1260(a)(3) was amended in 1976, 1978, and 1980. The limit is now $30,000.

See 8 Pacific L. J. 460; 10 Pacific L. J. 356.

(2) [§31] Property.

New Law: For the new Enforcement of Judgments law, see Supp., infra, §227A et seq.

(b) *Sources for Married Claimant.*

(4) *Joint tenancy or tenancy in common.* The citation should now be C.C. 1238(c), as amended in 1976.

(5) *Separate property of wife.* The separate property of both spouses is now governed by C.C. 1238(c), as amended in 1976. The special restrictions of former C.C. 1239 were repealed.

See 8 Pacific L. J. 460.

Cross-References: 7 Summary, Community Property, §§3 et seq., 127, 4.

(3) [§32] Value.

New Law: For the new Enforcement of Judgments law, see Supp., infra, §227A et seq.

(a) *Limits.* As amended in 1980, the limits prescribed by C.C. 1260 are $45,000, $45,000 and $30,000 respectively.

(c) *Retroactivity of Increased Limits.* C.C. 1260 was amended in 1976 to make the new limits (supra, this section) effective as to declarations filed prior to January 1, 1977, subject to the same conditions noted in the text.

See 8 Pacific L. J. 457; 10 Pacific L. J. 356.

A 1979 amendment deletes "January 1, 1977" and substitutes "the operative date of any amendment." (See 11 Pacific L. J. 615.)

On constitutionality of retroactive application of exemption statutes, see 9 Pacific L. J. 889.

(4) [§33] Procedure in Creation.

New Law: For the new Enforcement of Judgments law, see Supp., infra, §227A et seq.

p. 3413:

(a) *Homestead of Head of Family.* C.C. 1263 was amended in 1976 to provide that either spouse may make the declaration and that, if the other does not join, the declaring spouse must state that it is made for their joint benefit. The section was further amended to delete the provision for augmentation of value. (See Supp., supra, §32.)

See 8 Pacific L. J. 460.

(New) Property rights between spouses. C.C. 1263 was amended in 1976 to provide: "The declaration of a homestead shall not affect the property rights of spouses as between themselves other than as provided by this title." (See *Bonner v. Superior Court* (1976) 63 C.A.3d 156, 133 C.R. 592, 7 *Summary, Community Property,* Supp., §94 [on dissolution of marriage, court can order homesteaded community property sold to effect equal property division under C.C. 4800].)

p. 3414:

(e) *False Statements.* The requirement of an estimate of actual cash value was deleted from C.C. 1263 in 1969.

(5) [§34] Conveyance.

New Law: For the new Enforcement of Judgments law, see Supp., infra, §227A et seq.

(b) *Conveyance of Married Person's Homestead.* See *Katsivalis v. Serrano Reconveyance Co.* (1977) 70 C.A.3d 200, 208, 138 C.R. 620 [husband and wife must each personally execute and acknowledge; husband's execution pursuant to her recorded power of attorney would not suffice].

Cross-Reference: 7 *Summary, Community Property,* §80.

(6) [§35] Abandonment.

New Law: For the new Enforcement of Judgments law, see Supp., infra, §227A et seq.

Cross-Reference: 7 *Summary, Community Property,* §80.

(7) [§36] Disposition on Death or Dissolution of Marriage.

New Law: For the new Enforcement of Judgments law, see Supp., infra, §227A et seq.

(a) *Death.* Prob.C. 660 et seq. were amended in 1980 to repeal the right of survivorship in declared homesteads. (See 12 Pacific L. J. 533.) (For transitional provisions on homesteads declared prior to the effective date of the repeal, see Stats. 1980, Chap. 119, §22 [does not apply to declared homesteads which were previously *set apart* pursuant to Prob.C. 660 et seq.].)

Cross-References: 7 Summary, Wills and Probate, §513; 7 Summary, Community Property, §94.

(1) [§37] In General.

New Law: For the new Enforcement of Judgments law, see Supp., infra, §227A et seq.

On exemption of dwelling not homestead, see Supp., infra, §49A.

(New) Priority over tax lien: Although tax liens generally have priority over a recorded homestead (Rev.C. 2192.1), Rev.C. 2191.4, providing for a lien for personal property taxes, expressly states that the lien has the priority of a *judgment lien.* Hence, when the declaration of homestead is recorded, this particular tax lien, like a judgment lien, is inferior. (*Curtis v. Kern* (1974) 37 C.A.3d 704, 706, 113 C.R. 41.)

On the policy of the law, see *Katsivalis v. Serrano Reconveyance Co.* (1977) 70 C.A.3d 200, 212, 138 C.R. 620.

(2) [§38] Retroactive Effect.

New Law: For the new Enforcement of Judgments law, see Supp., infra, §227A et seq.

(a) *Defeats existing attachment lien:* In *Becker v. Lindsay* (1976) 16 C.3d 188, 127 C.R. 348, 545 P.2d 260, the long established rule that a declaration of homestead, recorded before judgment, defeats a prior attachment lien, was challenged on a highly technical theory of statutory interpretation. The rule was established by the case law prior to the 1951 amendment of C.C. 1241(4), dealing with the exception for debts secured by mortgages executed and recorded before recording of the homestead. The 1951 Legislature changed the word "mortgages" to "encumbrances" (see text, §42). Plaintiff, citing C.C. 1114 (encumbrances include "all liens") and C.C.P. 542a (attachment "shall be a lien upon all real property attached"), argued that the amendment changed the law. *Held,* the argument was untenable.

(1) The original "mortgage" language was construed by the courts to embrace deeds absolute, and it was intimated that it might apply to trust deeds. Thus, its language was misleading, and it was to be expected that the Legislature intended to codify the decisions rather than to modify the law. (16 C.3d 191, 192.)

(2) Two other reasons for this conclusion appear in the amended language: (a) The section speaks of "encumbrances executed and recorded"; an execution is issued, not executed. (b) To give the statute the construction urged would mean that an attachment which was not a valid lien would prevail; i.e., once signed by the clerk and recorded, the attachment would defeat the homestead even though an attachment does not become a valid lien until it is served (C.C.P. 542a). (16 C.3d 192, 193.)

(3) All commentators agree that, although the attachment is an encumbrance within many contexts, it is not "an encumbrance executed and recorded" for the purposes of C.C. 1241(4). (16 C.3d 193, quoting the text.)

(4) At the very least, the wording suggests that it is doubtful that the section subordinates a homestead to the attachment lien, and the court must follow the policy of liberal construction of the homestead exemption. (16 C.3d 193, 194, quoting the text, p. 3416.) This policy assumes peculiar importance because countless homesteaders undoubtedly relied on earlier pronouncements. (16 C.3d 194.)

(3) [§39] Temporary Exemption of Proceeds.

New Law: For the new Enforcement of Judgments law, see Supp., infra, §227A et seq.

See *Ortale v. Mulhern* (1976) 58 C.A.3d 861, 864, 130 C.R. 277 [proceeds of sale are those payable to seller from escrow after deduction of expenses of sale].

p. 3418:

In 1979, C.C. 1257 was repealed and replaced by a new section of the same number. (See Supp., infra, §45A.)

(5) [§41] Inequitable Conduct of Homestead Claimants.

New Law: For the new Enforcement of Judgments law, see Supp., infra, §227A et seq.

C.C. 1245 was repealed and replaced by a new section of the same number. (See Supp., infra, §45A.)

Cross-Reference: 3 *Summary, Real Property,* §169.

(1A)   [§42A]   (New) Prior Agreements Affecting Condominium and Similar Interests.

New Law: For the new Enforcement of Judgments law, see Supp., infra, §227A et seq.

C.C. 1237 was amended in 1970 and 1973 to provide that "an *agreement, covenant, or restriction* between or binding upon the owners of a title, interest, or estate in a *condominium, planned development, stock cooperative, or community apartment project,* or a *lien* arising under such agreement, covenant, or restriction, or an underlying *lease or sublease, indebtedness, security, or other interest or obligation* may be enforced in the same manner as if *no homestead were declared.* . . ." (See 5 Pacific L. J. 455.)

(2)   [§43]   Encumbrance Created by Homestead Claimant.

New Law: For the new Enforcement of Judgments law, see Supp., infra, §227A et seq.

C.C. 1256 was repealed and replaced by a new section of the same number. (See Supp., infra, §45A.)

(3)   [§44]   Favored Claimants.

New Law: For the new Enforcement of Judgments law, see Supp., infra, §227A et seq.

(b) *Defrauded Creditor.* See *Stoner v. Walsh* (1972) 24 C.A.3d 938, 942, 101 C.R. 485.

(1)   [§45]   Exclusive Procedure.

New Law: For the new Enforcement of Judgments law, see Supp., infra, §227A et seq.

C.C. 1260 was amended in 1976, 1978, and 1980. The limits are now $45,000 and $30,000. (See Supp., supra, §32.)

See *Swearingen v. Byrne* (1977) 67 C.A.3d 580, 136 C.R. 736 [judgment lien did not attach to excess value; procedure of C.C. 1245 et seq. is exclusive]; *Engelman v. Gordon* (1978) 82 C.A.3d 174, 179, 146 C.R. 835 [same, following *Blue v. Superior Court*]; *Wells Fargo Bank v. PAL Investments* (1979) 96 C.A.3d 431, 434, 157 C.R. 818 [same].

The procedure under C.C. 1245 is still exclusive for a *dwelling house which is homesteaded,* despite the enactment of C.C.P. 690.31. (*Krause v. Superior Court* (1978) 78 C.A.3d 499, 144 C.R. 194, Supp., infra, §49D.) However, in 1979 the procedural provisions on declared homesteads were amended to make them virtually identical with those in C.C.P. 690.31. (See Supp., infra, §45A.)

See C.E.B., Debt Collection Manual, §8.30 et seq.

(1A) [§45A] (New) Procedure in Effect on January 1, 1980.

New Law: For the new Enforcement of Judgments law, see Supp., infra, §227A et seq.

(a) *Nature and Purpose of Changes.* With the adoption of the dwelling house exemption (see Supp., infra, §49C), two separate statutory methods were provided for reaching the excess value of the residence of a judgment debtor. (See *Krause v. Superior Court* (1978) 78 C.A.3d 499, 508, 144 C.R. 194, Supp., infra, §49D.) The 1979 Legislature repealed C.C. 1245 et seq. and enacted new C.C. 1245 et seq. which, with a few exceptions, adopt the procedures prescribed by C.C.P. 690.31 for the dwelling house exemption. (See 11 Pacific L. J. 611.) The new provisions do not affect any benefits under C.C.P. 690.31, irrespective of whether a declaration of homestead has been recorded, or a judgment has been entered prior to the recordation of a declaration of homestead. (C.C. 1259.2.)

(b) *Application for Writ of Execution.* New C.C. 1245 contains the same basic provisions as C.C.P. 690.31(c), and C.C. 1250 and 1253 follow C.C.P. 690.31(f) and C.C.P. 690.31(i). (See Supp., infra, §49C.) When the value of the property exceeds the exemption, the application must state whether the property may be divided without "material injury." (See 11 Pacific L. J. 612.)

(c) *Order To Show Cause and Notice.* New C.C. 1246 and 1257 follow the provisions of C.C.P. 690.31(d)(l) and C.C.P. 690.31(o). (See Supp., infra, §49C.)

(d) *Hearing and Order.* New C.C. 1247(a) and 1250 follow the provisions of C.C.P. 690.31(e) and C.C.P. 690.31(f). (See Supp., infra, §49C.) C.C. 1247(b) has special provisions for appointment of appraisers, and C.C. 1248 and 1249 have special provisions for the court's order on the issue of division of the property without "material injury." (See 11 Pacific L. J. 614.)

(e) *When Debtor Fails To Appear.* C.C. 1251 and 1257 follow the provisions of C.C.P. 690.31(g) and C.C.P. 690.31(p), and C.C. 1252 follow those of C.C.P. 690.31(h). (See Supp., infra, §49C.)

(f) *Reaching Excess Value.* C.C. 1254 contains special provisions on sale of the residence. No bid may be accepted unless it exceeds the exemption and all liens and encumbrances and is "not less than 90 per cent of the appraised fair market value." (C.C. 1254(a).) If no such bid is received, the court may, on motion of the judgment creditor, permit acceptance of a bid which at least exceeds the exemption and all liens and encumbrances, or it may issue a new order for sale of the homestead. (C.C. 1254(b).) Sales authorized by the new law must be conducted within 6 months of the date of issuance of the writ of execution. (C.C. 1254(c).) (See 11 Pacific L. J. 614.)

Otherwise, new C.C. 1255 follows the provisions of C.C.P. 690.31(j), and C.C. 1256 follows those of C.C.P. 690.31(k). (See Supp., infra, §49C.)

(2) [§46] Levy, Petition and Appraisal.

New Law: For the new Enforcement of Judgments law, see Supp., infra, §227A et seq.

On the new procedures, effective January 1, 1980, see Supp., supra, §45A. On costs, see new C.C. 1259.

(b) *Petition for Appraisers.*

p. 3423:

No lien or possibility of execution if filing and service not made in time: See *Swearingen v. Byrne* (1977) 67 C.A.3d 580, 136 C.R. 736, Supp., supra, §45.

See C.E.B., Debt Collection Manual, §8.30 et seq.

(aa) [§47] In General.

New Law: For the new Enforcement of Judgments law, see Supp., infra, §227A et seq.

On the new procedures, effective January 1, 1980, see Supp., supra, §45A.

p. 3424:

Exemption of proceeds: See *Lee v. Brown* (1976) 18 C.3d 110, 116, 132 C.R. 649, 553 P.2d 1121, *Appeal,* Supp., §141B.

See C.E.B., Debt Collection Manual, §§8.36, 8.37.

(bb) [§48] Homestead on Undivided Interest.

New Law: For the new Enforcement of Judgments law, see Supp., infra, §227A et seq.

On the new procedures, effective January 1, 1980, see Supp., supra, §45A.

p. 3426:

Error: Line 15, C.C.P. 1254 should be C.C. 1254.

2A. (New) Dwelling Not Homesteaded.

(a) [§49A] (New) Nature and Purpose of Legislation.

New Law: For the new Enforcement of Judgments law, see Supp., infra, §227A et seq.

The policy of the homestead laws to prevent debtors from becoming homeless (see text, §37) has been largely unrealized, for most debtors fail to declare a homestead on their residences. (See 6 Pacific L. J. 213.) C.C.P. 690.235, adopted in 1974 and effective July 1, 1975, extended to such debtors an exemption substantially equivalent to that of a declared homestead. Its application, however, was prospective; it did not affect rights of a lienholder or encumbrancer vested prior to its operative date. (Stats. of 1974, Chap. 1251, §6.)

C.C.P. 682b, which was part of this statute, required notice of the right to claim an exemption *after* a writ of execution had issued. (See 64 Cal. L. Rev. 180.) In 1976 C.C.P. 682b and 690.235 were repealed and replaced by C.C.P. 690.31, effective July 1, 1977. The new law gives the debtor the right to a hearing on his claim of exemption *before* a writ of execution may issue. (See 8 Pacific L. J. 226.) Amendments enacted by 1977 urgency legislation were also effective July 1, 1977, and are therefore treated here as part of the new law.

The former procedure continued until July 1, 1977, and rights vested under that procedure are not affected by the new law. (Stats. of 1976, Chap. 1000, §5.) (On the former procedure, see Supp., infra, §49B; on the new procedure, see Supp., infra, §49C.)

(New) Retroactive effect: In *Daylin Medical & Surgical Supply, Inc. v. Thomas* (1977) 69 C.A.3d Supp. 37, 138 C.R. 878, the Los Angeles Superior Court Appellate Department held the exemption for an *undeclared* homestead ineffective against a judgment obtained before the operative date of former C.C.P. 690.235 but recorded thereafter; recognition of a residential exemption without a declared homestead would be an unconstitutional impairment of contract. (69 C.A.3d Supp. 41.) (See 9 Pacific L. J. 745.)

In *San Diego White Truck Co. v. Swift* (1979) 96 C.A.3d 88, 157 C.R. 745, the court refused to follow the Appellate Department decision in *Daylin.* (1) The statutory language reflects the legislative intent to include all debtors regardless of when the debt was incurred. (96 C.A.3d 92.) (2) Under the modern approach to the Contract Clause a statute furthering a legitimate state interest may be given valid retroactive effect. (96 C.A.3d 93, 94.)

See *San Diego etc. Group Ins. v. Lorea* (1980) 112 C.A.3d 221, 169 C.R. 157 [distinguishing *San Diego White Truck,* supra; abstract of judgment filed *before* effective date of C.C.P. 690.31].

(b) **[§49B]** (New) **Former Procedure.**

New Law: For the new Enforcement of Judgments law, see Supp., infra, §227A et seq.

(1) *Nature of Exemption.* An exemption could be claimed in "A

dwelling house in which the debtor, or the family of the debtor actually resides, to the same extent and in the same amount, except as otherwise provided in this section, as the debtor or the spouse . . . would be entitled to select *as a homestead . . . ; provided that neither such debtor nor the spouse . . . has an existing declared homestead* on any property in this state." (C.C.P. 690.235(a).) (On the nature, extent and amount of a declared homestead, see text, §30 et seq. and Supp.)

(2) *Notice of Exemption.* C.C.P. 682b (replaced on July 1, 1977 by C.C.P. 690.31(d)(g)) prescribed a form of notice which advised the debtor of the exemption and how to claim it. A copy of this notice had to accompany the application for a writ of execution against any real property containing a dwelling house. (C.C.P. 682b(a).) No writ could issue without such a copy, and the copy had to be served with the writ. (C.C.P. 682b(b)(c).) Proof of service of the notice also had to be made with the return of the writ. (C.C.P. 683, as amended effective July 1, 1975.)

(3) *Claim of Exemption.* The procedure for claiming and resisting the claim was the same as that for other exemptions (see text, §89 et seq.), with these differences: The affidavit of exemption had to be delivered within 20 rather than 10 days from the levy, and the counter-affidavit had to be delivered within 10 rather than 5 days after service of the affidavit of exemption. (C.C.P. 690.50(a)(b)(c), as amended effective July 1, 1975.) These amendments were repealed, and the procedural differences were eliminated, effective July 1, 1977. (See 9 Pacific L. J. 376.)

(4) *When Execution Allowed.* Exceptions to the exemption similar to those provided by C.C. 1241 for declared homesteads were recognized: (1) Judgment liens recorded "prior to the acquisition of the property . . . or the commencement of residence, whichever last occurs." (C.C.P. 690.235(b); see text, §42.) (2) Debts secured by various mechanics' liens. (C.C.P. 690.235(c)(1); see text, §44.) (3) Debts secured by encumbrances "executed and acknowledged by husband and wife, by a claimant of a married person's separate property, or by an unmarried claimant." (C.C.P. 690.235(c)(2); see text, §43.) (4) Debts secured by encumbrances "executed and recorded prior to or in connection with the acquisition of the property by the debtor or the spouse of the debtor." (C.C.P. 690.235(c)(3); see text, §42.)

(5) *Reaching Excess Value.* If the property was sold at an execution sale, the proceeds were applied "first, to the discharge of all liens and encumbrances, if any, on the property; second, to the debtor in the amount of the exemption . . . ; third, to the satisfaction of the execution; and fourth, to the debtor." (C.C.P. 690.235(d); see text, §45 et seq.) The portion which represented the exemption was

"exempt for a period of six months from the date of receipt of such proceeds." (C.C.P. 690.235(e); see *Ortale v. Mulhern* (1976) 58 C.A.3d 861, 864, 130 C.R. 277.)

(c) [§49C] (New) Procedure Effective July 1, 1977.

New Law: For the new Enforcement of Judgments law, see Supp., infra, §227A et seq.

(1) *Nature of Exemption.* New C.C.P. 690.31(a) is the same as C.C.P. 690.235(a) (see Supp., supra, §49B), except that the proviso regarding existing declared homesteads has been transferred to subsection (b), in which all exceptions are stated. (See infra, this section.) Section 690.31(a) also defines "dwelling house" to include the dwelling and "outbuildings and the land on which the same are situated," and, as amended in 1978, also applies to mobilehomes to the same extent. (See Supp., infra, §49E.)

(2) *When No Exemption Allowed.* C.C.P. 690.31(b) states the same basic exceptions as C.C.P. 690.235(a)(b), but with some changes: (a) When there is already a declared homestead on other property, *unless it is claimed under C.C. 1300* (see text, §30). (C.C.P. 690.31(b)(1).) (b) When the judgment or abstract thereof *or any other obligation which by statute is given the force and effect of a judgment lien* is recorded prior to the acquisition or residency of the dwelling by the debtor. (C.C.P. 690.31(b)(2).) (c) When the debt is secured by various mechanics' liens; by encumbrances on the premises by husband and wife, etc.; or by purchase money encumbrances. (C.C.P. 690.31(b)(3).)

(3) *Application for Writ of Execution.* Judgment creditors seeking to execute on a dwelling house must file a verified application with a superior, municipal, or justice court (as determined under C.C.P. 392(2)) in the county in which the dwelling is located. (C.C.P. 690.31(c).) The application must state that either or both of the following facts exist: (a) The dwelling is not exempt, and that a reasonable search has not disclosed a declared homestead, or valid claim of homeowner's exemption; or (b) the dwelling's current value, above liens and encumbrances, exceeds the allowable exemption. (C.C.P. 690.31(c)(1)(2).) If the judgment was rendered in another county, a filing fee must be paid: $4 if in a justice court, or $6 if in a municipal or superior court. An abstract of the judgment must also be filed. (C.C.P. 690.31(c); see 9 Pacific L. J. 375.) If the application is granted, the court clerk must send a copy of the order to the court rendering the judgment. (C.C.P. 690.31(f).)

If a prior application has been denied within the preceding 12 months, the application must also "be supported by a statement under oath alleging that there is a material change of circumstances affecting the exemption, and setting forth facts supporting such claimed material change of circumstances." (C.C.P. 690.31(i).)

(4) *Order To Show Cause and Notice.* The court sets a time and place for hearing and orders the debtor to show cause why the writ should not issue. Copies of the order, the judgment creditor's application, and a special notice must be served 10 days before the hearing, *by mail* on the defendant and the owner shown on the tax rolls, and *personally* on the occupant or the occupant's employee, agent, or family or household member found on the property. If there is no occupant when service is attempted, the copies must be posted. The notice must be in prescribed form and printed in 10-point type in English and Spanish. (C.C.P. 690.31(d)(*l*)(o).) Proof of service must accompany a return of the writ. (C.C.P. 683.) (See 9 Pacific L. J. 376.)

(5) *Hearing and Order.* The debtor has the burden of proving his right to the exemption. (C.C.P. 690.31(e)(1).) The creditor has the burden of proving an excess in value above the allowable exemption. (C.C.P. 690.31(e)(2).) If the court finds that the dwelling is not exempt, or, although it is exempt, the judgment creditor is entitled to levy on the excess, it must order that a writ of execution issue. The order must state "whether or not the dwelling house is exempt and, if not exempt, . . . that the judgment creditor is entitled only to execution against the excess over the exempt amount." (C.C.P. 690.31(f).) It must also specify the amount of the exemption. The writ of execution must state the names and addresses of encumbrancers and any exempt debtor and must specify the amounts for distribution under the levy and the exempt amount. (C.C.P. 690.31(f).)

(6) *When Debtor Fails To Appear.* If the debtor does not appear at the hearing, a second prescribed notice must be served with the writ 10 days before the execution sale. The required method and proof of service are the same as for the prehearing notice required by C.C.P. 690.31(d), supra. (C.C.P. 683, 690.31(g)(*l*).) The prescribed form contains a declaration stating that the prior absence was excusable, and requesting a new hearing. (C.C.P. 690.31(g); for Spanish version, see C.C.P. 690.31(p).) If the declaration is given to the levying officer 5 days prior to the scheduled sale date, the officer must cancel the sale pending further order of the court, and transmit the notice to the clerk who must set a hearing, giving the parties at least 10 days' notice, to determine if the writ should be recalled. (C.C.P. 690.31(h).)

(7) *Reaching Excess Value.* If the property is sold at an execution sale, the proceeds are applied as follows: "first, to the discharge of all liens and encumbrances, if any, on the property; second, to the debtor, or the debtor's spouse if such person is the exemption claimant, in the amount of the exemption if allowed pursuant to this

section; third, to the satisfaction of the execution; and fourth, to the debtor, or the debtor's spouse if such person is the exemption claimant." (C.C.P. 690.31(j).)

The proceeds representing the exemption remain exempt for 6 months, and if "used for the purchase of a dwelling house, in which the debtor or the family of the debtor actually reside, within a period of six months following receipt, the subsequently acquired dwelling shall be exempt from execution. The exemption for the subsequently acquired real property shall have the same effect as if allowed on the date of the acquisition of or the commencement of residence by the debtor or the spouse of the debtor, whichever last occurred, in the property previously determined to be exempt, except with respect to a judgment or other obligation which by statute is given the force and effect of a judgment lien against the subsequently acquired property prior to its acquisition." (C.C.P. 690.31(k).)

[§49D]   (New) Declared Homestead Procedure Not Superseded.

New Law: For the new Enforcement of Judgments law, see Supp., infra, §227A et seq.

In *Krause v. Superior Court* (1978) 78 C.A.3d 499, 144 C.R. 194, petitioner recorded a declaration of homestead on her dwelling valued at $66,000. Subsequently 6 abstracts of judgments, totalling in excess of $100,000, were recorded, and G, one of the judgment creditors, applied for a writ of execution pursuant to C.C.P. 690.31, to reach the excess value of the dwelling (over its encumbrance of $18,236 and the then exemption of $20,000). The lower court directed issuance of the writ, and petitioner sought a writ of review (treated as mandamus), contending that, where a dwelling was *homesteaded,* the procedure under C.C. 1245 et seq. (text, §45 et seq.) was exclusive. *Held,* mandamus granted.

(1) *Original dwelling statute.* The 1974 legislation (see Supp., supra, §§49A, 49B) created no conflict with the Civil Code sections: Former C.C.P. 690.235 expressly provided that the dwelling house exemption was not available if there was a declared homestead, and the procedure for claiming the exemption was similar to that for claiming any other exemption. (78 C.A.3d 503.)

(2) *Revised statute.* The 1977 legislation (see Supp., supra, §49C) introduced procedures inconsistent with those contemplated by C.C. 1245 et seq.

First, under the Civil Code, appraisers are not appointed and the value is not determined until after issuance and levy of the writ of execution; if the value exceeds the amount of the exemption and liens, the result may be a division of the property and sale of a portion or sale of the whole under supervision of the court. Under C.C.P. 690.31 no writ of execution may issue until application is made and a hearing is had on the value and availability of the exemption; if the value exceeds the exemption plus liens, the result is issuance of a writ of execution "and, apparently, an execution sale." (78 C.A.3d 504.)

Second, while the procedure under both statutes permits the judgment creditor to reach the excess value, a recorded abstract of judgment "appears to create a lien" for purposes of section 690.31 (see C.C.P. 674(c)), but not for purposes of C.C. 1245 et seq. (see C.C.P. 674(a)). (78 C.A.3d 505.)

(3) *No implied repeal of inconsistent Civil Code provisions.* The two statutory schemes apply to different situations: the Civil Code sections to homesteaded property including dwelling houses, and C.C.P. 690.31 to all other dwelling houses. (78 C.A.3d 505.) The broad language of C.C.P. 690.31(c) could be construed to cover all dwelling houses; and, since C.C. 1245 et seq. did not specifically provide a procedure for obtaining issuance of a writ of execution, "it is tempting" to construe the statutes so as to make the procedure under C.C.P. 690.31 exclusive for *obtaining a writ of execution,* leaving C.C. 1245 et seq. applicable to homesteaded dwellings *after issuance* of the writ. But the determination of value is made at a different stage and by different methods in the two statutory systems, and treatment of recorded abstracts of judgments in determining the existence of the exemption is also different; hence the suggested construction is not possible. (78 C.A.3d 506.) Moreover, the presumption is against repeal by implication, and there is abundant evidence in the legislative history and the text of C.C.P. 690.31 that the Legislature had C.C. 1245 et seq. in mind when it enacted C.C.P. 690.31. (78 C.A.3d 506, 507.)

The court concluded that persuasive arguments could be made for a single procedure, and that unresolved questions remain as to the interrelation of the sections of the Civil Code and Code of Civil Procedure; hence that there is an "urgent need for further consideration and action by the Legislature." (78 C.A.3d 508.)

In 1979, C.C. 1245 et seq. were repealed, and new C.C. 1245 et seq. were enacted, to provide substantially identical procedures for both residential exemptions. (See Supp., supra, §45A.)

(d)   [§49E]   (New) Dwelling Includes Mobilehome.

New Law: For the new Enforcement of Judgments law, see Supp., infra, §227A et seq.

C.C.P. 690.31 (see Supp., supra, §49C) was amended in 1978 to extend the dwelling house exemption to a mobilehome: For purposes of the section, "dwelling house" includes a mobilehome. (C.C.P. 690.30(a)(2); see 10 Pacific L. J. 356.)

(a) [§50] Scope of Exemption.

New Law: For the new Enforcement of Judgments law, see Supp., infra, §227A et seq.

See 12 Santa Clara Lawyer 155. On construction of the term "necessary" in statutes exempting "necessary" furniture, see 41 A.L.R.3d 607.

(c) [§52] Illustrations.

New Law: For the new Enforcement of Judgments law, see Supp., infra, §227A et seq.

Cross-Reference: 7 *Summary, Wills and Probate,* §511.

(b) [§54] New General Statute.

New Law: For the new Enforcement of Judgments law, see Supp., infra, §227A et seq.

(a) *Tools, books, etc.:* Like other exemptions, this is personal to an individual, i.e., a natural person, and cannot be claimed by a professional corporation. (*Canal-Randolph Anaheim v. Wilkoski* (1980) 103 C.A.3d 272, 291, 292, 163 C.R. 30, Supp., supra, §25.)

Automobile: In *Sun Ltd. v. Casey* (1979) 96 C.A.3d 38, 157 C.R. 576, the debtor, a licensed real estate agent, was confined to a wheelchair, and used her automobile to transport herself and prospective buyers to and from listed properties. The lower court concluded (1) that the car did not qualify as a "commercial vehicle" because it was not a taxi, bus, or other vehicle providing transportation for hire; and (2) that, although it was a "tool" or "implement," it was not exempt because it was not used "exclusively" in the debtor's trade or profession. *Held,* reversed. The "exclusive use" limitation is solely on the fourth category of "any other personal property" (text, p. 3422). Hence the automobile was exempt as a tool or implement, and "we need not reach the question of whether the trial court correctly interpreted the 'commercial vehicle' exemption." (96 C.A.3d 42.)

5. [§55] Motor Vehicle and House Trailer.

New Law: For the new Enforcement of Judgments law, see Supp., infra, §227A et seq.

(a) *Motor Vehicle.* C.C.P. 690.2 was amended in 1972 and 1974 to effect several changes. (1) The exemption was raised to $500. (2) The total value of the car is determined by "established used car price guides," or by fair market value if the car is not listed in such guides. (3) If the car is sold under execution, the proceeds are applied as follows: first, to the seller or mortgagee; second, to the debtor to the amount of the exemption; and third, in the manner of proceeds in an ordinary execution sale. (4) The proceeds representing the exemption remain exempt for three months. (See 4 Pacific L. J. 296; *Smith v. Rhea* (1977) 72 C.A.3d 361, 140 C.R. 116 [exemption is effective under 1974 amendment without being claimed by affidavit under C.C.P. 690.50, Supp., infra, §90].)

Former C.C.P. 690.2 was repealed, and new C.C.P. 690.2 was enacted, in 1976. (See 8 Pacific L. J. 229.) (1) The former ceiling of $1,000 on the value of the car was eliminated. A debtor is entitled to one motor vehicle in which his equity does not exceed $500 over and above liens and encumbrances. (C.C.P. 690.2(a).) (2) Value is determined by reference "to used car price guides customarily used by California automobile dealers, or, if not listed in such guides, fair market value, for a motor vehicle of that year and model." (C.C.P. 690.2(a).) (3) The levying officer must determine from the Department of Motor Vehicles if the debtor has any other vehicle registered in his name. A 1977 amendment to C.C.P. 690.2 altered the consequences of this determination:

(1) Under the 1976 version, if another vehicle was registered in the debtor's name, the exemption was denied unless the debtor established that he had no other car which was or could be made "safe, functional, and legally operable on the public roadway, with an expenditure which was reasonable in relation to its fair market value." (Former C.C.P. 690.2(b).) Any vehicle registered to the spouse of the debtor which was community property was deemed to be owned by the debtor when the spouses resided together. (Former C.C.P. 690.2(b).) If the debtor established that he had no second functional car, he was guaranteed either retention of the car or $500 from the proceeds of the sale. (Former C.C.P. 690.2(c)(d).)

(2) Under the 1977 amendment, if the debtor is the registered owner of another vehicle, the levying officer must notify him that he may claim the exemption for the vehicle being levied upon but will thereby waive it for other vehicles. The notice must accompany the notice of sale (see text, §77), and the exemption claim may be filed under C.C.P. 690.50 (text, §89 et seq.) at any time before sale; if not filed, it is denied. (C.C.P. 690.2(d) [omits attribution to debtor of community vehicle registered to spouse].) However, a debtor who has only one vehicle need not file a claim, and either gets back his car or is paid $500 from the sale proceeds. (C.C.P. 690.2(b)(c).)

(b) *House Trailer.* The exemption was raised to $9,500 in 1972, and to $15,000 in 1973. (See 4 Pacific L. J. 298; 5 Pacific L. J. 268.)

C.C.P. 690.3 was amended in 1976 in several respects. (1) The exemption was extended to houseboats, boats, or other "waterborne vessels"; (2) the amount was increased to $30,000 for heads of family and persons over 65 years of age; and (3) the exemption is also not available if the debtor or the debtor's spouse has obtained a prior judicial determination that the dwelling house of the debtor or the debtor's family is exempt. (See Supp., supra, §49A et seq.; 8 Pacific L. J. 458.) In 1978 and 1980, the limits of C.C.P. 690.3 were again raised: They are now $45,000 for heads of family and persons over 65 years of age, and $30,000 for others. (See 10 Pacific L. J. 356; 12 Pacific L. J. 533.)

7. [§58] Pensions and Similar Benefits.

New Law: For the new Enforcement of Judgments law, see Supp., infra, §227A et seq.

(a) *In General.* See 93 A.L.R.3d 711 [exemption of employee retirement pension benefits].

p. 3435:

(b) *Pension Money or Fund.*

(1) C.C.P. 690.18(a) was amended in 1975 to permit payments for child or spousal support to be satisfied from such funds. (See 7 Pacific L. J. 325.)

See *Roosevelt v. Roosevelt* (1981) 177 C.A.3d 397, 172 C.R. 641; *In Re Marriage of McGhee* (1982) 131 C.A.3d 408, 182 C.R. 456.

(2) In *Bonelli v. California* (1977) 71 C.A.3d 459, 465, 139 C.R. 486, Govt.C. 9359.3 (providing an exemption, equivalent to that of C.C.P. 690.18(b), for Legislators' Retirement Fund rights) was held to *preclude an offset by the state* under Govt.C. 12419.5 (permitting Controller to offset amounts due state against debts of a state agency). Govt.C. 12419.5 was amended in 1980, in light of the *Bonelli* decision, to provide that "an amount owing to a person or entity by any state agency shall include any tax refund." The Legislature also declared that tax refunds are "a simple debt and do not create a trust relationship between the taxpayer and the state." (Stats. 1980, Chap. 572, §2.)

C.C.P. 690.18(b) was amended in 1980 to exempt its provisions from court-ordered child and spousal support payments.

(3) C.C.P. 690.18(c) was amended in 1976 to delete the exclusion from the exemption of moneys held under the 1962 federal act, and to provide that, with the exceptions of moneys held for unemployment insurance purposes and court-ordered child support payments, the exemption of C.C.P. 690.18 applies to moneys held in self-employed and individual retirement annuities or accounts provided by the federal "Employee Retirement Income Security Act of 1974."

C.C.P. 690.18(c) was further amended in 1978, as follows: (1) the limitation of the exemption to bankruptcy proceedings was deleted; (2) the exemption is extended to qualifying funds deposited by the pensioner or beneficiary; (3) spousal as well as child support orders are excepted from the exemption; (4) plans provided by the Tax Reform Act of 1976 are also included; and (5) the exemption is limited to "the maximum amount exempt from federal income taxation" under any qualifying plan. (See 10 Pacific L. J. 355.)

In 1980 C.C.P. 690.18(c) was relettered C.C.P. 690.18(d). (See Supp., infra, §59.)

8. [§59] Workmen's Compensation, Unemployment and Welfare Benefits.

New Law: For the new Enforcement of Judgments law, see Supp., infra, §227A et seq.

(b) *Unemployment Compensation or Contributions.* C.C.P. 690.18(c), added in 1980, exempts money held, etc., by the state and its political subdivisions for payment or reimbursement of unemployment payments, etc.

Cross-Reference: 2 *Summary, Workmen's Compensation,* §258.

(a) [§60] Unconditional Exemption of One-Half.

New Law: For the new Enforcement of Judgments law, see Supp., infra, §227A et seq.

(New) Former Law (applicable until July 1, 1979).

(1) *Nature and Theory of Exemption.* C.C.P. 690.6(b) was amended in 1971 to exempt earnings "received" rather than earnings "due or owing." (See C.E.B., Debt Collection Manual §8.12.) C.C.P. 690.6(b) should be C.C.P. 690.6(a), effective January 1, 1976. (See Supp., infra, this section.) C.C.P. 690.6(a) was further amended in 1975 to apply to "his or her" personal services.

p. 3437:

First, federal statute: Since the federal law, incorporated into the California law by C.C.P. 690.6(b), limits garnishment to 25% of the debtor's earnings, at least 75% is exempt. (See *Raigoza v. Sperl* (1973) 34 C.A.3d 560, 563, 110 C.R. 296.)

Third, no need to claim: C.C.P. 688 should be C.C.P. 688(a), effective January 1, 1976. (See Supp., supra, §11.) Reference to C.C.P. 690.6 has been deleted from C.C.P. 688(a).

Fourth, exemption from attachment: C.C.P. 690.6(a) has been deleted from C.C.P. 690.6, effective January 1, 1976, to bring the section into conformity with the new attachment law. (See *Provisional Remedies,* Supp., §312A.) The remaining subsections were accordingly relettered. C.C.P. 543 has been repealed, effective January 1, 1976.

p. 3438:

(3) *Exception for Wife or Child Support.* In 1971 the Legislature created a statutory exception to the earnings exemption provided by C.C.P. 690.6. Welf.C. 11489 provides that in Aid to Dependent Children cases (Welf.C. 11200 et seq.) a writ of execution to enforce a support judgment against an absent parent may be issued against one-half of the parent's earnings and no claim of exemption is effective against its enforcement.

(4) *(New) Constitutionality of wage garnishment.* The rule of the *Sniadach* case (see *Provisional Remedies,* §224) applies to prejudgment garnishment, where the debtor has no opportunity for a hearing on his defense to the claim. After trial and judgment, garnishment without a further hearing is not a denial of due process. The statutory requirement that the debtor apply for and prove his exemption (see text, §88) is not arbitrary. (*Raigoza v. Sperl,* supra, 34 C.A.3d 567, 568.)

For the *Raigoza* holding applied to other exemptions, see Supp., infra, §88, and Supp., supra, §29A.

(New) Employees' Earnings Protection Law. The California Law Revision Commission made a number of proposals for revision of the law relating to garnishment of wages on execution and the earnings exemption. (See Cal. Law Rev. Com. 1971 Report, p. 709 et seq.; 1972 Report, p. 109 et seq.; 1974 Report, p. 905 et seq.) Its final drafts of a statute are discussed in 13 Cal. Law Rev. Com. Reports, p. 601 et seq. and 13 Cal. Law Rev. Com. Reports 1703 et seq.) The statute, enacted in 1978 and effective July 1, 1979, is entitled "Employees' Earnings Protection Law." (C.C.P. 723.010 et seq.) It creates an exclusive procedure, superseding other Code of Civil Procedure sections dealing with the subject. (For a full discussion of the statute, under a new Outline, see Supp., infra, §133A et seq.)

The enacting legislation (Stats. of 1978, Chap. 1133) repeals C.C.P. 690.6, and amends Welf. C. 11489 to provide that the court may order an assignment of wages pursuant to C.C. 4701. (See Law Rev. Com. Comment on repealed C.C.P. 690.6.)

(1) [§61] Statutory Conditions and Exceptions.

New Law: For the new Enforcement of Judgments law, see Supp., infra, §227A et seq.

(New) Former Law (applicable until July 1, 1979).

C.C.P. 690.6(c) should be C.C.P. 690.6(b), effective January 1, 1976. (See Supp., supra, §60.)

(a) *Exemption.* C.C.P. 690.6(c) (see Supp., supra, this section), was amended in 1971 and 1972. The exemption now applies to "all earnings of the debtor received for his personal services rendered at any time within 30 days next preceding the date of a withholding by the employer" pursuant to C.C.P. 682.3 (Supp., infra, §66A).

(b) *Condition.* The classification of debts incurred for the common necessaries of life and other debts is not a denial of equal protection: "[T]he purpose is to assure to the poor acquisition of the necessities of life by giving creditors who advance such supplies a preference over those who sell the non-essentials upon credit." (*Thayer v. Madigan* (1975) 52 C.A.3d 16, 20, 125 C.R. 28.)

C.C.P. 690.6(b) was amended in 1976 to apply also when the earnings are necessary for the debtor personally. (See Supp., infra, §63.)

(New) Employees' Earnings Protection Law. The new statute (see Supp., supra, §60, and Supp., infra, §133A et seq.) applies after July 1, 1979. C.C.P. 690.6 and 682.3 were repealed.

(aa)   [§62]   Debtor's Family Supported by Him.

New Law: For the new Enforcement of Judgments law, see Supp., infra, §227A et seq.

C.C.P. 690.6(c) should be C.C.P. 690.6(b), effective January 1, 1976. (See Supp., supra, §60.)

C.C.P. 690.6 has been repealed, as of July 1, 1979. (See Supp., supra, §60.)

Cross-Reference: 6 *Summary, Parent and Child,* §141.

(bb)   [§63]   Necessary for Use.

New Law: For the new Enforcement of Judgments law, see Supp., infra, §227A et seq.

C.C.P. 690.6(c) should be C.C.P. 690.6(b), effective January 1, 1976. (See Supp., supra, §60.)

C.C.P. 690.6(b) was amended in 1976 to apply to the debtor as well as the debtor's family. (See 8 Pacific L. J. 234.)

C.C.P. 690.6 has been repealed, as of July 1, 1979. (See Supp., supra, §60.)

(aa)   [§64]   Common Necessaries or Personal Services.

New Law: For the new Enforcement of Judgments law, see Supp., infra, §227A et seq.

(1) *Common Necessaries.* C.C.P. 690.6(c) should be C.C.P. 690.6 (b), effective January 1, 1976. (See Supp., supra, §60.)

(2) *Personal Services.* See Supp., supra, this section.

C.C.P. 690.6 has been repealed as of July 1, 1979. (See Supp., supra, §60.)

(bb) [§65] Wife or Child Support Claim.

New Law: For the new Enforcement of Judgments law, see Supp., infra, §227A et seq.

On enforcement of a support judgment against an absent parent in Aid to Dependent Children cases, see Welf.C. 11489, Supp., supra, §60.

p. 3441:

In re Marriage of Pallesi (1977) 73 C.A.3d 424, 140 C.R. 842, applied the *Henry* rule, that the exemption is unavailable against enforcement of an award for attorney's fees incurred by the debtor's spouse, even though the parties had *reconciled* before the levy of execution. The appellate court reasoned that (1) the nature of the attorney's services was not altered by the subsequent reconciliation; (2) the trial court's discretionary order of execution (see text, §9) was not challenged by motion to recall or quash the writ; (3) public policy favors payment of court-approved fees; and (4) nonenforcement would discourage representation of indigent spouses and encourage immediate execution on orders for fees and costs. (73 C.A.3d 428.)

On child and spousal support payments as exception to pension and benefits exemption, see C.C.P. 690.18, as amended in 1981.

Cross-Reference: 6 *Summary, Husband and Wife,* §190.

(c) [§66] Levy on Nonexempt Earnings.

New Law: For the new Enforcement of Judgments law, see Supp., infra, §227A et seq.

For the statutory authorization of a continuing levy, see Supp., infra, §66A.

C.C.P. 690.6(d)(e) should be C.C.P. 690.6(c)(d), effective January 1, 1976. (See Supp., supra, §60.)

C.C.P. 690.6 has been repealed, as of July 1, 1979. (See Supp., supra, §60.)

[§66A] (New) Continuing Levy.

New Law: For the new Enforcement of Judgments law, see Supp., infra, §227A et seq.

(New) Former law (applicable until July 1, 1979).

Formerly, nonexempt earnings were subject to *multiple levies.* California law permitted the judgment creditor to levy only on the amount of earnings owing to the debtor at the time of levy. Hence, if the amount levied on was insufficient to satisfy the judgment, the creditor typically made successive levies, serving a writ of execution each time, until the judgment was satisfied. This practice was criticized because it increased the costs of collection, imposing an unnecessary burden on the debtor and the public at large. (See 53 Cal. L. Rev. 1220; 4 U.C. Davis L. Rev. 81; Cal. Law Rev. Com. 1971 Report, p. 710.) The 1971 Legislature responded to the problem by enacting C.C.P. 682.3, effective March 4, 1972, and nonexempt earnings are now subject to execution by means of a 90-day continuing levy. (See 3 Pacific L. J. 221.) The procedure is as follows:

(1) *Levy on Employer.* The employer is served with a writ of execution. Thereafter, he must withhold the nonexempt earnings of the employee-debtor and pay them to the levying officer until the levy is terminated. If he fails to do so, he is liable to the judgment creditor for the amounts not paid. (C.C.P. 682.3(a).)

(2) *Termination of Levy.* The levy is terminated when: (a) The employer receives a direction to release from the levying officer (the officer must issue a release on written direction from the judgment debtor, on order of the court, or "[i]n all other cases provided by law"). (b) The employer has withheld the full amount specified in the writ of execution. (c) The judgment debtor's employment is terminated and he is not reemployed within 90 days. (d) A period of 90 days has elapsed after service of the writ. (C.C.P. 682.3(a).)

(3) *Claim of Exemption.* The debtor-employee may file a claim of exemption in accord with C.C.P. 690.50 (text, §89 et seq.) for full exemption of his earnings under C.C.P. 690.6 (text, §61 et seq.), and the claim extends to any earnings withheld whether before or after the claim was filed. (C.C.P. 682.3(b), as amended in 1972; see 4 Pacific L. J. 293.)

(4) *Duty of Levying Officer.* The levying officer must "account for and pay to the person entitled thereto" the sums collected under the writ, less his fees and expenses, every 30 days and make a return on the writ upon collection. (C.C.P. 682.3(c).)

(New) Employees' Earnings Protection Law. C.C.P. 682.3 was repealed, as of July 1, 1979, and the new statute covers this subject. (See Supp., supra, §60; Supp., infra, §133A et seq.)

10. [§67] Miscellaneous Exemptions.

New Law: For the new Enforcement of Judgments law, see Supp., infra, §227A et seq.

(c) *Money Deposits.* C.C.P. 690 should be C.C.P. 690.24. That section and Lab.C. 404 were amended, effective January 1, 1976, by deleting reference to attachment, to bring them into conformity with the new attachment law. (See *Provisional Remedies,* Supp., §§311A, 312A.)

(f) *(New) Relocation Assistance.* C.C.P. 690.8, added in 1972 and amended in 1974, provides that *"compensation* received from a *public entity* which acquires for a public use a *dwelling actually owned and occupied by the debtor"* is exempt for six months in "the amount, over and above all liens and encumbrances" of a declared homestead. (See 4 Pacific L. J. 298; 6 Pacific L. J. 433.) C.C.P. 690.8a, added in 1974, provides that "All *relocation benefits* for displacement from a *dwelling actually owned or rented by the debtor"* are exempt "without filing a claim of exemption." (See 6 Pacific L. J. 433.) (On relocation assistance, see 5 *Summary, Constitutional Law,* §598.)

(g) *(New) Direct Deposits Authorized by Social Security Administration.* C.C.P. 690.30, added in 1976, provides for a special exemption of regular retirement and survivors benefits, supplemental security income benefits, coal miners' benefits, and disability insurance benefits, which are deposited directly in accounts of financial institutions. (See 8 Pacific L. J. 228.) The exemption is for the first $500 in such accounts if there is one depositor, or $750 if there are two or more depositors. (C.C.P. 690.30(a).)

(a) [§68] Application and Time of Issuance.

New Law: For the new Enforcement of Judgments law, see Supp., infra, §227A et seq.

(1) *Application to Clerk.* C.C.P. 688 should be C.C.P. 688(e), effective January 1, 1978. (See Supp., supra, §11; Supp., infra, §73A.)

C.C.P. 686 was repealed in 1980. (See Supp., supra, §3.)

p. 3443:

(2) *Time of Issuance.*

Issuance within 10-year period: In *Alonso Inv. Corp. v. Doff* (1976) 17 C.3d 539, 131 C.R. 411, 551 P.2d 1243, the judgment creditor obtained the writ shortly before the end of the 10-year period, but it was not delivered to the levying officer until after the period had expired. The judgment debtor challenged the resulting levy and sale under execution, contending that C.C.P. 685 (on discretionary execution after 10 years) applied, and that the creditor had to make a motion and showing under that section (see text, §199). *Held,* the levy and sale were valid.

(a) C.C.P. 681, permitting "issuance" of the writ or order "at any time within 10 years" is controlling. The section contains no indication that a validly issued writ may later become unenforceable despite the fact that its execution and return are in conformity with C.C.P. 683 (returnable not less than 10 nor more than 60 days after receipt by levying officer) and C.C.P. 688 (no levy binding longer than 1 year after issuance of writ). (17 C.3d 543; see text, §§72, 74.)

(b) Nothing in C.C.P. 685 suggests that it limits the language of

C.C.P. 681. The statement in section 685 that the judgment may be "enforced or carried into execution" merely means that the section applies not only to execution but to any other means of enforcement. (17 C.3d 544, citing the text, §199.)

(c) The statutory form of the writ also supports this conclusion. (17 C.3d 545.)

See C.E.B., Debt Collection Manual, §8.2.

(c) [§70] Content and Form of Writ.

New Law: For the new Enforcement of Judgments law, see Supp., infra, §227A et seq.

(1) *Statutes and Forms.* With the exception of Writ of Execution (Joint Debtors) all the judicial Council Forms were revised, effective July 1, 1975. They were revised further in 1977 and 1978, and there are now only two optional forms: (1) Writ of Execution (EJ-130(79)), and (2) Writ of Execution Against Dwelling House (Money Judgment (EJ-140(79)).

(2) *Writ of Execution for Money Judgment.*

(a) C.C.P. 682 was amended in 1978 to add registered process servers to those persons authorized to serve the writ. (See Supp., infra, §71A.)

p. 3445:

(d) Against the *person:* C.C.P. 682 was amended in 1973 to delete reference to arrest and bail. (See *Provisional Remedies,* Supp., §7A.)

The form in C.C.P. 682.1 was amended to provide for service by a registered process server. (See supra, this section.)

(a) [§71] Duty and Liability of Officer.

New Law: For the new Enforcement of Judgments law, see Supp., infra, §226A et seq.

See C.E.B., Debt Collection Manual, Appendix D.

[§71A] (New) Service of Writ by Process Server.

New Law: For the new Enforcement of Judgments law, see Supp., infra, §227A et seq.

C.C.P. 687(b), added in 1978, authorizes a registered process server (see *Actions,* Supp., §609), to serve a writ of execution "against the property of a judgment debtor in the possession of another" when "the levy of execution does not require the person serving the writ to sell, deliver, or take cutody of such property." Conforming amendments were made in C.C.P. 682, 682a, and 682.1. (See 10 Pacific L. J. 352.)

The sheriff, constable, or marshal performs all other duties required, "as if . . . he . . . had served the writ himself." (C.C.P. 687(c).)

(b) [§72] Time of Levy and Return.

New Law: For the new Enforcement of Judgments law, see Supp., infra, §227A et seq.

See C.E.B., Debt Collection Manual, §8.2.

C.C.P. 683 was amended in 1971 to provide that where the levy is against the earnings of the judgment debtor, the return is to be made on termination of the levy in accord with C.C.P. 682.3 (Supp., supra, §66A).

A 1977 amendment to C.C.P. 683 enlarges the circumstances under which the returned writ is redelivered to the levying officer. The 1949 amendment, quoted in the text, remains applicable when the return *antedates* the execution sale; the *court* is thereupon empowered to direct redelivery at the judgment creditor's request. The 1977 amendment applies when "proceeds resulting from a levy of execution are received by the levying officer *after* the writ has been returned," and provides that "the *clerk shall redeliver* such execution" on request of the judgment creditor. (See 9 Pacific L. J. 372.)

A 1978 amendment of C.C.P. 683 adds subdivision (f), providing that if an earnings withholding order has been issued and served on the employer under C.C.P. 723.010 et seq. (see Supp., infra, §133A et seq.) prior to the time the writ of execution is made returnable under C.C.P. 683(a), the execution is returnable as provided in C.C.P. 723.026 (Supp., infra, §133J).

(c) [§73] Making of Levy.

New Law: For the new Enforcement of Judgments law, see Supp., infra, §227A et seq.

See C.E.B., Debt Collection Manual, §8.6 et seq.

C.C.P. 688 was amended and subdivided, effective January 1, 1974. (See Supp., supra, §11.) C.C.P. 688(b), as amended in 1977, provides:

"All property subject to execution may be levied upon or released from levy *in like manner* as like property may be levied upon or released from *attachment, except* that *tangible personal property in the possession of the judgment debtor* shall always be levied upon in the manner provided by subdivision (c). Notwithstanding the provisions of Title 6.5 (commencing with Section 481.010), *service* on the judgment debtor of a copy of the writ of execution shall be made either by *personal delivery or by mail* to the judgment debtor at the address furnished by the judgment creditor. To levy upon any property or debt owed to the judgment debtor which is subject to execution but for which *a method of levy of attachment is not provided,* the levying officer shall *serve* upon the person in possession of such property or owing such debt, or his agent (1) a copy of the *writ of execution* and (2) a *notice* that such property or debt is levied upon in pursuance of such writ."

On the procedure under C.C.P. 688(c), added in 1977, see Supp., infra, §73A.

[§73A]   (New) Keeper To Take Possession.

New Law: For the new Enforcement of Judgments law, see Supp., infra, §227A et seq.

When the new Attachment Law was enacted in 1976, C.C.P. 688(b) was revised to provide that levy on tangible personal property was to be made in the manner provided by C.C.P. 488.320 (see *Provisional Remedies,* Supp., §345A). It was not clear from this reference what were the proper uses, if any, of keepers (see C.C.P. 488.045, 488.360; *Provisional Remedies,* Supp., §§339, 349A, 350A). (See 14 Law. Rev. Com. Reports p. 53 et seq.) To resolve these doubts, C.C.P. 688(c) was added in 1977, and subdivision (b) was amended to refer to the new subdivision rather that to C.C.P. 488.320. (See 9 Pacific L. J. 373.) C.C.P. 688(c)–(f) were relettered C.C.P. 688(d)–(g).

The principal features of the new subsection are as follows:

(1) *Keeper Permitted.* Tangible personal property is levied upon by taking it into custody, and the levying officer may either remove the property to a place of safekeeping or install a keeper. (C.C.P. 688(c).)

(2) *Keeper Required for Dwellings.* When the property levied upon is a dwelling, such as a housetrailer, mobilehome, or vessel, a keeper must be placed in charge for at least 2 days, at the creditor's expense. Thereafter the occupants are removed, "unless other disposition is made by the court or agreed upon by the judgment creditor and the judgment debtor." (C.C.P. 688(c).)

(3) *Keeper Required for Business Property if Debtor Consents.* When the property is business property, other than money or a registered motor vehicle, and the judgment debtor consents, a keeper must be placed in charge for at least 2 days, during which period the business may be continued, at the judgment debtor's expense, "provided that all sales are final and are for cash or the equivalent of cash," including checks. All proceeds must be given to the keeper unless otherwise authorized by the judgment creditor. Thereafter, the officer must take the property into exclusive possession "unless other disposition is made by the court or agreed upon by the judgment creditor and the judgment debtor." (C.C.P. 688(c).)

(1) [§74] Creation and Duration.

New Law: For the new Enforcement of Judgments law, see Supp., infra, §227A et seq.

Levy on interest of heir, etc.: See *Estate of Badivian* (1973) 31 C.A.3d 737, 740, 107 C.R. 537.

(2) [§75] Priorities.

New Law: For the new Enforcement of Judgments law, see Supp., infra, §227A et seq.

(a) Creditor who first levies: See *Estate of Badivian* (1973) 31 C.A.3d 737, 739, 107 C.R. 537, citing the text.

See C.E.B., Debt Collection Manual, §12.19 et seq.

Cross-Reference: 3 Summary, Security Transactions in Real Property, §38.

(b) [§77] Notice Requirements.

New Law: For the new Enforcement of Judgments law, see Supp., infra, §227A et seq.

(3) *Real property or leasehold:* A 1971 amendment to C.C.P. 692 requires *personal notice* to be given to the judgment debtor prior to an execution sale of real property or a leasehold interest, in addition to the required posted and published notice (text, p. 3449). At least 20 days before the sale, notice of the time and place of sale must be given (1) by mailing it by certified mail to the judgment debtor's last known business or residence address, (2) by mailing it to his attorney, or (3) by delivering it to the judgment debtor. The party delivering the execution for levy must furnish the officer with the information necessary to comply with the notice requirements.

A 1977 amendment to C.C.P. 692(3) adds notice requirements for property having no street address or other common designation. The notice must contain the name and address of the beneficiary requesting the sale, and must state that directions may be obtained on submitting a written request within 10 days from the first publication. Directions must locate the property by distance and direction from the nearest crossroads or frontage or access road. Neither the validity of the notice nor of the *sale* is affected by error or omission in giving the street address, common designation, name and address of beneficiary, or directions as to location. (See 9 Pacific L. J. 633.)

(3) [§80] Real Property.

New Law: For the new Enforcement of Judgments law, see Supp., infra, §227A et seq.

On the levying officer's duty to notify the judgment debtor of his redemption rights, see Supp., infra, §98.

(a) [§84] Stay of Execution.

New Law: For the new Enforcement of Judgments law, see Supp., infra, §227A et seq.

See C.E.B., Debt Collection Manual, §8.56 et seq.

(New) Stay while another action pending: A court has inherent power to stay execution on a judgment where the judgment debtor has another action pending on a disputed claim against the judgment creditor; otherwise the judgment debtor would be deprived not only of his right of set-off, but with an impecunious creditor the right to receive any recovery. "In exercising its discretion, the court must consider the likelihood of the judgment debtor prevailing in the other action and the financial ability of the judgment creditor to satisfy a judgment on the disputed claim if such should be rendered." (*Airfloor Co. of Calif. v. Regents of Univ. of Calif.* (1979) 97 C.A.3d 739, 741, 158 C.R. 856, citing *Erlich v. Superior Court, Pleading,* §1023.)

(aa) [§85] Nature of Remedy.

New Law: For the new Enforcement of Judgments law, see Supp., infra, §227A et seq.

See C.E.B., Debt Collection Manual, §8.61.

(bb) [§86] Procedure.

New Law: For the new Enforcement of Judgments law, see Supp., infra, §227A et seq.

See C.E.B., Debt Collection Manual, §8.62; *In re Marriage of Barnes* (1978) 83 C.A.3d 143, 152, 147 C.R. 710, citing the text.

(1) [§88] Necessity of Claim.

New Law: For the new Enforcement of Judgments law, see Supp., infra, §227A et seq.

C.C.P. 690(a) was amended, effective January 1, 1976, to bring it into conformity with the new attachment law. The words "or attachment" were deleted "to avoid the implication that claims of exemption from attachment must always be made as provided in Section 690.50. In some circumstances . . . special claims procedures are provided by the Attachment Law. . . . This amendment does not, however, change the general rule that property exempt from execution is also exempt from attachment." (Law Rev. Com. Comment to C.C.P. 690.) (For a special prelevy procedure, see C.C.P. 484.070, *Provisional Remedies,* Supp., §317A.)

(New) Constitutionality of claim requirement: The contention that the levy on exempt property without a prior judicial hearing is a denial of due process under the *Sniadach* rule (see *Provisional Remedies,* §224) was rejected in *Raigoza v. Sperl,* dealing with the exemption of wages under C.C.P. 690.6 (see Supp., supra, §60). The *Raigoza* conclusion, that there is no arbitrary deprivation of property in the requirement that the judgment debtor claim and prove his exemption, was restated and applied to other exemptions in *Phillips v. Bartolomie* (1975) 46 C.A.3d 346, 121 C.R. 56.

In the *Phillips* case, the judgment creditor levied on the entire joint checking account of Mr. and Mrs. Phillips. They filed a complaint against the sheriff, alleging that all of the funds were received as benefits or pensions under programs of the Veterans Administration, the Social Security Administration, and the county welfare department, and thus exempt from execution (C.C.P. 690.18(a); see text, §58). In addition to seeking declaratory relief, plaintiffs demanded an injunction preventing further levies, in order that they might maintain their checking account without further interference. The lower court sustained a demurrer and entered judgment of dismissal. *Held,* affirmed.

(a) *Sniadach* and its progeny all relate to *prejudgment* remedies; there is little authority on *postjudgment* remedies. (46 C.A.3d 350, footnote 3.) But the reasoning of *Raigoza* is persuasive: The debtor is in a better position than the creditor or the bank to establish the facts relating to an exemption. "For us to impose the responsibilities on depositories to determine in advance where all deposits come from, or to keep track of all checks as sources, would seem an impossible burden and the law so recognizes this by requiring the filing of the affidavits of exemption by the debtors." (46 C.A.3d 352.)

(b) The claim requirement is burdensome in that the debtor must suffer delay during the period of its consideration; but there is a practical way to avoid this hardship: "[A] judgment debtor, like Phillips here, could well discourage the creditor from a futile execution by filing his affidavit of exemption with the depository immediately after the judgment is entered, with a copy to the creditor." (46 C.A.3d 354.)

p. 3456:

(1) Debtor's earnings: C.C.P. 690.6(b) should be C.C.P. 690.6(a), effective January 1, 1976. (See Supp., supra, §60.)

(4) Unemployment compensation benefits: C.C.P. 690.18(c), added in 1980. (See Supp., supra, §59.)

(7) Person in penal institution: C.C.P. 690.21 was amended, effective January 1, 1976, to delete reference to attachment. (See Supp., supra, §67.)

(aa) [§89] In General.

New Law: For the new Enforcement of Judgments law, see Supp., infra, §227A et seq.

(1) *Statutory Special Proceeding. Garnishment of state or subdivision:* The procedure set forth in C.C.P. 690.50 also applies to a claim of exemption where money owed to the judgment debtor by the state or one of its subdivisions has been garnished pursuant to C.C.P. 710. (See text, §134 et seq.) However, the procedure under C.C.P. 710 does not involve a levying officer; hence, in such cases, the court rendering judgment is considered to be the levying officer for the purposes of C.C.P. 690.50. (C.C.P. 710(c).)

C.C.P. 690.50 was amended in 1978 to delete references to repealed C.C.P. 690.6 (see Supp., supra, §60). (For the procedure under the new Employees' Earnings Protection Law, C.C.P. 723.010 et seq., see Supp., infra, §133A et seq.)

(bb) [§90] Affidavit and Counteraffidavit.

New Law: For the new Enforcement of Judgments law, see Supp., infra, §227A et seq.

On procedure where money owed by the state or one of its subdivisions has been garnished, see Supp., supra, §89.

(1) *Affidavit to Officer Within 10 Days.* C.C.P. 690.50(a) was amended in 1972 in conformity with new C.C.P. 682.3 providing for a continuous levy on earnings. (See Supp., supra, §66A.) With respect to earnings, "*each date* that *earnings are withheld* from the judgment debtor shall be deemed to be the date such earnings were levied on," and a separate claim of exemption may be filed each time a withholding occurs. However, if there has been a prior adjudication rejecting the claim (see text, §91), the affidavit must set forth "the changed circumstances which support the *new* claim of exemption." (See 4 Pacific L. J. 293.)

C.C.P. 690.50(a) was further amended in 1974 to provide a 20-day period for claims under former C.C.P. 690.235. (See Supp., supra, §49A.) This amendment was repealed as of July 1, 1977. (See Supp., supra, §49B.) The subsection was amended again in 1976, to delete reference to attachment and defendants. (See *Provisional Remedies,* Supp., §312A.)

(New) Officer's fee: Even though the levying officer must "serve" the debtor's claim of exemption on the creditor (C.C.P. 690.50(b); see text), he may not demand a fee from the debtor for service of process. "[T]he claim of exemption process is an integral part of the return required and for which the levying officer has received a fee from the

creditor." (*Lampley v. Alvares* (1975) 50 C.A.3d 124, 129, 123 C.R. 181.)

(New) Motor vehicle exemption: Under C.C.P. 690.2(d), as amended in 1977, a registered owner of multiple vehicles may file a claim to the motor vehicle exemption at any time before the execution sale. (See Supp., supra, §55.)

See C.E.B., Debt Collection Manual, §10.13 et seq.

(2) *Service on Creditor.* C.C.P. 690.50(b) was amended in 1974 to provide a 10-day period in cases under former C.C.P. 690.235. (See Supp., supra, §49A.) This amendment was repealed as of July 1, 1977. (See Supp., supra, §49B.)

(3) *Counteraffidavit.* C.C.P. 690.50(c) was amended in 1974 to provide a 10-day period in cases under former C.C.P. 690.235. (See Supp., supra, §49A.) This amendment was repealed as of July 1, 1977. (See Supp., supra, §49B.)

(New) Employees' Earnings Protection Law. C.C.P. 690.50 was amended in 1978 to delete references to repealed C.C.P. 690.6 (see Supp., supra. §60). (For the new procedure, see Supp., infra, §133A et seq.) C.C.P. 682.3 was also repealed. (See Supp., supra, §66A.)

See C.E.B., Debt Collection Practice, §10.20.

(cc) [§91] Hearing.

New Law: For the new Enforcement of Judgments law, see Supp., infra, §227A et seq.

On procedure where money owed by the state or one of its subdivisions has been garnished, see Supp., supra, §89.

(5) *(New) Reconsideration of Allowance of Claim to Earnings.* In 1971 a new procedure for continuous levy on earnings was introduced by C.C.P. 682.3. (See Supp., supra, §66A.) When a claim of exemption has been adjudicated as valid with respect to such a levy, the judgment creditor may "at any time during the effective period of the claim of exemption, . . . move the court for consideration of the claim previously granted on the grounds of a material change of circumstances affecting the debtor's exemption rights." He must support his motion by "a statement under oath alleging the changed circumstances." (C.C.P. 690.50(a), as amended in 1972.) (See 4 Pacific L. J. 294.)

C.C.P. 690.50 was amended in 1978 to delete references to repealed C.C.P. 690.6 (see Supp., supra, §60). (For the new procedure, see Supp., infra, §133A et seq.) C.C.P. 682.3 was also repealed. (See Supp., supra, §66A.)

See C.E.B., Debt Collection Manual, §10.22.

(dd)   [§92]   Judgment and Incidental Orders.

New Law: For the new Enforcement of Judgments law, see Supp., infra, §227A et seq.

On procedure where money owed by the state or one of its subdivisions has been garnished, see Supp., supra, §89.

C.C.P. 690.6 has been repealed. (See Supp., supra, §60.)

See C.E.B., Debt Collection Manual, §10.25.

(2)   [§94]   Inadequate Price: Sale Upheld.

New Law: For the new Enforcement of Judgments law, see Supp., infra, §227A et seq.

See 5 A.L.R.4th 794 [inadequacy of price as basis for setting aside execution sale].

(3)   [§95]   Inadequate Price and Fraud.

New Law: For the new Enforcement of Judgments law, see Supp., infra, §227A et seq.

See 5 A.L.R.4th 794 [inadequacy of price as basis for setting aside execution sale].

(f)   [§97]   Actions for Damages.

New Law: For the new Enforcement of Judgments law, see Supp., infra, §227A et seq.

Cross-References: 4 *Summary, Torts,* §§263 et seq., 328 et seq., 354 et seq., 176.

(1)   [§98]   In General.

New Law: For the new Enforcement of Judgments law, see Supp., infra, §227A et seq.

p. 3465:

(f) *Redemption After Statutory Period.* See *Smith v. Kessler* (1974) 43 C.A.3d 26, 31, 117 C.R. 470 [inadequate price and manifest unfairness; debtor allowed to collect rents and make tax and trust deed payments during period of redemption].

(g) *(New) Notice of Right To Redeem.* If property sold on execution is subject to redemption (see text, p. 3464), the levying officer must notify the judgment debtor within one week after the sale of his right to redeem. Failure to do so subjects the officer to liability for actual damages plus a penalty of $100. (C.C.P. 700a(b).)

Cross-Reference: 3 *Summary, Real Property,* §228.

(2) [§99] By Judgment Debtor or Successor.

New Law: For the new Enforcement of Judgments law, see Supp., infra, §227A et seq.

See *Lindsey v. Meyer* (1981) 125 C.A.3d 536, 544, 178 C.R. 1.

(1) [§104] Nature and Scope of Proceeding.

New Law: For the new Enforcement of Judgments law, see Supp., infra, §227A et seq.

The third party claim is in the nature of an equitable action to determine adverse claims to personal property; hence a person asserting equitable title to the property under a resulting trust is entitled to make the claim under C.C.P. 689. (*Canal-Randolph Anaheim v. Wilkoski* (1980) 103 C.A.3d 282, 294, 163 C.R. 30.)

See C.E.B., Debt Collection Manual, Chap. 12.

(aa) [§105] Verified Claim.

New Law: For the new Enforcement of Judgments law, see Supp., infra, §227A et seq.

See C.E.B, Debt Collection Manual, §12.3.

(bb) [§106] Bond To Prevent Release.

New Law: For the new Enforcement of Judgments law, see Supp., infra, §227A et seq.

p. 3472:

Justification of sureties: C.C.P. 689, as amended in 1980, requires notice of an exception to be *delivered* to the levying officer within 5 days of receipt of the notice of the undertaking.

See C.E.B., Debt Collection Manual, §12.5.

(cc) [§107] Hearing.

New Law: For the new Enforcement of Judgments law, see Supp., infra, §227A et seq.

See C.E.B., Debt Collection Manual, §12.8 et seq.

(dd) [§108] Judgment and Incidental Orders.

New Law: For the new Enforcement of Judgments law, see Supp., infra, §227A et seq.

See C.E.B., Debt Collection Manual, §12.10.

(1) [§110] Nature and Scope of Proceeding.

New Law: For the new Enforcement of Judgments law, see Supp., infra, §227A et seq.

Automobiles are excluded from the terms of the Uniform Commercial Code. (See 2 *Summary, Secured Transactions in Personal Property*, §23.)

Cross-Reference: 2 *Summary, Sales*, §210.

(aa) [§111] Verified Claim by Seller or Mortgagee.

New Law: For the new Enforcement of Judgments law, see Supp., infra, §227A et seq.

See C.E.B., Debt Collection Manual, §§12.12, 12.13.

(bb) [§112] Payment or Undertaking by Plaintiff.

New Law: For the new Enforcement of Judgments law, see Supp., infra, §227A et seq.

(3) *Statement and Undertaking of Plaintiff.* C.C.P. 689b(9) was amended in 1980, in conformity with the amendment of C.C.P. 689 (see Supp., supra, §106), to require an exception to the undertaking, and *delivery* of the notice of the exception to the levying officer, within 5 days of notice of receipt of the undertaking.

See C.E.B., Debt Collection Manual, §12.14.

(d) [§114] Undertaking To Release Property.

New Law: For the new Enforcement of Judgments law, see Supp., infra, §227A et seq.

See C.E.B., Debt Collection Manual, §§12.16, 12.17.

(1) [§116] In General.

New Law: For the new Enforcement of Judgments law, see Supp., infra, §227A et seq.

Cross-Reference: 3 *Summary, Real Property*, §66.

(2) [§117] Bona Fide Purchase.

New Law: For the new Enforcement of Judgments law, see Supp., infra, §227A et seq.

Judgment creditor: In *Torrance v. Castner* (1975) 46 C.A.3d 76, 120 C.R. 23, an artist sold some of his paintings to a dealer who, in turn, loaned them to the City of Torrance for an exhibit. Thereafter, the artist's former wife obtained judgment against him and levied execution on his property. The paintings were erroneously turned over to the levying officer, and the former wife purchased them at the execution sale by crediting her judgment. The city, on learning of the error, joined the dealer in seeking declaratory relief. The trial court granted summary judgment in favor of the dealer. *Held,* affirmed.

(1) The authorities are conflicting on whether a judgment creditor at an execution sale of *real* property is a bona fide purchaser when he merely credits his bid against the judgment. *Riley* and *Pepin* (see text) hold that the creditor can be a bona fide purchaser, but other cases, such as *Boye v. Boerner* (*Provisional Remedies,* §181) have held that the creditor only acquires whatever interest the judgment debtor has. (46 C.A.3d 80, 81.) And those cases which treat the creditor as a bona fide purchaser rely on the statutory duty to record any interest claimed in land. (46 C.A.3d 81.) The rule in *Riley,* therefore, does not control a case in which personal property is involved. (46 C.A.3d 82, citing *Sargent v. Sturm* (1863) 23 C. 359.)

(2) In addition, since the paintings were not in the judgment debtor's possession when taken, but in the possession of a stranger, the creditor was put on inquiry, and therefore failed to qualify as a purchaser without notice. (46 C.A.3d 82.)

See *20th Century Plumbing Co. v. Sfregola* (1981) 126 C.A.3d 851, 179 C.R. 144.

A. [§123] In General.

New Law: For the new Enforcement of Judgments law, see Supp., infra, §227A et seq.

(2) *Simplified Procedure.*

p. 3488:

See C.E.B., Debt Collection Manual, §9.9 et seq.

(4) *Arrest for Failure To Appear.* C.C.P. 714, 717 were amended in 1974 to require a boldface notice in the order that "Failure to appear may subject the party served to arrest and punishment for contempt of court." They were further amended to make it a misdemeanor to "willfully make . . . an improper service" of such an order which results in an arrest. And registered process servers were added to those who may serve the order. (See 6 Pacific L. J. 223.)

1. [§124] With or Without Execution.

New Law: For the new Enforcement of Judgments law, see Supp., infra, §227A et seq.

See C.E.B., Debt Collection Manual, §9.3 et seq.

On required notice of sanctions of arrest and contempt, see Supp., supra, §123.

p. 3489:

(b) *Second Order.* C.C.P. 1008 was repealed and reenacted in 1978. (See *Proceedings Without Trial,* Supp., §28B.) The citation in the text should now be C.C.P. 1008(b).

[§124A]   (New) Examination by Interrogatories.

New Law: For the new Enforcement of Judgments law, see Supp., infra, §227A et seq.

C.C.P. 714.5, added in 1976, permits examination of a judgment debtor *who is represented by counsel* by written interrogatories in the manner prescribed by C.C.P. 2030. (See 8 Pacific L. J. 231; *Cal. Evidence,* 2d, §978 et seq.; *MacDonald v. Superior Court* (1977) 75 C.A.3d 692, 141 C.R. 667 [singling out debtors represented by counsel does not deny them equal protection, as answering interrogatories is less onerous than appearing in court].)

Interrogatories may be used "in connection with" oral examination, and may be served "any time after execution against property of the judgment debtor may properly be issued." But the judgment debtor may not be required to respond more frequently than once in any 4-month period during which he has been subject to any examination pursuant to C.C.P. 714. (C.C.P. 714.5.)

The section may be enforced, "to the extent practicable," in the same manner as the section governing interrogatories in a civil action. (C.C.P. 714.5; see *Cal. Evidence,* 2d, §1027 et seq.; *MacDonald v Superior Court,* supra [trial court could not bar appeal from judgment as sanction for failure to answer interrogatories].)

2.   [§125]   Before Return of Execution.

New Law: For the new Enforcement of Judgments law, see Supp., infra, §227A et seq.

See C.E.B., Debt Collection Manual, §9.7.

1.   [§126]   In General.

New Law: For the new Enforcement of Judgments law, see Supp., infra, §227A et seq.

(c) *Order and Service.* See Supp., supra, §123.

p. 3491:

(d) *Hearing.* C.C.P. 717 was amended in 1972 to give the spouse of the judgment debtor the privilege not to testify provided by Ev.C. 970, 971. (See 4 Pacific L. J. 325.) (On the nature and extent of the husband-wife privilege, see *Cal. Evidence,* 2d, §828 et seq.)

See C.E.B., Debt Collection Manual, §§9.9 et seq., 9.13.

2. [§127] Adverse Claim or Denial of Debt.

New Law: For the new Enforcement of Judgments law, see Supp., infra, §227A et seq.

In *Mitchell v. Superior Court* (1972) 28 C.A.3d 750, 104 C.R. 921, Evans sued William M. Mitchell and others on a note and received a default judgment which was unpaid. He then, on noticed motion and hearing, obtained an order appointing a receiver for a partnership in which William M. Mitchell, William B. Mitchell and Sydney Karlin were members. The alleged partners refused to recognize the receiver's authority, and were held in contempt. *Held,* contempt orders annulled.

(a) The summary proceeding under C.C.P. 719 cannot be used where, as here, the purported debtor of the judgment debtor claims an adverse interest or denies the debt. (28 C.A.3d 763.) Pending the filing of an action under C.C.P. 720 the court may enjoin him from transferring the property (see text, p. 3492), but it has no jurisdiction to appoint a receiver. (28 C.A.3d 763.)

(b) The statute providing for a charging order against a partnership (Corp.C. 15028, text, §142) assumes that the partnership status is unchallenged, and authorizes appointment of a receiver only of a partner's share of the profits. Here the receiver was directed to take over all "assets" of William M. Mitchell; i.e., the court attempted to decide that the other two parties must recognize his supposed partnership interest. This was beyond its jurisdiction. (28 C.A.3d 764.)

See C.E.B., Debt Collection Manual, §9.12.

(a) [§128] Nature, Purpose and Effect.

New Law: For the new Enforcement of Judgments law, see Supp., infra, §227A et seq.

On garnishment of nonexempt earnings, see Supp., supra, §66A.

(1) *Other Remedies Compared.*

p. 3493:

The language from C.C.P. 688 quoted in the text was amended, effective January 1, 1976. (See Supp., supra, §11.) The current text of C.C.P. 688(b) is quoted in Supp., supra, §73.

See C.E.B., Debt Collection Manual, §8.10 et seq.

(b) [§129] What Interests May Be Garnished.

New Law: For the new Enforcement of Judgments law, see Supp., infra, §227A et seq.

(1) *Interests Subject to Garnishment.* See 60 A.L.R.3d 1190 [liability insurer's potential liability for failure to settle claim against insured; garnishment by insured's judgment creditors]; 60 A.L.R.3d

1301 [garnishment against executor or administrator by creditor of estate].

(2) [§132] Execution Sale of Garnished Debt.

New Law: For the new Enforcement of Judgments law, see Supp., infra, §227A et seq.

(a) *Nature of Problem.* C.C.P. 688 should be C.C.P. 688(f), effective January 1, 1978. (See Supp., supra, §§11, 73A.)

2A. (New) Employees' Earnings Protection Law.

EXPLANATORY NOTE ON 1978 LAW. The material which follows in this Supplement is a new and complete treatment of wage garnishment under the Employees' Earnings Protection Law, enacted in 1978, and effective July 1, 1979. It has a new topic heading (see supra), new section numbers (§§133A–133Z, inclusive), and a new Outline of the new topics with references to pages of this Supplement (see below).

EXPLANATORY NOTE ON NEW ENFORCEMENT OF JUDGMENTS LAW. The 1978 law was repealed in 1982, effective July, 1, 1983, and replaced with the Wage Garnishment Law, part of the new Enforcement of Judgments law). (C.C.P. 706.010 et seq.). (See Supp., infra, §338A et seq.)

NEW OUTLINE FOR 1978 LAW.

(a) (New) Nature and Purpose of Revision.

(1) [§133A] (New) Enactment of New Law.

New Law: For the new Enforcement of Judgments law, see Supp., infra, §227A et seq.

(a) *Former Wage Garnishment Procedure.* Our prior law authorized several methods of garnishment of an employee's earnings by a judgment creditor: (1) Levy of execution on the employer of a private employee. (See text, §128 et seq.) (2) Filing an abstract or transcript of judgment with a public entity employer of a public employee. (See text, §134 et seq.) (3) Mailed withholding orders to secure payment of a delinquent state tax liability, under special statutes. (See 13 Cal. L. Rev. Com. Reports (1976), p. 617; for criticisms of the law, see 13 Cal. Law Rev. Com. Reports (1976), p. 611 et seq.; 17 Santa Clara L. Rev. 631.)

(b) *Law Revision Commission Recommendation.* The Commission, after a series of studies and drafts, made its final proposal of a comprehensive statute establishing an exclusive procedure which "will significantly reduce the cost of wage garnishments, greatly alleviate the hardship such garnishments cause employers, and make numerous other improvements in wage garnishment procedure." (13 Cal. Law Rev. Com. Reports (1976) p. 617; see also pp. 603, 611 et seq.; 13 Cal. Law Rev. Com. Reports (1976) p. 1705 et seq.)

(c) *New Statute.* The 1978 Legislature followed the latest Commission Recommendation by adopting a new Chapter 2.5 of the Code of Civil Procedure with the title of the "Employees' Earnings Protection Law." (C.C.P. 723.010 et seq.; see 10 Pacific L. J. 327.)

(d) *Effective Date and Non-retroactivity.* The operative date of the statute is January 1, 1980. (Stats. 1978, Chap. 1133, §12, as amended by Stats. 1979, Chap. 66, §5.) The provisions on non-retroactivity (Stats. 1978, Chap. 1133, §11, as amended by Stats. 1979, Chap. 66, §4) are as follows:

(1) *Levy made before January 1, 1980.* A levy made under former C.C.P. 682.3, and served on the employer before January 1, 1980, is valid and is governed by the prior law.

(2) *Earnings withholding order made during period of levy.* Even if the order is served after the operative date, it is ineffective during the period of a prior valid levy.

(e) *Definitions.* C.C.P. 723.011 defines a number of important terms as follows: (a) *Earnings:* "compensation payable by an employer to an employee for personal services performed by such employee, whether denominated as wages, salary, commission, bonus, or otherwise." (b) *Employee:* "a public officer and any individual who performs services subject to the right of the employer to control both what shall be done and how it shall be done." (c) *Employer:* "a person for whom an individual performs services as an employee." (d) *Judgment creditor, as applied to the state:* "the specific state agency seeking to collect a judgment or tax liability." (e) *Judgment debtor:* "includes a person from whom the state is seeking to collect a tax liability under Article 4 (commencing with Section 723.070), whether or not a judgment has been obtained on such tax liability." (See Supp., infra, §133Q.) (f) *Person:* "includes an individual, a corporation, a partnership or other unincorporated association, and a public entity."

(f) *Amendment and Repeal of Other Statutes.* The following changes were made by the 1978 Legislature:

Repealed: C.C.P. 682.3 (see Supp., supra, §66A); C.C.P. 690.6 (see Supp., supra, §60).

Amended: C.C.P. 682 (see Supp., supra, §70); C.C.P. 683 (see Supp., supra, §72); C.C.P. 690.50 (see Supp., supra, §89); C.C.P. 710 (see Supp., infra, §134); Lab.C. 300 (see 1 *Summary, Agency and Employment,* §741 et seq.); Welf.C. 11489 (see Supp., supra, §60).

Added: Govt.C. 26750, establishing fee of $8.50 for serving an earnings withholding order, and prohibiting charge of any additional fees, costs or expenses.

(2) [§133B]   (New) Exclusive Procedure.

New Law: For the new Enforcement of Judgments law, see Supp., infra, §227A et seq.

Except as provided in C.C. 4701 (wage assignments for support; see Supp., infra, §133W), "the earnings of an employee shall not be required to be withheld by an employer for payment of a debt by means of any judicial procedure other than pursuant to this chapter." (C.C.P. 723.020; see also C.C.P. 723.021 [levy of execution on earnings made in accordance with this chapter, not under C.C.P. 688 (see text, §73)]; see Law. Rev. Com. Comment, pointing out that attachment of earnings before judgment is abolished by C.C.P. 487.020(c) (see *Provisional Remedies,* Supp., §312A); that the chapter applies to public entities as well as private persons, and imposes limitations on the State's ability to garnish wages for tax delinquencies (see C.C.P. 723.070, Supp., infra, §133Q).

The Commission Comment notes, however, that the new statute has no effect on matters preempted by federal law, such as bankruptcy proceedings and federal tax collection procedures; that it does not apply to an employer's deductions for insurance premiums and payments to health, welfare or pension plans; and that it does not affect procedures for examination of a debtor of the judgment debtor (see C.C.P. 717 et seq., text, §126).

(3) [§133C] (New) Administration and Enforcement.

New Law: For the new Enforcement of Judgments law, see Supp., infra, §227A et seq.

(a) *Judicial Council Rules.* The Council "may provide by rule for the practice and procedure" under the Chapter (except for the State's administrative hearings). (C.C.P. 723.100; see Law Rev. Com. Comment, observing that rules may prescribe the circumstances under which forms in languages other than English may or must be used; see C.C.P. 723.120.) However, "*No findings are required* in court proceedings under this chapter." (C.C.P. 723.106.)

(b) *Judicial Council Forms.* Except for witholding orders for taxes (prescribed by the State; C.C.P. 723.081, Supp., infra, §133Q), the Council "shall prescribe the form of the applications, notices, claims of exemption, orders, and other documents required by this chapter and only such forms may be used to implement this chapter." (C.C.P. 723.120; see Law Rev. Com. Comment, emphasizing complete authority to adopt and revise forms.)

Pursuant to this authority, the following forms were adopted and prescribed by new Rule 982.5, effective January 1, 1980: (1) Application for Earnings Withholding Order; (2) Earnings Withholding Order; (3) Earnings Withholding Order for Support; (4) Employer's Return; (5) Claim of Exemption and Financial Declaration; (6) Notice of Filing of Claim of Exemption; (7) Notice of Opposition to Claim of Exemption; (8) Notice of Hearing on Claim of Exemption; (9) Order Determining Claim of Exemption; (10) Notice of Modification or Termination of Earnings Withholding Order; (11) Application for Earnings Withholding Order for Taxes; (12) Earnings Withholding Order for Taxes; (13) Notice of Hearing (Earnings Withholding Order for Taxes); (14) Temporary Earnings Holding Order for Taxes; (15) Claim of Exemption and Financial Declaration (Earnings Withholding—State Tax Liability).

(c) *Judicial Council Instructions to Employers.* The Council must prepare "employers instructions" to provide the employer with the information needed to comply with the law; and, except to the extent that the instructions are included in the required forms, the levying officer must be provided with copies to give to employers along with withholding orders. (C.C.P. 723.127; see C.C.P. 723.103, Supp., infra, §133F.)

(d) *Judicial Council Liason With Federal Administrator.* The Council is authorized to "perform all acts" required by the Administrator of the Wage and Hour Division of the United States Department of Labor to obtain a state exemption from the earnings garnishment provisions of the Consumer Credit Protection Act of 1968. (C.C.P. 723.151; see Law Rev. Com. Comment.)

(e) *Fraudulent Withholding by Employer.* It is a *misdemeanor* for an employer to withhold earnings and, with intent to defraud either the judgment creditor or the judgment debtor, fail to pay the earnings over to the levying officer. (C.C.P. 723.152.)

(f) *Creditor's Remedies Against Employer.* (1) The judgment creditor may bring a civil action against an employer who *defers or accelerates a payment of earnings* to an employee with the intent to defeat or diminish the creditor's rights under a withholding order; the amount that should have been withheld and paid over may be recovered. (C.C.P. 723.153, stating that this remedy is not exclusive.) (2) The judgment creditor may also sue an employer who *fails to withhold or pay over,* and recover the amount he should have withheld or paid. (C.C.P. 723.154(a), also stating that the remedy is not exclusive.) (See Law Rev. Com. Comment, noting that supplemental proceedings are not a prerequisite to such a suit.)

(g) *Employer Not Liable for Mistaken Compliance.* "[A]n employer who complies with any written order or written notice which purports to be given or served in accordance with the provisions of this chapter is not subject to any civil or criminal liability for such compliance unless the employer has actively participated in a fraud." (C.C.P. 723.154(b); see Law Rev. Com. Comment.)

(b) (New) Withholding Orders: Judgments.

(1) [§133D] (New) Application for Withholding Order.

New Law: For the new Enforcement of Judgments law, see Supp., infra, §227A et seq.

(a) *Writ of Execution as Prerequisite.* The judgment creditor must first obtain a writ of execution to the county where the employer is to be served. He may then file an application with a levying officer in that county. (C.C.P. 723.102(a); see Law Rev. Com. Comment; and see subdivision (b), noting that the section does not apply to a withholding order for taxes, Supp., infra, §133Q.)

(b) *Form of Application.* The application must be executed under oath or by declaration under penalty of perjury, in the form prescribed by the Judicial Council, and containing specified information concerning the judgment debtor, the judgment creditor, the court, the writ, the amount to be collected, the employer and the person to whom the withheld money is to be paid. (C.C.P. 723.102, 723.121.)

(2) (New) Withholding Orders.

(aa) [§133E] (New) Issuance, Content and Form.

New Law: For the new Enforcement of Judgments law, see Supp., infra, §227A et seq.

The levying officer, on filing of the application (see Supp., supra, §133D), "shall promptly issue an earnings withholding order" in the prescribed form. (C.C.P. 723.102.)

The content of the order is specified in C.C.P. 723.125, and includes information concerning the debtor, employer, creditor, levying officer, judgment, writ of execution, amount that may be withheld, the withholding period, and the following orders to the employer: (1) to pay over to the levying officer the amount required; (2) to fill out and send to the officer by first-class mail within 15 days after service, the "employer's return" (see Supp., infra, §133H); (3) to deliver to the judgment debtor, within 10 days after service, a copy of the withholding order and the notice to employee (see Supp., infra, §133G), unless the judgment debtor is no longer employed and no earnings are owed.

(bb) [§133F] (New) Service on Employer.

New Law: For the new Enforcement of Judgments law, see Supp., infra, §227A et seq.

(1) *What Must Be Served.* The levying officer must serve the employer with an original and copy of the withholding order, the form for the employer's return, and the form of the notice to the

employee (see Supp., infra, §133G). (C.C.P. 723.103(a).) He must also provide the employer with a copy of his instructions (see Supp., supra, §133C), unless a Judicial Council rule excuses compliance. (C.C.P. 723.103(b).)

(2) *Who May Be Served.* The withholding order may be served on (1) a managing agent or person in charge of the branch or office where the employee works or from which he is paid; or (2) any person on whom a summons may be served under C.C.P. 416.10 et seq. (see *Actions,* §649 et seq.). (C.C.P. 723.101.)

(3) *Types of Service.* Service of the withholding order may ordinarily be made by personal delivery or by registered or certified mail; but if mailed service is ineffective personal service is required. (C.C.P. 723.101(b).) (See also C.C.P. 723.101(c), as amended in 1979, permitting service of any other notice or document by first class mail with postage prepaid; C.C.P. 723.101(d), added in 1979, permitting creditor to request personal service of earnings withholding order; C.C.P. 723.101(e), added in 1980, permitting registered process servers to serve earnings withholding orders; 11 Pacific L. J. 373.)

(4) *Time of Service.* No order may be served after the time for return of the writ of execution (C.C.P. 683(a), text, §72) has expired. (C.C.P. 723.103(c).)

(5) *Lien Created by Service.* Service of the order creates a lien on the earnings of the judgment debtor in the amount required to be withheld, which continues for 1 year from the date the earnings became payable. (C.C.P. 723.029; see Law Rev. Com. Comment, pointing out that service of the order is a form of levy of execution, and that the purpose of this section is to protect the employer against stale claims and to give the levying creditor priority over competing claims by third parties where priority is not already regulated by other sections (see Supp., infra, §133W et seq.).)

(cc) [§133G] (New) Notice to Employee.

New Law: For the new Enforcement of Judgments law, see Supp., infra, §227A et seq.

(1) *Duty To Deliver.* The employer served with a withholding order must, within 10 days from the date of service, deliver to the employee a notice of the order. (C.C.P. 723.104(a).) Failure to comply with this requirement does not subject the employer to civil liability, but in extreme cases he may be punished for contempt. (C.C.P. 723.104(a); see Law Rev. Com. Comment.)

(2) *Form of Notice.* The notice must inform the employee "in simple terms" of the nature of a wage garnishment, the right to an exemption and procedure for claiming it, certain specified additional

matters, and "any other information" which the Judicial Council considers useful. (C.C.P. 723.122.)

(dd) [§133H] (New) Employer's Return.

New Law: For the new Enforcement of Judgments law, see Supp., infra, §227A et seq.

(1) *Duty To Mail Return.* The employer served with a withholding order must, within 15 days from the date of service, complete and mail his "return" to the levying officer. (C.C.P. 723.104(b).) If the withholding order is *ineffective,* the employer must state in his return that he will not comply for this reason, and must return the order. (C.C.P. 723.104; on ineffective orders where others have priority, see Supp., infra, §133W et seq.)

(2) *Form of Return.* The "employer's return" must be executed under oath or by declaration under penalty of perjury; it must contain certain specified information about the judgment debtor's employment and his earnings, and must be on the form prescribed by the Judicial Council and provided by the levying officer. (C.C.P. 723.126, 723.104.)

(ee) [§133-I] (New) Employer's Duties To Withhold and Pay.

New Law: For the new Enforcement of Judgments law, see Supp., infra, §227A et seq.

(1) *Duty To Withhold.* "Except as otherwise provided by statute, an employer *shall withhold* the amounts required by an earnings withholding order from all earnings of the employee payable for any pay period of such employee which ends during the *withholding period,*" (C.C.P. 723.022(b); see C.C.P. 723.022(c) [not liable for amounts withheld and paid over to levying officer prior to service of notice of termination (see infra, this section)].)

The "withholding period" is defined in C.C.P. 723.022(a) as the period which *commences* on the 10th day after service of the withholding order, and *continues* until the earliest of the following dates: (1) The 100th day after the order was served. (2) The date the employer has withheld the full amount specified in the order. (3) The date of termination specified in a court order served on the employer. (4) The date of termination specified in a notice of termination served on the employer by the levying officer. (See elaborate Law Rev. Com. explanatory Comment, with the cautionary note that only earnings for the pay period ending during the withholding period are subject to levy; earnings for prior periods, even though still in the employer's possession, are not subject to the order.)

(2) *Duty To Pay Officer.* The amount withheld must normally be

paid to the levying officer not later than the 15th day of each month. (C.C.P. 723.025(a).) The employer, however, may elect to make more frequent payments; and, if he so elects, must make payments not later than 10 days after the close of the pay period. (C.C.P. 723.025(b).)

(ff) [§133J] (New) Officer's Duty To Pay and Make Return.

New Law: For the new Enforcement of Judgments law, see Supp., infra, §227A et seq.

(1) *Payment of Money Received.* The levying officer must pay the amounts received (see Supp., supra, §133H) "to the person entitled thereto" at least once every 30 days. (C.C.P. 723.026(a).)

(2) *Return on Writ.* Where the withholding order has been served before the time the writ of execution is returnable under C.C.P. 683(a) (text, §72), the levying officer may, in his discretion, return the writ at either of the following times: (1) After the withholding order terminates and the amount withheld has been paid over to him. (2) Earlier, by indicating the date of service of the withholding order on the employer, and making a supplemental return on the order. (C.C.P. 723.026(b); see Law Rev. Com. Comment, pointing out that ordinarily the levying officer will delay his return until the withholding order expires so as to avoid the need to make a supplemental return; but, if the judgment creditor desires to obtain another writ to levy on other property, the officer can return the writ and make a supplemental return later on the withholding order.) However, subdivision (b), supra, does not extend the time within which a levy may be made under the writ of execution. (C.C.P. 723.026(c); see Law Rev. Com. Comment.)

(3) (New) Judgment Debtor's Exemptions.

(aa) [§133K] (New) Types of Exemptions Allowed.

New Law: For the new Enforcement of Judgments law, see Supp., infra, §227A et seq.

(1) *Standard Exemption.* The standard or basic exemption is the amount specified in the Federal Consumer Protection Act of 1970. (C.C.P. 723.050.) That statute restricts garnishment for any workweek to 25% of disposable earnings or disposable earnings less 30 times the federal minimum hourly wage, whichever amount is less. (See 10 Pacific L. J. 331.) This standard exemption applies to ordinary earnings withholding orders, not to orders issued for child or spousal support (see Supp., infra. §113V) or withholding orders for taxes (see Supp., infra, §133Q et seq.). (See Law Rev. Com. Comment to C.C.P. 723.050.)

(2) *Hardship Exemption.* The "hardship exemption" of former C.C.P. 690.6 (see text, §61 et seq.) is continued in C.C.P. 723.051, with some modifications. (a) *The exemption:* That portion of the judgment debtor's earnings which he proves is necessary for the support of himself or his family supported in whole or in part by him. (b) *The exception:* The exemption is not allowed where the debt is incurred (1) for personal services rendered by an employee or former employee of the debtor, or (2) by the debtor, or his or her spouse or family for the "common necessaries of life." (See Law Rev. Com. Comment, pointing out that the limitation in former C.C.P. 690.6 to earnings received within 30 days prior to the date of withholding was eliminated; and see 10 Pacific L. J. 332.) (For the exemption applicable to withholding orders for support, and the power of the court to make an equitable division of earnings, see C.C.P. 723.052, and Law Rev. Com. Comment.)

See *J.J. MacIntyre Co. v. Duren* (1981) 118 C.A.3d Supp. 16, 173 C.R. 715.

(bb) [§133L] (New) Claim of Hardship Exemption.

New Law: For the new Enforcement of Judgments law, see Supp., infra, §227A et seq.

(1) *Circumstances.* A judgment debtor may claim an exemption under C.C.P. 723.051 (Supp., supra, §133K) under either of the following circumstances: "(1) No prior hearing has been held with respect to the earnings withholding order. (2) There has been a material change in circumstances since the time of the last prior hearing on the earnings withholding order." (C.C.P. 723.105(a); see Law Rev. Com. Comment.)

(2) *Procedure.* The claim is made by filing with the levying officer an original and one copy of (1) the judgment debtor's claim of exemption, and (2) his financial statement. (C.C.P. 723.105(b).) Both documents must be executed under oath or by declaration under penalty of perjury, and the contents are specified in C.C.P. 723.123 and 723.124. The levying officer has copies of the Judicial Council forms, available without charge. (C.C.P. 723.129.) (See Law Rev. Com. Comment to C.C.P. 723.105.)

(cc) [§133M] (New) Judgment Creditor's Contest.

New Law: For the new Enforcement of Judgments law, see Supp., infra, §227A et seq.

(1) *Levying Officer's Notice to Judgment Creditor.* On the filing of the claim of exemption, the levying officer must promptly send copies

of the claim of exemption and financial statement, together with a *notice of claim of exemption.* This notice, on a Judicial Council form, states that the claim has been filed and that the withholding order will be terminated or modified unless a *notice of opposition* is filed with the levying officer within 10 days after the date of mailing of the notice of claim. (C.C.P. 723.105(c); see Law Rev. Com. Comment.)

(2) *Judgment Creditor's Notice of Opposition.* Within the 10-day period (see supra) the judgment creditor who desires to contest must file a notice of opposition to the claim. (C.C.P. 723.105(c).) This notice must be executed under oath or by declaration under penalty of perjury, and must contain specified information. (C.C.P. 723.128.) (On effect of failure to file, see Supp., infra, §133N.)

See *Westervelt v. Robertson* (1981) 122 C.A.3d Supp. 1, 9, 176 C.R. 94.

(3) *Notice of Motion for Hearing.* If the notice of opposition is timely filed the judgment creditor is entitled to a hearing. To obtain it he must file a *notice of motion* within the same 10-day period (see supra). (C.C.P. 723.105(e).)

(4) *Hearing on Notice.* The hearing must be held not later than 20 days from the date the notice of motion was filed unless a continuance is granted for good cause. Not less than 10 days prior to the hearing the judgment creditor must (a) *give written notice* of the hearing to the levying officer; and (b) *serve a notice* of the hearing and copy of the notice of opposition *by mail* on the judgment debtor (and, if the claim of exemption so requested, on his attorney). Service is deemed made on proper deposit in the mail, and the judgment creditor must file proof of such service with the court. (C.C.P. 723.105(e).) On receipt of the notice of hearing the levying officer files the claim of exemption and the notice of opposition with the court. (C.C.P. 723.105.)

(dd)   [§133N]   (New) Termination or Modification of Order.

New Law: For the new Enforcement of Judgments law, see Supp., infra, §227A et seq.

(1) *Where No Notice of Opposition or Notice of Hearing.* If the levying officer does not receive a timely notice of opposition and timely notice of hearing (see Supp., supra, §133M), he must serve on the employer one of the following: (1) A notice that the *withholding order has been terminated* if all of the earnings were claimed to be exempt. (2) A *modified withholding order* "which reflects the amount of earnings claimed to be exempt" if only a portion were so claimed. (C.C.P. 723.105(f).)

(2) *Order After Hearing.* The court, after the hearing, may order that the withholding order be *modified* or *terminated.* If it does, the clerk must promptly transmit a certified copy of the order to the levying officer; and the levying officer must promptly serve on the employer (1) a copy of the modified withholding order or (2) a notice that the withholding order has been terminated. (C.C.P. 723.105(g).) The court may order that the withholding order be terminated as of *a date which precedes the date of hearing;* and it may order that any amount withheld in excess of the proper amount be promptly paid to the judgment debtor. (C.C.P. 723.105(g).)

(3) *After Judgment Satisfied.* If the judgment is satisfied the judgment creditor must promptly notify the levying officer, and he must promptly serve a notice of termination on the employer. (C.C.P. 723.027; see Law Rev. Com. Comment.)

(4) *Judgment Debtor's Recovery of Amounts Withheld.* (a) If an employer has withheld and *paid over* amounts after the date of termination but *prior to receipt of notice of it,* he is not liable to the judgment debtor; the latter may recover such amounts only from the levying officer (if he has the money) or from the judgment creditor (if it has been paid over). (C.C.P. 723.105(i).) (b) If the employer has withheld amounts after termination but has *not paid them over to the levying officer,* he must promptly pay them to the judgment debtor. (C.C.P. 723.105(i).)

(ee) [§133-O]   (New) **Appeals From Orders.**

New Law: For the new Enforcement of Judgments law, see Supp., infra, §227A et seq.

Appeals from orders under the exemption claim section are covered by C.C.P. 723.105(j):

(1) An appeal lies from any order denying a claim of exemption.

(2) The judgment creditor may appeal from an order modifying or terminating a withholding order. But the appeal does not stay the modifying or terminating order: Until it is set aside or modified, "the order allowing the claim of exemption in whole or in part shall be given the same effect as if the appeal had not been taken."

(4) [§133P]   (New) **New Withholding Orders.**

New Law: For the new Enforcement of Judgments law, see Supp., infra, §227A et seq.

(a) *After Court Termination of Withholding Order.* If the withholding order is terminated by the court (see Supp., supra, §133N), the judgment creditor cannot immediately apply for another order directed to the same employer with respect to the same judgment debtor. Unless the court otherwise orders or there is a material change in circumstances since the time of the last hearing, the judgment creditor is precluded from making such an application for (1) a period of 100 days following the date of service of the withholding order, or (2) 60 days after the date of its termination, whichever is later. (C.C.P. 723.105(h); see Law Rev. Com. Comment.)

(b) *After Prior Withholding Order.* If the judgment creditor has obtained a withholding order, and the employer withholds earnings pursuant thereto, the judgment creditor cannot have another withholding order served for 10 days following expiration of the prior order. (C.C.P. 723.107.) The purpose of this limitation is to give other judgment creditors a 10-day period to serve their withholding orders. (Law Rev. Com. Comment.)

(c) *To Recover Costs and Interest.* "Subject to Section 723.107" (see supra, this section), a judgment creditor may apply for another withholding order to recover costs and interest that may have accrued since the original application. (C.C.P. 723.028; see Law Rev. Com. Comment.)

(c)   (New) Withholding Orders: Taxes.

(1)   [§133Q]   (New) Nature and Scope of Statutes.

New Law: For the new Enforcement of Judgments law, see Supp., infra, §227A et seq.

(a) *Separate Treatment.* Withholding orders for taxes are separately treated in Article 4 of the new Chapter (C.C.P. 723.070 et seq.) A distinct procedure is created (C.C.P. 723.072; see Supp., infra, §133S et seq.); the forms are mainly prescribed by the state taxing agencies (C.C.P. 723.081); special provisions are made for service of notice, documents and orders (C.C.P. 723.080); a withholding order may be issued whether or not the tax liability has been reduced to judgment (C.C.P. 723.072(d)); and the debtor's hardship exemption provisions (see Supp., supra, §§133K, 133L) do not apply (C.C.P. 723.105(K)).

Special definitions are added for "State" and "State tax liability" (C.C.P. 723.070); and "levying officer" is deemed to mean the specific state agency seeking to collect a state tax liability (C.C.P. 723.073). A "withholding order for taxes" is an earnings withholding order issued pursuant to the Article "and shall be denoted as a withholding order for taxes on its face." (C.C.P. 723.072(a).) (See also C.C.P. 723.084 [when warrant, notice of levy, or notice of order to withhold shall be deemed to be a withholding order for taxes].)

Where no express exception is made, however, the general procedural provisions of the Chapter apply. (C.C.P. 723.073.)

(b) *Other State Remedies.* "This chapter does not limit the state's right to collect a state tax liability except that (a) no levy upon earnings of an employee held by an employer is effective unless such levy is made in accordance with the provisions of this chapter and (b) the methods of collection referred to in subdivision (b) of Section 723.070 may not be used to require an employer to withhold earnings of an employee in payment of a state tax liability." (C.C.P. 723.071.) The Law Revision Commission points out that this Article establishes an *exclusive procedure* for withholding earnings to collect *certain state taxes* (listed in C.C.P. 723.070(b)). Collection of federal taxes is governed by federal law; and, as to other taxes not within the scope of the Article, the tax obligation must be reduced to judgment and the ordinary procedure applies (see Supp., supra, §133D et seq.).

(2) [§133R] (New) Grounds for Issuance of Withholding Order.

New Law: For the new Enforcement of Judgments law, see Supp., infra, §227A et seq.

A withholding order for taxes may be issued only where (1) the existence of the state tax liability appears on the face of the taxpayer's return; or (2) the liability has been assessed or determined in an administrative proceeding under the Revenue and Taxation Code or Unemployment Insurance Code, and the taxpayer had notice and an opportunity for administrative review. In the latter case, if the taxpayer makes a timely request for review the order cannot be issued until the administrative review procedure is completed. (C.C.P. 723.072(b); see Law Rev. Com. Comment.)

(3) (New) Procedure.

(aa) [§133S] (New) Issuance of Order.

New Law: For the new Enforcement of Judgments law, see Supp., infra, §227A et seq.

(1) *By State.* The state may itself issue a withholding order for taxes, specifying the amount to be withheld. Unless a lesser amount is specified, the amount is the same as that specified by C.C.P. 723.050 for ordinary judgment creditor withholding orders (see Supp., supra, §133K). (C.C.P. 723.074.)

(2) *By Court, for Larger Amount.* In some cases the State may seek withholding of an amount in excess of that which could be withheld pursuant to an order obtained under C.C.P. 723.074 (supra, this section). This may be done by court order, under C.C.P. 723.076, as follows:

(a) The State may "at any time" file an application in a court of record in the county of the taxpayer's last known residence. The application must include an affidavit or declaration under penalty of perjury stating that the taxpayer has been served with a copy of the application and a notice informing him of its purpose and his right to a hearing. (C.C.P. 723.076(b)(c).)

(b) A hearing is held on notice deposited in the mail at least 10 days before the day set. (C.C.P. 723.076(d).)

(c) After the hearing the court issues an order requiring withholding of "all earnings of the taxpayer other than the amount which the taxpayer proves is exempt" under C.C.P. 723.051 (see Supp., supra, §133K), but not less than that permitted to be withheld under C.C.P. 723.050 (see Supp., supra, §133K). (C.C.P. 723.076(e); see Law Rev. Com. Comment.)

(3) *Temporary Earnings Holding Order.* (a) If the State intends to apply to the court for a withholding order and has determined that collection will be jeopardized during the period for court action on the application, C.C.P. 723.076(f) authorizes the State to issue "a temporary earnings holding order, which shall be denoted as such on its face," requiring the employer to retain earnings then or thereafter due. (b) A copy of this order and a notice to the taxpayer is served on the employer, who must deliver copies to the taxpayer. (c) The temporary order expires 15 days from the date it is served on the employer unless extended by the court on ex parte application for good cause shown. (d) The State may not, for a period of 6 months, serve another temporary order on the same employer for the same employee, unless the court for good cause shown otherwise orders. (e) C.C.P. 723.153 (employer's duty not to defer or accelerate earnings; Supp., supra, §133C), and C.C.P. 723.154 (remedies of judgment creditor and limitation of employer's liability; Supp., supra, §133C), apply to temporary orders issued under this section. (See Law Rev. Com. Comment, observing that such orders should be used only in rare and unusual cases.)

(bb) [§133T] (New) Service of Order and Notice.

New Law: For the new Enforcement of Judgments law, see Supp., infra, §227A et seq.

(1) The State must serve the employer with the withholding order and an additional copy and a notice informing the taxpayer of his rights. Within 10 days from the date of service the employer must deliver copies to the taxpayer, except that immediate delivery must be made where a jeopardy withholding order has been served. (C.C.P. 723.075(b).) (On priority of the order, see Supp., infra, §133Y.)

(2) Service of a withholding order may be made by mail, and is complete when received by the employer or an authorized person (C.C.P. 723.101(a)(1)(2), Supp., supra, §133F). (C.C.P. 723.080.)

(3) Service of any other notice or document may also be made by

mail, and is complete when it is deposited in the mail. (C.C.P. 723.080.)

(cc) [§133U] (New) Hearing.

New Law: For the new Enforcement of Judgments law, see Supp., infra, §227A et seq.

C.C.P. 723.074(c) requires an administrative hearing on the amount to be withheld, at the request of the taxpayer made at any time after service of the order. The matter must be determined within 15 days after the request is received by the State, and determination of the amount is subject to the standard provided in C.C.P. 723.051 (hardship exemption; Supp., supra, §133K).

No review of the taxpayer's *tax liability* is permitted. (C.C.P. 723.082.)

(d) [§133V] (New) Withholding Order for Support.

New Law: For the new Enforcement of Judgments law, see Supp., infra, §227A et seq.

C.C.P. 723.030 deals specifically with a "withholding order for support," defined as "an earnings withholding order on a writ of execution issued to collect delinquent amounts payable under a judgment for the support of a child, or spouse or former spouse, of the judgment debtor." (C.C.P. 723.030(a); see Law Rev. Com. Comment.)

This order does not terminate 100 days after service (see Supp., supra, §133-I); the employer must continue to withhold earnings until the ealiest of the dates specified in C.C.P. 723.022(a)(2)(3)(4) (see Supp., supra, §133-I). However, it will automatically terminate 1 year after the employment ceases. (C.C.P. 723.030(b)(1); see Law Rev. Com. Comment.) (On priority of the order, see C.C.P. 723.030(b)(2)(3), Supp., infra, §133X.)

(e) (New) Priorities.

(1) [§133W] (New) Wage Assignments.

New Law: For the new Enforcement of Judgments law, see Supp., infra, §227A et seq.

An order of assignment of wages for child support made pursuant to C.C. 4701 (see 6 *Summary, Parent and Child,* §139) has priority over any earnings withholding order, including one for support. An employer who is served with an order made under C.C. 4701 must comply with it, disregarding any earnings withholding order, and must notify the levying officer that a supervening wage assignment for support is in effect. (C.C.P. 723.031(a)(b); see Law Rev. Com.

[65]

Comment.) (On determining the amount to be withheld, see C.C.P, 723.031(d)(e), and Law Rev. Com. Comment.)

(2) [§133X] (New) Withholding Order for Support.

New Law: For the new Enforcement of Judgments law, see Supp., infra, §227A et seq.

A withholding order for support (see Supp., supra, §133V) has priority over *any other earnings withholding order.* (C.C.P. 723.030(b)(2); see Law Rev. Com. Comment; as to priority of a *wage assignment,* see Supp., supra, §133W.)

Although the support order has priority, it does not preclude another order; the employer must withhold earnings pursuant to both a withholding order for support and another earnings withholding order, deducting from the employee's earnings the amount withheld for support before withholding any amount pursuant to the other order. (C.C.P. 723.030(b)(3); see Law Rev. Com. Comment.)

(3) [§133Y] (New) Withholding Order for Taxes.

New Law: For the new Enforcement of Judgments law, see Supp., infra, §227A et seq.

(a) *Priority Over Other Orders.* A withholding order for taxes has priority over any earnings withholding order except one for support. When served the employer must cease withholding pursuant to an ordinary earnings withholding order and notify the levying officer that a supervening withholding order for taxes is in effect. (C.C.P. 723.077(a); see Law Rev. Com. Comment.)

(b) *Priority of First Order for Taxes.* If a withholding order for taxes is in effect, a subsequent withholding order for taxes is ineffective, and the employer must promptly notify the taxing agency that issued or obtained the second order of the reason for disregarding it. (C.C.P 723.077(b); C.C.P. 723.104(b); see Law Rev. Com. Comment.)

(4) [§133Z] (New) Other Withholding Orders.

New Law: For the new Enforcement of Judgments law, see Supp., infra, §227A et seq.

Ordinary withholding orders obtained by judgment creditors (see Supp., supra, §133D et seq.) are governed by the basic rule of first in time.

(a) *First Order Served.* Unless one of the exceptions for particular orders applies, the basic rule governs: The employer must comply with the first earnings withholding order served upon him. (C.C.P. 723.023(a); see Law Rev. Com. Comment.)

(b) *Orders Served on Same Day: First Judgment Entered.* If two or more earnings withholding orders are served on the same day, the employer must comply with the order issued pursuant to the judgment first entered. (C.C.P. 723.023(b); see C.C.P. 723.125(c) [order gives date of entry].) If the judgments were entered on the same day, the employer has discretion to select the one with which he will comply. (C.C.P. 723.023(b).)

(1) [§134] Nature of Statute.

New Law: For the new Enforcement of Judgments law, see Supp., infra, §227A et seq.

C.C.P. 710 was amended in 1976 to delete the special procedure for reaching wages and salaries of public employees: "This section shall not be construed to authorize the withholding of earnings of a public officer or employee. Except as otherwise expressly provided by law, the earnings of a public officer or employee may be withheld for payment of a judgment only pursuant to Section 682.3." (C.C.P. 710, as amended.) (See Supp., supra, §66A.)

C.C.P. 710(h) was amended in 1978 to refer to the superseding provisions of the Employees' Earnings Protection Law (see Supp., infra, §133B) instead of to former C.C.P. 682.3.

(3) [§136] State and Local Officers.

New Law: For the new Enforcement of Judgments law, see Supp., infra, §227A et seq.

C.C.P. 710 was amended in 1976 to eliminate the special procedure for reaching wages and salaries of public employees. (See Supp., supra, §134.)

(b) *Constitutional Officers.* The quoted language from C.C.P. 710(f) was deleted in 1976. (See supra, this section.)

Cross-Reference: 5 *Summary, Constitutional Law,* §449 et seq.

(1) [§137] Affidavit and Judgment.

New Law: For the new Enforcement of Judgments law, see Supp., infra, §227A et seq.

Money owing by state: C.C.P. 710a(1) was amended in 1971 to delete the reference to the Personnel Board. Hence, after filing with the proper board or department, all state claims are forwarded to the Controller.

(2) [§138] Payment.

New Law: For the new Enforcement of Judgments law, see Supp., infra, §227A et seq.

(a) *Payment into Court.* The language quoted from C.C.P. 710(a) was deleted in 1976. (See Supp., supra, §134.)

(a) [§140]   Nature and Scope of Remedy.

New Law: For the new Enforcement of Judgments law, see Supp., infra, §227A et seq.

See *Del Conte Masonry Co. v. N. T. Lewis* (1971) 16 C.A.3d 678, 94 C.R. 439, Supp., infra, §141A; *Takehara v. H. C. Muddox Co.* (1972) 8 C.3d 168, 172, 104 C.R. 345, 501 P.2d 913, Supp., infra, §141A, citing the text; *Roseburg Loggers v. U. S. Plywood-Champion Papers* (1975) 14 C.3d 742, 747, 122 C.R. 567, 537 P.2d 399, Supp., infra, §141A, citing the text; *Atiya v. Di Bartolo* (1976) 63 C.A.3d 121, 133 C.R. 611, Supp., infra, §141; *Abatti v. Eldridge* (1980) 103 C.A.3d 484, 486, 163 C.R. 82; *Abatti v. Eldridge* (1980) 112 C.A.3d 411, 169 C.R. 330; C.E.B., Debt Collection Manual, §8.40 et seq.

C.C.P. 688 is now C.C.P. 688(f). (See Supp., supra, §§11, 73A.)

Tax liens attach to a taxpayer's cause of action "[n]otwithstanding the provisions of Sections 688 and 688.1 of the Code of Civil Procedure." (See, e.g., Rev.C. 6757(f); 5 *Summary, Taxation,* Supp., §95B.)

(New) Lien against claim of defendant: In *Abatti v. Eldridge,* supra, plaintiffs sued defendants for specific performance of an option agreement for purchase of real property. L, judgment creditor of defendants, moved to impose a lien on any money defendants might recover from plaintiffs. Defendants contended that the statute authorized a lien only on a "cause of action," and that defendants had no cause of action. *Held,* the lien was properly imposed. In order for plaintiffs to obtain specific performance of their contract they had to pay the agreed purchase price of $246,500 to defendants. Hence defendants as well as plaintiffs had a right to relief in the proceeding; and, under a broad interpretation of "cause of action" as "the obligation sought to be enforced," a cause of action was vested in defendants and therefore was subject to L's lien. (103 C.A.3d 488, 489.)

(b) [§141]   Procedure.

New Law: For the new Enforcement of Judgments law, see Supp., infra, §227A et seq.

See C.E.B., Debt Collection Manual, §§8.41, 8.42.

p. 3502:

(2) *Granting of Lien.* In *Atiya v. Di Bartolo* (1976) 63 C.A.3d 121, 133 C.R. 611, an order denying the lien was based on defense counsel's declarations that the lien would make settlement virtually impossible. *Held,* order reversed. (a) Counsel's declarations were

insufficient because they only stated opinions without factual support. (b) Even an adequate evidentiary showing that settlement negotiations might be frustrated would not justify denial of the lien. (c) The defense of other available remedies failed for lack of proof of other assets subject to levy. (63 C.A.3d 126.)

(c) [§141A] (New) Priorities.

New Law: For the new Enforcement of Judgments law, see Supp., infra, §227A et seq.

(1) *First To Assert a Claim.* In *Del Conte Masonry Co. v. N. T. Lewis* (1971) 16 C.A.3d 678, 94 C.R. 439, Del Conte, a subcontractor, sued Lewis, the general contractor, for money due. Prior to judgment, L, a creditor of Del Conte, moved for an order under C.C.P. 688.1 granting a lien on the cause of action and anticipated judgment. On receiving notice of motion and before the hearing, Del Conte by written agreement granted a lien on the cause of action to its attorney B personally to secure his fees, and to him as trustee to secure payment to other materialmen creditors of Del Conte. The trial judge granted L's motion and determined that L's lien was entitled to priority over B's. *Held,* affirmed.

(a) The statute does not indicate priorities, and the general rule of first in time was urged by B, who contended that L's lien did not arise until the order granting the motion was entered and the lien thereby created. (16 C.A.3d 680.)

(b) But the equitable rule giving priority to the one who first asserts a claim is preferable; and priority may also be given to an equitable lien as of "the time of the occurrences which gave rise to the underlying substantive right." (16 C.A.3d 681.)

See *Cetenko v. United Cal. Bank* (1982) 30 C.3d 528, 179 C.R. 902, 638 P.2d 1299; *Nicoletti v. Lizzoli* (1981) 124 C.A.3d 361, 177 C.R. 685.

(2) *First in Time.* In *Takehara v. H. C. Muddox Co.* (1972) 8 C.3d 168, 104 C.R. 345, 501 P.2d 913, Muddox had a cause of action against certain persons. In October, 1965, Mission obtained an order granting a lien on it. In June, 1968, Muddox received judgment of $24,000 on the cause of action. The trial judge gave priority to the Mission lien, and this exhausted the recovery. The other creditors appealed, contending that recovery of judgment was analogous to a judgment debtor acquiring property; hence that, up to the time of judgment, there was nothing to which Mission's lien could attach, and when judgment was rendered all the liens attached simultaneously. *Held,* judgment affirmed. The lien attaches to the *cause of action,* before any judgment is recovered; and its priority, under the rule of first in time of *creation,* carries over to the judgment. (8 C.3d 172.)

(3) *Equitable Offset.* In *Salaman v. Bolt* (1977) 74 C.A.3d 907, 141 C.R. 841, plaintiff lessors leased property to defendant Bolt, lessee, and later brought unlawful detainer. The trial judge found that one of the lessors had been guilty of oppressive and inequitable conduct, and awarded Bolt $8,000 attorneys' fees and costs. Bolt then confessed to judgment in favor of Field, his attorney, in the amount of $31,036.52 for services rendered, and Field made a motion for a lien on Bolt's cause of action for fees. The motion was denied, but the Court of Appeal reversed, holding that Field had a judgment lien on Bolt's $8,000 judgment. In the meantime plaintiffs obtained judgment against Bolt for $6,214.44 on an unrelated cause of action, and moved to offset their judgment against Bolt's judgment for attorneys' fees. The trial judge gave priority to Field's judgment lien and denied plaintiffs' claim of offset. *Held,* reversed. (a) As between a statutory lien and a right of equitable offset, things are not equal, and the offset is given an equitable preference. (74 C.A.3d 918, quoting *Harrison v. Adams* and *Highsmith v. Lair,* text, §212.) (b) The language of C.C.P. 688.1 is consistent with this approach, and plaintiffs were therefore entitled to offset their judgment against Bolt's judgment, with Field's lien reaching only the excess, if any, remaining. (74 C.A.3d 919, 920.)

(4) *Unemployment Insurance Tax Lien Has No Special Priority.* In *Roseburg Loggers v. U. S. Plywood-Champion Papers* (1975) 14 C.3d 742, 122 C.R. 567, 537 P.2d 399, Roseburg sued Plywood for breach of contract. In February, 1970, the Director of Human Resources Development recorded a certificate of Roseburg's delinquency in payment of unemployment insurance contributions; in June, 1970, Standley, who had obtained a default judgment against Roseburg for $145,253.14, made a motion under C.C.P. 688.1 and the court granted a lien on the Roseburg cause of action against Plywood; in December, 1970, the Director made a similar motion and the court granted a similar lien, but made it effective as of February, 1970, when the Director's certificate of delinquency was filed. *Held,* the order giving priority to the Director's lien was error.

(a) The statute is silent on priorities, but, under the holding in *Takehara,* supra, Standley's lien would prevail as first in time (order granting it entered more than 8 months prior to order granting Director's lien). (14 C.3d 748.)

(b) The Director relied on Unemp.Ins.C. 1703, which gives his recorded certificate of delinquency "the force, effect and priority of a judgment lien." But a judgment which merely creates a lien on specific property is not a proper basis for execution; the remedy is an action to foreclose the lien. (14 C.3d 749, citing the text, §10.) Accordingly, Unemp.Ins.C. 1785 provides for a warrant of enforcement, with the effect of a writ of execution. However, since C.C.P. 688 prevents execution on a cause of action, the warrant cannot be enforced against a cause of action; the Director, like other creditors, must make a motion under C.C.P. 688.1. (14 C.3d 749.)

(c) Since nothing in the Unemployment Insurance Code suggests that the Director's lien has any special priority, the *Takehara* rule applies; i.e., the first lien created under C.C.P. 688.1 is prior. This follows the general rule that, regardless of the order in which judgment creditors obtain their judgments, the first to levy execution has priority (see text, §75): "[W]here the property is a cause of action, the first to 'levy,' e.g., obtain a lien under section 688.1, has priority." (14 C.3d 750, footnote 6.)

4. [§142] Charging Order Against Partnership.

New Law: For the new Enforcement of Judgments law, see Supp., infra, §227A et seq.

(a) *Normal Remedy.* See 51 Cal. S.B.J. 394 [discussion of procedure with suggested forms].

Evans v. Galardi (1976) 16 C.3d 300, 128 C.R. 25, 546 P.2d 313, involved an unsuccessful attempt to reach assets of limited partners.

In 1969, plaintiff E and defendants G and H formed El Dorado, a limited partnership, which built a motel in South Lake Tahoe, called Rodeway Inn. The general partner was E Corp., which operated the motel, and whose stock was initially owned by the three individuals. In 1970 plaintiff contracted to sell to defendants all of his interest in the limited partnership and all of his stock in the corporation, and defendants gave him their promissory note for the price. Defendants defaulted, and plaintiff sued and recovered judgment against them as individuals for the amount due. He then obtained a writ of execution and instructed the sheriff to levy on the Rodeway Inn. El Dorado filed a third party claim, contending that plaintiff could only reach the partnership assets by a charging order. The trial judge sustained the third party claim, and plaintiff appealed, contending that, since defendants as limited partners were each entitled to half the net profits of the business, and together owned all the equitable interest in the corporation general partner, El Dorado was not a bona fide third party. *Held,* judgment affirmed.

(1) Assets of the limited partnership were not available to satisfy the judgment against the limited partners in their individual capacities. (a) No California decision has considered the question, but authorities elsewhere and legal commentators are agreed that a limited partner has no interest in partnership property. By the very nature of the relationship he is primarily an investor who contributes capital and acquires the right to share in profits, but is not liable for debts except to the extent of his capital contribution. (16 C.3d 308; see 6 *Summary, Partnership,* §54.) (b) No contrary conclusion is

compelled simply because defendants were entitled to 100% of the net partnership profits. (16 C.3d 309.) And no showing was made that El Dorado was not a bona fide limited partnership or that it was used by defendants to perpetrate a fraud. (16 C.3d 310.)

(2) A charging order was the proper remedy. Plaintiff's argument, that an exception should be implied where the judgment debtors own the entire proprietary interest in the business, is not persuasive; the statutory remedy of charging order has replaced levies of execution in both general and limited partnership cases. (16 C.3d 310.)

(3) Plaintiff's final contention was that El Dorado, owned entirely by defendants, should not be considered a separate entity. But the statutes treat it as a separate entity for purposes of suing and being sued (C.C.P. 388(a); Corp.C. 15526), and it was not named as a party or in any way involved in plaintiff's action against defendants. (16 C.3d 311.)

See C.E.B., Debt Collection Manual, §8.23 et seq.

1.   [§143]   Nature of Remedy.

New Law: For the new Enforcement of Judgments law, see Supp., infra, §227A et seq.

See C.E.B., Debt Collection Manual, §9.39 et seq.

(a)   [§146]   In General.

New Law: For the new Enforcement of Judgments law, see Supp., infra, §227A et seq.

See 6 A.L.R.4th 862 [applicability of rule denying recovery for fraudulent conveyance where the claim motivating the conveyance was never established].

(1) *Nature of Fraudulent Conveyance.* See 90 Harv. L. Rev. 505 [related concepts of fraudulent conveyance, equitable subordination, dividend restraints, and piercing corporate veil].

(2) *Uniform Act.* The Act is now in 7A U.L.A. (Master Ed.) 161.

Construction to bring about uniformity: See *Kirkland v. Risso* (1979) 98 C.A.3d 971, 977, 159 C.R. 798.

(3) *Preferences Distinguished.* C.C. 3448 et seq., governing statutory assignments for the benefit of creditors, were repealed in 1980, pursuant to the recommendation of the California Law Revision Commission, because common law assignments are used in nearly all cases. (For the current law on preferences in assignments for the benefit of creditors, see C.C.P. 1800, added in 1979; 11 Pacific L. J. 339.)

Cross-Reference: 7 *Summary, Equity,* §12.

(1) [§147] Actual Intent To Defraud.

New Law: For the new Enforcement of Judgments law, see Supp., infra, §227A et seq.

(a) *In General.* Intent to defraud does not necessarily require a malicious desire to cause harm. (See *Economy Ref. & Service Co. v. Royal Nat. Bank* (1971) 20 C.A.3d 434, 441, 97 C.R. 706.)

(b) *Proof of Intent.* See *Hansford v. Lassar* (1975) 53 C.A.3d 364, 377, 125 C.R. 804 [finding of actual intent reversed where evidence negating insolvency erroneously excluded]; *Neumeyer v. Crown Funding Corp.* (1976) 56 C.A.3d 178, 128 C.R. 366 [finding of no intent affirmed].

(New) Burden of Proof. Actual intent to defraud must be established by clear and convincing evidence. (*Hansford v. Lassar*, supra, 53 C.A.3d 377; *Neumeyer v. Crown Funding Corp.*, supra, 56 C.A.3d 184.)

p. 3511:

(c) *Future or Subsequent Creditors.* Tort claimant: See *Estate of Blanco* (1978) 86 C.A.3d 826, 832, 150 C.R. 645.

p. 3512:

C.C. 3450 was repealed in 1980. (See Supp., supra, §146.)

Cross-References: 1 *Summary, Contracts,* §361 et seq.; 3 *Summary, Real Property,* §283.

(2) [§148] Transfer by Insolvent Without Consideration.

New Law: For the new Enforcement of Judgments law, see Supp., infra, §227A et seq.

(b) *Fair Consideration.* If the transferor was admittedly insolvent, the burden is on the transferee to prove fair consideration. (*Kirkland v. Risso* (1979) 98 C.A.3d 971, 978, 159 C.R. 798.)

p. 3514:

(c) *Insolvency.* See *Hansford v. Lassar* (1975) 53 C.A.3d 364, 375, 125 C.R. 804 [evidence insufficient to support finding of insolvency].

The burden of proof of insolvency was considered in *Neumeyer v. Crown Funding Corp.* (1976) 56 C.A.3d 178, 128 C.R. 366, where the voluntary transferor, S, disappeared. The transferee contended that the presumption of solvency was sufficient to support the trial court's finding of solvency, despite evidence of substantial unmatured liabilities on the date of transfer. *Held,* reversed. (1) Out-of-state cases establish that a voluntary transfer made when the transferror has existing debts is prima facie invalid if he has insufficient funds to pay them. (56 C.A.3d 187 et seq.) (2) Under C.C. 3901 and 3902 it is immaterial that those debts have not matured at the time of transfer.

(56 C.A.3d 189.) (3) Thus, "under the . . . Act a voluntary conveyance . . . made without fair consideration, when the evidence shows that there are existing indebtednesses, is presumptively fraudulent. It is then incumbent upon the grantee to prove that the conveyer was solvent. In the instant case respondent offered no evidence to show the value of Schmidt's nonexempt assets on the date of the conveyance." (56 C.A.3d 190.)

3. [§150] Transfers Violating Other Statutes.

New Law: For the new Enforcement of Judgments law, see Supp., infra, §227A et seq.

p. 3516:

(c) *(New) Preferences in Assignments for Benefit of Creditors.* C.C.P. 1800, added in 1979, provides for recovery of specifically defined transfers made within 90 days of assignment. (C.C.P. 1800(b)(f)(g).) (See 11 Pacific L. J. 342.)

Cross-References: 2 Summary, Sales, §§196, 197, 198, 199, 201, 202, 204, 203.

(1) [§152] In General.

New Law: For the new Enforcement of Judgments law, see Supp., infra, §227A et seq.

See 8 A.L.R.4th 1123 [right of secured creditor to set aside fraudulent transfer of *other property* of debtor].

(a) *No Lien Required.* It is no longer necessary that a creditor reduce his claim to judgment (see text, p. 3517); but in *Weisenburg v. Cragholm* (1971) 5 C.3d 892, 896, 97 C.R. 862, 489 P.2d 1126, the court made this distinction: Where the creditor does reduce his claim to judgment, and that judgment is the sole basis for the attack on the conveyance as fraudulent, reversal of the judgment on appeal deprives the creditor of any foundation for his action.

Thus, in *Weisenburg* plaintiff creditor brought his original action on a claim. While the action was pending the debtor transferred his property to third persons, allegedly to defraud plaintiff creditor; plaintiff then brought the present action to set aside the fraudulent transfer; judgment was rendered in his favor, and the debtor appealed. Thereafter the original judgment on the claim was reversed on appeal. *Held,* the fraudulent conveyance judgment should also be reversed.

See *Estate of Blanco* (1978) 86 C.A.3d 826, 837, 150 C.R. 645, following *Weisenburg.*

(c) [§156] Personal Action Against Transferee.

New Law: For the new Enforcement of Judgments law, see Supp., infra, §227A et seq.

See 11 A.L.R.4th 345 [creditor's right to damages for conspiracy to defraud him of claim].

(c) [§157A] (New) District Attorney Cannot Bring Proceeding.

New Law: For the new Enforcement of Judgments law, see Supp., infra, §227A et seq.

In *Safer v. Superior Court* (1975) 15 C.3d 230, 124 C.R. 174, 540 P.2d 14, United Farm Workers, a labor union, picketed several growers. The growers obtained a temporary restraining order limiting the spacing and number of pickets. The next day the sheriff arrested a number of union members for alleged violation of the order. They were charged with the misdemeanor of wilful disobedience of a lawful court order, pleaded not guilty, and requested jury trials. On the date set for the trials the judge required the personal attendance of defendants at a proceeding which the district attorney stated would be a motion for dismissal. When defendants appeared, however, he served them with orders to show cause in contempt proceedings under C.C.P. 1209, and then procured dismissal of the criminal charges "in furtherance of justice," on the ground that the defendants had become subject to the contempt proceedings. "In this manner the district attorney sought to convert a misdemeanor proceeding, in which defendants had the protection of a jury trial and other statutory safeguards, into a contempt proceeding, in which defendants would be stripped of these protections." (15 C.3d 234.) *Held,* prohibition granted.

(1) *Legislative intent.* The Legislature has indicated by specific enactments that the district attorney may exercise his power only in such civil litigation as it has found essential; and even where specifically authorized he enjoys neither plenary power nor unbridled discretion. (15 C.3d 236.)

"The intervention of the district attorney in these proceedings, springing from a civil suit is, indeed, the introduction of the government itself on one side of the litigation, casting the whole issue into a different framework. The weight of government tends naturally to tilt the scales of justice in favor of the party whom the government sponsors. Moreover, in cases like this the intrusion of the district attorney exposes the disadvantaged litigant to a special danger; the district attorney undertakes to bring about nothing less than his incarceration." (15 C.3d 238.)

(2) *District attorney's interest in administration of justice.* The argument that disobedience of a court order is an affront to the court and the People, such as to authorize the district attorney's appearance on the plaintiff's behalf, is unconvincing. His authority is limited to institution of a criminal proceeding under P.C. 166, in which the defendant has the right of trial by jury. (15 C.3d 240.)

[75]

The court added some strong words on the policy involved:

"This case presents a disturbing instance of intervention by a public authority in an acrimonious labor dispute. By imposing the weight of his office and the advantages of a public purse on the side of management, the district attorney at one stroke relieves one of the civil litigants of the necessity of financing his half of the battle, deprives defendants of the right to jury trial which they enjoyed in the previous criminal prosecution, and simultaneously suggests that public order necessitates management success in this private civil dispute. From such acts, even when well-intentioned, spring some of the bitterest chapters in the social history of our nation. The Legislature of this state has wisely refrained from empowering the public officer in question to play this role." (15 C.3d 242.)

Two justices dissented, arguing that public policy supports contempt actions by the district attorney, and that he may properly elect to proceed under the statute with the lesser penalty (C.C.P. 1218; see text, §170) than that with the right to a jury (P.C. 166). (15 C.3d 247.)

(b) [§158] Judgments and Orders Enforceable.

New Law: For the new Enforcement of Judgments law, see Supp., infra, §227A et seq.

See 1 C.E.B., Civ. Proc. Before Trial (1977 ed.), §5.72 et seq.; C.E.B., Family Law Act Practice (2d ed.), pp. 235 et seq., 306 et seq.; C.E.B., Debt Collection Manual, §9.29 et seq.

p. 3520:

(New) Property settlement agreement and division of community property: In re Fontana (1972) 24 C.A.3d 1008, 1011, 101 C.R. 465, held that an order to make payments pursuant to a property settlement agreement dividing the community property could not be enforced by contempt. The court thought that to apply the sanction of contempt to breach of the obligation would violate the constitutional prohibition of imprisonment for debt.

In re Marriage of Fithian (1977) 74 C.A.3d 397, 141 C.R. 506, not mentioning *Fontana,* reaches a different result on distinguishable facts. There was no property agreement; the lower court, in accordance with the Supreme Court's decision that the husband's military retirement pay was community property, ordered the husband to deposit in court the percentage constituting the wife's interest. *Held,* the order could be enforced by contempt proceedings. The wife's claim to a share in community property is not that of a creditor but of an owner; hence the husband's obligation to pay that share is not a debt within the meaning of the Constitution. (74 C.A.3d 404, 405.)

See also *Verner v. Verner* (1978) 77 C.A.3d 718, 729, 143 C.R. 826, following *Fithian.*

(New) Necessity of effective order: In *Ketscher v. Superior Court* (1970) 9 C.A.3d 601, 88 C.R. 357, two brothers were engaged in a violent dispute over land. Their counsel entered into a stipulation for judgment, and the judge said from the bench: "If either party attacks the other, I will consider this to be contempt of court, and I will punish accordingly." Two days later the brothers got into an argument and petitioner threw a rock. The judge held him in contempt and imposed a fine and jail sentence. *Held,* prohibition issued; there was no punishable contempt. (1) There was no effective order, because it was neither written and filed nor entered in the minutes (see *Judgment,* §56). (2) The statement was uncertain: The judge merely warned the parties as to his future action, and did not directly enjoin the provocative acts. (9 C.A.3d 604.)

See 84 A.L.R.3d 1047 [violation of compromise and settlement where terms approved by court but not incorporated in order or judgment].

Cross-References: 6 *Summary, Husband and Wife,* §§154, 171, 201 et seq.

(a) [§159] In General.

New Law: For the new Enforcement of Judgments Law, see Supp., infra, §227A et seq.

See C.E.B., Debt Collection Manual, §§9.30, 9.31.

(1) [§160] Requirements of Affidavit.

New Law: For the new Enforcement of Judgments law, see Supp., infra, §227A et seq.

See C.E.B., Debt Collection Manual, §9.29 et seq; C.E.B., Family Law Act Practice (2d ed.), pp. 236, 237, 307, 308.

p. 3522:

(b) *Child Support Cases.* On C.C.P. 1209.5, see *Lyons v. Municipal Court* (1977) 75 C.A.3d 829, 838, 142 C.R. 449, *Jurisdiction,* Supp., §307A, citing the text.

(2) [§161] Jurisdictional Rule Abrogated.

New Law: For the new Enforcment of Judgments law, see Supp., infra, §227A et seq.

p. 3523:

(2) Court may order or permit amendment: See *Mossman v. Superior Court* (1972) 22 C.A.3d 706, 710, 99 C.R. 638.

(c) [§162] Service of Order.

New Law: For the new Enforcement of Judgments law, see Supp., infra, §227A et seq.

See C.E.B., Family Law Act Practice (2d ed.), p. 129.

(a) [§163] In General.

New Law: For the new Enforcement of Judgments law, see Supp., infra, §227A et seq.

See C.E.B., Family Law Act Practice (2d ed.), p. 121.

p. 3525:

(3) *Quasi-Criminal Proceeding.* Since the proceeding is quasi-criminal it is governed by the criminal trial standard of proof beyond a reasonable doubt. But there is no requirement that the record show that the judge followed that standard; the presumption that official duty has been performed applies. (*Ross v. Superior Court* (1977) 19 C.3d 899, 913, 141 C.R. 133, 569 P.2d 727.)

(1) [§164] Invalidity of Order Violated.

New Law: For the new Enforcement of Judgments law, see Supp., infra, §227A et seq.

(a) *Injunction void for lack of jurisdiction:* See *Board of Med. Examiners v. Terminal-Hudson Electronics* (1977) 73 C.A.3d 376, 388, 140 C.R. 757.

(2) [§165] No Notice or Knowledge.

New Law: For the new Enforcement of Judgments law, see Supp., infra, §227A et seq.

(a) *General Rule.* See *International Molders etc. Union v. Superior Court* (1977) 70 C.A.3d 395, 410, 138 C.R. 794, citing the text.

p. 3527:

(b) *Child Support Cases.* C.C.P. 1209.5 is constitutional; challenges of the presumption as arbitrary and a denial of due process, and as a violation of the Fifth Amendment, were rejected in *Martin v. Superior Court* (1971) 17 C.A.3d 412, 94 C.R. 110, *Cal. Evidence,* 2d, Supp., §223.

See also *Lyons v. Municipal Court* (1977) 75 C.A.3d 829, 838, 142 C.R. 449, *Jurisdiction,* Supp., §307A, citing the text.

(c) *Knowledge of Attorney.* See *Mossman v. Superior Court* (1972) 22 C.A.3d 706, 711, 99 C.R. 638.

Cross-Reference: 1 *Summary, Agency and Employment,* §139.

(3) [§166] Inability To Pay.

New Law: For the new Enforcement of Judgments law, see Supp., infra, §227A et seq.

(a) *General Rule.* See *Mossman v. Superior Court* (1972) 22 C.A.3d 706, 712, 99 C.R. 638 [burden of proof on party charged with contempt].

Cross-Reference: 6 *Summary, Husband and Wife,* §171.

4. [§169] Order of Commitment.

New Law: For the new Enforcement of Judgments law, see Supp., infra, §227A et seq.

See *Ross v. Superior Court* (1977) 19 C.3d 899, 904, 141 C.R. 133, 569 P.2d 727, footnote 4, citing the text [oral statement from the bench, sufficient recital of facts]; C.E.B., Debt Collection Manual, §9.35.

The order of commitment must be promptly entered: "After an adjudication of contempt, it may not be practical for the court to prepare its written judgment the instant the defendant is committed, and we make no determination when such a judgment must be signed and entered. But eight days after a defendant is jailed is *too late.*" (*In re Jones* (1975) 47 C.A.3d 879, 881, 120 C.R. 914.)

Cross-Reference: 6 *Summary, Parent and Child,* §82.

(2) [§171] Imprisonment Until Performance.

New Law: For the new Enforcement of Judgments law, see Supp., infra, §227A et seq.

Order must contain finding of present ability to comply: See *Lake v. Superior Court* (1977) 67 C.A.3d 815, 817, 136 C.R. 830.

(New) Challenge of indefinite commitment: In re Farr (1974) 36 C.A.3d 577, 111 C.R. 649, examined the perplexing question of validity and duration of a commitment until compliance with an order. Petitioner, a newspaper reporter, was held in contempt for refusal to state which of the attorneys of record in the celebrated Manson murder case had violated the court's order prohibiting dissemination of the content of testimony involving questions of admissibility. On certiorari, the contempt judgment was held valid. (*Farr v. Superior Court* (1971) 22 C.A.3d 60, 99 C.R. 342, *Cal. Evidence,* 2d, Supp., §891A.) Petitioner then sought habeas corpus on several grounds, one of which was invalidity of indefinite commitment. The court, lacking any direct authority, set forth some novel conclusions:

(a) The commitment of a person until he complies with a valid order of court is not penal, but coercive; i.e., it is not to punish but to enforce compliance. (36 C.A.3d 583.) However, a coercive incarceration presents a special problem where disobedience is based on an articulated moral principle (claim of privilege): "in such a situation, it is necessary to determine the point at which the commitment ceases to serve its coercive purpose and becomes punitive in character. When that point is reached so that the incarceration of the contemner becomes penal, its duration is limited by the five-day maximum sentence provided in Code of Civil Procedure section 1218." (36 C.A.3d 584.) The test is "the presence or absence of a substantial likelihood that continued commitment will accomplish the purpose of the order." (36 C.A.3d 584.)

(b) By proper proceedings in the superior court a determination of that issue may be made; i.e., the trial court must determine the presence or absence of a substantial likelihood that his continued commitment will serve the purpose of supplementing the Manson record on appeal and the effective discipline of the offending attorneys "within a period in which the purpose will be effective." (36 C.A.3d 584.)

See 11 San Diego L. Rev. 1026.

(c) [§174] No Compensatory Damages.

New Law: For the new Enforcement of Judgments law, see Supp., infra, §227A et seq.

For the general law, see 85 A.L.R.3d 895.

Heinz was distinguished in *Moffat v. Moffat* (1980) 27 C.3d 645, 655, 656, 165 C.R. 877, 612 P.2d 967. In *Heinz* the order in excess of jurisdiction was annulled on direct attack—a review of the contempt order. In *Moffat* the attack was collateral—in a subsequent proceeding. The court, following *Pacific Mut. Life Ins. Co. v McConnell* (*Jurisdiction,* §228), held that, where the trial court had jurisdiction of the subject matter and parties, its order, though in excess of jurisdiction, was not subject to collateral attack. (27 C.3d 656.)

6. [§175] Review on Certiorari or Habeas Corpus.

New Law: For the new Enforcement of Judgments law, see Supp., infra, §227A et seq.

(a) *In General.* Certiorari to review and annul contempt order: See *Mitchell v. Superior Court* (1972) 28 C.A.3d 759, 762, 104 C.R. 921, citing the text; *In re Coleman* (1974) 12 C.3d 568, 572, 116 C.R. 381, 526 P.2d 533, footnote 2, citing the text [petition for habeas corpus improperly sought to review contempt order; treated as petition for certiorari and order reviewed].

1. [§177] Nature of Remedy.

New Law: For the new Enforcement of Judgments law, see Supp., infra, §227A et seq.

In 1973 C.C.P. 667, 682 and 684 were amended to delete references to arrest and bail, and C.C.P. 1154 was repealed. (See *Provisional Remedies,* Supp., §7A; 5 Pacific L. J. 268; C.E.B., Debt Collection Manual, §§2.9, 3.25, 9.7.)

2. [§178] Procedure for Release.

New Law: For the new Enforcement of Judgments Law, see Supp., infra, §227A et seq.

C.C.P. 1143, 1148, 1149, 1151 were repealed in 1973. (See *Provisional Remedies,* Supp., §7A; 5 Pacific L. J. 268; C.E.B., Debt Collection Manual, §9.7.)

2. [§180] To Enforce Judgment.

New Law: For the new Enforcement of Judgments law, see Supp., infra, §227A et seq.

Order for support of child: See *Sheridan v. Sheridan* (1972) 33 C.A.3d 917, 919, 109 C.R. 466.

In the *Sheridan* case defendant, the former husband, was a federal government employee. He contended that a garnishment of his salary was prohibited by the sovereign immunity doctrine, and that the same should be true of receivership. The court held, however, that appointment of a receiver and an order directing defendant to endorse his salary checks to him did not involve the government; i.e., that once the money was paid to the defendant sovereign immunity was no longer involved. (33 C.A.3d 921, 922.)

Cross-References: 6 *Summary, Husband and Wife,* §§154, 173.

4. [§182] In Aid of Execution.

New Law: For the new Enforcement of Judgments law, see Supp., infra, §227A et seq.

In a proper case a receiver can be appointed to collect a simple money judgment. (*Olsan v. Comora* (1977) 73 C.A.3d 642, 646, 140 C.R. 835.)

Receivers in aid of execution or supplementary proceedings or creditors' suits are "creatures of statute," and the power of the court to use this drastic remedy should be exercised sparingly and with caution. (*Morand v. Superior Court* (1974) 38 C.A.3d 347, 350, 113 C.R. 281.)

In the *Morand* case S Co. obtained a money judgment against Far East Corp. M was appointed receiver to take over and collect assets of the judgment debtor. On M's representation that Western Corp. and Surgical Corp. were claiming such assets, the court authorized him to employ an attorney to take "whatever action may become necessary" to gain possession of property in possession of Western. The receiver then commenced an action, naming as defendants the judgment debtor, Western Corp., Surgical Corp. and three others. *Held*, the receiver had no authority to sue the parties other than Western. The judgment creditor would normally be the proper person to sue third parties alleged to have property of the judgment debtor (C.C.P. 720, text, §143). And the "questionable authority to sue one defendant" (Western) "falls far short of leave" to sue the four others not named. (38 C.A.3d 352, 353.)

(New) Appointment without supplementary proceedings: In *Olsan v. Comora,* supra, the court, quoting the text, observed that "most, if not all, cases to date affirming the appointment of a receiver in a money judgment situation have done so in conjunction with a supplementary proceeding under one of the two sections" (i.e., C.C.P. 714 or 715, text, §§123, 124, 125). However, neither the statutes nor the decisions exclude direct appointment without supplementary proceedings; and "The current practice of superior courts in numerous counties is that a petitioning party has procedural alternatives, i.e., a proceeding under sections 714 or 715 or a direct proceeding by motion in the court under section 564, subdivision 4." (73 C.A.3d 648.) Here the declaration supporting the judgment creditor's motion showed that diligent efforts to discover assets other than business income had been unsuccessful, and that the judgment debtor had indicated his intention to prevent seizure of any assets that might be discovered. "Under such circumstances, the judge was not required to order a supplementary proceeding that would only establish anew the need for a receiver." (73 C.A.3d 648.)

Cross-Reference: 6 *Summary, Husband and Wife,* §200.

2.   [§184]   Writ of Possession or Assistance.

New Law: For the new Enforcement of Judgments law, see Supp., infra, §227A et seq.

See C.E.B., Debt Collection Manual, §§8.6 et seq.; 8.29.

Judicial Council forms: The two forms, as revised effective January 1, 1979, are Writ of Execution (EJ-130(79)), and Writ of Execution Against Dwelling House (Money Judgment) (EJ-140(79)).

C.C.P. 682 was resubsectioned in 1973. The citation in the text should now be to C.C.P. 682(4).

C.C.P. 686 was repealed in 1980. (See Supp., supra, §3.)

Proceedings to quiet title, etc.: C.C.P. 380 was repealed in 1972.

3. [§185] Writ of Restitution.

New Law: For the new Enforcement of Judgments law, see Supp., infra, §227A et seq.

(a) *Nature of Writ.* C.C.P. 1174 was amended and subdivided in 1974. Citations should now be to C.C.P. 1174(a) and 1174(d) respectively.

(b) *Procedure: Removal of Tenant.* C.C.P. 1174(d), as amended in 1982, provides that, subject to C.C.P. 1174(c), the judgment for possession of the premises is to be enforced pursuant to C.C.P. 712.010 et seq. (see Supp., infra, §397A et seq.).

(New) Notice to unnamed tenant: in *Arrieta v. Mahon* (1982) 31 C.3d 381, 182 C.R. 770, 644 P.2d 1249, tenant A was given no notice of the unlawful detainer action until a writ of execution and a notice to vacate were posted on her apartment door. The tenant named in the action had assisted A in obtaining the apartment and had paid the first month's rent, but had moved away before the writ was issued; A had thereafter made rental payments. A sought declaratory and injunctive relief, and the trial judge granted the relief by an order (1) barring removal of any adult not named in a writ of execution who claimed a right of possession and had entered the premises before commencement of the unlawful detainer action, and (2) requiring that the notice to vacate include a statement directing such a person to contact the marshal's office. *Held,* affirmed.

(a) The eviction of persons not named in the writ of execution was a violation of due process, for it denied them the right to a hearing at which to interpose any valid defenses to eviction. (31 C.3d 389.)

(b) The procedure adopted by the trial judge did not bar eviction of unnamed tenants; it merely required that a postjudgment order be obtained by the landlord directing those tenants to show cause why they should not be evicted. Landlords could avoid such procedure by naming all adults on the premises in the writ of execution. (31 C.3d 393.)

(c) *Procedure: Storage of Tenant's Personal Property.* C.C.P. 1174 was amended and subdivided in 1974 to bring its provisions into conformity with new C.C. 1980 et seq., enacted at the same time. (See 6 Pacific L. J. 374.)

(1) The section applies to *all property left on the premises.* If the landlord "reasonably believes" property left is lost, he must dispose of it pursuant to C.C. 2080 et seq. (see 3 *Summary, Personal Property,* §79 et seq.). (C.C.P. 1174(e).) Otherwise, he must "store the personal property in a place of safekeeping" and return or dispose of it as prescribed in C.C.P. 1174. (C.C.P. 1174(g).) If the police refuse to

accept property believed to be lost, it is "deemed not to have been lost." (C.C.P. 1174(e).)

(2) The landlord must give notice, as prescribed by C.C. 1983, to anyone he "reasonably believes" is the owner of the property, other than the tenant (who gets notice in the writ of restitution). (C.C.P. 1174(f).)

(3) The landlord must release the property to the tenant "or, at the landlord's option, to a person reasonably believed . . . to be its owner", if storage costs (see C.C. 1990) are paid and the demand is made within the period specified in the writ (if the tenant) or notice (if not the tenant). (C.C.P. 1174(h).)

(4) If not released to the tenant or owner, the property must be sold or disposed of pursuant to C.C. 1988. (C.C.P. 1174(i).)

(5) The landlord is not liable to anyone who had notice or to any other person, unless such other person "proves that . . . the landlord believed or reasonably should have believed that such person had an interest in the property *and* that the landlord knew or should have known upon reasonable investigation the address of such person." (C.C.P. 1174(j)–(l).)

p. 3543:

The reasoning and decision in *Gray v. Whitmore* were followed by the Supreme Court in *Love v. Keays* (1971) 6 C.3d 339, 98 C.R. 811, 491 P.2d 395.

(a) The tenant-judgment-debtor is not entitled to file an exemption claim since the only writ involved is one for restitution of the premises and no property of the tenant is levied upon.

(b) The statutory direction for storage of the tenant's personal property and for reimbursement of the landlord for storage costs satisfies the requirements of due process and equal protection.

(c) However, the provisions requiring the evicted tenant to satisfy the landlord's money judgment in order to redeem the property, and allowing the landlord to apply the proceeds of a sale in payment of his judgment, are void as a denial of due process and equal protection: They allow landlord creditors to reach property exempt from the claims of non-landlord creditors, and do not further the statutory purpose of restitution of the premises. And they also place the tenant-debtor in a more precarious position than all other judgment debtors in denying him the opportunity to dispute the landlord's claim to satisfaction of the judgment out of the stored property.

See 61 Cal. L. Rev. 406.

1. [§186] Nature of Remedy.

New Law: For the new Enforcement of Judgments law, see Supp., infra, §227A et seq.

(New) Contract obligation only: C.C.P. 989 refers to persons jointly indebted on "an obligation"; but it provides for a proceeding under C.C.P. 410.70, which covers persons liable "on a contract." Hence a joint debtor proceeding may not be brought on a judgment based on causes of action for fraud and conversion (tort) or in quasi-contract. (*Hillco v. Stein* (1978) 82 C.A.3d 322, 325, 326, 327, 147 C.R. 108.)

4. [§188A] (New) Amendment of Complaint.

New Law: For the new Enforcement of Judgments law, see Supp., infra, §227A et seq.

C.C.P. 993 permits amendments to pleadings "as in other cases." Hence it is permissible to amend the complaint in the joint debtor proceeding to substitute the true names for persons sued in fictitious names. (*Vincent v. Grayson* (1973) 30 C.A.3d 899, 905, 106 C.R. 733.) But the judgment against a joint debtor must be based on the cause of action set forth in the complaint in the main action; an attempt in the new proceeding to amend to recover on a different obligation is improper. As the court said in *Vincent v. Grayson,* supra, 30 C.A.3d 910:

"Having in mind that a joint debtor proceeding is in the nature of a summary action on the judgment, we construe section 993 to mean that the parties can amend their pleadings to cure technical defects or matters of form, such as to allow proof of compliance with the statutory requirement to file a certificate of doing business under a fictitious name, . . . or to substitute the true names of parties sued as fictitious defendants, as in the case at bench, but that it does not authorize a plaintiff to amend his complaint to raise new issues of fact giving rise to a different legal obligation. . . . To countenance this would be to permit a new lawsuit against a defendant without affording him the protection of the normal rules of procedure available in a plenary action. It would also render the statutory scheme for joint debtor proceedings incomprehensible in that a defendant would be summoned to show cause why a judgment which has not yet been entered should not be enforced against him." (30 C.A.3d 910.)

1. [§189] In General.

New Law: For the new Enforcement of Judgments law, see Supp., infra, §227A et seq.

p. 3545:

Law Revision Commission Recommendations: The California Law Revision Commission found the existing procedures on enforcement of claims and judgments against public entities defective in several respects. (See 15 Cal. L. Rev. Com. Reports 1261.) The Commission recommended that the statutes be amended to (1) more clearly impose a duty to pay an approved claim or final judgment; (2) provide that mandamus is an appropriate remedy to enforce this duty; (3) eliminate execution as a method of enforcing a money judgment against a public entity; and (4) provide for interest on a claim allowed in whole or in part. (See Com. Reports, supra, p. 1263 et seq.) These changes were enacted in 1980. (See Supp., infra, §190 et seq.)

Eminent domain: Former C.C.P. 1252 has been superseded by C.C.P. 1268.020, which continues the substance of the former section. (See 5 *Summary, Constitutional Law,* Supp., §741.) The section was amended in 1980 to require enforcement of eminent domain judgments against public entities pursuant to Govt.C. 810 et seq.

2. [§190] Claims and Judgments Against State.

New Law: For the new Enforcement of Judgments law, see Supp., infra, §227A et seq.

(b) *Where No Sufficient Appropriation Is Available.* In 1980 Govt.C. 955.5 was superseded by new Govt.C. 965.6, which continues the provisions and language quoted in the text. Govt.C. 942, erroneously cited in the text as C.C.P. 942, was also amended to limit the remedy of mandamus to claims "*required . . .* to be paid." Govt.C. 965.7, added in 1980, also recognizes that mandamus is the proper remedy, but provides that the Legislature may not be compelled (1) to make "an appropriation for payment," to "provide an offset for a claim, compromise, settlement, or judgment," or (3) to "authorize . . . a payment or offset."

(c) *(New) Exemption of University of California.* The provisions of Govt.C. 965 et seq. do not apply to "claims, settlements, and judgments against the Regents of the University of California." (Govt.C. 965.9, added in 1980.)

3. [§191] Judgments Against Local Public Entities.

New Law: For the new Enforcement of Judgments law, see Supp., infra, §227A et seq.

(a) *Tort Judgments.* Govt.C. 970.2 was amended in 1975 by deleting its limitation to tort judgments. The purpose of this and similar amendments to related sections was to permit payment of judgments in inverse condemnation actions. (See Govt.C. 970, Law Rev. Com. Comment; 7 Pacific L. J. 533.)

In 1980 Govt.C 970(b) was amended to make the provisions of Govt.C. 970 et seq. applicable to all "final judgments for the payment of money rendered against a local public entity."

(1) *Payment in First Fiscal Year.* Govt.C. 970.4 was amended in 1975 to delete the limitation to tort judgments, and to provide for

payment of interest. (For the general provisions on interest, see Supp., infra, §191B.)

Govt.C. 970.4 was amended in 1980, to authorize installment payments, rather than full payment in the fiscal year in which the judgment becomes final.

(2) *Payment in Ensuing Fiscal Year.* Govt.C. 970.6(a) was amended in 1975 to provide for payment of interest, and to delete the absolute discretion of the governing body to determine whether to pay in installments. (See infra, this section.) In 1980 the subsection was deleted and reenacted as Govt.C. 970.5. (For the general provisions on interest, see Supp., infra, §191B.)

(3) *Payment in Installments.* To prevent abuse of the right to pay in installments, Govt.C. 970.6(b) was substantially amended in 1975 to provide that the *court* which enters the judgment must order it paid in 10 installments if both these conditions are satisfied: (1) an ordinance or resolution is adopted finding that "an unreasonable hardship will result" unless payment is so made, and (2) the court, after hearing, finds that this is true. (See Govt.C. 970, Law Rev. Com. Comment.) The subsection is now Govt.C. 970.6(a) (see Supp., supra, this section), and it was amended in 1980 to authorize 10 *equal* annual installments. The purpose of this change was to avoid disproportionately larger payments during the earlier years, because of the interest on the principal being paid. (See Govt.C. 970.6, Law. Rev. Comment.)

(4) *Funding Judgments With Bonds.* Govt.C. 970.8 was amended in 1980 to substitute a requirement that the budget of the local entity include a provision for payment of all judgments. Govt.C. 971 was also amended to reflect the fact that all money judgments are now subject to the provisions of Govt.C. 970 et seq. (See Supp., supra, this section.)

(b) *Other Judgments.* Govt.C. 50170 et seq. were repealed in 1980, since the provisions of Govt.C. 970 et seq. now apply to all money judgments. (See Supp., supra, this section.) For the same reason, Educ.C. 35301 and 72501, and Water C. 31091 et seq., were also repealed.

[§191A]   (New) Claims Against Local Public Entities.

New Law: For the new Enforcement of Judgments law, see Supp., infra, §227A et seq.

Govt.C. 912.6(c), added in 1980, provides a means of enforcing payment of claims allowed or compromised by local entities. It requires payment of such claims "in the same manner as if the claimant had obtained a final judgment" for that amount. However, the claim may be paid in installments as provided in Govt.C. 970.6

(Supp., supra §191) "only if the claimant agrees in writing to that method of payment and in such case no court order authorizing installment payments is required." If such an agreement is made the local entity may, in its discretion, "prepay any one or more installments or any part of an installment." (Govt.C. 912.6(c).)

4.   [§191B]   (New) Statutes Applicable to State and Local Entities.

New Law: For the new Enforcement of Judgments law, see Supp., infra, §227A et seq.

(a) *Interest on Claims.* Govt.C. 906, added in 1980, deals with interest on claims not reduced to judgment. Unless varied by agreement, interest begins to accrue 30 days after the claimant accepts in writing the amount allowed in settlement of the entire claim, unless payment is subject to legislative approval of an appropriation, in which case interest begins to accrue 30 days after the effective date of the enactment. (Govt.C. 906(b).) Interest accrues at the rate provided for judgments, until paid. (Govt.C. 906(b)(3).)

These terms may be varied by agreement, and a public entity may condition its offer to settle or compromise on acceptance of a provision that varies the terms. (Govt.C. 906(c)(d).)

(b) *Judgment Not Enforceable by Execution.* No judgment against the State or any local public entity is enforceable by execution pursuant to C.C.P. 681 et seq. (Govt.C. 965.5(b), 970.1(b).)

(c) *Judgments Enforceable for 10 Years.* Judgments against the State and local public entities are enforceable "until 10 years after the time the judgment becomes final or, if the judgment is payable in installments, until 10 years after the final installment becomes due." (Govt.C. 965.5(a), 970.1(a).)

1.   [§192]   California Judgment.

New Law: For the new Enforcement of Judgments law, see Supp., infra, §227A et seq.

p. 3548:

(e) *Preserving priority of judgment lien:* C.C.P. 674 was subdivided in 1973 (see *Judgment,* Supp., §139), and the citation should now be C.C.P. 674(a). Its provisions were extended to sister-state judgments in 1974. (See Supp., infra, §195A et seq.)

C.C.P. 674(c), effective July 1, 1977, provides that a judgment lien attaches to real property containing a dwelling notwithstanding a judicial determination that it is exempt under C.C.P. 690.31 (see Supp., supra, §49C). (See *Judgment,* Supp., §141.)

Error: Page 3547, line 27, the citation should be 14 C.2d 355.

Cross-Reference: 4 *Summary, Torts,* §759.

(a) [§193]   When Action May Be Brought.

New Law: For the new Enforcement of Judgments law, see Supp., infra, §227A et seq.

See *Little v. Stevens* (1972) 23 C.A.3d 112, 99 C.R. 885, Supp., infra, §194; *Stevens v. Superior Court* (1972) 28 C.A.3d 1, 104 C.R. 369, Supp., infra, §194.

On validity and effect of sister-state judgments in general, see 1970/71 A.S. 43; on foreign judgments, see 1974/75 A.S. 24.

On conflict of laws, see *Petersen v. Petersen* (1972) 24 C.A.3d 201, 206, 100 C.R. 822 [California may apply our more liberal law on modification of an Illinois divorce decree]; *In re Marriage of Taylor* (1981) 122 C.A.3d 209, 213, 175 C.R. 716 [Missouri child support order; father's obligation under Missouri law to support child until 21 years old applied, rather than California termination age of 18].

(New) Codification of law. The 1974 Legislature added a new Title, "Sister State and Foreign Money-Judgments," with Chapter 1, C.C.P. 1710.10 et seq., on Sister State Money-Judgments, leaving Chapter 2, C.C.P. 1713 et seq., on Foreign Money-Judgments (text, §196 et seq.) intact. (For the new Act on Sister State Money-Judgments, see Supp., infra, §195A et seq.)

Cross-Reference: 6 *Summary, Husband and Wife,* §208 et seq.

(b) [§194]   Reasons for Denying Enforcement.

New Law: For the new Enforcement of Judgments law, see Supp., infra, §227A et seq.

(1) Judgment not final:

(New) Distinction: Appeal without stay. In *Little v. Stevens* (1972) 23 C.A.3d 112, 99 C.R. 885, plaintiff obtained a money judgment against defendant in Oklahoma, and defendant appealed without a stay bond. Under Oklahoma law the judgment was not stayed and execution could be had. Plaintiff then brought this action in California to enforce the Oklahoma judgment. *Held,* summary judgment for plaintiff affirmed. Under C.C.P. 1913, and the holding in a case decided before its enactment (*Taylor v. Shaw* (1870) 39 C. 536, 593) an action can be maintained in this state on a foreign judgment despite a pending appeal, where there is no stay in the foreign appeal. This is also the weight of the limited authority on the point. (See 2 A.L.R.3d 1384.) And it is also the Restatement view. (Rest. Conflict of Laws 2d §§107, comment e, 112, comment b; cf. Rest. Judgments §41, comment d.)

The court expressed no opinion on whether execution on the

present California judgment should be stayed until determination of the Oklahoma appeal. (23 C.A.3d 114, noting that C.C.P. 1713.6, text, p. 3552, authorizes a stay in an action under the Foreign Money-Judgments Recognition Act.)

Stevens v. Superior Court (1972) 28 C.A.3d 1, 104 C.R. 369, answered the question left open in *Little v. Stevens,* supra. After affirmance of plaintiff's judgment on appeal defendant sought a stay of execution, on adequate security, pending decision in the Oklahoma appeal from the underlying judgment. The lower court refused a stay, but the Court of Appeal issued mandamus to compel granting of a stay on an adequate undertaking. (a) The case law of other jurisdictions supports a post-judgment stay of execution in this situation, and the Restatement Second of Conflict of Laws, §107, comment e, §112, comment b, is in accord. (28 C.A.3d 3, 4.) (b) The Uniform Foreign Money-Judgments Recognition Act expressly authorizes a stay pending an appeal from the foreign judgment. (C.C.P. 1713.6, text, §197.) (c) The same is true as to our own local judgments, under C.C.P. 917.1. Thus, California policy "is to permit a judgment debtor to stay enforcement of the judgment pending appellate review if he provides an undertaking to secure payment in the event of affirmance." (28 C.A.3d 4.)

The new Act (see Supp., infra, §195E) contains an express provision on the point and, unlike C.C.P. 1713.6, supra, it is *mandatory:* The court "shall grant a stay" where "An appeal from the sister state judgment is pending or may be taken in the state which originally rendered the judgment." (C.C.P. 1710.50.)

(4) A penal judgment: On enforceability of a foreign judgment for *punitive damages,* see 44 A.L.R.3d 960.

Cross-References: 6 *Summary, Husband and Wife,* §§210, 211; 6 *Summary, Parent and Child,* §45; 6 *Summary, Husband and Wife,* §118.

(d)   (New) Sister State Money-Judgments Act.

(1)   [§195A]   (New) Nature, Purpose, Scope and Effect.

New Law: For the new Enforcement of Judgments law, see Supp., infra, §227A et seq.

(a) *Nature and Purpose.* The traditional method of *an action* to enforce a sister state judgment (see text, §193) has been criticized as time consuming and inefficient. The 1974 Sister State Money-Judgments Act provides a simple alternative method of *registration* for enforcement, but affords the judgment debtor an opportunity to present any available defenses. (See 11 Cal. Law Rev. Com. Reports, pp. 457–459; 6 Pacific L. J. 207, 211; 50 Cal. S.B.J. 483; *Tom Thumb*

Glove Co. v. Han (1978) 78 C.A.3d 1, 7, 144 C.R. 30, Supp., infra, §195B; *Liebow v. Superior Court* (1981) 120 C.A.3d 573, 575, 175 C.R. 26, citing the text.

A constitutional challenge on the ground that the statute fails to provide for notice and hearing prior to entry of the judgment by the clerk (see Supp., infra, §195C) was rejected in *Magalnick v. Magalnick* (1979) 98 C.A.3d 753, 758, 159 C.R. 889; the judgment debtor may move to vacate and set up defenses which would be available where a judgment creditor files an action (see Supp., supra, §194).

(b) *Scope: Judgment and Parties.* For purposes of the Act, a sister state judgment is *"that part* of any judgment, decree or order of a court of a state of the United States, other than California, which requires *the payment of money."* It does not, however, include a "support order" as defined in the Uniform Reciprocal Enforcement of Support Act. (C.C.P. 1710.10(c).) Support orders were excluded because they are enforceable under the Uniform Act (see 6 *Summary, Parent and Child,* §46 et seq.; *Husband and Wife,* §212). (Law Rev. Com. Comment to C.C.P. 1710.10.) And a new registration procedure was also enacted in 1974 for such orders. (See Supp., infra, §195F et seq.) Any portion of the judgment which requires something other than the payment of money must be enforced in the traditional way. (Law Rev. Com. Comment to C.C.P. 1710.10.) (See text, §193, and infra, this section.)

See *Fishman v. Fishman* (1981) 117 C.A.3d 815, 823, 173 C.R. 59 [although New York judgment awarding wife attorney's fees and costs had "incidents" of a support order, it was actually a nonmodifiable final money judgment for a liquidated sum and was therefore enforceable under C.C.P. 1710.10 et seq.].

C.C.P. 1710.10 defines *judgment creditor* as "the person or persons who can bring an action to enforce a sister state judgment," and *judgment debtor* as "the person or persons against whom an action to enforce a sister state judgment can be brought." These definitions incorporate the general law on such parties. (Law Rev. Com. Comment to C.C.P. 1710.10.)

The reference to "sister state judgment" is properly construed to include a judgment of a court of the District of Columbia. (*Richard A. Viguerire Co. v Noble* (1980) 101 C.A.3d 62, 64, 161 C.R. 435.)

(c) *Effect.* Except as otherwise provided, "a judgment entered pursuant to this chapter shall have the *same effect as a money judgment of a superior court of this state* and *may be enforced or satisfied in like manner."* (C.C.P. 1710.35.) This section incorporates the provisions respecting judgment liens (see *Judgment,* §139), execution (text, §5 et seq.) and supplemental proceedings (text, §123 et seq.). (Law Rev. Com. Comment to C.C.P. 1710.35.) (For special provisions regarding execution, see Supp., infra, §195D; on defenses to enforcement, see Supp., infra, §195C; for limitations on entry of judgment, see Supp., infra, this section.)

(d) *Limitations on Entry of Judgment.* C.C.P. 1710.55 provides:

"No judgment based on a sister state judgment may be entered pursuant to this chapter in any of the following cases:

(a) *A stay* of enforcement of the sister state judgment is currently in effect *in the sister state.*

(b) *An action* based on the sister state judgment *is* currently *pending* in any court *in this state.*

(c) *A judgment* based on the sister state judgment *has* previously *been entered in any proceeding in this state.*"

On entry of judgment here before a stay in the sister state, see Supp., infra, §195E; on action brought to enforce part of judgment not requiring payment of money, see Supp., infra, this section.

(e) *Optional Action on Money Judgment.* Unless a money judgment has already been entered under the new Act, a traditional action to enforce payment may be brought. (C.C.P. 1710.60.) But two money judgments may not be obtained in this state on the same sister state judgment. (Law Rev. Com. Comment to C.C.P. 1710.55, 1710.60.)

(f) *Separate Action To Enforce Portion of Judgment Not Requiring Payment of Money.* The new Act is limited to that part of a sister state judgment requiring payment of money; any other part of the judgment must be enforced by the traditional action. Accordingly C.C.P. 1710.65 provides that bringing such an action does not limit the right "to obtain entry of judgment based on the sister state judgment pursuant to this chapter." In other words, "use of the two separate procedures is not to be regarded as splitting a single cause of action." (Law Rev. Com. Comment to C.C.P. 1710.65.)

(2) [§195B] (New) Application for Entry of Judgment.

New Law: For the new Enforcement of Judgments law, see Supp., infra, §227A et seq.

(a) *Jurisdiction.* Enforcement of a sister state money judgment is begun by filing an application for entry of the judgment in the *superior court,* even though the amount of the judgment is below the California jurisdictional minimum for that court. (C.C.P. 1710.15(a), and Law Rev. Com. Comment.) This special rule is designed to "promote efficient and uniform operation" of the Act. (11 Cal. Law Rev. Com. Reports, p. 458, note 8.)

(b) *Venue.* The application must be filed in the superior court of the county "in which any judgment debtor resides," or, if none is a resident, of "any county in this state." (C.C.P. 1710.20(a).) If there is a mistake in venue, the judgment debtor may move to transfer, but the transfer "will not . . . affect the validity of actions already taken." (C.C.P. 1710.20(b), and Law Rev. Com. Comment.)

(c) *Form and Contents of Application.* C.C.P. 1710.15(b), as amended in 1982, provides that the application must be "*executed under oath*" and must include all of the following:

"(1) A statement that *an action* in this state on the sister state judgment *is not barred* by the applicable statute of limitations.

(2) A statement, based on the applicant's information and belief, that *no stay* of enforcement of the sister state judgment *is currently in effect* in the sister state.

(3) A statement of *the amount remaining unpaid* under the sister state judgment and, if accrued interest on the sister state judgment is to be included in the California judgment, a statement of the amount of interest accrued . . . (computed at the rate of interest applicable to the judgment under the law of the sister state), a statement of the rate of interest applicable to the judgment under the the law of the sister state, and a citation to the law of the sister state establishing such rate of interest.

(4) A statement that *no action* based on the sister state judgment *is currently pending* in any court in this state and that no judgment based on the sister state judgment has previously been entered in any proceeding in this state.

(5) Where the judgment debtor is *an individual,* a statement setting forth the *name and last known residence address* of the *judgment debtor.* Where the judgment debtor is *a corporation,* a statement of the corporation's name, place of incorporation, and whether the corporation, *if foreign, has qualified to do business* in this state . . . . Where the judgment debtor is a *partnership,* a statement of the *name* of the partnership, whether it is a foreign partnership, and, if it is a *foreign partnership,* whether it *has filed a statement* . . . *designating an agent for service of process.* Except for facts which are matters of public record in this state, the statements required by this paragraph may be made on the basis of the judgment creditor's information and belief.

(6) A statement setting forth the *name and address* of the *judgment creditor.*"

See 9 Pacific L. J. 369, 370.

In addition, "A properly authenticated copy of the sister state judgment shall be attached to the application." (C.C.P. 1710.15(c).)

(d) *Application by Corporate Creditor.* In *Tom Thumb Glove Co. v. Han* (1978) 78 C.A.3d 1, 144 C.R. 30, plaintiff corporation filed its application, signed by an officer, without representation by counsel.

Defendant contended that the application was similar to a pleading, and that a corporation, not entitled to appear in pro. per. (see *Jurisdiction,* §120), could file such an application only through a licensed attorney. *Held,* the application was properly made. Since entry of judgment is a ministerial act of the clerk (see *Judgment,* §49), the application merely requests performance of a ministerial duty, and is neither a pleading nor an appearance. Only in the event that the judgment debtor moves to vacate (see Supp., infra, §195C) is the court called upon to perform judicial acts, and in that proceeding the corporation must be represented by counsel. (78 C.A.3d 8.)

The Judicial Council adopted an optional form to implement the statute: Application for Entry of Judgment on Sister State Judgment (EJ-105(78)). The form was revised, effective January 1, 1978, to reflect the additional requirement of a statement of the applicable rate of interest, when sought. (See infra, this section.)

On statutes of limitation in actions on sister state judgments, see *Actions,* §§58, 349, 374; on the bar as a ground for vacating entry of the judgment, see *Epps v. Russell* (1976) 62 C.A.3d 201, 133 C.R. 30 [holding that 10-year statute of C.C.P. 337.5(3) was not a bar where the application under C.C.P. 1710.15 was made before the end of the period, even though the clerk's entry of judgment under C.C.P. 1710.25 was made 5 days after expiration of the period].

On a current stay of or prior action on the judgment as a bar to entry, see Supp., supra, §195A.

Paragraph (3), supra, is designed to prevent double recovery and, when the judgment is payable in installments, only those due and unpaid may be enforced by execution (see Supp., infra, §195C); the 1977 amendment makes clear that the applicable rate of interest is that of the sister state, but may not exceed California's rate; paragraph (5), supra, "will provide information necessary to determine whether a writ of execution may issue before notice of entry of judgment" (see Supp., infra, §195D). (Law Rev. Com. Comment to C.C.P. 1710.15.)

On authentication of judgment, see 28 U.S.C., §1738; Ev.C. 1452, 1453, 1530(a); *Cal. Evidence,* 2d, §§687, 703.

(3)   [§195C]   (New) Entry, Notice and Vacation.

New Law: For the new Enforcement of Judgments law, see Supp., infra, §227A et seq.

(a) *Entry of Judgment.* As amended in 1977, C.C.P. 1710.25(a) provides that, upon the filing of the application, "the clerk shall enter a judgment based upon the application for the total of the following amounts" as shown in the application: (1) "The amount remaining unpaid under the sister state judgment." (2) "The amount of interest accrued on the sister state judgment . . . ." (3) "The amount of the fee for filing the application for entry of the sister state judgment." Entry is made "in the same manner as entry of a judgment of the superior court" (see *Judgment, §49 et seq.*), and interest accrues at the rate of interest applicable to a judgment entered in this state. (C.C.P. 1710.25(b), as amended in 1982.) (See 9 Pacific L. J. 370.)

Where the judgment is payable in installments, the judgment is entered for the amount remaining unpaid, and execution may issue only as to installments which have accrued. (Law Rev. Com. Comment to C.C.P. 1710.25.)

The 1982 amendment is in conformity with the amendment of C.C.P. 1710.15 regarding interest (see Supp., supra, §195B), and make it clear that the filing fee is included, and that the California rate of interest applies after entry of the judgment here.

(b) *Notice of Entry.* Unlike C.C.P. 664.5 (see *Judgments, §59*), C.C.P. 1710.30(a) requires that notice of entry "be served promptly *by the judgment creditor* upon the judgment debtor in the manner provided for service of summons." It must be in the form prescribed by the Judicial Council, and must inform the judgment debtor that he has 30 days within which to make a motion to vacate the judgment. A form for optional use was adopted by the Judicial Council in 1976: Notice of Entry of Judgment on Sister State Judgment (EJ-110(76)). (On manner of service, see *Actions, §616 et seq.*; on execution before entry of judgment, see Supp., infra, §195D.)

The fee for service of the notice is a recoverable cost. (C.C.P. 1710.30(b), added in 1977.)

The usual proof of service of the notice is required. (See C.C.P. 1710.40(b), 1710.45(a)(d); *Actions, §666 et seq.*)

(c) *Vacation of Judgment.* The judgment debtor may move to vacate the judgment on *written* notice, not later than 30 days after service of notice of entry. (C.C.P. 1710.40(b).) The motion may be based "on any ground which would be a defense to an action in this state on the sister state judgment." (C.C.P. 1710.40(a); see text, §193; *Tom Thumb Glove Co. v. Han* (1978) 78 C.A.3d 1, 5, 144 C.R. 30 [defendant's declarations insufficient to sustain his burden of proof]; *Harris v. EMI Television Programs* (1980) 102 C.A.3d 214, 219, 162 C.R. 357 [judgment had already been discharged by accord and satisfaction]; *New York Higher Education Asso. Corp. v. Siegel* (1979) 91 C.A.3d 684, 688, 154 C.R. 200, *Attack on Judgment in Trial Court,* Supp., §192 [defense of extrinsic fraud unavailing where no showing of meritorious case]; *Krofcheck v. Ensign Co.* (1980) 112 C.A.3d 558, 564, 567, 169 C.R. 516 [Utah judgment against partnership improperly entered against individual partner who had not been named as party or served in the Utah proceedings]; *Fishman v.*

Fishman (1981) 117 C.A.3d 815, 819, 820, 173 C.R. 59 [whether New York judgment constituted a "support order" was not a ground for vacating the judgment under C.C.P. 1710.40(a)].)

The motion may also be based on the ground that the "amount of interest accrued on the sister state judgment and included in the judgment . . . is incorrect." (C.C.P. 1710.40(a), as amended in 1977; see supra, this section.)

The motion is a mandatory ground for stay of enforcement of the judgment. (See Supp., infra, §195E.) If execution will issue or be levied before the motion may be heard, the court may either shorten time (see *Proceedings Without Trial,* §16) or grant a stay; and equitable relief after the time for moving to vacate has expired may also be available (see *Attack on Judgment in Trial Court,* §175). (Law Rev. Com. Comment to C.C.P. 1710.40.)

After the hearing, the judgment may be vacated, and a different judgment entered, "including, but not limited to, another and different judgment for the judgment creditor." (C.C.P. 1710.40(c), added in 1977.)

Findings of fact and conclusions of law, if requested, are required for the decision on the motion to vacate, unless the judgment does not exceed $1,000. (C.C.P. 1710.40(c), added in 1977; see Law Rev. Com. Comment.)

(d) *(New) Appeal.* An order on a motion to vacate under C.C.P. 1710.40 is appealable. (*Fishman v. Fishman,* supra; *Liebow v. Superior Court* (1981) 120 C.A.3d 573, 576, 175 C.R. 26.)

(4)   [§195D]   (New) Execution.

New Law: For the new Enforcement of Judgments law, see Supp., infra, §227A et seq.

(a) *General Rule.* Since the judgment debtor has 30 days within which to move to vacate the judgment (see Supp., supra, §195C), normally "a writ of execution . . . shall not issue, nor may the judgment be enforced by other means, until at least 30 days after the judgment creditor serves notice of entry of judgment" and then only on proper proof of such service. (C.C.P. 1710.45(a), as amended in 1982.)

(b) *Execution Before Service of Notice.* If the *clerk* determines from the application (see Supp., supra, §195B) that the judgment debtor is a *nonresident individual, a foreign corporation* not qualified to do business in this state, or a *foreign partnership* which has not designated an agent for service of process, he may issue a writ of execution or seek other enforcement before service of the notice of entry of judgment. (C.C.P. 1710.45(b), as amended in 1982, and Law

Rev. Com. Comment.) The *court* also has discretion to order such issuance or permit such enforcement by other means if it "finds upon an ex parte showing that *great or irreparable injury would result* to the judgment creditor if issuance of the writ were delayed." (C.C.P. 1710.45(c), as amended in 1982.)

If a writ of execution is issued immediately or satisfaction of the judgment is sought by other means, no property may be sold or distributed before expiration of the period prescribed by C.C.P. 1710.45(a) (supra, this section), except that perishable property "may be sold in order to prevent its destruction or loss of value." But the proceeds of such a sale "shall not be distributed to the judgment creditor before the date sale of nonperishable property is permissible." (C.C.P. 1710.45(d), as amended in 1982.)

(5) [§195E] (New) Stay of Enforcement.

New Law: For the new Enforcement of Judgments law, see Supp., infra, §227A et seq.

The court may grant a stay on its own motion, on "ex parte motion," or on "noticed motion." (C.C.P. 1710.50(b).) And C.C.P. 1710.50(a) provides that it *must* grant a stay where:

"(1) *An appeal* from the sister state judgment *is pending or may be taken* in the state which originally rendered the judgment. Under this paragraph, enforcement shall be stayed until the proceedings on appeal have been concluded or the time for appeal has expired.

(2) *A stay of* enforcement of the sister state judgment *has been granted in the sister state.* Under this paragraph, enforcement shall be stayed until the sister state stay of enforcement expires or is vacated.

(3) The judgment debtor has made a *motion to vacate* pursuant to Section 1710.40. Under this paragraph, enforcement shall be stayed until the judgment debtor's motion to vacate is determined.

(4 a stay of enforcement."

C.C.P. 1710.50(c) gives the court broad discretion to protect the interests of both parties:

"The court shall grant a stay of enforcement under this section *on such terms and conditions as are just* including but not limited to the following:

(1) The court may require *an undertaking* in an amount it determines to be just, but the amount of the undertaking shall not exceed double the amount of the judgment creditor's claim.

(2) If *a writ of execution* has been issued, the court may order that it *remain in effect.*

(3) If property of the judgment debtor has been levied upon under a writ of execution, the court may order the *levying officer to*

retain possession of the property capable of physical possession and *to maintain the levy* on other property."

On relevant factors to consider in the matter of an undertaking, see Law Rev. Com. Comment to C.C.P. 1710.50.

(e)   (New)   Registration of Foreign Support Orders.

(1)   [§195F]   (New)   Nature and Purpose of Statute.

New Law: For the new Enforcement of Judgments law, see Supp., infra, §227A et seq.

In 1974 a registration procedure (C.C.P. 1698, 1698.1) was added to the Uniform Reciprocal Enforcement of Support Act. The new remedies are in addition to those already provided by the Act. (C.C.P. 1697.) Their purpose is to provide a more efficient method of enforcement of foreign support orders. (See 6 Pacific L. J. 204.)

As with the existing civil remedies under the Act (see 6 *Summary, Parent and Child,* §58), the prosecuting attorney represents the obligee. (C.C.P. 1698.2, 1698.3(b).)

(2)   [§195G]   (New)   Procedure for Registration.

New Law: For the new Enforcement of Judgments law, see Supp., infra, §227A et seq.

(a) *Filing of Papers by Obligee.* To register a foreign support order, the obligee must transmit to the clerk of the superior court having jurisdiction over the obligor or his property (see 6 *Summary, Parent and Child,* §§48, 49) the following: "(1) three certified copies of the order with all modifications thereof, (2) one copy of the *reciprocal enforcement of support act* of the state in which the order was made, and (3) a *statement* verified and signed by the obligee, showing the post office address of the obligee, the last known place of residence and post office address of the obligor, the amount of support remaining unpaid, a description and the location of any property of the obligor available upon execution, and a *list of the states in which the order is registered.*" (C.C.P. 1698.3(a).) The clerk must file the documents in the registry of foreign support orders without fee, and *that filing constitutes registration.* (C.C.P. 1698.3(a); see also C.C.P. 1698.1.)

The Judicial Council adopted an optional form in 1975: Statement for Registration of Foreign Support Order and Clerk's Notice (EJ-120(75)).

(b) *Effect of Registration.* When registered, the order is treated in the same manner as a local support order. "It has the same effect and is subject to the same procedures, defenses, and proceedings for reopening, vacating, or staying as a support order of this state and may be enforced and satisfied in like manner." (C.C.P. 1699(a).)

(3) [§195H] Notice, Opposition, and Hearing.

New Law: For the new Enforcement of Judgments law, see Supp., infra, §227A et seq.

(a) *Clerk's Notice to Obligor.* The clerk dockets the case, notifies the prosecuting attorney, and "promptly" mails notice of the registration, together with a copy of the support order and the obligee's address, to the obligor at the address given, "by any form of mail requiring a return receipt from the addressee only." (C.C.P. 1698.3(b).) Proof of personal notice is made by a return receipt signed by the obligor. (C.C.P. 1698.3(b).) (On the 1976 Judicial Council form, see Supp., supra, §195G.)

(b) *Obligor's Petition To Vacate.* The obligor has 20 days after the notice is *mailed* to petition to vacate the registration or for other relief. If no petition is filed the registered support order is confirmed. (C.C.P. 1699(b).)

(c) *Hearing.* At the hearing, only matters which would be a defense to the enforcement of a support order may be presented. (C.C.P. 1699(c).) A temporary stay may be obtained if there is an appeal pending, one is to be taken, or a stay of execution has been granted, but only "upon satisfactory proof that the obligor has furnished security for payment . . . as required by the rendering state." If grounds for stay of enforcement of a support order of this state are shown, a stay will be granted for an appropriate period "if the obligor furnishes the same security . . . that is required for a support order of this state." (C.C.P. 1699(c).)

(a) [§196] Nature and Purpose of Act.

New Law: For the new Enforcement of Judgments law, see Supp., infra, §227A et seq.

(1) *Former Law and Uniform Act.* C.C.P. 1915 was repealed in 1974. It had largely been ignored and served no useful purpose, particularly after enactment of the Uniform Act in 1967 (text, §196). "With the repeal of Section 1915, the enforcement of foreign nation judgments is determined by other statutory provisions and the decisions of the courts under principles of the common law and private international law." (11 Cal. Law Rev. Com. Reports, p. 473.) (See 6 Pacific L. J. 210.)

The Uniform Act is now in 13 U.L.A. (Master Ed.) 417.

On construction and application of the Act, see 100 A.L.R.3d 792. See also 13 A.L.R.4th 1109 [enforcement of judgment of court of foreign country].

p. 3551:

(3) C.C.P. 1713.3 was amended in 1974 to provide that foreign nation money judgments may not be enforced pursuant to the new procedures for sister state money judgments (see Supp., supra, §195A et seq.). "Foreign nation money judgments are enforced by bringing an action in California to obtain a domestic judgment." (Law Rev. Com. Comment to C.C.P. 1713, as amended.)

(b) [§197] Scope of Act.

New Law: For the new Enforcement of Judgments law, see Supp., infra, §227A et seq.

(1) *Foreign State.*

p. 3552:

In 1974 the Ryukyu Islands were deleted from the exceptions to the definition of foreign state in C.C.P. 1713.1(1).

(c) [§198] Grounds for Denying Enforcement.

New Law: For the new Enforcement of Judgments law, see Supp., infra, §227A et seq.

(c) *No personal jurisdiction:* In *Julen v. Larson* (1972) 25 C.A.3d 325, 101 C.R. 796, plaintiff filed suit in Switzerland against defendant and received a money judgment. In this California action on the judgment the trial court gave summary judgment for defendant. *Held,* affirmed. The process, consisting of enclosures in letters by certified mail from the Swiss Consulate in San Francisco, was inadequate, for the enclosed documents were in German, a language defendant did not understand, and the letters did not indicate their nature.

The court said: "While we do not require documents in a foreign language to be translated into English in order to be validly served, we think at a minimum a defendant should be informed in the language of the jurisdiction in which he is served . . . that a legal action of a specific nature is pending against him at a particular time and place. Normally this information should include the location of the pending action, the amount involved, the date defendant is required to respond, and the possible consequences of his failure to respond." (25 C.A.3d 328.)

The court found support for its conclusion in the requirements in the Convention on the Service Abroad of Judicial and Extrajudicial Documents in Civil and Commercial Matters, effective February 10, 1969. (25 C.A.3d 328.)

(2) *Other Grounds for Refusing Recognition.*

Repugnant to this state's public policy: See *Pentz v. Kuppinger* (1973) 31 C.A.3d 590, 597, 107 C.R. 540 [Mexican judgment enforcing payment of alimony to divorced wife despite her remarriage;

contrary to our statutory rule and in conflict with our earlier judgments].

2. [§200] Procedure.

New Law: For the new Enforcement of Judgments law, see Supp., infra, §227A et seq.

p. 3554:

(b) *Affidavits and Counteraffidavits.* See *In re Marriage of Hudson* (1979) 95 C.A.3d 72, 76, 156 C.R. 849 [order to show cause with accompanying declaration and subsequent testimony was substantial compliance with affidavit requirement].

(a) [§203] In General.

New Law: For the new Enforcement of Judgments law, see Supp., infra, §227A et seq.

(1) *Nature of Statute.* A revised compulsory financial responsibility law was enacted in 1974. Former Chapter 1 (Veh.C. 16000 et seq.) was repealed and a new Chapter 1 was enacted. (See Supp., infra, §205A et seq.) Technical and conforming changes were also made in Chapter 2 (Veh.C. 16250 et seq.), and suspension is now required for failure to satisfy judgments in excess of $350 rather than $200. (Veh.C. 16251, as amended in 1978.)

(2) *Constitutionality.* Veh.C. 16372 was repealed in 1973 in response to the *Perez* decision (text, §203). (See 5 Pacific L. J. 447.) The provisions for pre-judgment suspension were held unconstitutional in *Rios v. Cozens* (1972) 7 C.3d 792, 799, 103 C.R. 299, 499 P.2d 979, 5 *Summary, Constitutional Law,* §303, because no hearing was provided before suspension, and the *Escobedo* and *Orr* cases (text, §203) were overruled insofar as they were inconsistent with that conclusion. Over 20,000 persons demanded hearings in reliance on *Rios* (see 6 Pacific L. J. 340), and former Veh.C. 16080.5 was enacted in 1973 to suspend all proceedings pending outcome of review of *Rios* by the United States Supreme Court. (See 4 Pacific L. J. 565.) That Court, however, remanded the case to the California court because it was not clear whether the decision rested exclusively on the federal Constitution. (*Dept. of Motor Vehicles v. Rios* (1973) 410 U.S. 425, 93 S.Ct. 1019, 35 L.Ed.2d 398.) On remand, our court certified that the decision rested on the state Constitution as an independent ground. (*Rios v. Cozens* (1973) 9 C.3d 454, 455, 107 C.R. 784, 509 P.2d 696.) The 1974 Legislature responded by adopting a new approach to the problem, and repealed former Chapter 1 (see supra, this section), including Veh.C. 16080.5. (See Supp., infra, §205A et seq.) (See also *Anacker v. Sillas* (1976) 65 C.A.3d 416, 420–421, 135 C.R. 537, Supp., infra, §205E.)

Cross-References: 5 Summary, Constitutional Law, §§405, 4.

(1) [§204] Requirement of Security.

New Law: For the new Enforcement of Judgments law, see Supp., infra, §227A et seq.

(a) Report of Accident. The 1974 law continues the same reporting requirements, but suspension for failure to report is now mandatory. (See Supp., infra, §205C.)

(b) Deposit of Security. The provisions for deposit of security were repealed in 1974. Under the new law maintenance of one of the prescribed forms of financial responsibility is mandatory (Supp., infra, §205B), and the driving privilege is suspended for 3 years for failure to prove compliance with the law or until proof of current compliance and continued compliance for 3 years is filed with the Department (Supp., infra, §205D).

(c) Exemptions From Security Requirement. The security requirements were repealed in 1974. Some of the former exemptions outlined in the text are similar to the prescribed methods of complying with the new compulsory requirement to maintain financial responsibility. (See Supp., infra, §205B.)

(2) [§205] Suspension for Noncompliance.

New Law: For the new Enforcement of Judgments law, see Supp., infra, §227A et seq.

Former Chapter 1 was repealed in 1974. New Veh.C. 16020 imposes a mandatory duty to maintain one of the prescribed forms of financial responsibility, and new Veh.C. 16022 requires proof of such compliance in the event of an accident involving property damage of more than $250, bodily injury or death. (See Supp., infra, §205B.) Pre-judgment suspension is now covered by new Veh.C. 16070 et seq. (See Supp., infra, §§205D, 205E.)

(3) (New) Compulsory Financial Responsibility Law.

(aa) [§205A] (New) No Fault Approach.

New Law: For the new Enforcement of Judgments law, see Supp., infra, §227A et seq.

The Rios decision (Supp., supra, §203) resulted in a new approach to pre-judgment suspension: "The Legislature finds that as a result of the difficulty of ascertaining a likelihood of fault in connection with vehicle operation, the number of financially irresponsible motor vehicle owners and operators has increased dramatically. The Legislature further finds that such fault determinations, and the costs associated therewith, do not further the purpose of the financial responsibility laws. Therefore, *the Legislature declares* that *it is the policy of this state* that those owning or operating motor vehicles on the streets or highways of this state *shall be financially capable of providing monetary protection* to those suffering injury to their person or property by reason of the ownership or use of such vehicles *without regard to the negligence, liability, carelessness, or culpability of the owners or operators* thereof, and further, that *such capability shall be deemed a concurrent responsibility* of such motor vehicle *ownership or operation*. The Legislature further declares that it is the public policy of this state that those owning or operating motor vehicles on the streets or highways thereof shall *evidence such financial capability* by the methods specified in this act." (1974 Stats., ch. 1409, §1; see note to Veh.C. 16000, Deering's Vehicle Code, Pocket Supplement.)

Former Chapter I (Veh.C. 16000 et seq.) was repealed, a new Chapter I (Veh.C. 16000 et seq.) was enacted, and minor and technical changes were made in other sections, to effectuate the new policy. (See 6 Pacific L. J. 336; see also 6 Pacific L. J. 344.)

(New) Injury to driver himself: The constitutionality of the new law was upheld in *Anacker v. Sillas* (1976) 65 C.A.3d 416, 135 C.R. 537. A's license was suspended on a finding that he was involved in a motor vehicle accident in which he suffered bodily injury. He contended that to require proof of financial responsibility without a showing of fault on his part was a denial of equal protection, and the trial judge, agreeing, construed the statute as requiring property damage or bodily injury to another person. *Held*, reversed.

(1) The requirement of financial responsibility is imposed not only on negligent drivers but on all owners and drivers; and involvement in the accident does not create the obligation, but "merely provides the occasion for demonstrating that a preexisting obligation has been satisfied." (65 C.A.3d 422.) And, although compliance with the law as a condition to issuance of a license might be more effective than the "random spot-check" at the time of an accident, the legislative scheme is not irrational. (65 C.A.3d 423.)

(2) The reference to "any person" shows a clear legislative intent to include the driver himself. "Admittedly, the Legislature could have narrowed its sampling of drivers in a number of ways, including one which would exclude respondent and others similarly situated from the category which must prove financial responsiblity. It can still do so. But until that time even the person who suffers bodily injury in a motor vehicle accident may be obliged to demonstrate his financial responsibility." (65 C.A.3d 425.)

[103]

(bb)   [§205B]   (New) Mandatory Duty.

New Law: For the new Enforcement of Judgments law, see Supp., infra, §227A et seq.

Pursuant to the new policy (see Supp., supra, §205A), Veh.C. 16020 requires every driver and owner of a motor vehicle to "at all times, maintain in force one of the forms of financial responsibility specified in Section 16021." The methods designated by Veh.C. 16021, as amended in 1978, are: (1) self-insurance (see Veh.C. 16052, 16053 [limited to owners of more than 25 vehicles]); (2) maintenance of an insurance policy or bond with minimum coverage of $15,000, $30,000, and $5,000 "and which covers the driver for the vehicle involved in the accident" (see Veh.C. 16056); (3) establishment of public ownership (see Veh.C. 16051); (4) deposit of cash with the department in the minimum amount required for insurance (see Veh.C. 16054.2(a)); or (5) "compliance with the requirements authorized by the department by any other manner which effectuates the purposes of this chapter" (see Veh.C. 16054.2(b)).

Any driver or owner who, after having filed proof of financial responsibility, drives or permits a vehicle to be driven without one of the prescribed forms of financial responsibility in effect is guilty of a criminal infraction, and is subject to a fine not exceeding $100 for each offense. (Veh.C. 16023, as amended in 1975.)

(cc)   [§205C]   Report of Accident and Proof of Compliance.

New Law: For the new Enforcement of Judgments law, see Supp., infra, §227A et seq.

Drivers involved in an accident in which property damage to any one person exceeds $350, or in which anyone is injured or killed, must report the accident on a prescribed form to the department within 15 days. (Veh.C. 16000, as amended in 1978 [exempting public owned or leased vehicles]; see also Veh.C. 16001 [owner deemed driver of driverless runaway vehicle].) If the driver is physically incapacitated, the owner must report the accident. (Veh.C. 16003.) Employee drivers must report the accident to their employers within 5 days, and the employers must make the report. (Veh.C. 16002 [exempting public, self-insured, and adequately insured or bonded employers].) As under the former law (see text, §204), the report is confidential. (Veh.C. 16005.) But suspension of the driving privilege for wilful failure to report is now mandatory. (Veh.C. 16004(a).) (See 10 Pacific L. J. 540.)

Every driver (or his employer) and every owner of a vehicle involved in a reported accident, who fails to prove financial responsibility for the accident, must file such proof with the department within 60 days after the accident, and maintain it for 3 years thereafter. (Veh.C. 16022; see also Veh.C. 16050 [every driver or employer required to report accident must do so].) If such proof is established by filing a vehicle liability policy or bond, and coverage thereafter terminates, the insurer must inform the department of the date of termination. (Veh.C. 16022, as amended in 1975.)

(dd)   (New) Suspension for Non-Compliance.

(i)   [§205D]   (New) Duration and Scope.

New Law: For the new Enforcement of Judgments law, see Supp., infra, §227A et seq.

Besides possible criminal sanctions (see Supp., supra, §205B), failure to prove financial responsibility as required by Veh.C. 16020 results in suspension of the driving privilege. (Veh.C. 16070(a); see also Veh.C. 16071 [when suspended in another state on same ground].) But suspension is not authorized unless evidence that the accident resulted in property damage in excess of $350 or bodily injury or death is submitted to the Department within 60 days following the accident. (Veh.C. 16070(b), as amended in 1978.)

Suspension may not be made effective "earlier than the 76th day after receipt of the first accident report." (Veh.C. 16070(a).) The period of suspension is 3 years from the date of the accident or until the driver or owner "files and thereafter maintains proof of ability to respond in damages pursuant to Section 16022." (Veh.C. 16072, as amended in 1978; see also Veh.C. 16023 [current compliance may be condition of probation].)

An *employee* "whose *occupation requires* the use of a motor vehicle in the course of his employment" may continue to drive "a *vehicle not registered in his name* and in the course of his employment . . . even though his privilege to drive is otherwise suspended." (Veh.C. 16073.)

See 10 Pacific L. J. 540.

(ii)   [§205E]   (New) Notice and Hearing.

New Law: For the new Enforcement of Judgments law, see Supp., infra, §227A et seq.

(a) *Notice of Intent To Suspend.* Suspension may not be made effective until 20 days after notice of intent to suspend and the right to a hearing is sent to the driver or owner. (Veh.C. 16075(a).)

(b) *Demand for Hearing and Stay of Suspension.* The person receiving notice of intent to suspend may obtain a written hearing by demanding one in writing within 20 days of "receiving" the notice. (Veh.C. 16075(c), added in 1978.) The demand "shall operate to stay the suspension . . . from the date of such demand until the hearing is completed and a decision has been made." (Veh.C. 16075(c).) (See 10 Pacific L. J. 540.)

(c) *Hearing.* A hearing must be held, within 60 days of the written demand for one, in the county of residence of the person requesting it. (Veh.C. 16075(b)(d), as amended in 1978.) The hearing is conducted pursuant to the procedure prescribed by Veh.C. 14100 et seq. (Veh.C. 16075(d), as amended in 1978.)

The only issues to be determined are (1) whether the accident falls within the terms of Veh.C. 16000 (see Supp., supra, §205C), and (2) whether the driver or owner "has established that proof of financial responsibility . . . was in effect at the time of the accident." (Veh.C. 16075(b).)

Accident reports are now available for public inspection. (Veh.C. 1808, added in 1974.) This provision makes it possible for the driver or owner to examine the evidence upon which the suspension is to be based. (See 6 Pacific L. J. 340.)

(c) [§206] Suspension Following Unsatisfied Judgment.

New Law: For the new Enforcement of Judgments law, see Supp., infra, §227A et seq.

(1) *Mandatory Suspension.* The provisions for suspension of registration cards and license plates were deleted from Veh.C. 16370 in 1975.

p. 3560:

(2) *Exceptions.* In 1974 reference to former Veh.C. 16020, and the exception outlined in the text, were deleted from Veh.C. 16370.

(4) *Effect of Discharge in Bankruptcy.* Veh.C. 16372 was repealed in 1973 in response to the *Perez* decision. (See 5 Pacific L. J. 447.)

2. [§207] Other Licenses.

New Law: For the new Enforcement of Judgments law, see Supp., infra, §227A et seq.

(a) *Contractor's License.*

p. 3561:

The suggestion in the text that B. & P.C. 7113.5 was subject to constitutional challenge under the Supremacy Clause was confirmed in *Grimes v. Hoschler* (1974) 12 C.3d 305, 314, 115 C.R. 625, 525 P.2d 65. The court, following *Perez v. Campbell* (text, p. 3561) and overruling *Tracy v. Contractors' State License Board* (5 *Summary, Constitutional Law,* §8), held the section invalid. The 1975 Legislature then added this statement to B. & P.C. 7113.5: "No disciplinary action shall be commenced against a licensee for avoiding or settling in bankruptcy, or by composition, arrangement, or reorganization with creditors under federal law, the licensee's lawful obligations incurred as a contractor for less than the full amount of such obligations."

Cross-Reference: 5 *Summary, Constitutional Law,* §8.

A. [§208] Payment or Compromise by Judgment Debtor.

New Law: For the new Enforcement of Judgments law, see Supp., infra, §227A et seq.

On the power to impose terms and conditions, including installment payments, in the satisfaction of money judgments of municipal and justice courts, see C.C.P. 85, added in 1974, reenacted in 1976, and amended in 1977.

Cross-References: 1 *Summary, Contracts,* §§551, 555.

1. [§209] Joint Obligor: Contribution.

New Law: For the new Enforcement of Judgments law, see Supp., infra, §227A et seq.

Contribution among joint judgment debtors is now dealt with in C.C.P. 875 et seq. The substance of former C.C.P. 709 is continued in new C.C.P. 882, operative July 1, 1983.

Cross-References: 7 *Summary, Equity,* §123; 4 *Summary, Torts,* §44 et seq.

2. [§210] Surety: Reimbursement.

New Law: For the new Enforcement of Judgments law, see Supp., infra, §227A et seq.

On new C.C.P. 882, see Supp., supra, §208.

Cross-Reference: 7 *Summary, Equity,* §122.

3. [§211] Procedure.

New Law: For the new Enforcement of Judgments law, see Supp., infra, §227A et seq.

New C.C.P. 883, operative July 1, 1983, supersedes former C.C.P. 709 and codifies the practice of requiring a hearing on noticed motion.

Cross-Reference: 4 *Summary, Torts,* §49.

1. [§212] Nature of Right and Procedure.

New Law: For the new Enforcement of Judgments law, see Supp., infra, §227A et seq.

(New) Judgment Debtor's Right To Elect Among Claims. In

Margott v. Gem Properties (1973) 34 C.A.3d 849, 111 C.R. 1, defendant moved to have an *unsecured* claim against an insolvent plaintiff offset against a proposed judgment announced by the court. Plaintiff then submitted proposed findings, conclusions and a judgment which offset a *secured* claim, and these were signed by the court before hearing defendant's motion. *Held,* reversed. In the absence of some equitable ground established by the judgment creditor, the judgment debtor (1) has a *right* to offset when the judgment creditor is insolvent (34 C.A.3d 854, citing the text), and (2) also has the right to setoff an unsecured claim and preserve his right to a secured claim (34 C.A.3d 855).

2. [§213] Limitations on Right.

New Law: For the new Enforcement of Judgments law, see Supp., infra, §227A et seq.

(New) No state setoff against pension rights: See *Bonelli v. California* (1977) 71 C.A.3d 459, 465, 139 C.R. 486, Supp., supra, §58.

1. [§214] In General.

New Law: For the new Enforcement of Judgments law, see Supp., infra, §227A et seq.

See 21 U.C.L.A. L. Rev. 381 et seq. [symposium issue on 1973 bankruptcy reform]; C.E.B., Debt Collection Manual, §11.16 et seq.

On the proposed new Bankruptcy Act and its impact on consumer-debtors, see 18 Santa Clara L. Rev. 291.

Bankruptcy Reform Act of 1978: The substance of former 11 U.S.C., §§32(f)(1), 35(a), and 35(c) were continued by new 11 U.S.C., §§524(a)(1), 523(a), and 523(c)(d). (For a detailed discussion of the new law, see 19 Santa Clara L. Rev. 817 [Consumer Insolvency Counseling for Californians in the 1980's]; 53 So. Cal. L. Rev. 1527 [Adequate Disclosure Under Chapter 11 of the Bankruptcy Code]; 17 San Diego L. Rev. 1113 [automatic stay under the Bankruptcy Code]; 28 U.C.L.A. L. Rev. 953 [Bankruptcy Law in Perspective]; 1980 A.S. 689 [Judicial Standards for Rejection of Executory Contracts in Bankruptcy Code Reorganization Cases].)

(a) [§215] Discharge as a Defense.

New Law: For the new Enforcement of Judgments law, see Supp., infra, §227A et seq.

Bankruptcy Reform Act of 1978: Former 11 U.S.C., §35(a)(3) was superseded by new 11 U.S.C., §523(a)(3).

(1) [§217] Fraud and Malicious Conversion.

New Law: For the new Enforcement of Judgments law, see Supp., infra, §227A et seq.

Fraud: See *Stoner v. Walsh* (1972) 24 C.A.3d 938, 942, 101 C.R. 485 [false promise]; *Brown v. Felsen* (1979) 442 U.S. 127, 99 S.Ct. 2205, 2211, 60 L.Ed.2d 767, 776 [in considering issue bankruptcy court is not limited to record and judgment in prior state court proceeding to collect the debt; creditor may submit additional evidence that debt is nondischargeable].

Bankruptcy Reform Act of 1978: Former 11 U.S.C., §35(a)(2) was superseded by new 11 U.S.C., §523(a)(2).

(2) [§218] Misappropriation or Defalcation by Fiduciary.

New Law: For the new Enforcement of Judgments law, see Supp., infra, §227A et seq.

Bankruptcy Reform Act of 1978: Former 11 U.S.C., §35(a)(4) was superseded by new 11 U.S.C., §523(a)(4).

Cross-References: 6 *Summary, Corporations,* §13; 4 *Summary, Torts,* §177.

(3) [§219] Wilful and Malicious Injury.

New Law: For the new Enforcement of Judgments law, see Supp., infra, §227A et seq.

See *Terzian v. Calif. Cas. Ind. Exch.* (1974) 42 C.A.3d 942, 947, 117 C.R. 284 [judgment resulting from reckless driving while drunk; finding of "wilful and malicious" injury affirmed].

Pleading: A personal injury plaintiff may plead on alternative theories of negligence and wilful misconduct, even though he does not seek punitive damages. The wilful misconduct count is proper and the issue must be determined, to avoid the possibility of wiping out of the judgment by the defendant's bankruptcy. (*Savage v. Van Marle* (1974) 39 C.A.3d 241, 246, 114 C.R. 51.)

Bankruptcy Reform Act of 1978: Former 11 U.S.C., §35(a)(8) was superseded by new 11 U.S.C., §523(a)(6).

(1) [§220] Alimony and Child Support.

New Law: For the new Enforcement of Judgments law, see Supp., infra, §227A et seq.

See 25 U. C. L. A. L. Rev. 96 [Putative Spousal Support Rights and the Federal Bankruptcy Act]; C.E.B., Debt Collection Manual, §11.17.

Bankruptcy Reform Act of 1978: Former 11 U.S.C., §35(a)(7) was superseded by new 11 U.S.C., §523(a)(5).

Cross-Reference: 6 *Summary, Husband and Wife,* §207.

(2) [§221] Taxes.

New Law: For the new Enforcement of Judgments law, see Supp., infra, §227A et seq.

Bankruptcy Reform Act of 1978: Former 11 U.S.C., §35(a)(1) was superseded by new 11 U.S.C., §523(a)(1).

(3) [§222] Wages.

New Law: For the new Enforcement of Judgments law, see Supp., infra, §227A et seq.

Bankruptcy Reform Act of 1978: Former 11 U.S.C., §35(a)(5) was not continued. The priority of *payment* of such claims, provided by former 11 U.S.C., §104(a), is continued by new 11 U.S.C., §507(a)(3), which increases the amount to $1,200.

5. [§224] Estoppel To Set Up Defense.

New Law: For the new Enforcement of Judgments law, see Supp., infra, §227A et seq.

Cross-Reference: 1 *Summary, Contracts,* §183 et seq.

1. [§225] Conditions and Procedure.

New Law: For the new Enforcement of Judgments law, see Supp., infra, §227A et seq.

C.C.P. 675(a) was amended in 1977 to provide for entry of the satisfaction in the register of actions in all trial courts, including justice courts.

p. 3574:

Abstract of judgment: C.C.P. 675(b) was amended in 1974 to require that the acknowledgment also show the *full name* of the judgment debtor being released and "identify the judgment debtor as such." His name must "appear on the acknowledgment as it appears on the abstract of judgment." In 1976, the subsection was amended to require, when an abstract of judgment has been recorded, that the creditor both file an acknowledgement of satisfaction and deliver a copy to the debtor or his attorney, either personally or by first class mail. (See 8 Pacific L. J. 233.)

The Judicial Council approved an optional form in 1975: Acknowledgment of Full Satisfaction of Judgment (EJ-100(75)).

On judgment "satisfied in fact," see *Yanchor v. Kagan* (1971) 22

C.A.3d 544, 552, 99 C.R. 367, Supp., infra, §226 [covenant not to execute].

2. [§226] Compelling Acknowledgment of Satisfaction.

New Law: For the new Enforcement of Judgments law, see Supp., infra, §227A et seq.

Power of court: See *George S. Nolte etc. v. Magliocco* (1979) 93 C.A.3d 190, 193, 155 C.R. 348, citing the text.

Satisfaction by another method: Theoretically a covenant not to execute does not have a self-executing effect; the judgment remains. But where there is a single judgment debtor, a covenant not to execute is the equivalent of a release, and the judgment debtor is entitled to have satisfaction of judgment entered. (*Yanchor v. Kagan* (1971) 22 C.A.3d 544, 552, 99 C.R. 367, *Attorneys,* Supp., §116.) (See also C.C.P. 675(b), as amended in 1976, Supp., supra, §225.)

p. 3575:

(c) *Penalty for refusal:* See *Bartneck v. Dunkin* (1969) 1 C.A.3d 58, 60, 81 C.R. 428.

(d) *State agency:* C.C.P. 675(d) was relettered C.C.P. 675(e) in 1975.

Cross-Reference: 1 *Summary, Contracts,* §555.

VI. (NEW) ENFORCEMENT OF JUDGMENTS LAW.

EXPLANATORY NOTE: The material which follows is a new and complete treatment of the law governing enforcement of judgments enacted by the 1982 Legislature. It has a new topic heading, corresponding to the new statutory title (C.C.P. 680.010, the Enforcement of Judgments Law), new "A" sections (§§227A to 436A, inclusive), and a new Outline of the new topics with references to pages of this Supplement (see below).

See 14 Pacific L.J. 397.

NEW OUTLINE:

A. **(New) In General.**

  1. **(New) Nature of Revision.**

    (a) **[§227A] (New) Law Revision Commission Report.**

(1) *Defects in Prior Law.* The Introduction to the Commission's explanatory Pamphlet (see Supp., infra, this section) commences as follows (p. 1029):

"The law relating to enforcement of judgments has long been in need of a thorough study and revision. Many provisions in existing law date from the 1872 enactment of the Code of Civil Procedure and some have remained largely unchanged since 1851, and piecemeal amendments have accumulated over the last century. As a result, the statutory law falls far below the standards of the modern California codes. There are long and complex sections that are difficult to read and more difficult to understand. There are duplicating and inconsistent provisions. There are provisions that are obsolete and inoperative. Judicial decisions interpreting the statutory language are conflicting and obscure. Important matters are not covered at all in the existing statute or are covered inadequately. The principles and terminology of the Commercial Code are not recognized in the statutes governing enforcement of judgments, even though portions of the Commercial Code deal with the same or related subject matter."

(2) *Recommendation of the Commission.* The Commission drafted a comprehensive statute to provide a full and clear statutory treatment of the law, and to streamline procedures so as to reduce procedural costs and provide better remedies for creditors and protections for debtors. The scope of the new statute is essentially the same as that of existing law, but it separates the provisions on enforcement of various types of judgments, and clarifies the extent to which general provisions apply to nonmoney judgments. (Pamphlet, p. 1029 and footnote 2.) Much of the existing law was retained, but important substantive changes were made. (Pamphlet, p. 1011.)

(3) *Law Revision Commission Explanatory Pamphlet.* The Commission's Report was reproduced in edited form with additional material in a Pamphlet published in cooperation with, and distributed by, California Continuing Education of the Bar. The Pamphlet, entitled *1982 Creditors' Remedies Legislation,* is cited herein as Pamphlet, p ____. It includes the following material on the new Enforcement of Judgments Law:

(a) Recommendation of the Commission: (1) Summary of the Report (p. 1011 et seq.). (2) The Recommendation, preceded by a detailed Outline (p. 1025 et seq.). This material was revised to reflect the changes made by the Legislature after the proposed legislation was introduced, with omissions and additions indicated.

(b) The Enforcement of Judgments Law: The entire statute as enacted, together with the Commission's Comments, and Comments by Legislative Committees of the Senate and Assembly, preceded by a detailed Outline (p. 1183 et seq.).

(c) Conforming Additions, Amendments and Repeals (p. 1763 et seq.).

(d) Disposition of Existing Enforcement of Judgments Statute (p. 1861 et seq.).

The Pamphlet also covers the changes made in the Attachment Law. (See p. 1608 et seq.; *Provisional Remedies,* Supp., §297A et seq.)

(b)   [§228A]   (New) Enactment of New Statute.

(1) *Short Title and Operative Date.* The new statute may be cited as "the Enforcement of Judgments Law." (C.C.P. 680.010.) Its operative date is July 1, 1983. (C.C.P. 694.010.) (For transitional provisions, see Supp., infra, §229A.) Chapter 5 of Division 2, replacing the "Employees' Earnings Protection Law" (former C.C.P.

723.010, Supp., supra, §133A), may be separately cited as the "Wage Garnishment Law." (C.C.P. 706.010, Supp., infra, §____.)

(2) *Structure and Scope.* The new statute, Title 9 of part 2 of the Code of Civil Procedure, entitled "Enforcement of Judgments," replaces the existing Title 9. It consists of 5 Divisions, each containing Chapters; and most of the Chapters are further subdivided into Articles. The Divisions are as follows:

Division 1. Definitions and General Provisions. (See Supp., infra, §229A et seq.)

Division 2. Enforcement of Money Judgments. (See Supp., infra, §241 et seq.)

Division 3. Enforcement of Nonmoney Judgments. (See Supp., infra, §397A et seq.)

Division 4. Third-Party Claims and Related Procedures. (See Supp., infra, §407A et seq.)

Division 5. Satisfaction of Judgments. (See Supp., infra, §428A et seq.)

The decimal numbering system starts out with C.C.P. 680.010 and concludes with C.C.P. 724.260.

(3) *Severability.* The statute contains the standard severability clause. (C.C.P. 681.050.)

(c) [§229A] (New) Transitional Provisions.

The general rule governing application of the new law to pending matters is stated in C.C.P. 694.020:

"Except as otherwise provided in this chapter, this title on and after its operative date applies to all proceedings commenced prior thereto unless in the opinion of the court application of a particular provision of this title would substantially interfere with the effective conduct of the proceedings or the rights of the parties or other interested persons, in which case the particular provision of this title does not apply and prior law applies."

On application of the provisions dealing with judgment liens on personal property, see Supp., infra, §246A-1.

Specific transitional rules for particular provisions are set forth in succeeding sections:

(1) *Period For Enforcement of Judgments.* The period for enforcement and renewal of judgments entered prior to July 1, 1983, is governed by the new law (C.C.P. 694.030(a)), with these exceptions: (a) A judgment that is not renewable because of expiration of the time for filing an application for renewal may be renewed on noticed motion filed within 2 years after July 1, 1983, if the court which entered the judgment determines that a motion for discretionary

enforcement under former C.C.P. 685 (see text and Supp., supra, §199 et seq.) would have been granted and if the court authorizes renewal of the judgment. (C.C.P. 694.030(b).) (b) The time limitations of the new law do not apply to judgments under the Family Law Act (C.C. 4000 et seq.; see 6 *Summary, Parent and Child,* text and Supp., §§136 et seq., *Husband and Wife,* text and Supp., §§171 et seq.), or to money judgments against public entities subject to Govt.C. 965.5 or Govt.C. 970.1 (see Supp., supra, §191B). (See Legislative Com. Comment—Senate, Pamphlet, p. 1262.)

(2) *Execution and Return of Writs and Orders.* Writs and orders for enforcement of judgments served prior to July 1, 1983, are governed by prior law (C.C.P. 694.040(a)(b)), but any sale of property after July 1, 1983, is governed by the credit transaction provision of the new law (C.C.P. 701.590, Supp., infra, §285A). (C.C.P. 694.040(c)).

(3) *Redemption Rights.* Property which has been sold or levied upon, or as to which foreclosure or other proceedings for sale have been commenced, prior to July 1, 1983, remains subject to the right of redemption provided under prior law (see text and Supp., §98 et seq.), unless the parties agree in writing to application of the new law. (C.C.P. 694.050.)

(4) *Creditor's Suit.* A 1-year grace period is provided to bring a creditor's suit that could have been brought under prior law on the day before July 1, 1983, even though it would be barred by the statute of limitations of the new law. (C.C.P. 694.060; see Law Rev. Com. Comment, Pamphlet, p. 1264, 1511.)

(5) *Third-Party Proceedings.* Prior law governs third-party claims and demands for third-party claims filed or served prior to July 1, 1983. (C.C.P. 694.070.)

(6) *Exemptions.* Whether property subjected to a lien is exempt from enforcement of a money judgment is determined by the law in effect at the time the lien was created. (C.C.P. 694.080; see also C.C.P. 703.050; Law Rev. Com. Comment, Pamphlet, p. 1381.)

(7) *Effect of Homestead Declaration.* A homestead declaration made under prior law is effective only to the extent provided by the new law. (C.C.P. 694.090.)

(d) [§230A] (New) Principal Changes in New Law.

The Enforcement of Judgments Law (C.C.P. 680.010 et seq.) is a comprehensive revision and modernization of our former law. The following are among the more significant changes made:

(1) *Changes in Exemptions.* The most significant changes include: (a) Extension of the homestead exemption to include *any* property in which the debtor or his spouse resides, and simplification and unifica-

tion of the procedures governing homestead exemptions (see Supp., infra, §328A et seq.); (b) increase of the motor vehicle exemption from $500 to $1,200 (see Supp., infra, §306A); (c) a general exemption for household furnishings and personal effects, rather than a listing of specific household items (see Supp., infra, §307A); (d) a new $2,500 exemption for jewelry, heirlooms, and works of art (see Supp., infra, §309A); (e) elimination of the general deposit account exemption and replacement with a paid earnings exemption (see Supp., infra, §312A); (f) consolidation and revision of the life insurance exemption provisions (see Supp., infra, §315A); (g) expansion of the exemption for private retirement plans to reflect recent changes in federal law (see Supp., infra, §318A); (h) total exemption of disability and health benefits except as against a health care provider (see Supp., infra, §320A); (i) new exemptions for damages for personal injury or wrongful death (see Supp., infra, §321A, 322A), strike benefits paid by a union (see Supp., infra, §319A), and student financial aid (see Supp., infra, §326A); (j) increase of the prisoner's trust fund exemption from $40 to $1,000 (see Supp., infra, §314A); (k) elimination of the exemption for church pews (see text, §20; Law Rev. Com. Recommendation, Pamphlet, p. 1091).

(2) *Abolition of Redemptions.* The statutory right of redemption on execution sales of real property (see text, §98 et seq.) was initially adopted for the purposes of preventing sacrifice sales and permitting a debtor one last opportunity to save his property. (See Law Rev. Com. Recommendation, Pamphlet, p. 1117.) Under the prior law the right of redemption prevented a purchaser from obtaining clear title until 12 months after the sale. The effect of the statute was therefore to deter purchasers and the purpose of precluding sacrifice sales, rather than being advanced, was in fact hindered. The new law therefore abolishes the right of redemption and, with limited exceptions (see Supp., infra, §286A) makes all sales absolute. (See Law Rev. Com. Recommendation, Pamphlet, p. 1019 [Summary], 1118.) However, the new law still gives the debtor an opportunity to save his property or to sell it for a higher price by providing a grace period of 120 days between service of the notice of levy and the notice of sale. (C.C.P. 701.545, Supp., infra, §283A; see Law Rev. Com. Recommendation, Pamphlet, p. 1019 [summary], 1118.)

The right of redemption is continued in one area: when a creditor foreclosing a mortgage or deed of trust pursuant to C.C.P. 726 seeks a deficiency judgment. (See 3 *Summary, Security Transactions in Real Property,* §87 et seq., 139 et seq.; Law Rev. Com. Recommendation, Pamphlet, p. 1019 [summary], 1122.) In such cases, the right of redemption is governed by new C.C.P. 729.010 et seq. The property may be redeemed only by the judgment debtor or his successor in interest (C.C.P. 729.020), and the redemption period is 3 months (if the proceeds are sufficient to satisfy the debtor's obligation) or 1 year (if the proceeds are not sufficient (C.C.P. 729.030). (See Law Rev. Com. Recommendation, Pamphlet, p. 1122.)

(3) *Third Party Claim Procedure.* Prior law limited the third-party claims procedure to claims to personal property. (See text, §104.) The new law extends the right to make third-party claims to claims to real property. (See Supp., infra, §407A et seq.) The new law also changes the requirements concerning a creditor's undertaking to prevent release of the property; the undertaking must be either $7,500 in the superior court, $2,500 in the municipal and justice courts, or twice the amount of the creditor's lien, whichever is the lesser. (See Supp., infra, §411A.) The new law also requires that the debtor be given notice of a third-party claim. (See Supp., infra, §417A.)

(4) *Judgment Liens.* Under prior law only real property was subject to a judgment lien. (See *Judgment,* §141.) The new law provides a procedure for obtaining a judgment lien on certain types of personal property. (See Supp., infra, §246A et seq.)

(5) *Registered Process Servers.* The new law expands and clarifies the authority of a registered process server to levy on property. (See Supp., infra, §254A.)

(6) *Levy on Property.* Prior law provided only 60 days to levy on property after receipt of the writ of execution (see text, §72) and required that personal property be levied on before real property (see text, §70). The new law provides a period of 180 days from the date of issuance of the writ within which to levy on property and has eliminated the mandatory order of levy. (See Supp., infra, §258A.)

(7) *Collection of Collectible Property.* The new law encourages collection rather than sale of certain types of property that are particularly susceptible to sacrifice sales. (See Supp., infra, §282A-1.)

(8) *Enforcement and Renewal of Judgments.* Under prior law a judgment was enforceable for a period of 10 years, but a stay of enforcement extended the period; enforcement after 10 years was permitted only at the court's discretion. The new law retains the 10-year period, but the period may not be extended. However, a procedure is provided for renewal of a judgment as a matter of right for additional 10-year periods. See Supp., infra, §237A et seq.)

(e) [§231A] (New) Amendments to Other Statutes.

The 1982 Legislature amended, added, and repealed a great many other statutes in numerous codes to conform them to the provisions of the new Enforcement of Judgments Law. The more significant changes are noted in Pamphlet, p. 1763 et seq.

See 14 Pacific L. J. 397.

2. [§232A] (New) Definitions.

A number of definitions are set forth in C.C.P. 680.120 et seq., to govern unless the provision or context otherwise requires. (C.C.P. 680.110.) (For special definitions governing construction of the Wage Garnishment Law (C.C.P. 706.010 et seq.), see Supp., infra, §338A; for special definitions governing third-party claims and related procedures (C.C.P. 720.010 et seq.), see Supp., infra, §407A.)

(a) *Persons and Entities.* A number of terms are defined:

(1) "Person": a natural person, a corporation, a partnership or other unincorporated association, or a public entity. (C.C.P. 680.280; see Law Rev. Com. Comment, Pamphlet, p. 1201.)

(2) "Court": "the court where the judgment sought to be enforced was entered." (C.C.P. 680.160; see Law Rev. Com. Comment, Pamphlet, p. 1198.)

(3) "Financial institution": a state or national bank, state or federal savings and loan association or credit union, or a similar organization, (including a corporation engaged in the safe deposit business. (C.C.P. 680.200.)

(4) "Levying officer": a sheriff, marshal, or constable. (C.C.P. 680.260; see Legislative Com. Comment—Assembly, Pamphlet, p. 1200.)

(5) "Judgment creditor": the person in whose favor a judgment is rendered or, if there is an assignee of record, the assignee of record. "Unless the context otherwise requires, the term also includes the guardian or conservator of the estate, personal representative, or other successor in interest of the judgment creditor or assignee of record." (C.C.P. 680.240; see Law Rev. Com. Comment, Pamphlet, p. 1200.)

(6) "Judgment debtor": "the person against whom a judgment is rendered." (C.C.P. 680.250; see Law Rev. Com. Comment, Pamphlet, p. 1200.)

(7) "Registered process server": a person registered as a process server pursuant to B. & P.C. 22350 et seq. (C.C.P. 680.330.)

(b) *Commercial Code Definitions.* Many terms are defined by reference to the Commercial Code: "Account debtor" (C.C.P. 680.120; U.C.C. 9105); "Account receivable" (C.C.P. 680.130; U.C.C. 9106 [definition of "account"]; see Law Rev. Com. Comment, Pamphlet, p. 1197); "Chattel paper" (C.C.P. 680.140; U.C.C. 9105); "Deposit account" (C.C.P. 680.170; U.C.C. 9105); "Document of title" (C.C.P. 680.180; U.C.C. 9105 [definition of "document"]; negotiability is determined by reference to U.C.C. 7104); "General intangibles" (C.C.P. 680.210; U.C.C. 9106; see Legislative Com. Comment—Assembly, Pamphlet, p. 1199); "Instrument" (C.C.P. 680.220; U.C.C. 9105; see Legislative Com. Comment—Assembly, Pamphlet p. 1199); "Secured party" (C.C.P. 680.340; U.C.C. 9105); "Security" (C.C.P.

680.345; U.C.C. 8102); "Security agreement" (C.C.P. 680.350; U.C.C. 9105); "Security interest" (C.C.P. 680.360; U.C.C. 1201).

(c) *Property.* "Property" includes real and personal property and any interest therein. (C.C.P. 680.310.) "Real property" includes any right in real property, including but not limited to a leasehold interest. (C.C.P. 680.320; see Legislative Com. Comment—Senate, Pamphlet, p. 1202.) "Personal property" includes both tangible and intangible personal property. (C.C.P. 680.290.) "Tangible personal property" includes chattel paper, documents of title, instruments, securities, and money. (C.C.P. 680.370.)

(d) *Judgment.* "Judgment": "a judgment, order, or decree entered in a court of this state." (C.C.P. 680.230; see Law Rev. Com. Comment, Pamphlet, p. 1199.) "Money judgment": "that part of a judgment that requires the payment of money." (C.C.P. 680.270; see Legislative Com. Comment—Senate, Pamphlet, p. 1201.) "Principal amount of the judgment": "the total amount of the judgment as entered or as last renewed, together with the costs thereafter added to the judgment pursuant to Section 685.090, reduced by any partial satisfactions of such amount and costs and by any amounts no longer enforceable." (C.C.P. 680.300; see Law Rev. Com. Comment, Pamphlet, p. 1201.)

(e) *Costs.* "Costs": "costs and disbursements, including but not limited to statutory fees, charges, commissions, and expenses." (C.C.P. 680.150; see Law Rev. Com. Comment, Pamphlet, p. 1197.)

(f) *Equity.* "Equity": "the fair market value of the interest of the judgment debtor in property, or in the case of community property the fair market value of the interest of the judgment debtor and the spouse of the judgment debtor in the property, over and above all liens and encumbrances on the interest superior to the judgment creditor's lien." (C.C.P. 680.190; see Law Rev. Com. Comment, Pamphlet, p. 1198.)

(g) *Spousal Support.* "Spousal support" includes support for a former spouse. (C.C.P. 680.365; see Legislative Com. Comment— Senate, Pamphlet, p. 1203.)

(h) *Writ.* "Writ" includes a writ of execution, a writ of possession of personal property, a writ of possession of real property, and a writ of sale. (C.C.P. 680.380; see Law Rev. Com. Comment, Pamphlet, p. 1203.)

3.   (New) Practice and Procedure.

(a)   [§233A]   (New) In General.

(1) *Methods of Enforcing Judgments.* The new law contains provisions governing enforcement of money judgments (C.C.P.

695.010 et seq., Supp., infra, §§241A et seq.), judgments for possession of personal property (C.C.P. 714.010, Supp., infra, §401A), judgments for possession of real property (C.C.P. 715.010 et seq., Supp., infra, §§402A et seq.), judgments for sale of real or personal property (C.C.P. 716.010, Supp., infra, §405A), and judgments not falling within any of the above categories (C.C.P. 717.010, Supp., infra, §406A). (C.C.P. 681.010.) The methods provided by the new law are not the exclusive methods of enforcing judgments; various other statutes provide methods of enforcement of specific types of judgments. (See Law Rev. Com. Comment, Pamphlet, p. 1204.)

A sister state money-judgment is enforceable under the new law if a California judgment has been entered in accordance with the Sister State Money-Judgments Act (C.C.P. 1710.10 et seq., Supp., supra, §§195A et seq.). (See Law Rev. Com. Comment, Pamphlet, p. 1204.) Foreign nation money judgments are enforceable pursuant to the Uniform Foreign Money-Judgments Recognition Act (see text and Supp., supra, §§196 et seq.). (See Law Rev. Com. Comment, Pamphlet, p. 1205.)

(2) *Enforcement by Assignee.* Under former practice an assignee of a judgment was not permitted to enforce the judgment unless the assignment was a matter of court record, but no method was prescribed for becoming an assignee of record. The new law codifies existing practice by providing that an assignee of a judgment may not enforce the judgment "unless an acknowledgment of assignment of judgment to that assignee has been filed" under new C.C.P. 673 "or the assignee has otherwise become an assignee of record." (C.C.P. 681.020.) C.C.P. 673, added in 1982, requires that an acknowledgment of assignment be filed "with the clerk of the court which entered the judgment" (C.C.P. 673(a)) and specifies the contents and manner of execution of the acknowledgment (C.C.P. 673(b)(c)). The new law does not limit other methods of becoming an assignee of record. (C.C.P. 673(d).)

Under prior law, if there were conflicting assignments of a judgment the assignee who first gave written notice of the assignment to the judgment debtor had priority. (Former C.C. 955.1.) Under the new law the assignee who first files an acknowledgment of assignment of judgment or otherwise becomes an assignee of record has priority. (C.C. 954.5(b).) However, the existing rule, that a judgment debtor without notice of the assignment may continue to pay the judgment creditor, is retained; filing of an acknowledgment of assignment of judgment does not of itself constitute such notice. (C.C. 954.5(c), 955.1.)

See Law Rev. Com. Recommendation, Pamphlet, pp. 1023 [Summary], 1165; Law Rev. Com. Comment, Pamphlet, p. 1205.

(3) *Procedural Provisions Continued.* "Provisions concerning en-

forcement of judgments after the death of the judgment debtor or the judgment creditor [see Supp., infra, §238], contribution among judgment debtors [see text and Supp., supra, §209 et seq.], entry of costs on writs [see Supp., infra, §240A], execution of commercial paper by the levying officer [see Supp., infra, §236A], judgment creditor's instructions to the levying officer [see Supp., infra, §236A], the manner of custody of property levied upon [see Supp., infra, §236A], and the deposit of fees prior to performance of a duty by the levying officer [see Supp., infra, §236A] are continued in the proposed law without substantial change." (Law Rev. Com. Recommendation, Pamphlet, p. 1170.)

(b) [§234A] (New) Forms.

(1) *Authority of Judicial Council.* The Judicial Council is authorized to adopt rules of practice and procedure and to prescribe forms of the various documents required under the new law. (C.C.P. 681.030(a)(b).) Forms so adopted are deemed to comply with the new law and supersede any corresponding forms provided in the law. Forms may be adopted in languages other than English. (C.C.P. 681.030(b).) The Council must also prepare a form containing a list of the federal and California exemptions from enforcement of a money judgment against a natural person, with citations to the relevant federal or California statutes creating each exemption. (C.C.P. 681.030(c).) (See Law Rev. Com. Recommendation, pp. 1023 [Summary], 1169; Law Rev. Com. Comment, Pamphlet, p. 1206.)

(2) *Interim Forms.* The new law includes statutory forms to be used until the Council adopts superseding forms. These forms include: Writ of execution, possession, and sale (C.C.P. 693.010); notice of levy (C.C.P. 693.020); garnishee's memorandum (C.C.P. 693.030); notice of renewal of judgment (C.C.P. 693.040); notice of hearing for order for sale of dwelling (C.C.P. 693.050); notice of order for sale upon default (C.C.P. 693.060).

(c) [§235A] (New) Service of Papers.

(1) *In General.* The new law contains general provisions on manner and proof of service which apply unless a particular provision provides otherwise. (See Law Rev. Com. Recommendation, Pamphlet, p. 1167.) With the exception of provisions requiring a judgment creditor to supply the name and address of a person being served (C.C.P. 684.130, infra, this section), permitting service by a person authorized by the levying officer (C.C.P. 684.140, infra, this section), and governing proof of service (C.C.P. 684.210 et seq., infra, this section), the general provisions on service of papers are inapplicable to

proceedings under the Wage Garnishment Law (C.C.P. 706.010 et seq.), which has its own provisions on service of papers (see Supp., infra, §350A, 354A, 356A et seq.)). (C.C.P. 684.310.)

The new law also expands significantly the authority of registered process servers to make levies. (See Law Rev. Com. Recommendation, Pamphlet, p. 1022 [Summary]; Supp., infra, §254A.)

(2) *Service on Attorney.* Subject to statutes which govern the withdrawal, discharge, and substitution of attorneys (see *Attorneys,* text and Supp., §35 et seq.) and which require service on the party in certain Family Law Act matters (see *Proceedings Without Trial,* §15), a paper that is required to be served on the judgment creditor must be served on the judgment creditor's attorney of record, if he has one. (C.C.P. 684.010; see Law Rev. Com. Comment, Pamphlet, p. 1221.) Papers required to be served on the judgment debtor must be served on the judgment debtor, not his attorney, unless the judgment debtor has requested that service be made on his attorney. A judgment debtor's request for service on his attorney must be filed with the court and served personally or by mail on the judgment creditor, and must include the attorney's signed consent to receive service. (C.C.P. 684.020(a)(b).) A request or consent may be revoked by filing a notice of revocation with the court, and serving it personally or by mail on the judgment creditor. (C.C.P. 684.020(c).)

Service on an attorney must be made by personal delivery, by service as provided by C.C.P. 1011 (see *Proceedings Without Trial,* §17) or by mail as provided in C.C.P. 684.120 (see infra, this section). (C.C.P. 684.040.)

See Law Rev. Com. Recommendation, Pamphlet, p. 1167.

(3) *Service on Party.* Subpenas, other process to require a party's attendance, and papers to bring a party into contempt must be served on the party. (C.C.P. 684.030.)

(4) *Manner of Service.* When personal service is required, service must ordinarily be made in the manner provided by C.C.P. 413.10 et seq. (see *Actions,* text and Supp., §611 et seq.). (C.C.P. 684.110.) Exceptions to this rule are: (a) Service on an attorney must be made in the manner provided in the new law (see supra, this section) (C.C.P. 684.110(b)); (b) service on a financial institution, a title insurer or underwritten title company, or an industrial loan company must be made at the office or branch that either actually possesses the property levied upon or carries a deposit account levied upon and must be made on "the officer, manager, or other person in charge of the office or branch at the time of service" (C.C.P. 684.110(c)); (c) service of a copy of a writ and notice of levy on any other third person must be made in the manner provided by C.C.P. 415.10 or C.C.P. 415.20 (see *Actions,* text and Supp., §616 et seq.) (C.C.P.

684.110(d)). (See Legislative Com. Comment—Assembly, Pamphlet, p. 1224.)

Unless otherwise provided, service by mail must be sent by first-class mail in a sealed, postage paid envelope, addressed as follows: (1) If an attorney is being served, to the attorney's last address as given on any paper filed in the proceeding and served on the party making service; (2) if any other person is being served, to the person's current mailing address if known or, if unknown, to the person's last address as given on any paper filed in the proceeding and served on the party making service; (3) if service cannot be made in accordance with (1) or (2), to the person's last known address. (C.C.P. 684.120(a).) Service is complete at the time of deposit in the mail, but any required period of notice and the time within which to exercise any right or duty to do any act or make any response are extended 5 days if the place of address is within California, 10 days if it is anywhere else within the United States, and 20 days if it is outside the United States. However, the court may prescribe a shorter period of time. (C.C.P. 684.120(b).) The paper served must "bear a notation of the date and place of mailing or be accompanied by an unsigned copy of the affidavit or certificate of mailing," but this requirement is directory only. (C.C.P. 684.120(c).)

A judgment creditor must use reasonable diligence to ascertain, and must include in the instructions to the levying officer, the correct name and address of any person on whom the levying officer is required by the law to serve any paper. (C.C.P. 684.130(a).) The levying officer may rely on such instructions unless he has actual knowledge that the name or address is incorrect. (C.C.P. 684.130(b).) (See Legislative Com. Comment—Assembly, Pamphlet, p. 1226.)

The new law permits a person (or his agent) in whose favor an order, notice, or other paper (other than a writ or notice of levy) runs to personally serve such paper, provided the levying officer who would otherwise make service gives permission. (C.C.P. 684.140.)

See Law Rev. Com. Recommendation, Pamphlet, p. 1167.

(5) *Proof of Service.* When service of notice of a court hearing is required, proof of such service must be made at or before the hearing to the court's satisfaction. (C.C.P. 684.210.)

The new law specifies several ways in which proof of service or of posting or publication *may* be made: (a) When personal service is made in the manner specified by C.C.P. 413.10 (see supra, this section), proof of service may be made in the manner provided in C.C.P. 417.10 (see *Actions,* text and Supp., §666 et seq.). (C.C.P. 684.220(a).) (b) If service is made in the manner specified by C.C.P. 415.10 or 415.20 (see supra, this section), the person making service may execute an affidavit which shows the time, place, and manner of service, the facts showing that service was made in accordance with statutory requirements, and (by recital or otherwise) the name and and, if appropriate, title or capacity, of the person actually served. (C.C.P. 684.220(b).) (c) Proof of service by mail may be made as provided in C.C.P. 1013a (see *Proceedings Without Trial,* text and Supp., §20). (C.C.P. 684.220(c).) (d) "Proof of posting may be made by the affidavit of the person who posted the notice, showing the time and place of posting." (C.C.P. 684.220(d).) (e) "Proof of publication may be made by the affidavit of the publisher or printer," (or either's foreman or principal clerk) "showing the time and place of publication." (C.C.P. 684.220(e).) (f) "Proof of service may be made by the written admission of the person served." (C.C.P. 684.220(f).) (g) Testimonial evidence may be used to show any type of proof of service, posting, or publication. (C.C.P. 684.220(g).)

(d) [§236A] (New) Levying Officers.

(1) *Instructions to Officer and Deposit of Costs.* The judgment creditor must give the levying officer written instructions, signed either by the judgment creditor's attorney of record or, if he has none, by the judgment creditor. The instructions must adequately describe any property to be levied upon; state whether the property is a dwelling and, if so, whether it is real or personal property; and contain any other "information needed or requested by the levying officer to comply with the provisions" of the new law. (C.C.P. 687.010(a).) The levying officer must act in accordance with and may rely on the information contained in the instructions, unless he has actual knowledge that the information is incorrect. (C.C.P. 687.010(b)(c).) (See Law Rev. Com. Comment, Pamphlet, p. 1238.)

A paper is considered filed with a levying officer when actually received by him, and there is no extension of time for papers which are mailed. (C.C.P. 681.040; see Legislative Com. Comment—Assembly, Pamphlet, p. 1206.)

Unless otherwise provided by law, the judgment creditor must deposit in advance with the levying officer money sufficient to pay the levying officer's costs of performing any duty. If property is to be taken into custody, the deposit must be sufficient to pay the costs of taking and safely keeping the property for a period up to 15 days. If continuation of custody is required, the levying officer may periodically make oral or written demands for additional deposits to cover estimated costs for periods up to 30 days each. The judgment creditor must be given at least 3 business days after receipt to comply with a demand. The levying officer must release the property if the amount demanded is not paid within the time specified in the demand. (C.C.P. 685.100(a); on exceptions to the general rule, see Law Rev. Com. Comment, Pamphlet, p. 1236.) If the judgment creditor does not comply with the provisions of C.C.P. 685.100 the levying officer is not liable for failure to take or hold property. (C.C.P. 685.100(b).)

(2) *Endorsement and Collection of Instructions.* C.C.P. 687.020 states the duty of a levying officer who obtains possession of an instrument, defined as "a check, draft, money order, or other order for the withdrawal of money from a financial institution, the United States, any state, or any public entity within any state" (C.C.P. 687.020(a)), payable to the judgment debtor on demand. The officer must "promptly endorse and present the instrument for payment." (C.C.P. 687.020(b).) The written endorsement must state the judgment debtor's name, the levying officer's name and official title, the title of the court where the judgment is entered, and the judgment's date of entry and where entered in the court's records. (C.C.P. 687.020(c).) If the instrument on its face appears to have been tendered to the judgment debtor in satisfaction of a claim or demand, so that endorsement would be considered a release and satisfaction, the levying officer may not endorse the instrument unless the judgment debtor first endorses it to the officer. If the debtor does not so endorse the instrument, the officer must hold it for 30 days, then return it to the maker. (C.C.P. 687.020(d).)

A financial institution or public entity drawee is not liable to any person for paying an instrument to a levying officer on his proper endorsement. (C.C.P. 687.020(c).) A levying officer is not liable either for endorsing, presenting, and obtaining payment of an instrument, or for delay in presenting for payment an instrument tendered in satisfaction of a claim which the judgment debtor does not endorse. (C.C.P. 687.020(c)(d).)

On the similarities and dissimilarities between new C.C.P. 687.020 and former C.C.P. 688(g), see Law Rev. Com. Comment, Pamphlet, p. 1239.

(3) *Custody or Control of Property.* Unless otherwise provided by statute, the levying officer when required or directed to take custody of property may do so by removing the property to a place of safekeeping, by installing a keeper, or by otherwise obtaining possession or control of the property. (C.C.P. 687.030.) The latter alternative is intended to allow levying officers flexibility in determining the best means of securing custody of diverse types of personal property. (Law Rev. Com. Comment, Pamphlet, p. 1240.)

(4) *Levying Officer's Lien.* "The levying officer has a special lien, dependent upon possession, on personal property levied upon" for any of his costs not advanced. (C.C.P. 687.050.)

(5) *Nonliability of Officer.* The new law contains a general provision exempting the levying officer from liability for actions taken in conformance with the law, including actions taken in reliance on

information contained in the judgment creditor's written instructions (see supra, this section) or provided by a registered process server (see Supp., infra, §254A), "except to the extent the levying officer has actual knowledge that the information is incorrect." The officer's immunity does not limit any liability of the judgment creditor or registered process server for providing incorrect information. (C.C.P. 687.040(a).) Unless he "is negligent in the care or handling of the property, the levying officer is not liable to either the judgment debtor or the judgment creditor for loss by fire, theft, injury, or damage" to personal property while in the levying officer's possession in, or in transit to or from, a warehouse or other storage place, or while in the custody of a keeper. (C.C.P. 687.040(b).)

See Law Rev. Com. Recommendation, Pamphlet, p. 1169; Legislative Com. Comment—Assembly, Pamphlet, p. 1241.

4. (New) Enforcement and Renewal of Judgments.

(a) [§237A] (New) In General.

Prior law permitted the enforcement of a judgment at any time within 10 years after its entry, with time extended by any stay of enforcement. (Former C.C.P. 681; see text and Supp., supra, §68.) A judgment could be renewed by bringing an action on it within the 10-year statute of limitations period. (C.C.P. 337.5; see text and Supp., supra, §192.) Discretionary enforcement after 10 years was also possible. (Former C.C.P. 685, text and Supp., supra, §199 et seq.) (See Law Rev. Com. Recommendation, Pamphlet, p. 1030.)

The new law retains the 10-year period for enforcement of a judgment, but does not exclude stays of enforcement from the 10-year period (C.C.P. 683.020, Supp., infra, §237A-1); retains the right to renew a judgment by an action under C.C.P. 337.5; codifies case law concerning the time for enforcement of installment judgments (C.C.P. 683.030, Supp., infra, §237A-1); and provides a simple procedure, based on the Sister State Money-Judgments Act (see Supp., supra, §195A et seq.), for renewal of the period of enforceability (C.C.P. 683.110 et seq., Supp., infra, §237A-2). (See Law Rev. Com. Recommendation, Pamphlet, pp. 1011 [Summary], 1031.)

The new law's provisions on enforcement and renewal of judgments do not apply to judgments under the Family Law Act (C.C. 4000 et seq.; see Supp., supra, §8, 9; 6 *Summary, Parent and Child*, §124; 6 *Summary, Husband and Wife*, §172) (C.C.P. 683.310; see Legislative Com. Comment—Senate, Pamphlet, p. 1220), or to money judgments against state or local public entities subject to Govt.C. 965.5 or 970.1 (see Supp., supra, §191B) (C.C.P. 683.320; see Law Rev. Com. Comment, Pamphlet, p. 1220).

(b) [§237A-1] (New) Period For Enforcement.

(1) *Judgment Enforceable on Entry.* "Except as otherwise provided by statute or in the judgment, a judgment is enforceable under this title upon entry." (C.C.P. 683.010; on stay of enforcement, see Law Rev. Com. Comment, Pamphlet, p. 1207.)

(2) *Ten-Year Period for Enforcement.* Unless renewed by an action on the judgment (see Supp., supra, §237) or by means of the renewal procedures set out in the new law (see Supp., infra, §237A-2), a judgment is enforceable only for 10 years after the date of entry. At the expiration of the 10-year period the judgment becomes unenforceable, all enforcement procedures must cease, and any lien created by any enforcement procedures taken is extinguished. (C.C.P. 683.020.) The holding of *Alonso Inv. Corp. v. Doff* (1976) 17 C.3d 539, 131 C.R. 411, 551 P.2d 1243 (see Supp., supra, §68), that a writ issued within the 10-year period may be enforced after expiration of that period, is not continued. Nor is the 10-year period extended or tolled for any reason. (See Law Rev. Com. Recommendation, Pamphlet, pp. 1011 [Summary], 1030; Law Rev. Com. Comment, Pamphlet, p. 1207.)

If a judgment is payable in installments, the period of enforceability begins to run only from the time each instalment falls due; the period of enforceability of costs on an instalment judgment runs from the date the costs are added to the judgment. These provisions codify case law. (C.C.P. 683.030; see Law Rev. Com. Recommendation, Pamphlet, p. 1031; Law Rev. Com. Comment, Pamphlet, p. 1208; text, supra, §68.)

The 10-year period of enforceability applies only to money judgments and judgments for possession or sale of property. (C.C.P. 683.020.) (On enforcement of other judgments, see Supp., infra, §406A; on transitional provisions for the period of enforceability, see Supp., supra, §229A.)

- (3) *Application for Writ Over 10 Years After Entry.* When a writ for enforcement of a judgment is sought more than 10 years after the judgment's entry or renewal, the application must "be accompanied by an affidavit of a person having knowledge of the facts stating facts showing that the issuance of the writ . . . is not barred." A copy of the affidavit must be attached to the writ when issued. (C.C.P. 683.040.) This requirement is designed to give the court clerk and levying officer sufficient information concerning enforceability of a judgment more than 10 years old. For example, an affidavit might be essential to show that a particular installment of an installment judgment is not barred by the 10-year period. (Law Rev. Com. Comment, Pamphlet, p. 1209.)

(c) [§237A-2] (New) Renewal of Judgments.

(1) *Right To Renew.* The new law permits renewal of a judgment

and extension of the period for its enforcement in accordance with a procedure drawn from the Sister State Money-Judgments Act (see Supp., supra, §195A et seq.). There is no limit on the number of times a judgment may be renewed, except that it may not be renewed more than once every 5 years. (C.C.P. 683.110; see Law Rev. Com. Recommendation, Pamphlet, p. 1032; Law Rev. Com. Comment, Pamphlet, p. 1210.) The new procedure supersedes the provisions of former C.C.P. 685 governing discretionary enforcement of a judgment after 10 years (see text, §199 et seq.). The right to renew is automatic, provided that the renewal application is timely filed; no showing of diligence on the judgment creditor's part is required. (See Law Rev. Com. Recommendation, Pamphlet, p. 1033; Law Rev. Com. Comment, Pamphlet, p. 1210; 14 Pacific L.J. 401.)

(2) *Application for Renewal and Effect.* An application for renewal is filed with the court which entered judgment and has the effect of renewing the judgment and extending the period of enforceability until 10 years from the date the application is filed. (C.C.P. 683.120(a)(b).) A money judgment payable in installments may be renewed with respect to any past due amounts not barred by the 10-year period; the amount (including principal and interest) of the renewed judgment must be treated as a lump-sum money judgment from the date the application is filed. (C.C.P. 683.120(c), 683.130(b); see Law Rev. Com. Comment, Pamphlet, p. 1212, 1213.)

(3) *Time for Filing Application.* Except for installment judgments, an application for renewal may be filed at any time during the period of enforceability of the original or renewed judgment. (C.C.P. 683.130(a).) With respect to an installment money judgment that has not previously been renewed, an application for renewal may be filed at any time as to past due amounts not barred by expiration of the applicable 10-year period of enforceability. With respect to an installment judgment that has previously been renewed, a subsequent application for renewal of the previously renewed amount may be filed at any time within the renewed 10-year period, while an application for renewal of any amounts that became due and payable after the previous renewal may be filed at any time before expiration of the applicable 10-year period of enforceability. (C.C.P. 683.130(b); see Law Rev. Com. Comment, Pamphlet, p. 1213.)

(4) *Contents of Application.* C.C.P. 683.140 requires that the application be executed under oath and include all the following:

"(a) The title of the court where the judgment is entered and the cause and number of the action.

(b) The date of entry of the judgment and of any renewals of the judgment and where entered in the records of the court.

(c) The name and address of the judgment creditor and the name and last known address of the judgment debtor.

(d) In the case of a money judgment, the information necessary to compute the amount of the judgment as renewed. In the case of a judgment for possession or sale of property, a description of the performance remaining due." (See Law Rev. Com. Comment, Pamphlet, p. 1214.)

(5) *Entry of Renewal by Court Clerk.* C.C.P. 683.150 governs the entry of the renewal of the judgment in the court records. The court clerk must enter the renewal upon the filing of the application, the entry of renewal being a ministerial act. (C.C.P. 683.150(a); see Law Rev. Com. Comment, Pamphlet, p. 1215.) The entry of renewal of a money judgment must show the amount of the judgment as renewed, which amount includes the filing fee for the renewal application. (C.C.P. 683.150(b)–(d).) In the case of a money judgment other than an installment judgment the amount also includes the amount required to satisfy the judgment on the date the application was filed. (C.C.P. 683.150(b).) In the case of an installment money judgment not previously renewed, the amount also includes, to the extent still enforceable, the total of past due unsatisfied installments, costs added to the judgment pursuant to C.C.P. 685.090 (see Supp., infra, §240A), and accrued interest. (C.C.P. 683.150(c).) In the case of an installment money judgment previously renewed, the amount also includes, to the extent unsatisfied and still enforceable, the total of the amount owed under the previous renewal, past due instalments that became due and payable thereafter, costs added to the judgment pursuant to C.C.P. 685.090 after the previous renewal, and interest accrued on those amounts since the last renewal. (C.C.P. 683.150(d).)

The entry of renewal of a judgment for possession or sale of property must describe the performance remaining due. (C.C.P. 683.150(e).)

(6) *Service of Notice of Renewal.* The judgment creditor must make personal service of a notice of renewal of the judgment on the judgment debtor, with proof of service filed with the court clerk. Unless superseded by a form adopted by the Judicial Council (see supra, §234A), the notice must be in the form prescribed by C.C.P. 693.040 and must inform the judgment debtor that he has 30 days within which to move to vacate or modify the renewal. (C.C.P. 683.160(a).) Until proof of service is filed, enforcement proceedings are permissible only to the extent that the judgment would be enforceable without the renewal. (C.C.P. 683.160(b); see Law Rev. Com. Comment, Pamphlet, p. 1215 [notice of renewal may be served after expiration of 10-year period if application for renewal is timely filed].)

(7) *Vacation or Modification of Renewal.* The judgment debtor may, not later than 30 days after service of notice of renewal, make a noticed motion to vacate the renewal. The notice of motion must be served, personally or by mail, on the judgment creditor. (C.C.P. 683.170(b).) The motion may be based "on any ground that would be a defense to an action on the judgment, including the ground that the amount of the renewed judgment . . . is incorrect." (C.C.P. 683.170(a).) At the hearing the renewal may be ordered vacated and, if the court determines that the amount of the judgment as renewed is incorrect, a renewal in the correct amount may be entered. (C.C.P. 683.170(c); see Law Rev. Com. Comment, Pamphlet, p. 1216.) A renewal must be vacated if the application was filed within 5 years of a previous renewal. (C.C.P. 683.170(a).)

(8) *Extending Duration of Judgment Lien on Real Property.* Renewal of a money judgment has the effect of extending a judgment lien on an interest in real property created pursuant to the judgment for an additional 10 years, provided that, prior to expiration of the judgment lien, a certified copy of the renewal application is recorded with the county recorder where the property subject to the lien is located. (C.C.P. 683.180(a).) This extension is analogous to the result obtained by an action on the judgment to preserve the priority of a judgment lien under the holding in *Provisor v. Nelson* (1965), 234 C.A.2d Supp. 876, 44 C.R. 894 (see text, §192). (See Law Rev. Com. Comment, Pamphlet, p. 1217.) If the judgment creditor fails to extend the judgment lien in the manner provided by C.C.P. 683.180(a), he may still record an abstract of the renewed judgment and obtain a new judgment lien dating from such recording. (See Law Rev. Com. Comment, Pamphlet, p. 1217.)

If the interest in real property has been transferred subject to the judgment lien and the transfer has been recorded prior to filing of the renewal application, the lien is not extended unless the transferee is personally served with a copy of the renewal application and proof of such service is filed within 30 days after filing of the renewal application. (C.C.P. 683.180(b); see Law Rev. Com. Comment, Pamphlet, p. 1217.)

(9) *Continuation of Other Liens.* C.C.P. 683.190 provides that renewal of the judgment extends the duration of a lien, other than a judgment lien on real property or an execution lien, for an additional 10 years, provided that, before expiration of the lien, a certified copy of the renewal application "is served on or filed with the same person and in the same manner as the notice or order that created the lien." The duration of a lien of limited duration may not be increased, but may be permitted to continue beyond the 10-year period of enforceability. (See Law Rev. Com. Comment, Pamphlet, p. 1218.)

(10) *Continuation of Enforcement Proceedings.* Renewal of the judgment permits continuation of any previously commenced enforcement proceedings that would otherwise have ceased due to expiration of the 10-year period of enforceability, if, before expiration of such period, a certified copy of the renewal application "is filed with the levying officer, receiver, or other officer acting pursuant to such writ or order or, in other cases, is filed in the enforcement proceeding." (C.C.P. 683.200; see Law Rev. Com. Comment, Pamphlet, p. 1219.)

(11) *Renewal During Stay of Enforcement.* A judgment may be renewed during a stay of enforcement. Such a renewal prevents termination of the period of enforceability but does not affect the stay. (C.C.P. 683.210; see Law Rev. Com. Comment, Pamphlet, p. 1219.)

(12) *Limitation Period for Action on Renewed Judgment.* The period during which an action on a renewed judgment may be brought under C.C.P. 337.5 runs from the date the renewal application is filed. (C.C.P. 683.220; see Law Rev. Com. Comment, Pamphlet, p. 1219.)

5. [§238A] (New) Enforcement After Death.

Prior law on enforcement after death is continued. (See Law Rev. Com. Comment, Pamphlet, p. 1237; text and Supp., §§3, 68.) Thus, the executor, administrator, or successor in interest of the judgment creditor may enforce a judgment in the same manner as the judgment creditor (C.C.P. 686.010), while enforcement against a judgment debtor's estate is governed by the Probate Code (C.C.P. 686.020).

6. (New) Enforcement of State Tax Liability.

(a) [§239A] (New) In General.

Prior law permitted a state agency which issued a warrant for tax liability under certain sections of the Revenue and Taxation Code and the Unemployment Insurance Code to use all the remedies available to judgment creditors. (Former C.C.P. 722.5; see text, §2.) When a warrant was issued the tax debtor was entitled to the exemptions available to a judgment debtor (former C.C.P. 690.51; see text, §26), and a third party could claim ownership or right to possession of property levied on by the state (former C.C.P. 689d; see text, §104.) The new law continues and extends these provisions to other warrant provisions, and also permits security interests and other liens to be claimed by third parties. (See Law Rev. Com. Recommendation, Pamphlet, p. 1152; on detailed provisions, see Supp., infra, §239A-1.)

The new law continues jurisdiction of proceedings for enforcement of tax liability in the superior court, but also provides for concurrent jurisdiction in the municipal or justice court under specified circumstances. (See Law Rev. Com. Recommendation, Pamphlet, p. 1153; Supp., infra, §239A-1.)

Statutory provisions permitting tax enforcement in certain situations by means of a notice to withhold or notice of delinquency to a person who has personal property of or owes a debt to a tax debtor are unchanged by the new law. When enforcement is pursuant to such provisions the tax debtor may not claim exemptions. (See Law Rev. Com. Recommendation, Pamphlet, p. 1153.)

(b) [§239A-1] (New) Pursuant to Warrant or Notice.

(1) *Jurisdiction of Courts; Venue.* Jurisdiction of proceedings for enforcement of a tax liability is conferred on the superior court. In addition, the municipal or the justice court has concurrent jurisdiction if: (a) The amount being sought does not exceed the court's jurisdictional limit; and (b) the person against whom enforcement is sought does not contest the legality of the tax liability. (C.C.P. 688.010; see Law Rev. Com. Comment, Pamphlet, p. 1242.)

An action for enforcement may be brought in the county of the debtor's residence, the county where the property is located, or, if the debtor is a nonresident of the state, in any county. (C.C.P. 680.020(b).) However, any claim of exemption or third-party claim (see infra, this section) must be heard in the county where the property levied upon is located. (C.C.P. 688.030(c).)

(2) *Remedies When Warrant Issued.* C.C.P. 688.020(a) provides that whenever any provision of the Public Resources Code, Revenue and Taxation Code, or Unemployment Insurance Code authorizes the state or its department or agency to properly issue a warrant, and permits the warrant to "be levied with the same effect as a levy pursuant to a writ of execution," the state or its department or agency "may use any of the remedies available to a judgment creditor." The statute permits the state to use the miscellaneous remedies available to judgment creditors (see Supp., infra, §367A et seq.), if a warrant *may* properly be issued, regardless of whether one is actually issued. The statute by its general language is broader than former C.C.P. 722.5, which applied only to enumerated sections of the Revenue and Taxation Code and Unemployment Insurance Code. (See Law Rev. Com. Comment, Pamphlet, p. 1243.)

On special provisions applicable to wage garnishment for collection of state taxes, see Supp., infra, §347A et seq.

(3) *Exemptions and Third-Party Claims.* When property is levied upon pursuant to a warrant (other than a warrant to enforce a lien for postponed real property taxes under Rev. C. 3201 et seq.) or notice of levy, the debtor may claim the same exemptions as a judgment debtor (see Supp., infra, §291A et seq.), and a third person

may claim ownership of, the right to possession of, a security interest in, or a lien on the property. Claims of exemptions and third-party claims must be made, heard, and determined as provided by the new law "in the same manner as if the property were levied upon under a writ of execution." (C.C.P. 680.030(a).) However, in the case of a notice of levy, the claim must be filed with the state department or agency which issued the notice of levy, and that department or agency must perform the levying officer's duties, with the exception that it need not give itself the notices that a levying officer and a judgment creditor or creditor are required to give each other. The department or agency is not obligated to seek to determine the existence of any lien or encumbrance on the property. (C.C.P. 688.030(b).) (See Legislative Com. Comment—Assembly, Pamphlet, p. 1244.)

For the purpose of applying exemption provisions that depend on the date of creation of a lien, "the date of creation of a tax lien is the earliest of the following times:" "(a) The time when a notice of state tax lien is recorded or filed pursuant to" Govt.C. 7150 et seq.; "(b) the time when the property is levied upon pursuant to a warrant or notice of levy or notice to withhold issued by the state or by" its department or agency; (c) the time of performance of any other act "that creates or perfects a lien on specific property as distinguished from a lien on the debtor's property generally." (C.C.P. 688.050; see Legislative Com. Comment—Assembly, Pamphlet, p. 1246.)

(c)   [§239A-2]   (New) Pursuant to Judgment.

C.C.P. 688.110 provides that, except as otherwise provided by statute, a judgment on a public entity's tax claim "is enforceable pursuant to this title in the same manner as any other money judgment." (On special provisions governing wage garnishment for collection of state taxes, see Supp., infra, §347A et seq.)

7.   [§240A]   (New) Interest.

(a) *Rate.* The rate of interest on money judgments is 10%. (C.C.P. 685.010(a).) The Legislature has reserved the right to lower the interest rate and to make the lower rate applicable prospectively. (C.C.P. 685.010(b).) (See Legislative Com. Comment—Senate, Pamphlet, p. 1229.)

(b) *Accrual and Cessation.* Interest on an installment money judgment accrues as to each installment on the date it becomes due, unless the judgment otherwise provides. (C.C.P. 685.020; see Legislative Com. Comment—Senate, Pamphlet, p. 1229.)

In the case of other money judgments, prior law allowed interest on the unpaid principal amount of a judgment until it was satisfied.

(See Law. Rev. Com. Recommendation, Pamphlet, p. 1035.) This remains the rule where a money judgment is satisfied in full other than pursuant to a writ; interest accrues until satisfaction of the judgment in full. (C.C.P. 685.030(b).) Prior law also provided that, if a judgment was satisfied in full pursuant to a levy under writ of execution, accrual of interest ceased on the date of levy. (See former C.C.P. 682.2; Law Rev. Com. Recommendation, Pamphlet, p. 1035.) This rule is continued when the proceeds of collection are paid in a lump sum; interest then ceases to accrue on the date of levy. In any other case where a judgment is satisfied in full pursuant to a writ, accrual of interest ceases on the date the levying officer actually receives the proceeds of sale or collection. (C.C.P. 685.030(a).) The new law thus facilitates satisfaction in a case where the garnishee pays the full amount due, while reducing the interest lost by the judgment creditor in other situations. (See Law Rev. Com. Recommendation, Pamphlet, p. 1035; Legislative Com. Comment—Senate, Pamphlet, p. 1230.)

When a money judgment is partially satisfied, pursuant to a writ or otherwise, accrual of interest on the part satisfied ceases on the date of satisfaction. (C.C.P. 685.030(c).)

The date of full or partial satisfaction of a money judgment (other than one fully satisfied pursuant to a writ) is the earliest of the date the judgment creditor actually receives satisfaction, the date satisfaction is tendered to or deposited in court for the judgment creditor, or "the date of any other performance that has the effect of satisfaction." (C.C.P. 685.030(d); see Legislative Com. Comment—Senate, Pamphlet, p. 1231.)

See 14 Pacific L.J. 402.

On the levying officer's duty to collect interest, see Supp., infra, §240A-1.

(c) *Prejudgment Interest.* The provisions of C.C.P. 685.010 et seq. do not affect the law relating to prejudgment interest (see *Judgment*, §136). (C.C.P. 685.110.)

(d) *Interest on Costs.* Under prior law it was unclear whether interest accrued on costs incurred during the enforcement process. The new law provides that costs added to the judgment are included in the principal amount of the judgment (C.C.P. 685.090(b)); interest therefore accrues on costs from the date they are added to the judgment. (Law Rev. Com. Recommendation, Pamphlet, p. 1036; 14 Pacific L.J. 402.)

8. [§240A-1] (New) Costs.

(a) *Right to Costs.* C.C.P. 685.040 permits recovery of "the reasonable and necessary costs of enforcing a judgment." Attorneys fees are not collectible as costs unless otherwise provided by law. Also, specific provisions may impose procedural restrictions or limit or prevent recovery of costs in certain circumstances. (See Legislative Com. Comment—Assembly, Pamphlet, p. 1231.)

(b) *Costs and Interest Under Writ.* When a writ is issued to enforce a judgment the levying officer must collect, and where necessary compute or determine, the costs and interest to be satisfied in the levy under the writ. This includes: (1) the statutory fee for the writ's issuance; (2) interest from the date of the judgment's entry or renewal to the date of the writ's issuance, as adjusted for partial satisfactions, if the judgment creditor has filed an affidavit stating the amount with the court clerk; (3) interest on the unsatisfied principal amount of the judgment from the date of the writ's issuance until interest ceases to accrue, as determined by reference to the daily interest entered on the writ; (4) the levying officer's statutory costs for performance under the writ. (C.C.P. 685.050; see Law Rev. Com. Comment, Pamphlet, p. 1232.)

(c) *Memorandum of Costs of Enforcing Judgment.* C.C.P. 685.070, which permits a judgment creditor to file a memorandum of costs, continues in substance most of the provisions of former C.C.P. 1033.7 (see *Judgment,* §§108, 109, 112) but extends the time for filing the memorandum from 6 months to 2 years after the costs have been incurred. (C.C.P. 685.070(b); see Law Rev. Com. Recommendation, Pamphlet, p. 1036; Legislative Com. Comment—Assembly, Pamphlet, p. 1233.)

The costs which may be claimed include: (1) "Statutory fees for preparing and issuing, and recording and indexing, an abstract of judgment or a certified copy of a judgment." (2) "Statutory fees for filing a notice of judgment lien on personal property." (3) To the extent not satisfied pursuant to C.C.P. 685.050, supra, statutory fees for issuing a writ to enforce the judgment. (4) To the extent not satisfied pursuant to C.C.P. 685.050, supra, or pursuant to a wage garnishment (see Supp., infra, §338A et seq.), the levying officer's statutory costs and fee for performing under a writ or under the Wage Garnishment Law (see Supp., infra, §338A et seq.). (5) Costs incurred in connection with any proceeding pursuant to the miscellaneous creditors' remedies provided by C.C.P. 708.010 et seq. (Supp., infra, §367A et seq.) "that have been approved as to amount, reasonableness, and necessity by the judge or referee conducting the proceeding." (C.C.P. 685.070(a).)

The memorandum of costs must be executed under oath by a person with knowledge of the facts, must "state that to the person's best knowledge and belief the costs are correct, are reasonable and necessary, and have not been satisfied," and must be filed with the court clerk and served personally or by mail on the judgment debtor.

(C.C.P. 685.070(b).) The judgment debtor may, within 10 days after service of the memorandum, make a noticed motion to have the costs taxed by the court. The notice of motion must be served personally or by mail on the judgment creditor. The motion may be determined in chambers, and the court must order the costs allowed or disallowed "to the extent justified under the circumstances of the case." (C.C.P. 685.070(c); see Legislative Com. Comment—Assembly, Pamphlet, p. 1234.) If a motion to tax costs is not made within the 10-day period, "the costs claimed in the memorandum are allowed." (C.C.P. 685.070(d).)

See 14 Pacific L.J. 403.

(d) *Motion for Costs of Enforcing Judgment.* C.C.P. 685.080, which permits a judgment creditor to claim costs by a noticed motion, continues the substance of former C.C.P. 1033.7 (see *Judgment,* §112), but extends the time for such a motion from 6 months to 2 years. (C.C.P. 685.080(a); see Law Rev. Com. Recommendation, Pamphlet, p. 1036; Legislative Com. Comment—Assembly, Pamphlet, p.1235.)

The costs that may be claimed under such a motion include the costs of enforcing a judgment (C.C.P. 685.040, supra), costs that could have been claimed by filing a memorandum of costs, and "costs incurred but not approved by the court or referee in a proceeding" pursuant to the miscellaneous creditors' remedies provided by the new law (C.C.P. 708.010 et seq., Supp., infra, §367A et seq.). (C.C.P. 685.080(a).)

The notice of motion must describe the costs claimed, state their amount, and be supported by an affidavit of a person with "knowledge of the facts stating that to the person's best knowledge and belief the costs are correct, are reasonable and necessary, and have not been satisfied." The notice of motion must be served personally or by mail on the judgment debtor. (C.C.P. 685.080(b).) The court must allow or disallow the costs "to the extent justified under the circumstances of the case." (C.C.P. 685.080(c).)

(e) *Addition of Costs to Judgment.* Costs are added to and are included in the principal amount of the judgment: (1) on the filing of an order allowing costs; or (2) if a memorandum of costs is filed and no motion to tax is made, on expiration of the time for making the motion. (C.C.P. 685.090(a)(b).) If costs are added to the judgment while a writ is outstanding, the levying officer must add such costs to the amount to be collected under the writ if, before return of the writ, he receives either a certified copy of the court order allowing the costs or a certificate from the court clerk that the costs have been added to the judgment. (C.C.P. 685.090(c).) If the certified copy or the clerk's certificate is received before distribution, the levying officer must include such costs in the amount distributed to the judgment creditor. (C.C.P. 685.090(d).)

B. (New) Enforcement of Money Judgments.

1. (New) In General.

(a) [§241A] (New) Amount To Satisfy Judgment.

"The amount required to satisfy a money judgment is the total amount of the judgment as entered or renewed," with the addition of costs added pursuant to C.C.P. 685.090 (see Supp., supra, §240A-1) and interest added pursuant to C.C.P. 685.010 et seq. (see Supp., supra, §240A), and the subtraction of any partial satisfactions and any portion no longer enforceable. (C.C.P. 695.210; see Law Rev. Com. Comment, Pamphlet, p. 1270.)

(b) [§242A] (New) Application of Money Received.

Money received in satisfaction of a money judgment is credited (1) first, against costs collected by the levying officer pursuant to C.C.P. 685.050 (see Supp., supra, §240A-1); (2) next, against accrued interest that remains unsatisfied; and (3) finally, "against the principal amount of the judgment remaining unsatisfied." On installment judgments, money is credited against installments in the order of maturity. (C.C.P. 695.220; see Law Rev. Com. Comment, Pamphlet, p. 1271.)

(c) [§243A] (New) Property Subject to Enforcement.

(1) *All Property of Judgment Debtor.* "Except as otherwise provided by law, all property of the judgment debtor is subject to enforcement of a money judgment." (C.C.P. 695.010.) The new law thus continues the basic rule of prior law (see former C.C.P. 688(a), text and Supp., supra, §11; Law Rev. Com. Recommendation, Pamphlet, p. 1037; Law Rev. Com. Comment, Pamphlet, p. 1265), but, like prior law, the general statement is subject to many exceptions (see Supp., infra, §§243A-1, 243A-2; Law Rev. Com. Comment, Pamphlet p. 1265).

(2) *Community Property.* Community property, including a non-debtor spouse's interest, generally is subject to enforcement of a money judgment, as provided in C.C. 5100 et seq. (C.C.P. 695.020; see Law Rev. Com. Recommendation, Pamphlet, p. 1038; Law Rev. Com. Comment, Pamphlet, p. 1266; 7 *Summary, Community Property,* §88 et seq.)

(3) *Real Property Leases.* A leasehold interest may be applied to satisfaction of a money judgment: (a) If the lessee has the right to sublet the property or assign the lease; (b) if the lessee has such right "subject to standards or conditions" and the purchaser or other

assignee "agrees to comply with the standards or conditions"; (c) if the lessee has such right "with the consent of the lessor," in which case the lessor's obligation to consent is subject to the standard applicable to a voluntary sublease or assignment; (d) if the lessor consents in writing. (C.C.P. 695.035(a); see Legislative Com. Comment—Assembly, Pamphlet, p. 1268.)

A provision against involuntary transfer or assignment is ineffective if the lessee's interest may be reached under C.C.P. 695.035(a). (C.C.P. 695.035(b); see Legislative Com. Comment—Assembly, Pamphlet, p. 1268.)

(4) *Property Subject to Lien After Transfer.* Property transferred or encumbered subject to a lien created under the new law remains subject to enforcement "in the same manner and to the same extent as if it had not been transferred or encumbered." (C.C.P. 695.070; see Legislative Com. Comment—Assembly, Pamphlet, p. 1270.)

(5) *Spendthrift Trust.* An interest in a spendthrift trust is subject to enforcement "to the extent provided by law." (C.C.P. 695.030(b)(1); see Legislative Com. Comment—Senate, Pamphlet, p. 1267; 7 *Summary, Trusts,* §94 et seq.)

(6) *Cause of Action.* "A cause of action for money or property that is the subject of a pending action or special proceeding" is subject to enforcement. (C.C.P. 695.030(b)(2); see Legislative Com. Comment—Senate, Pamphlet, p. 1267.)

See 14 Pacific L.J. 403.

(d) [§243A-1] (New) Property Not Subject to Enforcement.

(1) *Property Not Assignable or Transferable.* "Except as otherwise provided by statute, property of the judgment debtor that is not assignable or transferable is not subject to enforcement of a money judgment." (C.C.P. 695.030(a); see Legislative Com. Comment—Senate, Pamphlet, p. 1267.) This provision continues prior law. (Law Rev. Com. Recommendation, Pamphlet, p. 1037.)

(2) *License To Engage in Business.* With the exception of an alcoholic beverage license (see Supp., infra, §389A), "a license issued by a public entity to engage in any business, profession, or activity is not subject to enforcement of a money judgment." (C.C.P. 695.060.) This provision, with the exception of the liquor license exclusion, continues prior law (see former C.C.P. 688(f); Legislative Com. Comment—Assembly, Pamphlet, p. 1269; text and Supp., supra, §17.)

(3) *Release of Property.* Property not subject to enforcement "may not be levied upon or in any other manner applied to the satisfaction of a money judgment" (C.C.P. 695.040); as to such property it is unnecessary to make a claim of exemption (C.C.P. 704.210). (See Law

Rev. Com. Comment, Pamphlet, p. 1265.) If such property is levied upon, the claim of exemption procedure (see Supp., infra, §300A et seq.) may be used to obtain its release. (C.C.P. 695.040; see Law Rev. Com. Comment, p. 1269.)

(e) [§243A-2] (New) Enforcement Against Public Entity.

Prior law, under which properties of state and local public entities were not subject to enforcement, is continued. (C.C.P. 695.050; see Law Rev. Com. Recommendation, Pamphlet, p. 1037; Law Rev. Com. Comment, Pamphlet, p. 1269; Supp., supra, §189 et seq.)

2. (New) Liens.

(a) [§244A] (New) General Provisions.

(1) *Amount of Lien.* "Except as otherwise provided by statute," a lien is "for the amount required to satisfy the money judgment." (C.C.P. 697.010; see Law Rev. Com. Comment, Pamphlet, p. 1271.)

(2) *Relation Back of Liens.* C.C.P. 697.020 codifies case law that the priority of a judgment creditor's lien relates back to the date of creation of the first in a series of overlapping liens on the same property. The last lien may relate back either to an attachment lien or to an earlier lien created in the process of enforcement. (C.C.P. 697.020(a)(b); see Law Rev. Com. Recommendation, Pamphlet, p. 1039; Legislative Com. Comment—Assembly, Pamphlet, p. 1272.) However, the relation back doctrine does not affect the "priorities or rights of third persons established while the earlier lien was in effect under the law governing the earlier lien." (C.C.P. 697.020(c); on situations in which third party's lien might prevail, see Law Rev. Com. Recommendation, Pamphlet, p. 1040; Legislative Com. Comment—Assembly, Pamphlet, p. 1272.)

(3) *Duration of Liens.* Unless a shorter period is provided by statute, a lien "is effective during the period of enforceability of the judgment"; a lien remains effective under a renewed judgment, provided that the provisions of C.C.P. 683.180 et seq. (see Supp., supra, §237A-2) are complied with. (C.C.P. 697.030; see Law Rev. Com. Recommendation, Pamphlet, p. 1040; Legislative Com. Comment—Assembly, Pamphlet, p. 1273.) However, a lien may be extinguished by a stay of enforcement of judgment. (See infra, this section.)

(4) *Effect of Extinction of Lien.* When a lien is extinguished, property held subject to the lien must be released, unless the property is subject to another lien or the court orders it retained "pending resolution of a dispute concerning its proper disposition." (C.C.P. 697.050; see Law Rev. Com. Comment, Pamphlet, p. 1275.)

(5) *Effect of Stay of Enforcement of Judgment.* "If enforcement of the judgment is stayed on appeal by the giving of a sufficient undertaking under" C.C.P. 916 et seq. (see *Appeal,* §155 et seq.), existing liens are extinguished and new liens may not be created during the stay. (C.C.P. 697.040(a).) However, "[u]nless the court otherwise expressly orders," a limited stay under C.C.P. 918 (see *Appeal,* Supp., §149) does not extinguish or prevent the creation of a judgment lien on real or personal property, but does prevent the creation or continuance of other liens during the stay. (C.C.P. 697.040(b).) "Unless the court expressly orders otherwise," a stay of enforcement of a sister state support order under C.C.P. 1699 (Supp., supra, §195H) or a sister state money judgment under C.C.P. 1710.50 (Supp., supra, §195E) extinguishes existing liens and prevents creation of new liens during the stay. (C.C.P. 697.040(c).)

See Law Rev. Com. Recommendation, Pamphlet, p. 1040, 1164; Legislative Com. Comment—Assembly, Pamphlet, p. 1274.

(b)   (New) Judgment Lien on Real Property.

(1)   [§245A]   (New) Creation and Duration.

(a) *In General.* "Except as otherwise provided by statute, a judgment lien on real property is created under this section by recording an abstract of a money judgment with the county recorder." (C.C.P. 697.310(a); see Law Rev. Com. Recommendation, Pamphlet, p. 1041.) In the case of a federal court money judgment, an abstract or certified copy may be recorded to create the lien. (C.C.P. 697.060(a); see Law Rev. Com. Recommendation, Pamphlet, p. 1041; Legislative Com. Comment—Assembly, Pamphlet, p. 1275.) A judgment lien on real property continues for 10 years from the date of entry of judgment, but may be renewed under the provisions for renewal of judgment (see Supp., supra, §237A-2). (C.C.P. 697.310(b); Law Rev. Com. Recommendation, Pamphlet, pp. 1012 [Summary], 1043; Legislative Com. Comment—Assembly, Pamphlet, p. 1276; 14 Pacific L.J. 404.)

The above provisions are applicable to lump-sum money judgments, including municipal, justice, and small claims court judgments payable in installments, certain vehicle accident judgments payable in installments, and "similar" judgments payable in installments. (C.C.P. 697.310(c); Law Rev. Com. Recommendation, Pamphlet, p. 1044; Legislative Com. Comment—Assembly, Pamphlet, p. 1276.)

(b) *Installment Judgment for Support or Against Health Care Provider.* In the case of an installment judgment for spousal or child support or a judgment under C.C.P. 667.7 against a health care provider requiring periodic payments, a judgment lien on real property is created by recording a certified copy of the judgment with the county recorder. (C.C.P. 697.320(a).) The lien continues for 10 years from the date of its creation, but may be renewed for additional 10-year periods by rerecording a certified copy of the judgment. (C.C.P. 697.320(b).)

See Law Rev. Com. Recommendation, Pamphlet, p. 1044; Legislative Com. Comment—Senate, Pamphlet, p. 1277.

(c) *Workers' Compensation Award.* When a money judgment is entered on a workers' compensation award, the manner of creating a judgment lien on real property depends on whether the judgment is for a lump-sum or installments. If the judgment is for a lump-sum, the lien is created in the manner provided by C.C.P. 697.310 for lump-sum judgments generally; if the judgment is for installments, a lien is created in the manner provided by C.C.P. 697.320 for installment support judgments. In either case the lien is subject to the provisions of Lab.C. 3200 et seq. (2 *Summary, Workmen's Compensation*). (C.C.P. 697.330; see Law Rev. Com. Recommendation, Pamphlet, p. 1044; Law Rev. Com. Comment, Pamphlet, p. 1278.)

(2) [§245A-1] (New) Interests Subject to Lien.

Except as to declared homesteads (see Supp., infra, §334A et seq.), a judgment lien "attaches to all interests in real property in the county where the lien is created (whether present or future, vested or contingent, legal or equitable) that are subject to enforcement of the money judgment," but does not reach a right to rents, a leasehold interest with less than 2 years to run, or a beneficiary's interest under a trust. (C.C.P. 697.340(a).) The new law thus expands the interests that may be reached; under former C.C.P. 674, a judgment lien reached only vested legal ownership interests. (See Law Rev. Com. Recommendation, Pamphlet, p. 1042; Legislative Com. Comment—Senate, Pamphlet, p. 1279; *Judgment,* §§141, 142.)

A judgment lien attaches to an after-acquired property interest at the time of acquisition. (C.C.P. 697.340(b); Legislative Com. Comment—Senate, Pamphlet, p. 1280.)

See 14 Pacific L.J. 404.

(3) [§245A-2] (New) Amount of Lien.

(a) *In General.* "Except as otherwise provided by statute, a judgment lien on real property is a lien for the amount required to satisfy the money judgment." (C.C.P. 697.350(a); see Law Rev. Com. Recommendation, Pamphlet, p. 1045; Law Rev. Com. Comment, Pamphlet, p. 1280.)

(b) *Installment Judgments.* Liens under Municipal, justice, and small claims court installment judgments, certain vehicle accident installment judgments, or "similar" judgments, are for the full amount required to satisfy the judgment, but only the matured installments are enforceable unless the court orders otherwise. (C.C.P. 697.350(b); Law Rev. Com. Comment, Pamphlet, p. 1280.) A judgment lien created under an installment judgment for support, an installment judgment against a health care provider, or an installment judgment based on a workers' compensation award, is for the amount of the installments as they mature, with interest and costs as they are added to the judgment, but does not become a lien for any installment until it is due and payable. (C.C.P. 697.350(c); see Law Rev. Com. Recommendation, Pamphlet, p. 1045; Law Rev. Com. Comment, Pamphlet, p. 1281.)

(c) *Effect of Modification of Judgment.* When a judgment is modified as to amount, an abstract of the modified judgment or a certified copy of the order of modification may be recorded in the normal manner (see Supp., supra, §245A) and has the effect of conforming the terms of the judgment lien with the modified judgment. (C.C.P. 697.360(a); see Law Rev. Com. Comment, Pamphlet, p. 1281.) If the modification reduces the amount of the judgment, a previously-created judgment lien is considered modified, whether or not the modification is recorded. (C.C.P. 697.360(b); see Law Rev. Com. Recommendation, Pamphlet, p. 1045; Law Rev. Com. Comment, Pamphlet, p. 1282.) If the amount of the judgment is increased, the lien continues under its original terms until the modification is recorded. Once recorded, the lien extends to the modified judgment, but the priority for the increased amount dates from the time of recording. (C.C.P. 397.360(c); see Law Rev. Com. Recommendation, Pamphlet, p. 1046; Law Rev. Com. Comment, Pamphlet, p. 1282.)

(4) [§245A-3] (New) Release or Subordination of Lien.

A judgment creditor may either release all or part of the property from a judgment lien on real property, or subordinate to another lien or encumbrance the judgment lien on all or part of the real property subject to the lien. (C.C.P. 697.370(a).)

"A release or subordination is sufficient if it is executed by the judgment creditor in the same manner as an acknowledgement of satisfaction of judgment and contains all of the following:" (1) A description of the property which is the subject of the release or subordination, showing the record owner's name if the judgment debtor has no interest of record in the property; (2) the lien's date of creation and where in the county records the abstract of judgment or certified copy of the judgment creating the lien was recorded; (3) the title of the court which entered judgment and the cause and number of the action; (4) the dates of entry of the judgment and any renewals and where entered in the court's records; (5) the judgment creditor's and judgment debtor's names and addresses. (C.C.P. 697.370(b).)

A release or subordination "substantially complying" with these requirements is effective "even though it contains minor errors that are not seriously misleading." (C.C.P. 697.380(c).)

See Legislative Com. Comment—Senate, Pamphlet, p. 1283.

(5) [§245A-4] (New) Priority of Liens.

"Except as otherwise provided by law," the priorities of judgment liens on real property are as follows (C.C.P. 697.380(b):

(1) A lump-sum judgment lien (one created under C.C.P. 697.310; see Supp., supra, §245A) has priority over later lump-sum judgment liens. (C.C.P. 697.380(a), (c).)

(2) A lump-sum judgment lien has priority over an installment judgment lien (one created under C.C.P. 697.320; see Supp., supra, §245A) as to installments that mature on, interest that accrues on, and costs that are added to, the installment judgment after creation of the lump-sum judgment lien; in other respects the installment judgment lien has priority. (C.C.P. 697.380(a)(d)(e).)

(3) Where there are competing installment judgment liens, each lien has priority as to installments that have matured, interest that has accrued, and costs that have been added prior to those of the other. (C.C.P. 697.380(f).)

See Law Rev. Com. Recommendation, Pamphlet, p. 1046; Law Rev. Com. Comment, Pamphlet, p. 1284.

If two judgment liens attach to after-acquired property (see Supp., supra, §245A-1), the judgment lien that was first created has priority over the other. (C.C.P. 697.380(g).) This is a change from prior law, under which existing judgment liens attached with equal status to after-acquired property, with the creditor who levied first obtaining priority. (See Law Rev. Com. Recommendation, Pamphlet, p. 1047; Law Rev. Com. Comment, Pamphlet, p. 1285.)

(6) [§245A-5] (New) Transfer or Encumbrance of Interest.

When an interest in real property that is subject to a judgment lien is transferred or encumbered, the interest remains subject to an unsatisfied judgment lien created pursuant to C.C.P. 697.310 (see Supp., supra, §245A) "in the same amount as if the interest had not been transferred or encumbered" (C.C.P. 697.390(a)), and subject to a lien created pursuant to C.C.P. 697.320 (see Supp., supra, §245A) "in the amount of the lien at the time of transfer or encumbrance plus interest thereafter accruing on such amount" (C.C.P. 697.390(b)). (See Law Rev. Com. Comment, Pamphlet, p. 1285.)

(7) [§245A-6] (New) Recording Satisfaction of Judgment.

C.C.P. 697.400 provides for recording in the office of the county recorder certain documents which extinguish judgment liens in whole or in part. These include: (1) An acknowledgment of satisfaction of judgment pursuant to C.C.P. 724.060 or a clerk's certificate of satisfaction of judgment pursuant to C.C.P. 724.100 (C.C.P. 697.400(a); see Supp., infra, §429A et seq.); (2) an acknowledgement of satisfaction of matured installments pursuant to C.C.P. 724.250 (C.C.P. 697.400(b); see Supp., infra, §434A et seq.); (3) a release or subordination of a judgment lien on real property executed as provided in C.C.P. 697.370 (C.C.P. 697.400(c); see Supp., supra, §245A-3). The documents may be recorded by the judgment creditor, the judgment debtor, or the owner of the real property. (C.C.P. 697.400.)

(8) [§245A-7] (New) Release of Erroneous Lien.

C.C.P. 697.410, drawn from former C.C.P. 675(e)(f)(g) (see *Judgment,* Supp., §145A), provides remedies for a real property owner whose property appears subject to a judgment lien because his name is the same or similar to that of the judgment debtor. (C.C.P. 697.410(a); see Law Rev. Com. Comment, Pamphlet, p. 1288.)

(a) *Demand for Release.* The "owner may deliver to the judgment creditor a written demand for a recordable document releasing the lien." The demand must be accompanied by proof to the creditor's satisfaction that the owner "is not the judgment debtor and that the property is not subject to enforcement of the judgment against the judgment debtor." (C.C.P. 697.410(a).)

(b) *Delivery of Release.* The creditor must, within 15 days after receipt of the demand and accompanying proof, "deliver to the property owner a recordable document releasing the lien on the property of such owner." Improper failure to do so results in liability "for all damages sustained by reason of such failure" and $100. (C.C.P. 697.410(b).)

(c) *Motion for Release.* If the creditor fails to deliver the recordable document, the owner may make a noticed motion, served personally or by mail on the creditor, for an order releasing the lien. On presentation of satisfactory evidence that the "owner is not the judgment debtor and that the property is not subject to enforcement of the judgment," the court must "order the judgment creditor to prepare and deliver a recordable document releasing the lien or shall itself order the release of the judgment lien," which order may be recorded in the county recorder's office "with the same effect as the recordable document demanded by the property owner." (C.C.P. 697.410(c).) Attorney's fees must be awarded to the prevailing party. (C.C.P. 697.410(d).)

(d) *Other Damages or Penalties.* The damages recoverable under C.C.P. 697.410 (b), supra, "are not in derogation of any other damages or penalties to which an aggrieved person may be entitled by law." (C.C.P. 697.410(e).)

(c)   (New)   Judgment Lien on Personal Property.

(1)   [§246A]   (New)   In General.

Under prior law personal property was not subject to a judgment lien. (See text, §141.) The new law provides a procedure for obtaining a lien on certain types of business personal property in a manner analogous to the commercial code procedure for perfecting a security interest. (C.C.P. 697.510 et seq.; Law Rev. Com. Recommendation, Pamphlet, pp. 1012 [Summary], 1048; Law Rev. Com. Comment, Pamphlet, p. 1288.)

The primary advantage of the new procedure is that it provides a judgment creditor a fast and inexpensive method of obtaining priority over certain other creditors, and thus may enable the creditor to avoid the delay, expense, and uncertainty involved in seeking a levy of execution. A lien on personal property will also pressure a debtor to reach settlement with the creditor, since the lien prevents the debtor from pledging the property to finance the business. (Law Rev. Com. Recommendation, Pamphlet, p. 1051; Law Rev. Com. Comment, Pamphlet, p. 1289.)

A creditor may use the new procedure alone or in conjunction with other enforcement procedures. If the lien does not result in satisfaction of the judgment, the normal remedy will be by levy of execution. (Law Rev. Com. Recommendation, Pamphlet, p. 1051; Law Rev. Com. Comment, Pamphlet, p. 1289.) Unless the judgment debtor consents, the judgment creditor may not use the remedies, such as self-help repossession or private sale, provided in U.C.C. 9501 et seq. (See Law Rev. Com. Comment, Pamphlet, p. 1289; 2 *Summary, Secured Transactions in Personal Property;* §63 et seq.)

The details of the new procedure are covered in §246A-1 et seq., infra.

See 14 Pacific L.J. 405.

(2)   [§246A-1]   (New)   Creation and Duration.

A judgment lien on personal property is available only with respect to money judgments first entered in California on or after July 1, 1983. The lien "is created by filing a notice of judgment lien in the office of the Secretary of State." With certain exceptions (see Supp., infra, §246A-3), a lien on personal property is not available on an installment judgment unless all the installments have become due and payable at the time of filing. (C.C.P. 697.510(a); see Legislative Com. Comment—Assembly, Pamphlet, p. 1290.) A lien on personal property may also be created under a federal money judgment that is enforceable in California. (C.C.P. 697.060(b); see Legislative Com. Comment—Assembly, Pamphlet, p. 1275.)

The lien continues for 5 years from the date of filing and may not be extended. (C.C.P. 697.510(b); see Legislative Com. Comment—Assembly, Pamphlet, p. 1291.) The priority of a judgment lien on personal property does not relate back to the date of creation of an earlier lien. (C.C.P. 697.510(c); see Legislative Com. Comment—Assembly, Pamphlet, p. 1291.)

The procedure for creating a lien on personal property may be used alone or in addition to other enforcement procedures, such as levy of execution (see Supp., infra, §249A et seq.) or examination proceedings (see Supp., infra, §368A et seq.). (C.C.P. 697.520; see Law Rev. Com. Comment, Pamphlet, p. 1291.)

(3) [§246A-2] (New) Property Subject to Lien.

(a) *In General.* The lien attaches to all interests subject to enforcement of the judgment (see Supp., supra, §243A) in six types of personal property, "at the time the lien is created *if* a security interest in the property could be perfected under the Commercial Code by filing a financing statement at that time *with the Secretary of State.*" (C.C.P. 697.530(a).) Thus, the lien does not attach to items as to which a security interest is generally perfected by (1) taking possession (see 2 *Summary, Secured Transactions in Personal Property,* §35 et seq.), or (2) filing with the county recorder (see 2 *Summary, Secured Transactions in Personal Property,* §41). (See Legislative Com. Comment—Assembly, Pamphlet, p. 1293.)

The enumerated types of property are: (1) Accounts receivable; (2) chattel paper; (3) equipment; (4) farm products; (5) inventory; (6) negotiable documents of title. (C.C.P. 697.530(a).)

(b) *After-Acquired Property.* The lien attaches to after-acquired property at the time of acquisition. (C.C.P. 697.530(b); see Legislative Com. Comment—Assembly, Pamphlet, p. 1294.)

(c) *Exceptions.* The lien does not attach to: (1) A vehicle or boat required to be registered with the Department of Motor Vehicles, or a mobilehome or commercial coach required to be registered with the Department of Housing and Community Development; or (2) the inventory of a retail merchant that does not have a unit retail value of at least $500. The definition of "retail merchant," and the exclusion of agricultural and fish marketing cooperative associations from the definition, parallel those contained in U.C.C. 9102(4). (C.C.P. 697.530(d); see Law Rev. Com. Recommendation, Pamphlet, p. 1048;

Legislative Com. Comment—Assembly, Pamphlet, p. 1294; 2 *Summary, Secured Transactions in Personal Property,* text and Supp., §25.)

If personal property subject to a lien becomes a fixture, as defined in U.C.C. 9313 (see 2 *Summary, Secured Transactions,* Supp., §50D), the judgment lien on the property is extinguished. (C.C.P. 697.530(e).)

A person obligated on an account receivable or chattel paper as to which a notice of judgment lien has been filed may, subject to the provisions on miscellaneous remedies (C.C.P. 708.010 et seq., Supp., infra, §367A et seq.), "pay or compromise the amount without notice to or consent of the judgment creditor" unless and until there is a levy of execution pursuant to C.C.P. 699.010 (see Supp., infra, §249A et seq.). (C.C.P. 697.530(f).)

(4)   [§246A-3]   (New)   Amount of Lien.

"Except as otherwise provided by statute, a judgment lien on personal property is a lien for the amount required to satisfy the money judgment." (C.C.P. 697.540(a).)

A lien created under an installment judgment entered in the municipal, justice, or small claims court, or in connection with certain vehicle accident actions (Veh.C. 16380) is for the full amount required to satisfy the judgment, but may not be enforced as to unmatured installments unless the court so orders. (C.C.P. 697.540(b); see Law Rev. Com. Comment, Pamphlet, p. 1294.)

(5)   [§246A-4]   (New)   Notice of Lien.

(a) *Content and Form of Notice.* C.C.P. 697.550 requires a notice of judgment lien on personal property to be executed under oath by the judgment creditor's attorney if there is an attorney of record or, if not, by the judgment creditor. The notice must contain: (1) The judgment creditor's name and mailing address; (2) the judgment debtor's name and last known mailing address; (3) a statement that: "All property subject to enforcement of a money judgment against the judgment debtor to which a judgment lien on personal property may attach under Section 697.530 of the Code of Civil Procedure is subject to this judgment lien."; (4) the title of the court which entered judgment and the cause and number of the action; (5) the dates of entry of the judgment and any renewals and where entered in the court's records; (6) the amount required to satisfy the judgment on the notice date; (7) the notice date. (C.C.P. 697.550.)

The Secretary of State may prescribe a form of notice of judgment lien. (C.C.P. 697.670; see Law Rev. Com. Comment, Pamphlet, p. 1303.)

(b) *Service of Copy.* The creditor must, when the notice of lien is filed "or promptly thereafter," serve a copy on the debtor, either personally or by mail. Failure to make such service does not affect the lien's validity, but does not exempt the creditor from any potential liability to the debtor. (C.C.P. 697.560; see Law Rev. Com. Comment, Pamphlet, p. 1296.)

(c) *Filing, Marking and Indexing.* On presentation of the notice and tender of the filing fee to the Secretary of State's office, the notice must "be filed, marked, and indexed in the same manner as a financing statement." The filing fee "is the same as the fee for filing a financing statement in the standard form." A notice presented for filing more than 10 days after the date of the notice may not be filed. (C.C.P. 697.570; see Law Rev. Com. Comment, Pamphlet, p. 1296; on filing of financing statements under the U.C.C., see 2 *Summary, Secured Transactions in Personal Property,* §42.)

(d) *Certificate and Copies.* On request by any person, the Secretary of State must "issue a certificate showing whether there is on file in that office on the date and hour stated therein any notice of judgment lien on personal property filed against the property" of the person named. If a notice is on file, the certificate must "state the date and hour of filing of each such notice and any notice affecting any such notice of judgment lien" and the creditor's name and address. (C.C.P. 697.580(a).) On request, the Secretary of State must "furnish a copy of any notice of judgment lien or notice affecting a notice of judgment lien." (C.C.P. 697.580(b).) The fee for a certificate or for a copy of a notice is the fee prescribed by U.C.C. 9407 (see 2 *Summary, Secured Transactions in Personal Property,* §42). (C.C.P. 697.580(a)(b).)

See Law Rev. Com. Comment, Pamphlet, p. 1297.

(6) [§246A-5] (New) Priority of Lien.

(a) *Priority Against Security Interests.* The priority of a judgment lien on personal property as against a security interest is determined as provided in U.C.C. 9301. (C.C.P. 697.590(a); see Law Rev. Com. Recommendation, Pamphlet, p. 1050; Legislative Com. Comment—Assembly, Pamphlet, p. 1297; 2 *Summary, Secured Transactions in Personal Property,* §48.)

With respect to after-acquired property, a secured party having a purchase money security interest under U.C.C. 9107 has priority if he files a financing statement within 10 days after the debtor receives possession of the property; otherwise a lien on personal property filed prior to the financing statement has priority. (C.C.P. 697.590(b); see Law Rev. Com. Recommendation, Pamphlet, p. 1050; Legislative Com. Comment—Assembly, Pamphlet, p. 1298; 2 *Summary, Secured Transactions in Personal Property,* §51.) However, in a circular priority situation in which a perfected purchase money security interest in inventory has priority over the lien on after-acquired inventory, a conflicting security interest has priority over the purchase money security interest under U.C.C. 9312(3), and the lien would otherwise have priority over the conflicting security interest, the conflicting security interest will take priority over the lien. (C.C.P. 697.590(c); see Legislative Com. Comment—Assembly, Pamphlet, p. 1298; 2 *Summary, Secured Transactions in Personal Property*, §51.)

(b) *Priority Against Other Judgment Liens.* A lien on personal property has priority over later liens. (C.C.P. 697.600(a).) When two liens attach to after-acquired property at the same time, the lien first filed has priority. (C.C.P. 697.600(b); see Law Rev. Com. Comment, Pamphlet, p. 1298.)

(7) [§246A-6] (New) Transfer of Property.

(a) *Continuation of Lien on Property.* Except when disposed of after default as provided in U.C.C. 9504 (see 2 *Summary, Secured Transactions in Personal Property*, §§67 et seq.), "a judgment lien on personal property continues notwithstanding the sale, exchange, or other disposition of the property, unless the person receiving the property is": (1) A buyer in the ordinary course of business who, under U.C.C. 9307, "would take free of a security interest created by the seller" (see 2 *Summary, Secured Transactions in Personal Property*, §54); (2) "a holder to whom a negotiable document of title has been duly negotiated within the meaning of" U.C.C. 7501 (see 2 *Summary, Sales*, §125; 2 *Summary, Secured Transactions in Personal Property*, §56); or (3) a purchaser giving new value and taking possession of chattel paper in the ordinary course of business. (C.C.P. 697.610; see Law Rev. Com. Recommendation, Pamphlet, p. 1050; Legislative Com. Comment—Senate, Pamphlet, p. 1298.)

(b) *Lien on Proceeds.* A lien on personal property continues with the same priority on the identifiable cash proceeds (money, checks, deposit accounts, and the like) received on disposition of the property. (C.C.P. 697.620(a)(b); see Law Rev. Com. Recommendation, Pamphlet, p. 1050; Law Rev. Com. Comment, Pamphlet, p. 1299.) However, if insolvency proceedings are instituted by or against the judgment debtor, the lien continues only in the following proceeds: (1) "Proceeds in a separate deposit account containing only proceeds"; (2) money which is "neither comingled with other money nor deposited in a deposit account prior to the insolvency proceedings"; (3) "checks and the like which are not deposited in a deposit account prior to the insolvency proceedings." (C.C.P. 697.620(c).)

The judgment lien will attach to proceeds which do not qualify as identifiable cash proceeds only if such proceeds qualify as after-acquired property under C.C.P. 697.530(b) (see Supp., supra, §246A-2). (See Law Rev. Com. Comment, Pamphlet, p. 1299.)

(8) [§246A-7] (New) Recording Satisfaction of Judgment.

A judgment lien on personal property is extinguished as a matter of record on the filing in the Secretary of State's office of an acknowledgment of satisfaction of judgment or a court clerk's certificate of satisfaction of judgment. The acknowledgment or clerk's certificate may be filed by the creditor, the debtor, the owner of property subject to the lien, or a person with a security interest in or lien on the property. (C.C.P. 697.640(a); see Legislative Com. Comment—Assembly, Pamphlet, p. 1300.)

The filing officer must treat the acknowledgment or clerk's certificate in the same manner as a termination statement filed pursuant to U.C.C. 9404 (C.C.P. 697.640(b)), and the filing fee is the same as the fee for a termination statement (C.C.P. 697.640(a)). (On termination statements under U.C.C., see 2 *Summary, Secured Transactions in Personal Property,* §45.)

On acknowledgment of satisfaction and certificate of satisfaction, see Supp., infra, §429A et seq.

(9) [§246A-8] (New) Release or Subordination of Lien.

The judgment creditor may in writing either release the judgment lien on all or part of the property or subordinate the lien on all or part of the property to a security interest or other lien or encumbrance. (C.C.P. 697.650(a).) The release or subordination is sufficient if the creditor signs it and it contains a description of the property that is the subject of the release or subordination, the debtor's name and address, and the file number of the notice of lien. (C.C.P. 697.650(b).) The filing officer must treat the release or subordination in the same manner as a statement of release filed pursuant to U.C.C. 9405, and the filing fee is the same as provided in U.C.C. 9405. (C.C.P. 697.650(c).) (See Law Rev. Com. Comment, Pamphlet, p. 1301; on statements under U.C.C. 9405, see 2 *Summary, Secured Transactions in Personal Property.* §46.)

C.C.P. 697.670 authorizes the Secretary of State to prescribe forms of statement of release or subordination. (See Law Rev. Com. Comment, Pamphlet, p. 1303.)

(10) [§246A-9] (New) Release of Erroneous Lien.

C.C.P. 697.660 provides a procedure for release of an erroneous lien on personal property comparable to the procedure provided by C.C.P. 697.410 for release of an erroneous lien on real property. (Legislative Com. Comment—Assembly, Pamphlet, p. 1303; see Supp., supra, §245A-7.)

(a) *Demand for Release.* Either "the erroneously identified property owner or a person having a security interest in or a lien on the property may deliver to the judgment creditor a written demand" that he file in the Secretary of State's office a statement releasing the lien. The demand must be accompanied by proof to the creditor's satisfaction that the "owner is not the judgment debtor and that the property is not subject to enforcement of the judgment against the judgment debtor." (C.C.P. 697.660(a).)

(b) *Delivery of Release.* The creditor must, within 15 days after receipt of the demand and accompanying proof, file in the Secretary of State's office a statement releasing the lien on the property. Improper failure to do so results in liability "to the person who made the demand for all damages sustained by reason of such failure" and $100. (C.C.P. 697.660(b).)

(c) *Motion for Release.* If the creditor does not file the demanded statement of release, the person who made the demand may make a noticed motion, served personally or by mail on the creditor, for an order releasing the lien. On presentation of satisfactory evidence that the "owner is not the judgment debtor and that the property is not subject to enforcement of the judgment," the court must "order the judgment creditor to prepare and file the statement of release or shall itself order the release of the judgment lien." The court order may be filed in the Secretary of State's office with the same effect as a statement of release. (C.C.P. 697.660(c).) The fee for filing a statement of release or court order is the same as provided in U.C.C. 9405. (C.C.P. 697.670(f).) Attorney's fees must be awarded to the prevailing party. (C.C.P. 697.660(d).)

(d) *Other Damages or Penalties.* The damages provided by C.C.P. 697.660 "are not in derogation of any other damages or penalties to which an aggrieved person may be entitled by law." (C.C.P. 697.660(e).)

(d) (New) Execution Lien.

(1) [§247A] (New) Creation and Duration.

The new law continues the prior rule that an execution lien is created by a levy on property under a writ of execution. However, the new law increases the maximum duration of an execution levy to 2 years after the date of issuance of the writ. (C.C.P. 697.710; see Law Rev. Com. Recommendation, Pamphlet, p. 1051, 1059; Legislative Com. Comment—Assembly, Pamphlet, p. 1303; text, §74.)

(2) [§247A-1] (New) Transfer or Encumbrance of Real Property.

C.C.P. 697.720 codifies the case law rule that an interest in real property remains subject to an execution lien despite the transfer or encumbrance of the interest. (See Law Rev. Com. Recommendation, Pamphlet, p. 1051; Law Rev. Com. Comment, Pamphlet, p. 1304.)

(3) [§247A-2] (New) Transfer or Encumbrance of Personal Property.

(a) *Property in Custody of Officer.* Tangible personal property in the custody of a levying officer remains subject to an execution lien despite its transfer or encumbrance. (C.C.P. 697.730.) This rule is based on the principle that a potential transferee or encumbrancer of personal property has a duty to inquire whether the person making the transfer has possession and can deliver the property. (See Law Rev. Com. Recommendation, Pamphlet, p. 1051; Law Rev. Com. Comment, Pamphlet, p. 1304.)

(b) *Property not in Custody of Officer.* C.C.P. 697.740 provides that if personal property not in the custody of a levying officer is transferred or encumbered, the property remains subject to a previously-created execution lien "except where the transfer or encumbrance is made to one of the following persons:"

(1) A person who, without knowledge of the lien, acquires an interest in the property under California law for fair consideration, as defined in C.C. 3439.03.

(2) A buyer in the ordinary course of business who, under U.C.C. 9307, "would take free of a security interest created by the seller or encumbrancer." (See 2 *Summary, Secured Transactions in Personal Property,* §54.)

(3) A holder in due course of a negotiable instrument within the meaning of U.C.C. 3104. (See 2 *Summary, Negotiable Instruments,* §§6 et seq., 63.)

(4) A holder to whom a negotiable document of title has been duly negotiated within the meaning of U.C.C. 7501. (See 2 *Summary, Sales,* §125.)

(5) A bona fide purchaser, as defined in U.C.C. 8302, of a security.

(6) A purchaser giving new value and taking possession of chattel paper or an instrument in the ordinary course of business.

(7) A holder of a purchase money security interest, as defined in U.C.C. 9107. (See 2 *Summary, Secured Transactions in Personal Property,* §26.)

(8) A collecting bank holding a security interest in items being collected and accompanying documents and proceeds, pursuant to U.C.C. 4208.

(9) A person acquiring any right or interest in letters of credit, advices of credit, or money.

(10) A person acquiring any right or interest in property subject to another jurisdiction's certificate of title statute under which perfection of the security interest requires indication of the interest on the certificate of title.

See Law Rev. Com. Recommendation, Pamphlet, p. 1052; Law Rev. Com. Comment, Pamphlet, p. 1305.

(c) *Crops, Timber, or Minerals.* The following remain subject to an execution lien despite transfer or encumbrance: (1) Growing crops; (2) timber to be cut; (3) minerals or the like to be extracted, or accounts receivable resulting from their sale at wellhead or minehead. (C.C.P. 697.750.) A potential transferee has constructive notice of a levy on such items, since the levy is created by recording the writ and notice of levy with the county recorder. (See Law Rev. Com. Recommendation, Pamphlet, p. 1052; Law Rev. Com. Comment, Pamphlet, p. 1306.)

(e) [§248A] (New) Other Liens.

A lien on real or personal property that is created in an examination proceeding (see Supp., infra, §368A), a creditor's suit (see Supp., infra, §373A), or a charging order proceeding (see Supp., infra, §378A) has the same effect as an execution lien on personal property not in the custody of a levying officer. Thus, such property remains subject to the lien despite the property's transfer or encumbrance, unless the transfer or encumbrance is to a person listed in C.C.P. 697.740 (see Supp., supra, §247A-2). (C.C.P. 697.920; see Law Rev. Com. Recommendation, Pamphlet, p. 1054; Legislative Com. Comment—Assembly, Pamphlet, p. 1307.)

The effect of liens not covered by the C.C.P. 697.920 or by other statutory provisions is determined by judicial decision. (See Law Rev. Com. Recommendation, Pamphlet, p. 1054; Law Rev. Com. Comment, Pamphlet, p. 1307.)

3. (New) Execution.

(a) (New) General Provisions.

(1) [§249A] (New) Application of Chapter.

The simplest and most common procedure for enforcing a money judgment is by means of execution, under which all the judgment debtor's nonexempt property may be levied upon and either collected or sold. (Law Rev. Com. Recommendation, Pamphlet, p. 1054.) Except as otherwise provided by statute, C.C.P. 699.010 et seq.

governs enforcement of a money judgment by writ of execution. (C.C.P. 699.010; see Law Rev. Com. Comment, Pamphlet, p. 1307.)

(2) [§250A] (New) Levy in Private Place.

(a) *Limitation on Levying Officer's Authority.* The right to seize personal property from a judgment debtor's possession is limited by the debtor's right of privacy. (See Law Rev. Com. Recommendation, Pamphlet, p. 1061.) In recognition of these competing interests, C.C.P. 699.030 specifies the procedure to be followed when levying upon personal property in a private place. The levying officer must demand that the debtor deliver the property and must advise the debtor that he may be liable for costs and attorney's fees incurred in further proceedings to obtain delivery. If the debtor fails to deliver the property, the officer may not make further efforts to obtain custody, but must promptly notify the creditor of the failure to obtain custody. (C.C.P. 699.030(a); see Law Rev. Com. Comment, Pamphlet, p. 1309.)

(b) *Application for Order Directing Seizure.* Regardless of whether a writ has been issued or a demand pursuant to C.C.P. 699.030(a) has been made, a "judgment creditor may apply to the court ex parte, or on noticed motion if the court so directs or a court rule so requires, for an order directing the levying officer to seize the property." The application must "describe with particularity" the property to be levied upon and its location, according to the creditor's best knowledge, information, and belief, and the order may not issue unless the creditor shows "probable cause to believe that property sought to be levied upon is located in the place described." (C.C.P. 699.030(b); see Law Rev. Com. Recommendation, Pamphlet, p. 1061; Law Rev. Com. Comment, Pamphlet, p. 1309; 14 Pacific L.J. 407.)

(c) *Levy Pursuant to Order.* The levying officer, when he demands delivery of the property pursuant to the order, must announce his identity, purpose, and authority. If the property is not voluntarily delivered, the place where the property is believed to be located may be broken open in the manner "the levying officer reasonably believes will cause the least damage, but if the levying officer reasonably believes that entry and seizure of the property will involve a substantial risk of death or serious bodily harm to any person," the officer must not enter and must "promptly make a return to the court setting forth the reasons for believing that the risk exists." The court must then "make such orders as may be appropriate." (C.C.P. 699.030(b).)

If the levying officer gains entry, his authority to levy on property is restricted by the terms of the court order. (See Law Rev. Com. Comment, Pamphlet, p. 1309.)

(3) [§251A] (New) Turnover Order.

C.C.P. 699.040 makes available the remedy of a turnover order which is derived from the claim and delivery and attachment laws. (See Law Rev. Com. Recommendation, Pamphlet, p. 1062; Law Rev. Com. Comment, Pamphlet, p. 1310; *Provisional Remedies,* Supp., §§285A, 308A.) C.C.P. 699.040(a) permits the creditor, if a writ of execution is issued, to "apply to the court ex parte, or on noticed motion if the court so directs or a court rule so requires," for an order directing transfer by the debtor to the levying officer of either or both: (a) Possession of property which is to be levied upon by taking it into custody; (b) possession of documentary evidence of title to property or a debt sought to be levied upon. An order for such documentary evidence "may be served when the property or debt is levied upon or thereafter."

The court may issue a turnover order on a showing of need (C.C.P. 699.040(b)), which order must be personally served on and must contain a notice to the debtor that failure to comply may subject him to arrest and punishment for contempt of court (C.C.P. 699.040(c)).

The use of a turnover order may avoid the need for an order for a levy on property in a private place, and may generally facilitate reaching assets and collecting debts. (See Law Rev. Com. Recommendation, Pamphlet, p. 1062.)

See 14 Pacific L.J. 407

(4) [§252A] (New) Release of Property.

The new law generally continues the substance of prior law with respect to the release of property. (See Law Rev. Com. Recommendation, Pamphlet, p. 1062.) C.C.P. 699.060(a) provides that the levying officer must release property levied upon when: (a) The officer receives a written direction to do so from the creditor's attorney of record or, if he has no attorney of record, from the creditor; (b) the officer "receives a certified copy of a court order for release"; or (c) when the officer is "otherwise required to release the property." Any execution lien or attachment lien of the creditor on the property is extinguished by the release.

If the property has been taken into custody under the levy, it must be released to the person from whom it was taken unless the court orders otherwise. If the person does not claim the property, the officer must retain custody and serve notice on the person, personally or by mail, of where possession may be obtained. In a departure from prior law, the levying officer must sell the property (other than cash) if the person does not claim the property within 30 days after service of the notice. After deducting his costs, the levying officer must deposit the proceeds of sale and cash with the treasurer of the county where the property is located, payable to the order of the person. The person or his legal representative may claim the deposit within 5 years after it is made by applying to the treasurer or other official designated by the county; if such an application is not made, the deposit must be paid into the county general fund. (C.C.P. 699.060(b).)

In the case of property not taken into custody the levying officer must release the property by issuing a written notice of release and serving it, personally or by mail, on the person who was served with the writ and notice of levy that created the lien. (C.C.P. 699.060(c).)

In the case of property which was levied upon by recording or filing a copy of the writ and notice of levy, the officer must record or file a written notice of release in the same office. (C.C.P. 699.060(d).)

C.C.P. 699.060(e) protects the levying officer from liability for releasing property in accordance with the section and protects other persons from liability for acting in conformity with the release.

(5) [§253A] (New) Receiver, Sale or Other Action To Preserve Value.

The court, if it determines that the property levied upon "is perishable or will greatly deteriorate or greatly depreciate in value or that for some other reason the interests of the parties will be best served by the order," may "appoint a receiver or order the levying officer to take any action the court orders that is necessary to preserve" the property's value, including sale of the property. The creditor, the debtor, or a person who has filed a third-party claim may apply for such an order. If the court directs or a court rule requires, the application must be made on noticed motion; otherwise, it may be made ex parte. (C.C.P. 699.070(a).)

The levying officer, if he determines that the property "is extremely perishable or will greatly deteriorate or greatly depreciate in value before a court order" could be obtained, "may take any action necessary to preserve" the property's value or may sell the property. The officer is not liable for a good faith determination to take such action. (C.C.P. 699.070(b).)

Except as the court otherwise orders, the property must be sold and the proceeds applied to satisfaction of the judgment in the manner provided generally for execution sales (see Supp., infra, §282A et seq., 288A et seq.). However, the time limitations contained in C.C.P. 701.530(b)(d) (see Supp., infra, §283A) are not applicable; instead, notice of sale must "be posted and served at a reasonable time before the sale," considering the property's character and condition. (C.C.P. 699.070(c).)

The court must fix the daily fee of the receiver, if one is appointed, and may either order advance payment by the judgment creditor of the receiver's fees and expenses or direct payment of all or part of the fees and expenses from the sale proceeds. In other respects the general law (C.C.P. 564 et seq., 571 et seq., see *Provisional Remedies,* §247 et seq.) governs "the appointment, qualifications, powers, rights, and duties" of the receiver. (C.C.P. 699.070(d).)

See Law Rev. Com. Recommendation, Pamphlet, p. 1062; Law Rev. Com. Comment, Pamphlet, p. 1312.

(6) [§254A] (New) Levy by Registered Process Server.

(a) *Expansion of Authority.* Under prior law a registered process server could levy on property not in the judgment debtor's possession, provided the levy did not involve taking possession of the property. (Former C.C.P. 687; see Supp., supra, §71A.) C.C.P. 699.080 continues to limit the authority of a registered process server to levies where he need not take possession of the property, but otherwise expands the types of property on which he may levy, and clarifies other aspects of a registered process server's role. (See Law Rev. Com. Recommendation, Pamphlet, p. 1060; Legislative Com. Comment—Assembly, Pamphlet, p. 1314; 14 Pacific L.J. 407.)

(b) *Types of Property.* C.C.P. 699.080(a) specifies the property on which a registered process server may levy pursuant to a writ of execution: (1) real property, pursuant to C.C.P. 700.015 (see Supp., infra, §263A); (2) growing crops, timber to be cut, or minerals or the like to be extracted or accounts receivable from their sale at the wellhead or minehead, pursuant to C.C.P. 700.020 (see Supp., infra, §264A); (3) personal property in a levying officer's custody, pursuant to C.C.P. 700.050 (see Supp., infra, §265A); (4) personal property used as a dwelling, pursuant to C.C.P. 700.080(a) (see Supp., infra, §267A); (5) deposit accounts, pursuant to C.C.P. 700.140 or C.C.P. 700.160 (see Supp., infra, §272A); (6) property in a safe deposit box, pursuant to C.C.P. 700.150 or C.C.P. 700.160 (see Supp., infra, §273A); (7) accounts receivable or general intangibles, pursuant to C.C.P. 700.170 (see Supp., infra, §274A); (8) final money judgments, pursuant to C.C.P. 700.190 (see Supp., infra, §276A); (9) a judgment debtor's interest in personal property in a decedent's estate, pursuant to C.C.P. 700.200 (see Supp., infra, §277A). (See Law Rev. Com. Recommendation, Pamphlet, p. 1060; Legislative Com. Comment—Assembly, Pamphlet, p. 1314; 14 Pacific L.J. 407.)

(c) *Ancillary Duties.* A registered process server who levies on property must: (1) comply with applicable levy, posting, and service provisions of C.C.P. 700.010 et seq. (see Supp., infra, §262A et seq.); (2) deliver any undertaking required by C.C.P. 700.160 (see Supp., infra, §§272A, 273A); (3) request that any third person who has been served give the levying officer a garnishee's memorandum pursuant to C.C.P. 701.030 (see Supp., infra, §278A). (C.C.P. 699.080(b); see Legislative Com. Comment—Assembly, Pamphlet, p. 1314.)

(d) *Information Provided to Levying Officer.* The registered process server must, within 5 days after levy, file with the levying officer: (1) the writ of execution; (2) the registered process server's affidavit stating the manner of levy performed; (3) proof of any required service of the writ and notice of levy on other persons; and (4) written instructions to the levying officer, as required by C.C.P. 687.010 (see Supp., supra, §236A). (C.C.P. 699.080(c); see Law Rev. Com. Recommendation, Pamphlet, p. 1061; Legislative Com. Comment—Assembly, Pamphlet, p. 1314.) On payment of the fee provided by Govt.C. 26721, the levying officer then must perform the remaining duties under the writ and return the writ to the court. (C.C.P. 699.080(d); see Law Rev. Com. Recommendation, Pamphlet, p. 1061; Legislative Com. Comment—Assembly, Pamphlet, p. 1314.).

(e) *Fee as Recoverable Cost.* Whether the registered process server's fee was a recoverable cost of collection was unclear under prior law. C.C.P. 699.080(e) grants the court discretion to allow the fee as a recoverable cost on a motion for costs under C.C.P. 685.080 (see Supp., supra, §240A-1). If the fee is allowed, the amount is governed by C.C.P. 1032.8. (See Law Rev. Com. Recommendation, Pamphlet, p. 1061; Legislative Com. Comment—Assembly, Pamphlet, p. 1314.)

(7) [§255A] (New) Levy Based on Record Ownership.

C.C.P. 699.090 protects the creditor, the levying officer, and the sureties on the creditor's undertaking from liability to a third person for a levy based on record ownership of property. The section applies if the property is required by law to be registered or recorded in the owner's name, the debtor was the registered or record owner at the time of the levy, and the creditor acted in good faith and in reliance on that fact in causing the levy to be made and the lien maintained. (See Legislative Com. Comment—Assembly, Pamphlet, p.1315.)

(8) [§255A-1] (New) Payment by Debtor of Judgment Debtor.

C.C.P. 699.020 continues prior law by permitting a judgment debtor's debtor to pay the levying officer the entire debt or as much as is necessary to satisfy the judgment. Such payment may be made any time after delivery and before return of the writ of execution, and the levying officer must give a receipt which is a discharge for the amount paid. (See Law Rev. Com. Comment, Pamphlet, p. 1308; text, §§126, 128.)

(b) (New) Writ of Execution and Notice of Levy.

(1) [§256A] (New) Issuance of Writ.

(a) *Issuance on Application.* On the creditor's application the court clerk must issue a writ of execution for enforcement of a money judgment, "directed to the levying officer in the county where the levy is to be made and to any registered process server." A separate writ must be issued for each county where a levy is to be made. (C.C.P. 699.510(a).) These provisions are in accord with prior law. (See Law Rev. Com. Recommendation, Pamphlet, p. 1055; Legislative Com. Comment—Assembly, Pamphlet, p. 1316.)

(b) *Multiple Writs Outstanding.* C.C.P. 699.510(a) permits issuance of successive writs until the judgment is satisfied, but a new writ for a particular county may be issued only once every 180 days, unless the prior writ is first returned. This changes prior law, under which only one writ could be outstanding in a county. Under the new law a second writ may be obtained while the sale or collection process continues on the first writ. However, although several writs might be outstanding in a particular county, only one writ at a time provides authority for levy. (See Law Rev. Com. Recommendation, Pamphlet, p. 1055; Legislative Com. Comment—Assembly, Pamphlet, p. 1316.)

(c) *Family Law Act Judgments.* A judgment creditor seeking a writ of execution to enforce a Family Law Act support judgment (C.C. 4000 et seq.) must, in addition to the general requirements, also satisfy the requirements imposed by C.C. 4380 et seq. (Supp., supra, §8, 9; 6 *Summary, Parent and Child,* §124; 6 *Summary, Husband and Wife,* §172). (C.C.P. 699.510(b); see Legislative Com. Comment—Assembly, Pamphlet, p. 1317.

(2) [§257A] (New) Contents of Writ.

C.C.P. 699.520 prescribes the essential elements of a writ of execution. The writ must require the levying officer to enforce the money judgment and must include:

(1) The writ's date of issuance.

(2) The title of the court which entered judgment and the action's cause and number.

(3) The judgment creditor's name and address and the judgment debtor's name and last known address.

(4) The dates of entry of the judgment and any renewals and where entered in the court's records.

(5) The total amount of the initial or renewed judgment, together with costs thereafter added and accrued interest from the date of the judgment's entry or renewal to the date of the writ's issuance, reduced by partial satisfactions and amounts no longer enforceable.

(6) The amount required to satisfy the judgment on the date the writ is issued.

(7) The amount of daily interest accruing on the principal amount of the judgment.

(8) The name and mailing address of any person who has requested notice of sale under the judgment.

See Law Rev. Com. Comment, Pamphlet, p. 1318.

C.C.P. 693.010 contains a statutory form of writ of execution, possession, and sale, for use unless superseded by a Judicial Council form prescribed pursuant to C.C.P. 681.030. (See Supp., supra, §234A.)

(3) [§258A] (New) Delivery and Execution of Writ.

(a) *Duty of Levying Officer.* The levying officer, after receipt of the writ of execution and the creditor's written instructions (see Supp., supra, §236A), must "execute the writ in the manner prescribed by law." (C.C.P. 699.530(a).) The mandatory order of levy contained in former C.C.P. 682(1) (see text, §70) is not continued; thus, personal property need not be levied on before real property. However, the judgment creditor may designate the order of levy in his written instructions. (see Law Rev. Com. Recommendation, Pamphlet, p. 1057; Legislative Com. Comment—Assembly, Pamphlet, p. 1318.)

(b) *Limitation on Time for Levy.* Under former C.C.P. 683, 688(e), a writ of execution could remain in force for one year from the date of issuance, but its return was required within 60 days after its receipt by the levying officer. (See text, §72.) It was believed that the 60-day period provided insufficient time to locate and levy on property. Accordingly, new C.C.P. 699.530(b) permits a levy under the writ for a period of "180 days *from the date the writ was issued*." (see Law Rev. Com. Recommendation, Pamphlet, p. 1055; Legislative Com. Comment—Assembly, Pamphlet, p. 1319.)

(4) [§259A] (New) Notice of Levy.

(a) *Contents.* The notice of levy (see Supp., infra, §262A et seq.) must inform the person notified of (1) the capacity in which he is notified; (2) the property that is levied upon; (3) his rights under the levy, including the rights to claim an exemption (see Supp., infra, §291A et seq.) and to make a third-party claim (see Supp., infra, §407A et seq.); and (4) his duties under the levy. (C.C.P. 699.540; see Legislative Com. Comment—Assembly, Pamphlet, p. 1319.)

A statutory form of notice of levy is provided in C.C.P. 693.020, but the Judicial Council has authority to prepare a superseding form (C.C.P. 681.030(b)). (see Supp., supra, §234A.)

(b) *Failure To Give Notice.* C.C.P. 699.550 preserves the validity of a levy in a case where certain required notices have been omitted. When property has been levied upon, failure to comply with a statutory requirement to post, serve, or mail a copy of the writ of execution and a notice of levy to the debtor or other person "does not affect the execution lien created by the levy." Likewise, the lien is not affected by failure to serve or mail a list of exemptions to the judgment debtor. (See Law Rev. Com. Comment, Pamphlet, p. 1320.)

(5) [§260A] (New) Return of Writ.

(a) *In General.* The writ of execution must be returned, "with a report of the levying officer's actions and an accounting of amounts collected and costs incurred, at the earliest of the following times:" (1) 2 years from the writ's date of issuance; (2) promptly after performance of all duties under the writ; (3) when the judgment creditor makes a written request for return; (4) if no levy occurs within 180 days after issuance, "promptly after the expiration of the 180-day period"; (5) on expiration of the time for enforcement of the judgment. (C.C.P. 699.560(a); see Law Rev. Com. Recommendation, Pamphlet, p. 1056; Legislative Com. Comment—Assembly, Pamphlet, p. 1321; 14 Pacific L.J. 407.)

(b) *Levy on Interest in Estate Personal Property.* If a levy has been made under C.C.P. 700.200 on an interest in personal property in a decedent's estate, the writ must be returned within the time prescribed in that section (see Supp., infra, §277A). (C.C.P. 699.560(b); see Legislative Com. Comment—Assembly, Pamphlet, p. 1321.)

(c) [§261A] (New) Property Subject to Execution.

"Except as otherwise provided by law, all property that is subject to enforcement of a money judgment" (see Supp., supra, §243A) "is subject to levy under a writ of execution to satisfy a money judgment." (C.C.P. 699–710; see Legislative Com. Comment—Assembly, Pamphlet, p. 1321.)

(d) [§261A-1] (New) Property Not Subject to Execution.

Under C.C.P. 699.720(a), certain types of property are not subject to execution:

(1) A transferable alcoholic beverage license.

(2) A partner's interest in a non-judgment debtor partnership.

(3) A cause of action that is the subject of a pending action or special proceeding.

(4) A judgment in the debtor's favor prior to expiration of the time for appeal or final determination of an appeal that is filed.

(5) A debt, other than earnings, owing and unpaid by a public entity.

(6) An unmatured life insurance, endowment, or annuity policy's loan value.

(7) A franchise, and the rights and privileges thereof, granted by a public entity.

(8) A trust beneficiary's interest.

(9) A contingent remainder, executory interest, or other unvested interest in property.

(10) A guardianship or conservatorship estate's property.

However, a judgment creditor may use other available enforcement procedures to reach such property in satisfaction of the judgment. (C.C.P. 699.720(b); see Legislative Com. Comment—Assembly, Pamphlet, p. 1323.)

(e)   (New) Methods of Levy.

(1)   [§261A-2]   (New) General Rules.

Levy procedures under the new law are largely the same as under prior law. However, rather than incorporating the methods of levy under attachment, as the prior law did, the new law contains specific provisions governing the manner of levy on various types of property. The new law also uses Commercial Code terminology whenever practicable to replace terminology used in the prior law. (see Law Rev. Com. Recommendation, Pamphlet, p. 1013 [Summary], 1058, 1065.)

The Law Revision Commission Recommendation (Pamphlet, p. 1058) states that property is levied upon in four ways under the new law:

(1) "By taking custody and serving a writ and notice of levy." This method is used to levy on tangible personal property in the debtor's possession. (See Supp., infra, §265A.)

(2) "By serving a writ and notice of levy without taking custody (garnishment)." This method is used to levy on intangible personal property, tangible personal property under a third person's control, or property under estate administration. (See Supp., infra, §§265A, 274A, 277A.)

(3) "By filing or recording of a writ and a notice of levy." This method is used to levy on real property, growing crops, standing timber, minerals to be extracted, or a final money judgment. (See Supp., infra, §§263A, 264A, 276A.)

(4) "By delivering a writ and instructions to levy to the levying officer." This method is a "paper levy" on property which has already been levied upon. (See Supp., infra, §265A.)

On the specific provisions governing service of papers and the method of levy on particular types of property see infra, §262A et seq.

See 14 Pacific L.J. 409.

(2)   [§262A]   (New)   Service of Papers.

The levying officer must serve on the debtor copies of the writ of execution, a notice of levy, and, if the debtor is a natural person, the Judicial Council form listing state and federal exemptions. (C.C.P. 700.010(a); see Law Rev. Com. Recommendation, Pamphlet, p. 1109; Law Rev. Com. Comment, Pamphlet, p. 1324.) Service must be made at the time of levy or promptly thereafter (C.C.P. 700.010(a)), and may be made personally or by mail (C.C.P. 700.010(b)). However, failure to make such service does not affect the validity of the execution lien. (See Supp., supra, §259A.)

(3)   [§263A]   (New)   Real Property.

(a) *Property Subject to Levy.* Any interest in real property that is subject to enforcement of a money judgment may be levied on, unless another exclusive method of enforcement is specified. (See Supp., supra, §§243A, 261A, 261A-1; Legislative Com. Comment—Assembly, Pamphlet, p. 1325.) Under prior law some leases were treated as personal property and some as real property; the new law treats leasehold interests in real property as real property for purposes of levy. (See Law Rev. Com. Recommendation, Pamphlet, p. 1065; Legislative Com. Comment—Assembly, Pamphlet, p. 1326; on definition of real property as including leasehold interests, see C.C.P. 680.320, Supp., supra, §232A.)

(b) *Recording With County Recorder.* A copy of the writ of execution and a notice of levy must be recorded with the county recorder where the property is located. The notice of levy must describe the property and state that the debtor's interest in the property has been levied upon. If the county records list the debtor's interest in the name of a third person, the notice of levy must identify that person and the recorder must index the writ and notice of levy in both names. (C.C.P. 700.015(a).)

Prior law did not require recordation if there was already a judgment lien on the property, but the practice was to levy in every case. C.C.P. 700.015 continues this practice by making it a legal requirement. (See Law Rev. Com. Recommendation, Pamphlet, p. 1065; Legislative Com. Comment—Assembly, Pamphlet, p. 1326.)

(c) *Service on Third Person.* A copy of the writ and a notice of levy must be served on any third person in whose name the debtor's interest in the property is recorded in county records. Service must be made at the time of levy or promptly thereafter, and may be made personally or by mail. If service is by mail, it must be sent to the third person's address as shown by the county tax assessor's records; if no address is shown, service must be sent to the address used by the county recorder for return of the instrument creating the third person's interest in the property. (C.C.P. 700.015(b).)

(d) *Service on Occupant.* A copy of the writ and a notice of levy must be served on one occupant of the property, at the time of levy or promptly thereafter. Service must be left with the occupant personally or, in the occupant's absence, with his employee, agent, or a member of his household of "suitable age and discretion found upon the real property when service is attempted." If unable to serve the occupant when service is attempted, the levying officer must "post the copy of the writ and the notice of levy in a conspicuous place on the real property." If the property consists of distinct lots, parcels, or governmental subdivisions, some of which form one or more continuous, unbroken tracts, only one service or posting is required as to each continuous, unbroken tract. (C.C.P. 700.015(c).)

See 14 Pacific L.J. 409.

(4) [§264A] (New) Crops, Timber and Minerals.

(a) *Recording With County Recorder.* A copy of the writ of execution and a notice of levy must be recorded with the county recorder when levying upon (1) growing crops, (2) timber to be cut, or (3) minerals or the like, including oil and gas, to be extracted, or accounts receivable resulting from their sale at the wellhead or minehead. The notice of levy must describe the property levied upon, state that the debtor's interest in the property has been levied upon, and describe the real property where the property levied upon is located. If the debtor's interest in the property levied upon, or if the real property where the property levied upon is located, is listed in the county records in a third person's name, the notice of levy must identify that person and the recorder must index the writ and notice of levy in both names. (C.C.P. 700.020(a); Law Rev. Com. Recommendation, Pamphlet, p. 1065, 1066; Legislative Com. Comment—Assembly, Pamphlet, p. 1328.)

(b) *Service on Third Person.* At the time of levy or promptly thereafter, a copy of the writ and a notice of levy must be served personally or by mail on any third person in whose name either the debtor's interest in the property levied upon or the real property is listed in the county records. If service is by mail, it must be sent to the third person's address as shown by the county tax assessor's records; if no address is shown, service must be sent to the address used by the county recorder for the return of the instrument creating the third person's interest in the property. (C.C.P. 700.020(b)(1).)

(c) *Service on Secured Party.* At the time of levy or promptly thereafter, a copy of the writ and a notice of levy must be served personally or by mail on any secured party who, prior to the date of the levy, has filed a financing statement with respect to the property levied upon. (C.C.P. 700.020(b)(2).) This requirement is new and was included to enable the secured party to obtain protection in the event of an execution sale or other action concerning the property. (See Law Rev. Com. Recommendation, Pamphlet, p. 1065; Legislative Com. Comment—Assembly, Pamphlet, p. 1328.)

(d) *Service on Occupant.* A copy of the writ and a notice of levy must be served on an occupant of the real property where the property levied upon is located, at the time of levy or promptly thereafter. Such service is effected in the same manner as service on the occupant in the case of a levy on real property (see Supp., supra, §263A). (C.C.P. 700.020(c).)

(5)   (New) Tangible Personal Property.

(aa)   [§265A]   (New) In General.

(1) *Property in Possession of Judgment Debtor.* "Unless another method of levy is provided", the levying officer must levy upon tangible personal property in the judgment debtor's possession or control by taking it into custody. (C.C.P. 700.030; see Legislative Com. Comment—Assembly, Pamphlet, p. 1328; on other methods, see Supp., infra, §§266A [property of going business], 267A [property used as dwelling].)

(2) *Property in Possession of Third Person.* "Unless another method of levy is provided", the levying officer must levy upon tangible personal property in a third person's possession or control by personally serving a copy of the writ of execution and a notice of levy on that person. (C.C.P. 700.040(a); see Legislative Com. Comment—Assembly, Pamphlet, p. 1329.)

When a bailee has possession of goods for which he has issued a negotiable document of title, the goods may not be levied upon. However, the negotiable document of title may be levied upon pursuant to C.C.P. 700.120 (see Supp., infra, §271A). (C.C.P.

700.040(b); see Law Rev. Com. Recommendation, Pamphlet, p. 1067; Legislative Com. Comment—Assembly, Pamphlet, p. 1329.)

(3) *Property in Custody of Levying Officer.* C.C.P. 700.050 is a new provision governing "paper levies" on property already in a levying officer's custody. (See Law Rev. Com. Recommendation, Pamphlet, p. 1066; Legislative Com. Comment—Assembly, Pamphlet, p. 1330.) To levy upon personal property in such a case, the creditor must deliver the writ of execution to the levying officer, if the writ is directed to the officer with custody. If the writ is directed to an officer other than the one with custody, the officer to whom the writ is directed must serve, personally or by mail, a copy of the writ and a notice of levy on the officer with custody. (C.C.P. 700.050(a); see Law Rev. Com. Recommendation, Pamphlet, p. 1066; Legislative Com. Comment—Assembly, Pamphlet, p. 1330.) The levying officer having custody must comply with the writs in the order received and is not subject to the provisions governing the duties and liabilities of third persons after levy (see Supp., infra, §278A et seq.). (C.C.P. 700.050(b); see Legislative Com. Comment—Assembly, Pamphlet, p. 1330.)

(4) *Bailed Goods Not Covered by Negotiable Document of Title.* When a bailee possesses goods for which he has not issued a negotiable document of title, a levy is accomplished by personal service of a copy of the writ of execution and a notice of levy on the bailee. (C.C.P. 700.060(a); see Law Rev. Com. Recommendation, Pamphlet, p. 1067.) If the goods are subject to a security interest, the levying officer must, if instructed by the creditor, serve, personally or by mail, a copy of the writ of execution and a notice of levy on the secured party. (C.C.P. 700.060(b).) A levy on secured goods establishes the creditor's lien, but it does not affect any superior rights of the secured party. (See Law Rev. Com. Recommendation, Pamphlet, p. 1067; Legislative Com. Comment—Assembly, Pamphlet, p. 1330; Supp., infra, §279A.)

See 14 Pacific L.J. 410.

(bb) [§266A] (New) Property of Going Business.

Former C.C.P. 688(c) required use of a keeper for at least 2 days when levying on tangible personal property of a going business. (See Law Rev. Com. Recommendation, Pamphlet, p. 1067; Legislative Com. Comment—Senate, Pamphlet, p. 1331; Supp., supra, §73A.) The new law permits, but does not make mandatory, the use of a keeper. A levy upon tangible personal property of a going business in the debtor's possession or control is accomplished in the same manner as a levy on other tangible personal property in the debtor's possession (see Supp., supra, §265A), unless the creditor instructs that a keeper be used. (C.C.P. 700.070.)

If the creditor elects to levy by means of a keeper, and the debtor does not object, a keeper must be placed in charge of the business for the period, not to exceed 10 days, requested by the judgment creditor. During this period "the business may continue to operate in the ordinary course of business provided that all sales are final and are for cash or its equivalent," including checks. The keeper must take custody of all proceeds unless the creditor otherwise directs. (C.C.P. 700.070(a)(b); see Law Rev. Com. Recommendation, Pamphlet, p. 1067.)

The levying officer must take the property into exclusive custody if the creditor at any time so requests or the debtor at any time objects to placement of a keeper; otherwise the property must be taken into custody 10 days after placement of the keeper. (C.C.P. 700.070(b); see Law Rev. Com. Recommendation, Pamphlet, p. 1067; Legislative Com. Comment—Senate, Pamphlet, p. 1332.)

(cc) [§267A] (New) Property Used as Dwelling.

(a) *Service on Occupant.* A copy of the writ of execution and a notice of levy must be served on an occupant to levy upon personal property used as a dwelling, such as a housetrailer, mobilehome, or vessel. Service must be left with the occupant personally or, in the occupant's absence, with a member of the occupant's family or household of "suitable age and discretion found at the property." If unable to so serve the occupant, the levy is made "by posting the copy of the writ and the notice of levy in a conspicious place on the property." (C.C.P. 700.080(a); see Legislative Com. Comment—Assembly, Pamphlet, p. 1333.)

(b) *Placement of Keeper.* Former C.C.P. 688(c) required placement of a keeper for at least 2 days, followed by the occupant's removal unless some other disposition was ordered or agreed on. (See Law Rev. Com. Recommendation, Pamphlet, p. 1068; Legislative Com. Comment—Assembly, Pamphlet, p. 1333; Supp., supra, §73A.) This procedure was considered defective because it ignored the occupant's right to a judicial determination of the right to possession and was needlessly expensive. (See Law Rev. Com. Recommendation, Pamphlet, p. 1068; Legislative Com. Comment—Assembly, Pamphlet, p. 1333.) Under the new law, use of a keeper is no longer mandatory, but if the creditor so instructs, a keeper must be placed "in charge of the property for a period requested by the judgment creditor." (C.C.P. 700.080(b); see Law Rev. Com. Recommendation, Pamphlet, p. 1069.)

(c) *Removal of Occupants.* If the occupants do not voluntarily vacate the property, the judgment creditor may apply on noticed motion for an order directing their removal. Notice must be served, personally or by mail, on any legal owner who was served pursuant to C.C.P 700.090 (see Supp., infra, §268A), on the occupant, and on the debtor if he is not the occupant. At the hearing the court must determine the occupant's right to possession and make an order with "such terms and conditions as are appropriate under the circumstances of the case." (C.C.P. 700.080(c); see Law Rev. Com. Recommendation, Pamphlet, p. 1069; Legislative Com. Comment—Assembly, Pamphlet, p. 1333.)

(dd) [§268A] (New) Vehicles, Mobilehomes and Vessels.

When levy is made on a vehicle, vessel, mobilehome, or commercial coach for which a certificate of ownership or title is in effect, the levying officer must determine from either the Department of Motor Vehicles (vehicle or vessel) or the Department of Housing and Community Development (mobilehome or commercial coach) the legal owner's name and address. If the legal owner is neither the debtor nor in possession of the property, a copy of the writ of execution and a notice of levy must be served, personally or by mail, on the legal owner at the time of levy or promptly thereafter. (C.C.P. 700.090; on elimination of the requirement of duplicate notice where the legal owner has already received notice, see Law Rev. Com. Recommendation, Pamphlet, p. 1069; Law Rev. Com. Comment, Pamphlet, p. 1334.)

(6) [§269A] (New) Chattel Paper.

(a) *Method of Levy.* If chattel paper is in the debtor's possession, the levying officer must take it into custody. If the chattel paper is in a third person's possession, a levy is accomplished by personally serving a copy of the writ of execution and a notice of levy on that person. (C.C.P. 700.100(a); see Legislative Com. Comment—Assembly, Pamphlet, p. 1334.)

(b) *Service on Account Debtor.* Under prior law service was always required on the account debtor. (See Law Rev. Com. Recommendation, Pamphlet, p. 1069.) Under the new law the account debtor may be given notice only if: (1) the levying officer obtains custody of the chattel paper; or (2) a security agreement leaves the judgment debtor the liberty to collect or compromise the chattel paper or to enforce or accept the return of goods under the chattel paper. In such cases the levying officer must, if the judgment creditor so instructs, serve, personally or by mail, a copy of the writ of execution and a notice of levy on the account debtor. (C.C.P. 700.100(b); see Law Rev. Com. Recommendation, Pamphlet, p. 1069; Legislative Com. Comment—Assembly, Pamphlet, p. 1335.)

This change in procedure, in conjunction with the provisions governing the duty of an account debtor (see Supp., infra, §280A), is intended to provide greater protection to a secured party on the chattel paper. (See Law Rev. Com. Recommendation, Pamphlet, p. 1069; on the alternatives available to the secured party, see Legislative Com. Comment—Assembly, Pamphlet, p. 1334.)

(c) *Lien on Goods.* The levy also creates a lien on the debtor's rights in the property subject to the chattel paper, thus reaching all the debtor's rights in the property. (C.C.P. 700.100(c); see Legislative Com. Comment—Assembly, Pamphlet, p. 1335.)

(7) [§270A] (New) Instruments.

An instrument, whether negotiable or nonnegotiable, is levied upon: (a) by taking it into custody, if it is in the debtor's possession; (b) by personally serving a copy of the writ of execution and a notice of levy on a third person having possession of the instrument. (C.C.P. 700.110(a).) This is a departure from prior law, under which nonnegotiable instruments were treated as choses in action and levied upon by service on the obligor; the new law conforms procedures more closely to the Commercial Code. (See Law Rev. Com. Recommendation, Pamphlet, p. 1071; Legislative Com. Comment—Assembly, Pamphlet, p. 1336.)

The obligor may be given notice only if the levying officer takes custody of the instrument. In such a case, the obligor must, if the judgment creditor so instructs, be served, personally or by mail, a copy of the writ of execution and a notice of levy. (C.C.P. 700.110(b).) The limitation on notice to the obligor is intended to protect the rights of secured parties and holders in due course. (See Law Rev. Com. Recommendation, Pamphlet, p. 1071; Legislative Com. Comment—Assembly, Pamphlet, p. 1336.)

(8) [§271A] (New) Documents of Title and Securities.

(a) *Negotiable Documents of Title.* A negotiable document of title is levied upon: (1) By taking it into custody, if it is in the debtor's possession; (2) by personally serving a copy of the writ of execution and a notice of levy on a third person having possession. (C.C.P. 700.120; see Legislative Com. Comment—Assembly, Pamphlet, p. 1336.) The requirement under prior law that the obligor be given notice of levy has been eliminated, since the obligor (a bailee) cannot deliver the goods to anyone not in possession of the negotiable document. (See Law Rev. Com. Recommendation, Pamphlet, p. 1071.)

(b) *Securities.* The new law continues the substance of prior law by providing that a levy upon a security must be accomplished in compliance with U.C.C. 8317. (C.C.P. 700.130; see Law Rev. Com. Recommendation, Pamphlet, p. 1072; Legislative Com. Comment—Assembly, Pamphlet, p. 1337; 6 *Summary, Corporations,* §126.)

(9) [§272A] (New) Deposit Accounts.

(a) *Service on Financial Institution.* A deposit account is levied upon by personal service of a copy of the writ of execution and a notice of levy on the financial institution holding the account. (C.C.P. 700.140(a); see Law Rev. Com. Comment, Pamphlet, p. 1338.)

(b) *Service on Third Person.* "At the time of levy or promptly thereafter," service of a copy of the writ of execution and a notice of levy must be made personally or by mail on any third person in whose name the account is held. (C.C.P. 700.140(b).)

(c) *Duties of Financial Institution.* If the account is held solely in the debtor's name, the financial institution must not honor checks or other orders for payment of money, and must not permit withdrawals, that would reduce the account to an amount less than that levied upon, while the execution lien is in effect. Deposits in the process of collection may not be considered in determining the amount in the account. (C.C.P. 700.140(c).)

(d) *Nonliability of Institution.* While the execution lien is in effect, the financial institution is not liable to any person for (1) performance of a garnishee's duties under the levy; (2) nonpayment of checks or other orders for payment of money pursuant to the requirements of C.C.P. 700.140(c) (see supra); (3) refusal to pay withdrawals pursuant to the requirements of C.C.P. 700.140(c) (see supra). (C.C.P. 700.140(d).)

(e) *Undertaking Where Account in Third Person's Name.* C.C.P. 700.160 imposes additional requirements when the account levied on is held either in a third person's name or in both the debtor's and a third person's name. At the time of levy the levying officer must deliver to the financial institution an undertaking provided by the creditor and given by a qualified corporate surety (C.C.P. 1056, *Provisional Remedies,* text and Supp., §3), which undertaking must be for at least twice the amount of the judgment or the amount levied upon, whichever is less. The undertaking must indemnify any third person (who need not be specifically named) "rightfully entitled to the property against actual damage by reason of the levy" and must "assure to the third person the return of the property upon proof of the person's right thereto." The levy is ineffective, and the financial institution is prohibited from complying with the levy, if these requirements are not met. (C.C.P. 700.160(b).)

The financial institution must, immediately upon delivery of the undertaking to it, mail or deliver a notice thereof to the third person. A mailed notice must be sent by registered or certified mail to the person's last address known to the financial institution. The undertaking must be delivered as directed by the third person. (C.C.P. 700.160(c).)

The prohibition against honoring checks or permitting withdrawals, and the financial institution's nonliability therefor (see supra), is in effect from the time of levy and delivery of the undertaking to the financial institution until: (1) 15 days after mailing or delivery of the notice to the third party, if no objection to the undertaking is made; or (2) the court determines that the undertaking is sufficient, if objection is made. (C.C.P. 700.160(d)(1), (e)(1)(2).) On expiration of this period, the financial institution must comply with the levy and the provisions of C.C.P. 700.140 (see supra). (C.C.P. 700.160(g).)

Any person claiming to be rightfully entitled to the property may make an objection to the undertaking, which objection must be made as provided in C.C.P. 720.710 et seq. (see Supp., infra, §425A et seq.). (C.C.P. 700.160(f).)

See Law Rev. Com. Recommendation, Pamphlet, p. 1072; Law Rev. Com. Comment, Pamphlet, p. 1341.

(f) *Termination of Lien.* The lien terminates when the amount levied upon is paid to the levying officer. (C.C.P. 700.140(e).)

(10) [§273A] (New) Safe Deposit Boxes.

(a) *Service on Financial Institution.* A levy upon property in a safe deposit box is accomplished by personal service of a copy of the writ of execution and a notice of levy on the financial institution holding the box. (C.C.P. 700.150(a); see Legislative Com. Comment—Assembly, Pamphlet, p. 1339.)

(b) *Service on Third Person.* "At the time of levy or promptly thereafter," a copy of the writ of execution and a notice of levy must be served, personally or by mail, on any third person in whose name the box is held. (C.C.P. 700.150(b); see Legislative Com. Comment—Assembly, Pamphlet, p. 1339.)

(c) *Duties of Financial Institution.* If the box is held exclusively in the debtor's name, the financial institution must not, while the execution lien is in effect, permit removal of any of the box's contents except pursuant to the levy. (C.C.P. 700.150(c).) The financial institution may require the creditor to pay in advance the costs of forcibly opening and of repairing the box before allowing a forcible opening to permit removal of the property levied upon (C.C.P. 700.150(d)), but such costs may later be recovered from the debtor (see Legislative Com. Comment—Assembly, Pamphlet, p. 1339). To avoid such costs, the levying officer may give the boxholder an opportunity to open the box to permit removal of the property. (C.C.P. 700.150(d); see Law Rev. Com. Recommendation, Pamphlet, p. 1073.)

(d) *Nonliability of Institution.* While the execution lien is in effect, the financial institution is not liable to any person for: (1) Performing a garnishee's duties under the levy; (2) refusing to permit the boxholder access to the box; (3) removal of the box's contents pursuant to the levy. (C.C.P. 700.150(e).)

(e) *Undertaking Where Box Not Exclusively in Judgment Debtor's Name.* When the box is held in a third person's name or in both the debtor's and a third person's names, an undertaking must be provided in the same manner as in the case of a levy on a deposit account not exclusively in the debtor's name. (C.C.P. 700.160; on requirements of and objections to the undertaking, see Supp., supra, §272A.) The prohibition against removal of the box's contents, and the financial institution's nonliability for refusing access to or removal of the box's contents, are in effect during the period following delivery of the undertaking to the financial institution, for the same time as in the case of a levy on a deposit account. (C.C.P. 700.160(d)(2)(e)(3)(4); see Supp., supra, §272A.) On expiration of that period, the financial institution must comply with the levy and the provisions of C.C.P. 700.150 (supra). (C.C.P. 700.170(g).)

(11) [§274A] (New) Accounts Receivable and General Intangibles.

"Unless another method of levy is provided," an account receivable or general intangible is levied upon by personal service of a copy of the writ of execution and a notice of levy on the account debtor. (C.C.P. 700.170(a); see Legislative Com. Comment—Assembly, Pamphlet, p. 1342.) This continues the substance of prior law. (See Law Rev. Com. Recommendation, Pamphlet, p. 1073.)

If payments on the property levied upon are being made to a third person, the levying officer must, if the creditor so instructs, personally serve a copy of the writ of execution and a notice of levy on such person. Service on the third person creates a levy on any amounts owed by the person to the debtor, and thus protects the creditor's rights to any surplus payments. (C.C.P. 700.170(b); see Law Rev. Com. Recommendation, Pamphlet, p. 1073; Legislative Com. Comment—Assembly, Pamphlet, p. 1342; on rights and duties of secured party, see Supp., infra, §279A; on duty of account debtor, see Supp., infra, §280A.)

(12) [§275A] (New) Property Subject of Pending Action.

(a) *In General.* Prior law was unclear as to the effect of a levy on property that was the subject of a pending action or special proceeding. C.C.P. 700.180 clarifies the law by providing that certain types of property are subject to levy and prohibiting levy on any other type of property. (See Law Rev. Com. Recommendation, Pamphlet, p. 1074.) Under C.C.P. 700.180(d), an action or proceeding is pending from the time it is commenced until entry of judgment and expiration of the time for or final determination of an appeal.

(b) *Property Subject to Levy.* Under C.C.P. 700.180(a) the following types of property may be levied upon despite the pending action: (1) Real property; (2) growing crops, timber to be cut, or minerals or the like to be extracted or accounts receivable resulting from their sale at the wellhead or minehead; (3) tangible personal property in the judgment debtor's possession or control or the levying officer's custody; (4) a judgment debtor's interest, whether arising by testate or intestate succession, in personal property in a decedent's estate. Such property is levied upon in the same manner as required for any other levy on the property. (See Law Rev. Com. Recommendation, Pamphlet, p. 1074; Legislative Com. Comment—Assembly, Pamphlet, p. 1343.)

(c) *Property not Subject to Levy.* A levy upon any other property that is the subject of a pending action or special proceeding is ineffective. (C.C.P. 700.180(b).) Thus, tangible personal property not in the debtor's possession, as well as intangible personal property, cannot be levied on. (See Law Rev. Com. Recommendation, Pamphlet, p. 1075; Legislative Com. Comment—Assembly, Pamphlet, p. 1344.) Under C.C.P. 700.180(c), if a levy is attempted on such property and a garnishee's memorandum is requested under C.C.P. 701.030 (see Supp., infra, §278A), the memorandum must, in addition to the other required information, include (1) a statement that the levy is not effective because the property is the subject of a pending action or special proceeding; and (2) the title of the court, cause, and number of that action or proceeding.

(d) *Right to Lien in Pending Action Unaffected.* A judgment creditor's right to obtain a lien in the pending action or proceeding pursuant to the provisions of C.C.P. 708.410 et seq. (see Supp., infra, §379A et seq.) is not affected by C.C.P. 700.180. (C.C.P. 700.180(e); see Law Rev. Com. Recommendation, Pamphlet, p. 1075; Legislative Com. Comment—Assembly, Pamphlet, p. 1344.)

(13) [§276A] (New) Final Money Judgment.

C.C.P. 700.190 clarifies prior law by permitting a levy on a final money judgment and prescribing the manner and effect of the levy. (See Law Rev. Com. Recommendation, Pamphlet, p. 1075; Law Rev. Com. Comment, Pamphlet, p. 1345.) It must be a *final money judgment,* i.e., time for appeal must have expired or an appeal taken must have been finally determined. (C.C.P. 700.190(a); see Law Rev. Com. Comment, Pamphlet, p. 1345.)

The levy is made by filing a copy of the writ of execution and a notice of levy with the clerk of the court that entered the judgment. The court clerk must endorse upon the judgment a statement of the lien's existence and its time of creation, and any abstract of judgment must include a statement of the lien in the creditor's favor. (C.C.P. 700.190(b).)

"At the time of levy or promptly thereafter," a copy of the writ of execution and a notice of levy must be personally served on the debtor obligated to pay the judgment. Such service is not essential to create the levy, but absent such service, the debtor may make payment in satisfaction of the judgment to the creditor. (C.C.P. 700.190(c); see Law Rev. Com. Recommendation, Pamphlet, p. 1075; Law Rev. Com. Comment, Pamphlet, p. 1346.)

(14) [§277A] (New) Interest in Estate Personal Property.

The interest of a judgment debtor in personal property of a decedent's estate is levied upon by personal service of a copy of the writ and a notice of levy on the decedent's personal representative. (C.C.P. 700.200(a); see Law Rev. Com. Recommendation, Pamphlet, p. 1076; Law Rev. Com. Comment, Pamphlet, p. 1347.) Unlike prior law, no filing with the court clerk is required. (See Law Rev. Com. Recommendation, Pamphlet, p. 1076.) The execution lien continues for a one-year period after the decree distributing the interest becomes final, unless the judgment is sooner satisfied (C.C.P. 700.200(d)), and the writ must be returned within that one-year period (C.C.P. 700.200(e)). (See Law Rev. Com. Comment, Pamphlet, p. 1347.) However, the levy does not impair the personal representative's powers of administration. (C.C.P. 700.200(a).)

The personal representative must report the levy to the court administering the estate when a petition for distribution is filed. If the decree orders distribution to the debtor, the court must order the property delivered to the levying officer, but actual delivery to the officer may not occur until the decree has become final. The officer must release to the debtor any excess not necessary to satisfy the judgment. (C.C.P. 700.200(b).)

Promptly after delivery of the property to him, the levying officer must serve on the debtor, personally or by mail, a notice describing the property. The debtor has 10 days after service of the notice to make a claim of exemption. (C.C.P. 700.200(c); see Law Rev. Com. Recommendation, Pamphlet, p. 1076; Law Rev. Com. Comment, Pamphlet, p. 1347.)

(f)   (New) Duties and Liabilities of Third Persons.

(1)   [§278A]   (New) Duty of Garnishee.

(a) *Delivery or Payment to Levying Officer.* When property is levied upon by serving a copy of the writ of execution and a notice of levy on a third person, that person must, unless otherwise provided by statute or good cause exists for not doing so: (1) unless he claims the right to possession, deliver to the levying officer any of the property in his possession or control at the time of levy; (2) to the extent that he does not deny an obligation levied upon, or claim a priority over the judgment creditor's lien, pay to the levying officer any amounts that are, or during the period of the execution lien become, due and payable to the judgment debtor. (C.C.P. 701.010(a)(b)(1)(2)); see Law Rev. Com. Recommendation, Pamphlet, p. 1014 [Summary], 1076; Law Rev. Com. Comment, Pamphlet, p. 1348.) Such delivery or payment must be made "at the time of levy or promptly thereafter" (C.C.P. 701.010(a)), and the third person must execute and deliver any documents necessary to transfer the property (C.C.P. 701.010(b)(3)).

Good cause for failure to comply with these requirements "includes, but is not limited to, a showing that the third person did not know or have reason to know of the levy from all the facts and circumstances known to the third person." (C.C.P. 701.010(c).)

(b) *Liability for Noncompliance With Levy.* A third person who without good cause fails or refuses to deliver property or make payments is liable to the creditor for the lesser of: (1) the value of the debtor's interest in the property; (2) the amount of the payments required to be made; or (3) the amount required to satisfy the judgment. (C.C.P. 701.020(a); see Law Rev. Com. Recommendation, Pamphlet, p. 1076; Law Rev. Com. Comment, Pamphlet, p. 1349.)

Liability continues until the property is delivered or the payments are made to the levying officer, the property is released pursuant to C.C.P. 699.060 (see Supp., supra, §252A), or the judgment is satisfied or discharged, whichever occurs first. (C.C.P. 701.020(b).) The third person may, at the discretion of the court, be required to pay the costs and reasonable attorney's fees incurred in establishing liability. (C.C.P. 701.020(c).)

(c) *Garnishee's Memorandum.* The levying officer must, at the time of service on a third person, request a garnishee's memorandum. Regardless of whether the levy is effective, the third person must mail or deliver the memorandum to the levying officer within 10 days after the request. (C.C.P. 701.030(a); see Law Rev. Com. Recommendation, Pamphlet, p. 1077; Law Rev. Com. Comment, Pamphlet, p. 1351.) On receipt of the memorandum, the levying officer must promptly mail or deliver a copy to the judgment creditor; the original is attached to the writ on its return. If the memorandum is not received, the return must so state. (C.C.P. 701.030(c).)

The memorandum must be executed under oath and must (1) describe any property sought to be levied upon that is not delivered to the levying officer and state the reason for nondelivery; (2) state the amount and terms of any obligation sought to be levied upon that is due and payable and is not paid to the levying officer, and the reason for nonpayment, as well as the amount and terms of any obligation sought to be levied upon that is not due and payable; (3) describe any other property of the judgment debtor in the third person's possession or control and the amount and terms of any other obligation to the debtor; and (4) describe any claims and rights of other persons to the property or obligation levied upon known to the third person, with the names and addresses of the other persons. (C.C.P. 701.030(b); see Law Rev. Com. Recommendation, Pamphlet, p. 1078.) The information thus provided may render an examination proceeding (see Supp., infra, §368A et seq.) unnecessary. (See Law Rev. Com. Comment, Pamphlet, p. 1351.) If the third person fails to give the memorandum within the required time or fails to provide complete information, the court may, in its discretion, require him to pay costs and reasonable attorney's fees in any proceedings necessary to obtain the required information. (C.C.P. 701.030(d); see Law Rev. Com. Recommendation, Pamphlet, p. 1013 [Summary], 1078.)

In the case of a levy on a deposit account (see Supp., supra, §272A) or a safe deposit box (see Supp., supra, §273A), the financial institution need not give a memorandum if it fully complies with the levy; if a memorandum is required, it need only provide information with respect to property carried on records available at the office or branch where the levy is made. (C.C.P. 701.030(e); see Law Rev. Com. Recommendation, Pamphlet, p. 1078.)

A memorandum is not required if the third person has delivered or paid to the levying officer all the property sought to be levied upon and the amount due at the time of levy on any obligation to the debtor that was levied upon, and if no additional amount will thereafter become payable on the obligation. (C.C.P. 701.030(f); see Law Rev. Com. Recommendation, Pamphlet, p. 1077.)

See 14 Pacific L.J. 410.

(2) [§279A] (New) Rights and Duties of Secured Party.

If property not in the levying officer's custody is subject to a security interest that attached prior to levy, the security interest may be enforced without regard to the levy. However, if the execution lien has priority over the security interest, the secured party is liable for any proceeds received to the extent of the execution lien. Also, the court may order the security interest not enforced if it determines that the creditor's lien has priority. (C.C.P. 701.040(a); see Law Rev. Com. Recommendation, Pamphlet, pp. 1065, 1078; Legislative Com. Comment—Senate, Pamphlet, p. 1352.)

After satisfaction of the security interest, the secured party, unless otherwise ordered by the court or directed by the levying officer, must deliver any excess property and pay any excess proceeds to the levying officer as provided in U.C.C. 9504 (see 2 *Summary, Secured Transactions in Personal Property* §69). (C.C.P. 701.040(b); Law Rev. Com. Recommendation, Pamphlet, p. 1067, 1078.)

(3) [§280A] (New) Duty of Account Debtor.

C.C.P. 701.050 specifies the duties of an account debtor obligated on an account receivable, chattel paper, or general intangible, after service on the account debtor of a copy of the writ of execution and a notice of levy. If the account debtor has been paying or is required to pay the judgment debtor, the account debtor is to pay the levying officer "unless otherwise directed by court order or by the levying officer." (C.C.P. 701.050(a); see Law Rev. Com. Recommendation, Pamphlet, p. 1079; Law Rev. Com. Comment, Pamphlet, p. 1353.) If the account debtor has been paying or is required to pay a third person, such payments must be continued until the account debtor is notified "that the obligation to the third person is satisfied or is otherwise directed by court order or by the third person." After receipt of notice that the obligation is satisfied, the account debtor must pay the levying officer "unless otherwise directed by court order or by the levying officer." (C.C.P. 701.050(b); see Law Rev. Com. Recommendation, Pamphlet, p. 1079; Law Rev. Com. Comment, Pamphlet, p. 1353.)

If the judgment debtor has liberty under a security agreement to accept the return of goods or make repossessions, the account debtor must "deliver to the levying officer property returnable to the judgment debtor unless otherwise directed by court order or by the levying officer." (C.C.P. 701.050(c); see Law Rev. Com. Recommendation, Pamphlet, p. 1079; Law Rev. Com. Comment, Pamphlet, p. 1353.)

(4) [§281A] (New) Duty of Obligor Under Instrument.

The obligor on an instrument levied upon must make payments to the levying officer if the officer obtains custody of the instrument and serves the obligor pursuant to the levy. Payments made to another person after the obligor's receipt of notice of the levy do not discharge the obligor's obligation. (C.C.P. 701.060; see Law Rev. Com. Recommendation, Pamphlet, p. 1079; Legislative Com. Comment—Senate, Pamphlet, p. 1354.)

(g) (New) Sale and Collection.

(1) (New) In General.

(aa) [§282A] (New) Sale of Property Levied Upon.

Ordinarily the levying officer must sell property levied upon. However, his general authority is subject to the provisions governing collection of instruments (see Supp., supra §236A) and collectible property (see Supp., infra, §282A-1). Also, the officer may not sell tangible personal property until he obtains custody of it, and cash may not be sold unless its value exceeds its face value. (C.C.P. 701.510; see Law Rev. Com. Comment, Pamphlet, p. 1354.)

(bb) [§282A-1] (New) Collection or Sale of Collectible Property.

(1) *Collection of Collectible Property.* The new law encourages collection rather than sale of types of property that are particularly susceptible to sacrifice and speculative sales. Except as otherwise provided in C.C.P. 701.520, the following types of property must be collected rather than sold: (a) Accounts receivable; (b) chattel paper; (c) general intangibles; (d) final money judgments; (e) instruments not customarily transferred in an established market; (f) instruments arising out of consumer transactions involving property, services, or the loan of money. (C.C.P. 701.520(a); see Law Rev. Com. Recommendation, Pamphlet, p. 1110; Law Rev. Com. Comment, Pamphlet, p. 1356; 14 Pacific L.J. 411.)

(2) *Sale of Collectible Property.* The creditor must serve on the debtor personally or by mail, and must file (with proof of service) with the court and the levying officer, a notice of intended sale. The notice must describe the property and state that it will be sold at an execution sale unless the debtor objects as provided by the statute. (C.C.P. 701.520(b).) Within 10 days after service of the notice, the debtor may make a noticed motion for an order that the property be collected rather than sold. A copy of the notice of motion must be

served, personally or by mail, on the creditor and filed with the levying officer. If the notice of motion is timely filed with the officer, he must continue to collect the property until the court otherwise orders; otherwise, the officer must sell the property. (C.C.P. 701.520(c).)

The court has discretion to order collection, sale, or sale on specific terms and conditions, "depending on the equities and circumstances of the particular case." An order for collection may be conditioned on the debtor's assignment of the property to the creditor pursuant to C.C.P. 708.510 et seq. (see Supp., infra, §385A et seq.). (C.C.P. 701.520(d).) (See Law Rev. Com. Recommendation, Pamphlet, p. 1110; Law Rev. Com. Comment, Pamphlet, p. 1356.)

(2) [§283A] (New) Notice of Sale.

(a) *Notice of Sale of Personal Property.* C.C.P. 701.530 generally continues the substance of former C.C.P. 692. (See Legislative Com. Comment—Assembly, Pamphlet, p. 1357; text, §77.) Notice of sale must be written, must state the date, time, and place of sale, and must describe the property to be sold. (C.C.P. 701.530(a).) Not less than 10 days before sale, notice of sale must be served, personally or by mail, on the judgment debtor and must be posted in three public places in the city or judicial district of sale. (C.C.P. 701.530(b)(c); see Legislative Com. Comment—Assembly, Pamphlet, p. 1357.)

An individual's personal property may not be sold until the time for making an exemption claim under C.C.P. 703.520(a) (see Supp., §301A) has expired. (C.C.P. 701.530(d).) This gives the judgment debtor until 10 days after service of the notice of levy to claim the exemption; under prior law, the 10-day period ran from the date of the levy. (See Law Rev. Com. Recommendation, Pamphlet, p. 1111; Legislative Com. Comment—Assembly, Pamphlet, p. 1357.)

(b) *Notice of Sale of Real Property.* C.C.P. 701.540 continues some requirements of former C.C.P. 692(3) (see text and Supp., supra, §77) while adding others. Notice of sale of an interest in real property must be written, must state the date, time, and place of sale, and must give a legal description of the property and its street address or other common designation, if any. For property having no street address or other common designation, the notice must either contain directions or must state that directions may be obtained on written or oral request. Directions may locate the property by direction and distance from the nearest crossroads or frontage or access road. If the legal description is accurate, the validity of the notice and sale is not affected by error or omission of the street address, common designation, or directions. (C.C.P. 701.540(a); see Law Rev. Com. Recommendation, Pamphlet, p. 1111; Law Rev. Com. Comment, Pamphlet, p. 1359.)

Notice must be given at least 20 days before the sale (C.C.P. 701.540(b)) in the following manner: (1) notice must be served personally or by mail on the debtor (C.C.P. 701.540(c)); (2) notice must be posted in one public place in the city or judicial district of sale and in a conspicuous place on the property (C.C.P. 701.540(d)); (3) notice must be served or attempted on one occupant of the property in the same manner provided for service of the writ of execution and notice of levy (see Supp., supra, §263A); if an occupant cannot be served at the time notice is posted on the property, no further attempts are necessary (C.C.P. 701.540(e)). When the property consists of distinct lots, parcels, or governmental subdivisions, only one service on an occupant and one posting on the property is required as to each continuous, unbroken tract. (C.C.P. 701.540(f).) (See Law Rev. Com. Recommendation, Pamphlet, p. 1111; Law Rev. Com. Comment, Pamphlet, p. 1359.)

In addition, at least 20 days before the sale notice must be mailed to each lienholder of record in the county recorder's office on the date of levy. The creditor must determine the names of such lienholders no earlier than 30 days after the date of levy, and must instruct the levying officer to mail the notice to each lienholder at the address used by the county recorder to return the instrument that created the lien. (C.C.P. 701.540(h); see Law Rev. Com. Recommendation, Pamphlet, p. 1111; Law Rev. Com. Comment, Pamphlet, p. 1359.)

Beginning at least 20 days before the sale, notice must be published once a week pursuant to Govt.C. 6063 in a newspaper of general circulation published in the city, judicial district, or county in which the property or some part thereof is situated. (C.C.P. 701.540(g); see Law Rev. Com. Comment, Pamphlet, p. 1359.)

Under C.C.P. 701.545, the notice of sale may not be given until 120 days after service of the notice of levy on the judgment debtor; this restriction does not apply to sale of a leasehold interest with less than 2 years to run. The delay gives the judgment creditor an opportunity either to redeem the property before sale or to seek potential purchasers, and compensates for the elimination of the statutory right of redemption (see Supp., supra, §230A). (See Law Rev. Com. Recommendation, Pamphlet, p. 1111; Legislative Com. Comment—Assembly, Pamphlet, p. 1360.)

See 14 Pacific L.J. 411.

(c) *Notice to Prospective Bidders.* C.C.P. 701.547 requires that a notice of sale contain the substance of this statement: "Prospective bidders should refer to Sections 701.510 to 701.680, inclusive, of the Code of Civil Procedure for provisions governing the terms, conditions, and effect of the sale and the liability of defaulting bidders."

(d) *Notice to Persons Requesting Notice.* Any person may request notice of sale. A request made prior to issuance of the writ is filed with the court clerk; the request must be written, must specify the title of the court, the cause and number of the action, and the judgment's date of entry, and must state the address to which notice is to be mailed. The court must note the request for notice on the writ. (C.C.P. 701.550(b).) A request made after the property has been levied upon is filed with the levying officer who will conduct the sale and must contain the information specified by the officer. (C.C.P. 701.550(c).) At the time notice of sale is posted, notice of sale must be mailed to any person who has requested it. (C.C.P. 701.550(a).) (See Legislative Com. Comment—Assembly, Pamphlet, p. 1361.)

(e) *Effect of Sale Without Notice.* Failure to give the required notice of sale does not invalidate the sale, but the levying officer is liable to the creditor and the debtor for actual damages caused by such failure. (C.C.P. 701.560; see Law Rev. Com. Comment, Pamphlet, p. 1361; 14 Pacific L.J. 414.)

(f) *Advertising by Creditor or Debtor.* C.C.P. 701.555 permits the judgment creditor to advertise the sale in the advertising section of a newspaper of general circulation or other publication and to recover reasonable costs of such advertising. The debtor may also advertise the sale at his own expense. Such advertising may be appropriate where property with a specialized market is to be sold. (See Law Rev. Com. Recommendation, Pamphlet, p. 1111; Legislative Com. Comment—Assembly, Pamphlet, p. 1361.)

(3) [§284A] (New) Place, Time and Manner of Sale.

(a) *In General.* The substance of former C.C.P. 694 (see text, §78) is largely continued in the new law. A sale must be held in the county where the property or a part thereof is situated, between 9:00 a.m. and 5:00 p.m., "at auction to the highest bidder." (C.C.P. 701.570(a)(b).) Real property situated in two or more counties generally "may be sold in one county as instructed by the judgment creditor." (C.C.P. 701.570(a).)

The requirement of former C.C.P 694 that personal property capable of manual delivery be within view of those attending the sale (see text, §79) has been replaced by a requirement that such property be within view "unless, upon application of the judgment creditor or the judgment debtor, the court orders otherwise." (C.C.P. 701.570(c); see Law Rev. Com. Recommendation, Pamphlet, p. 1112; Law Rev. Com. Comment, Pamphlet, p. 1363.)

"After sufficient property has been sold to yield the amount required to satisfy the money judgment, no more shall be sold."

(C.C.P. 701.570(e); see Law Rev. Com. Comment, Pamphlet, p. 1363.)

(b) *Debtor's Request for Sale in Certain Manner.* Property must "be sold separately or in such groups or lots as are likely to bring the highest price." The judgment debtor may make a request (in writing if he does not attend the sale) concerning the manner or order of sale, which request must be honored if, in the levying officer's opinion, the requested manner "is likely to yield an amount at least equal to any other manner of sale or the amount required to satisfy the money judgment." The levying officer is not liable for his good faith decision on the request. (C.C.P. 701.570(d); see Law Rev. Com. Recommendation, Pamphlet, p. 1112; Law Rev. Com. Comment, Pamphlet, p. 1363.)

(c) *Postponement of Sale.* The substance of former C.C.P. 694 (see text, §78) is continued. (See Law Rev. Com. Comment, Pamphlet, p. 1364.) The debtor and creditor may jointly request in writing a postponement "to an agreed day and hour." The request must be delivered to the levying officer conducting the sale, who must, "by public declaration at the time and place originally fixed for the sale, postpone the sale to the day and hour fixed in the request." Notice of subsequent postponements must be given in the same manner. "No other notice of postponed sale need be given. A postponed sale shall be held at the place originally fixed for the sale." (C.C.P. 701.580.)

(4) [§285A] (New) Bid and Payment.

(a) *Levying Officer Cannot Purchase.* "The levying officer may not be a purchaser or have an interest in any purchase at a sale." (C.C.P. 701.610.) This continues the substance of former C.C.P. 694. (See Law Rev. Com. Comment, Pamphlet, p. 1367; text, §83.)

(b) *Minimum Bid.* The sale of property is prohibited unless the amount bid exceeds the total of: (1) all preferred labor claims under C.C.P. 1206; (2) state tax liens superior to the judgment creditor's lien; (3) any deposits, with interest thereon, made by the judgment creditor (unless he is the purchaser) in response to third-party claims pursuant to C.C.P. 720.260 (see Supp., infra, §415A); and (4) any proceeds exemption on a motor vehicle (see Supp., infra, §306A), household furnishings and personal effects (see Supp., infra, §307A), or tools of trade (see Supp., infra, §311A). (C.C.P. 701.620(a)(b); see Law Rev. Com. Recommendation, Pamphlet, p. 1113; Legislative Com. Comment—Assembly, Pamphlet, p. 1368.) If a minimum bid is not received, the levying officer must promptly release the property. (C.C.P. 701.620(c).)

See 14 Pacific L.J. 414.

On the minimum bid required on sale of a homestead, see C.C.P. 704.800, Supp., infra, §333A.

(c) *Manner of Payment.* A purchaser other than the creditor generally must pay in cash or by certified check or cashier's check. (C.C.P. 701.590(a).) If the creditor bids, he may give the levying officer a written receipt for the amount of the judgment, but must give cash or a certified check or cashier's check for the officer's costs, preferred labor claims, exempt proceeds, and other superior claims that must be satisfied. (C.C.P. 701.590(b).) These provisions codify prior law. (See Law Rev. Com. Recommendation, Pamphlet, p. 1112; Legislative Com. Comment—Senate, Pamphlet, p. 1365; text, §81.)

The new law, to encourage more bidders, also provides for credit bids under specified circumstances. (See Law Rev. Com. Recommendation, Pamphlet, p. 1112.) When the highest bid on real property exceeds $5,000, the high bidder may treat the sale as a credit transaction by depositing at least $5,000 or 10 percent of the amount bid, whichever is greater. (C.C.P. 701.590(c).) When the highest bid for personal property exceeds $2,500, the high bidder may treat the sale as a credit transaction by depositing at least $2,500 or 10 percent of the amount bid, whichever is greater. (C.C.P. 701.590(d).) In each case, the balance, with costs and interest, must be paid within 10 days. (C.C.P. 701.590(c)(d).) A credit bidder is not entitled to possession of the property until payment in full has been made. (C.C.P. 701.590(e); see Legislative Com. Comment—Senate, p. 1365.)

See 14 Pacific L.J. 414.

(5) [§285A-1] (New) Defaulting Bidder.

(a) *Resale of Property.* If the high bidder fails to pay, the levying officer must resell the property. When the default occurs at the sale, the property must be sold to the next highest bidder (if he agrees) or at an immediate new sale. (C.C.P. 701.600(a)(1); see Legislative Com. Comment—Assembly, Pamphlet, p. 1367.)

When the default occurs after sale to a credit bidder on real property, the property must be resold at a new sale. (C.C.P. 701.600(a)(2).) The same procedure is to be followed in the event of a default after a credit sale of personal property (see Law Rev. Com. Recommendation, Pamphlet, p. 1113; Legislative Com. Comment—Assembly, Pamphlet, p. 1367), although C.C.P. 701.600(a)(2) on its face is limited to sales under C.C.P. 701.590(c) (real property).

At a resale, the levying officer has discretion to reject a bid from the defaulting bidder. (C.C.P. 701.600(d).)

(b) *Application of Deposit.* Any deposit made on a credit sale of real property must be applied in the following order: (1) to satisfaction of costs accruing between the sale and the resale, including costs of resale; (2) to satisfaction of interest on the amount bid between the sale and the resale; (3) to satisfaction of the judgment. (C.C.P. 701.600(b); see Law Rev. Com. Recommendation, Pamphlet, p. 1112; Legislative Com. Comment—Assembly, Pamphlet, p. 1367.) A deposit on a credit sale of personal property is to be applied in the same order (see Law Rev. Com. Recommendation, Pamphlet, p. 1113; Legislative Com. Comment—Assembly, Pamphlet, p. 1367), although C.C.P. 701.600(b) on its face is limited to sales under C.C.P. 701.590 (c) (real property).

(c) *Action Against Defaulting Bidder.* If there is a resale, either the creditor or the debtor may sue the defaulting bidder, who is liable for the difference between the unpaid bid and a lower price obtained on resale, plus costs and interest on the amount bid between the original sale and the resale, and costs and attorney's fees incurred in the action against the defaulting bidder. (C.C.P. 701.600(c); see Legislative Com. Comment—Assembly, Pamphlet, p. 1367; 14 Pacific L.J. 414.)

(6) [§286A] (New) Effect of Sale.

(a) *Extinction of Liens.* A sale extinguishes the lien under which the property is sold, subordinate liens, and state tax liens. (C.C.P. 701.630; see Legislative Com. Comment—Assembly, Pamphlet, p. 1368.)

(b) *Interest Acquired by Purchaser.* The purchaser acquires the debtor's entire interest in the property. (C.C.P. 701.640; see Law Rev. Com. Comment, Pamphlet, p. 1369.) The sale is absolute and, except as provided in C.C.P. 701.680(c)(1) (see infra, this section), "may not be set aside for any reason." (C.C.P. 701.680(a); see Legislative Com. Comment—Assembly, Pamphlet, p. 1371.) The right of redemption of real property under prior law (see text, §98 et seq.) *has been repealed.* (See Legislative Com. Comment—Assembly, Pamphlet, p. 1371; Supp., supra, §230A.)

(c) *Where Judgment Is Set Aside.* If the judgment is set aside, the judgment debtor may recover from the judgment creditor the proceeds of the sale with interest on that part of the proceeds applied to satifaction of the judgment. (C.C.P. 701.680(b).)

(d) *Where Sale Is Improper.* If the sale is improper for any reason, the judgment debtor may recover damages caused by the impropriety. The damages, if recovered against the creditor or the levying officer, must either be offset against or applied to the judgment to the extent it is not satisfied. (C.C.P. 701.680(c)(2).)

In addition, if the creditor purchased the property, an action to set aside the sale may be brought within 6 months after the sale. If the sale is set aside, the judgment (with interest) is revived, but any damages recovered by the debtor are offset against the judgment. (C.C.P. 701.680(c)(1).)

(7)   [§287A]   (New) Possession, Certificate, or Deed.

(a) *Delivery of Possession.* Personal property, if capable of manual delivery, must be delivered to the purchaser on payment of the amount due. (C.C.P. 701.650(a)(1).) The levying officer must also sign or endorse and deliver to the purchaser any document or instrument in the officer's possession relating to title or possession. (C.C.P. 701.650(b).) (See Law Rev. Com. Comment, Pamphlet, p. 1370.)

(b) *Certificate of Sale.* The levying officer must execute and deliver a certificate of sale to a purchaser of property that is not capable of manual delivery (C.C.P. 701.650(a)(2)), as well as to a purchaser of deliverable property who requests such a certificate (C.C.P. 701.650(a)(1)). The officer must also sign or endorse and deliver to the purchaser any document or instrument in the officer's possession relating to title or possession of the property. (C.C.P. 701.650(b).) (See Law Rev. Com. Comment, Pamphlet, p. 1370.)

(c) *Deed of Sale of Real Property.* On payment of the amount due, the levying officer must execute and deliver a deed of sale to the purchaser of an interest in real property, and a duplicate deed must be recorded in the county recorder's office. (C.C.P. 701.660; see Law Rev. Com. Comment, Pamphlet, p. 1370.)

(d) *Contents of Certificate or Deed.* A certificate or deed of sale must contain: (1) the title of the court which entered judgment and the cause and number of the action; (2) the dates of entry of the judgment and any renewals and where entered in the court's records; (3) the judgment creditor's name and address and the judgment debtor's name and last known address; (4) a description of the property sold; (5) the date of sale. (C.C.P. 701.670; see Legislative Com. Comment—Senate, p. 1370.)

(h)   (New) Distribution of Proceeds.

(1)   [§288A]   (New) Manner of Distribution.

Prior law contained incomplete and somewhat contradictory provisions concerning distribution of the proceeds of a sale; the new law has a general section specifying the order of distribution. (See Law Rev. Com. Recommendation, Pamphlet, p. 1114; Legislative Com. Comment—Senate, Pamphlet, p. 1373.) Under C.C.P. 701.810 the proceeds of sale or collection must, except as otherwise provided by statute, be distributed in the following order:

(1) To persons with preferred labor claims under C.C.P. 1206. (C.C.P. 701.810(a); see Law Rev. Com. Recommendation, Pamphlet,

p. 1114; Legislative Com. Comment—Assembly, Pamphlet, p. 1374; *Provisional Remedies,* §183.)

(2) To payment of superior state tax liens. (C.C.P. 701.810(b); see Law Rev. Com. Recommendation, Pamphlet, p. 1114; Legislative Com. Comment—Senate, Pamphlet, p. 1374.)

(3) If he is not the purchaser, to the creditor to repay with interest any deposit made pursuant to C.C.P. 720.260 (see Supp., infra, §415A) in connection with a third-party claim. (C.C.P. 701.810(c); see Law Rev. Com. Recommendation, Pamphlet, p. 1114; Legislative Com. Comment—Senate, Pamphlet, p. 1374.)

(4) Where he is entitled to an exemption of proceeds from a motor vehicle (see Supp., infra, §306A), household furnishings and personal effects (see Supp., infra, §307A), or tools of trade (see Supp., infra, §311A), to the debtor in the amount of such exemption. However, consensual liens and encumbrances and liens for labor for materials subordinate to the judgment creditor's lien, as well as recorded or filed state tax liens subordinate to the judgment creditor's lien, must first be satisfied out of the exempt proceeds. (C.C.P. 701.810(d); see Law Rev. Com. Recommendation, Pamphlet, p. 1114; Legislative Com. Comment—Senate, Pamphlet, p. 1374.)

(5) To the levying officer for reimbursement of any costs not advanced. (C.C.P. 701.810(e); see Law Rev. Com. Recommendation, Pamphlet, p. 1114; Legislative Com. Comment—Senate, Pamphlet, p. 1374.)

(6) To the creditor, first to satisfy costs and interest accruing after issuance of the writ, and then to satisfy the amount due on the judgment with costs and interest, as entered on the writ. (C.C.P. 701.810(f); see Law Rev. Com. Recommendation, Pamphlet, p. 1114; Legislative Com. Comment—Senate, Pamphlet, p. 1374.)

(7) To any other judgment creditor who has delivered a writ to the levying officer with instructions to levy on the same property, or to any other person actually known to the levying officer who has a subordinate claim, lien, or other interest that is extinguished by the sale, in the order of their respective priorities. (C.C.P. 701.810(g); see Law Rev. Com. Recommendation, Pamphlet, p. 1114; Legislative Com. Comment—Senate, Pamphlet, p. 1375.)

(8) To the debtor. (C.C.P. 701.810(h).

(2) [§289A] (New) Time For Distribution.

Unless there are conflicting claims, the levying officer must make prompt distribution of the proceeds of a sale or collection. (C.C.P. 701.820(a); see Legislative Com. Comment—Assembly, Pamphlet, p. 1376.) Generally, the proceeds must be paid out within 30 days after the officer receives them. (C.C.P. 701.820(b); see Law Rev. Com.

Recommendation, Pamphlet, p. 1114.) Where the proceeds are not received in one payment, the officer may accumulate proceeds over a 30-day period and pay them out within 20 days after the 30-day period ends. (C.C.P. 701.820(c).)

Proceeds in the form of checks or other noncash payments are not considered received until actually honored on presentation for payment. (C.C.P. 701.820(d).)

A levying officer may be held liable under Govt.C. 26680 for failure to pay the money collected only if, after failure to distribute the proceeds as required, the officer also fails to make payment within 10 days to a person entitled to payment who has filed a written demand for payment with the officer. (C.C.P. 701.820(e).)

(3)   [§290A]   (New) Conflicting Claims to Proceeds.

C.C.P. 701.830 provides a new procedure for resolving conflicting claims to all or part of the proceeds of a sale or collection. (See Legislative Com. Comment—Assembly, Pamphlet, p. 1377.) If the levying officer knows of such conflicting claims, he may deposit the proceeds with the court instead of distributing them. Any interested person may then make a noticed motion for an order for the distribution of such proceeds, with service on such persons and in such manner as the court orders. On any interested person's request, the court must "grant a continuance for a reasonable time" for filing a response to the motion, for discovery proceedings, or for other preparation for the hearing. (C.C.P. 701.830(a).)

At the hearing the court must determine the issues and make an order for distribution of the proceeds, unless abatement of the hearing is required. (C.C.P. 701.830(b).) The hearing must be abated until the issues can be determined in a civil action if: (a) the court, under any other provision of law, is not the proper court to try a civil action involving the subject matter of the motion, and any interested person objects at or prior to the hearing; (b) another court has obtained jurisdiction in a pending civil action with respect to the subject matter of the motion; or (c) "the court determines that the matter should be determined in a civil action." (C.C.P. 701.830(c).)

4.   (New) Exemptions.

(a)   (New) General Provisions.

(1)   [§291A]   (New) Scope of Statute.

(a) *Application of Exemptions.* Laws exempting property from enforcement of a money judgment are intended to protect sufficient property of the debtor and his family and to facilitate his financial rehabilitation. Such laws also shift the cost of social welfare for debtors from the community to creditors. (Law Rev. Com. Recommendation, Pamphlet, p. 1079; 14 Pacific L.J. 415.)

Unless otherwise provided by statute, the exemptions provided by the Enforcement of Judgments Law (C.C.P. 703.010(a); on former law, see text, §25 et seq.) or any other statute apply to all procedures for enforcement of a money judgment, but do not apply if the judgment involved is for the foreclosure of a mortgage, deed of trust, or other lien or encumbrance on property other than a lien created pursuant to a money judgment or by virtue of attachment proceedings. (C.C.P. 703.010(b); see Law Rev. Com. Comment, Pamphlet, p. 1378; on proceedings to obtain an attachment lien, see *Provisional Remedies,* Supp., §313A et seq.)

On the exemptions available to an assignor of a general assignment for the benefit of creditors, see C.C.P. 1801, added in conforming legislation and operative July 1, 1983.

(b) *Time of Lien Governs.* The determination whether property is exempt, and the amount of an exemption, is made by application of the exemption statutes in effect either: (1) At the time the creditor's lien on the property was created; or (2) if the creditor's lien is the latest in a series of overlapping liens created when an earlier lien on the property in favor of the creditor was in effect, at the time the earliest lien in the series was created. (C.C.P. 703.050(a); see Law Rev. Com. Recommendation, Pamphlet, p. 1100.) However, the procedures involving a levy of execution are governed by the law in effect at the time the levy is made on the property. (C.C.P. 703.050(c).)

"This section applies to all judgments, whether based upon tort, contract, or other legal theory or cause of action that arose before or after the operative date of this section, and whether the judgment was entered before or after the operative date of this section." (C.C.P. 703.050(b).)

(c) *Reserved Power of State To Change Exemptions.* The Legislature retains the right to make changes in exemptions applicable in any enforcement proceeding after the operative date of the change, regardless of whether the judgment was entered before or after the operative date of the change, and regardless of when the underlying obligation or liability was created or arose. (C.C.P. 703.060(a); see Law Rev. Com. Comment, Pamphlet, p. 1382.)

All contracts are deemed to be made, and all liens created, in recognition of the State's power to make changes in the allowable exemptions from enforcement of money judgments. (C.C.P. 703.060(b).)

See 14 Pacific L.J. 425.

(d) *Continuing Review by Law Revision Commission.* The California Law Revision Commission must review the exempt amounts provided by law and recommend changes to the Governor and Legislature every 10 years. (CCP 703.120(a).) It may make such recommendations more frequently. (C.C.P. 703.120(b); see Law Rev. Com. Recommendation, Pamphlet, p. 1106.)

(2)   [§292A]   (New) **Persons Entitled to Exemptions.**

The exemptions in the Enforcement of Judgments Law (C.C.P. 703.010 et seq.) apply only to property of a natural person. (C.C.P. 703.020(a).) They may be claimed in all cases by the debtor or a person acting on his behalf (C.C.P. 703.020(b)(1)), or in the case of community property, by the debtor's spouse, whether or not the spouse is also a debtor (C.C.P. 703.020(b)(2)).

See Law Rev. Com. Comment, Pamphlet, p. 1378; 14 Pacific L.J. 424.

(3)   [§293A]   (New) **Claim and Waiver.**

(a) *Claim and Failure To Claim.* An exemption is waived and the property is subject to enforcement of a money judgment unless the exemption is claimed within the time and in the manner prescribed in the applicable enforcement procedure. (C.C.P. 703.030(a); see Law Rev. Com. Comment, Pamphlet, p. 1379.) Unless specifically provided otherwise, any property described in any statute as exempt without making a claim is not subject to any procedure for enforcement. (C.C.P. 703.030(b); see Law Rev. Com. Comment, Pamphlet, p. 1379.)

Under its authority to grant relief to a person from proceedings taken against him through mistake, inadvertence, suprise or excusable neglect (see C.C.P. 473, Attack On Judgment in Trial Court, §126 et seq.), the court may relieve a person upon such terms as may be just from failure to claim an exemption within the time and in the manner prescribed. (C.C.P. 703.030(c); see Law Rev. Com. Comment, Pamphlet, p. 1380.)

(b) *Prior Waiver of Exemptions.* Other than a waiver by failure to claim an exemption required to be made at the time enforcement of a judgment is sought (see supra), a purported contractual or other prior waiver of an exemption is against public policy and void. (C.C.P. 703.040; see Law Rev. Com. Comment, Pamphlet, p. 1380.)

(4)   [§294A]   (New) **Judgment for Child or Spousal Support.**

Except as otherwise provided by statute, the exemptions in the

Enforcement of Judgments Law or any other statute also apply to a judgment for child or spousal support. (C.C.P. 703.070(a); on procedure for claiming exemptions, see Supp., infra, §300A et seq.)

If property is exempt without making a claim, it may not be applied to satisfy a judgment for child or spousal support. (C.C.P. 703.070(b).)

Except as to property which is exempt without making a claim (see supra), if property sought to be applied to the satisfaction of a judgment for child or spousal support is claimed as exempt, the court must, upon noticed motion of the creditor, determine the extent to which the exempt property may nevertheless be applied to the satisfaction of the judgment. In making this determination, the court must take into account all relevant circumstances, including the needs of the creditor and of the debtor and his dependents. The court's determination is effectuated by an order specifying the extent to which the exempt property is to be applied to the satisfaction of the judgment. (C.C.P. 703.070(c); see Law Rev. Com. Comment, Pamphlet, p. 1383.)

(5) [§295A] (New) Tracing Exempt Funds.

An exemption for money from a particular source is illusory if the exemption is lost when the benefits are deposited in a bank or held in the form of a check or cash. (Law Rev. Com. Recommendation, Pamphlet, p. 1105.) Hence, an exempt fund remains so to the extent that it can be traced into deposit accounts or in the form of cash or its equivalent, subject to any limitation provided by a particular exemption. The burden of tracing an exempt fund is on the exemption claimant. (C.C.P. 703.080(a)(b); see Legislative Com. Comment—Assembly, Pamphlet, p. 1384.)

The tracing of exempt funds in a deposit account must be by application of the lowest intermediate balance principle, unless the claimant or creditor shows that some other method of tracing would be more equitable. (C.C.P. 703.080(c); see Legislative Com. Comment—Assembly, Pamphlet, p. 1384 [under lowest intermediate balance rule, exempt fund may not exceed *lowest balance* occuring at any time between the deposit of the exempt amount of money and the time of levy].)

(6) [§296A] (New) Costs Where Subsequent Levy Made.

If a creditor fails to oppose a claim of exemption within the time allowed (see Supp., infra, §303A), or if a court has determined that the property is exempt, and the creditor thereafter seeks to apply it toward satisfaction of the same money judgment, the creditor is not entitled to recover the subsequent costs of collection unless the property is applied to the satisfaction of the judgment. (C.C.P. 703.090; see Law Rev. Com. Comment, Pamphlet, p. 1385.)

(7) [§297A] (New) Time For Determination of Exemptions.

Subject to the court's power to consider changed circumstances (see infra, this section), the determination whether property is exempt must be made under the circumstances existing at the *earliest* of the following times: (a) The time of the levy; (b) the time of the commencement of court proceedings for application of property to satisfaction of the judgment; or (c) the time a lien is created under the Enforcement of Judgments Law or the provisions relating to attachment. (C.C.P. 703.100(a); see Legislative Com. Comment—Assembly, Pamphlet, p. 1386 [increased or new exemptions are enacted to take account of inflation or recognize importance of new forms of assets; this intention would be defeated if the fortuity of the time of contract or tort liability determined the applicable exemption]; on creation of attachment liens, see *Provisional Remedies,* Supp., §358A et seq.)

The court may take into consideration the following changes that have occurred between the time of levy, the time proceedings for enforcement were commenced, or the time the lien was created, and the time of hearing: (1) A change in the use of the property where the exemption was based on its use for exempt purposes but, at the time of the hearing, it is used for a non-exempt purpose; (2) a change in the value of the property if the exemption is based on such value; (3) a change in the financial circumstances of the debtor and his spouse and dependents if the exemption was based on their needs. (C.C.P. 703.100(b); see Legislative Com. Comment—Assembly, Pamphlet, p. 1386.)

See 14 Pacific L.J. 425.

(8) [§298A] (New) Application of Exemptions to Marital Property.

A matter of particular concern in the formulation of exemptions is the treatment of property of a married debtor and his spouse. (Law Rev. Com. Recommendation, Pamphlet, p. 1080.) Hence, C.C.P. 703.110 establishes the following special rules if the debtor is married:

(a) All exemptions provided by law apply to all property that is subject to enforcement of a money judgment, including the community property interest of the spouse in the property of the debtor. The number or amount of exemptions is not increased or decreased by the fact that one or both spouses are debtors or that property sought to be applied is separate or community.

(b) In determining an exemption based upon the needs of the debtor and his spouse and dependents, the court must take into account all of their property, including community and separate property of the spouse, whether or not such property is subject to enforcement.

(c) If an exemption is required to be applied first to property not before the court and then to property before the court, the application of the exemption not before the court must be made to the community property and separate property of both spouses, whether or not such property is subject to enforcement.

(d) If the same exemption is claimed by the debtor and his spouse for different property, and the property claimed by one spouse, but not both, is exempt, the exemption must be applied as the spouses agree. If the spouses cannot agree, the court may use its discretion in applying the exemption.

See Legislative Com. Comment—Assembly, Pamphlet, p. 1387.

(9) [§299A] (New) Exemptions in Bankruptcy.

The Bankruptcy Act permits each state to preclude use of the federal exemptions in bankruptcy and to require a debtor in bankruptcy to be subject to state exemptions. (11 U.S.C., §522(b)(1); Law Rev. Com. Recommendations, Pamphlet, p. 1099.) Pursuant to this authority, the federal exemptions are not authorized in this State (CCP 703.130(a)), except in the following situations:

(a) If a husband and wife are joined in a bankruptcy proceeding, they may jointly elect to utilize either the applicable federal or state exemptions, but not both. (CCP 703.130(b).)

(b) If a petition is filed individually, and not jointly, for a husband or a wife, the federal exemptions are authorized if the husband and wife each effectively waive in writing the right to claim, during the pendency of the proceeding, the exemptions provided by state law in any proceeding commenced by filing a bankruptcy petition for either of them. (CCP 703.130(c).)

(c) If a bankruptcy petition is filed for an unmarried person, the unmarried person may elect to utilize the applicable state exemptions or federal exemptions, but not both. (C.C.P. 703.130(d).)

See Legislative Com. Comment—Assembly, Pamphlet, p. 1390.

(b) (New) Procedure for Claiming Exemptions.

(1) [§300A] (New) In General.

(a) *Application of Article.* The procedure for claiming exemptions is governed by a separate article of the Enforcement of Judgments Law (C.C.P. 703.510 et seq.). Except as otherwise provided by statute (see, for example, C.C.P. 704.080, Supp., infra, §313A [deposit accounts consisting of Social Security benefits]; C.C.P. 704.710 et seq., Supp., infra, §328A et seq. [real property homestead]), property that has been levied upon may be claimed as exempt. (C.C.P. 703.510; see Legislative Com. Comment—Assembly, Pamphlet, p. 1390.)

Property that is not subject to enforcement of a money judgment is exempt without making any claim (C.C.P. 704.210), and may be released in the same manner as property claimed as exempt (C.C.P. 695.040; 703.510; see Legislative Com. Comment—Assembly, Pamphlet, p. 1390).

On exemption procedure under the new law, see 14 Pacific L.J. 423.

(b) *Extension of Time.* If the court extends the time allowed for an act required in connection with claiming an exemption, written notice of the extension must be filed with the levying officer and, unless waived, must be *promptly* served on the opposing party either personally or by mail. (C.C.P. 703.590.)

(c) *Appeal.* Any order made in a procedure relating to exemption claims may be appealed under the general rules governing appeals in the court where the proceedings take place. (C.C.P. 703.600.)

(2) [§301A] (New) Claim of Exemption.

(a) *Time of Filing.* Within 10 days after a notice of levy on property claimed to be exempt is served on a debtor, he may claim the exemption by filing a claim and a copy thereof with the levying officer. (C.C.P. 703.520(a); see Legislative Com. Comment—Assembly, Pamphlet, p. 1392.)

(b) *Form and Content of Claim.* The claim must be executed under oath and include all of the following: (1) The claimant's name and mailing address; (2) the name and last known address of the debtor if the claimant is not the debtor; (3) a description of the property claimed to be exempt (the description varies depending on the particular basis of the claim of exemption); (4) a financial statement if required (see infra, this section); (5) a citation of the provision of the Enforcement of Judgments Law or other statute upon which the claim is based; and (6) a statement of facts necessary to support the claim. (C.C.P. 703.520(b); see Legislative Com. Comment —Assembly, Pamphlet, p. 1392.)

(c) *Financial Statement.* A claim of exemption must include a financial statement if property is claimed to be exempt as necessary for the support of the debtor and his spouse and dependents. (C.C.P. 703.530(a).) The statement must be executed under oath by the debtor and, unless the spouses are living separate and apart, his spouse. (C.C.P. 703.530(c).)

The financial statement must include all of the following: (1) The name of the spouse of the debtor; (2) the name, age and relationship of all persons dependent on the debtor or his spouse for support; (3) all sources and the amounts of earnings and other income of the debtor and his spouse and dependents; (4) a list of assets of the debtor and his spouse and dependents, and the value of such assets; and (5) all outstanding obligations of the debtor and his spouse and dependents. (C.C.P. 703.530(b); see Law Rev. Com. Comment, Pamphlet, p. 1393.)

(3) [§302A] (New) Notice of Claim.

Promptly after filing a claim of exemption, the levying officer must serve on the creditor, either personally or by mail, a copy of the claim. He must likewise serve on the creditor a notice of claim of exemption stating that it has been made and that he will release the property unless, within the time specified in the notice, both of the following are filed with the levying officer: (a) A copy of the notice of opposition to the claim of exemption; and (b) a copy of the notice of motion for an order determining the claim. (C.C.P. 703.540; see Supp., infra, §303A.)

(4) [§303A] (New) Opposition to Claim.

Within 10 days after service of the notice of claim of exemption, a creditor who opposes the claim must file with the court and the levying officer (a) a notice of opposition to the claim of exemption, and (b) a notice of motion for an order determining the claim. The levying officer must then promptly file the claim of exemption with the court. If copies of the notices are not filed with the levying officer within the time allowed, he must *immediately* release the property to the extent it is claimed to be exempt. (C.C.P. 703.550; see Legislative Com. Comment—Assembly, Pamphlet, p. 1394.)

The notice of opposition must be executed under oath and include (1) an allegation either that the property is not exempt or that the equity in the property is in excess of the amount provided in the applicable exemption; and (2) a statement of the facts necessary to support the allegation. (C.C.P. 703.560.)

(5) [§304A] (New) Hearing and Order.

(a) *Notice of Hearing.* A hearing on a motion to determine a claim of exemption must be held not later than 20 days from the date the notice of motion is filed with the court, unless continued for good cause. (C.C.P. 703.570(a).) Not less than 10 days prior to the hearing, the creditor must serve a notice of the hearing and a copy of the notice of opposition to the claim personally or by mail on the claimant and the debtor, if other than the claimant. (C.C.P. 703.570(b); see Legislative Com. Comment—Assembly, Pamphlet, p. 1395.)

(b) *Hearing.* Subject to the power of the court to permit amendments in the interest of justice, the claim of exemption and notice of opposition constitute the pleadings. (C.C.P. 703.580(a).) At the hearing, the exemption claimant has the burden of proof. (C.C.P. 703.580(b).)

The claim of exemption is deemed controverted by the notice of opposition to it and both must be received in evidence. If no other evidence is offered and the court is satisfied that sufficient facts are shown by the claim and notice of opposition, it may make its determination thereon. If not so satisfied, the court must order the hearing continued for the production of other evidence. (C.C.P. 703.580(c).)

(c) *Order.* At the conclusion of the hearing, the court must determine by order whether or not the property is exempt in whole or in part. No findings are required. Subject to the right of appeal (see Supp., supra, §300A), the order is determinative of the right of the creditor to apply the property to the satisfaction of the judgment. (C.C.P. 703.580(d).)

The clerk must promptly transmit a certified copy of the order to the levying officer, who, subject to the provisions relating to disposition of property (see Supp., infra, §305A), must release the property or apply it to the satisfaction of the judgment. (C.C.P. 703.580(e).)

(6) [§305A] (New) Disposition of Property During Proceedings.

Except as otherwise provided by statute, the levying officer may not release, sell or otherwise dispose of any property claimed to be exempt until final determination of the exemption. (C.C.P. 703.610(a); see Legislative Com. Comment—Assembly, Pamphlet, p. 1397.) At any time during the pendency of the exemption proceedings, upon motion of the creditor or claimant, or on its own motion, the court may make such orders for disposition of the property as are proper under the circumstances. Such orders may be modified or vacated by the court at any time upon just terms. (C.C.P. 703.610(b); see Legislative Com. Comment—Assembly, Pamphlet, p. 1397.)

If an appeal of the determination of a claim of exemption is taken, notice of the appeal must be given to the levying officer and he must hold, release or dispose of the property in accordance with the provisions governing enforcement and stay of enforcements of money judgments pending appeal (see *Appeal,* §147 et seq.). (C.C.P.

703.610(c); see Legislative Com. Comment—Assembly, Pamphlet, p. 1397.)

(c) (New) Exempt Property.

(1) [§306A] (New) Motor Vehicles.

The exemption for motor vehicles is $1,200, derived from any combination of (a) the aggregate equity in vehicles; (b) proceeds from an execution sale of a vehicle; and (c) insurance or other indemnification proceeds for the loss, damage or destruction of a vehicle. (C.C.P. 704.010(a).) The proceeds are exempt for a period of 90 days from the time they are actually received by the debtor. (C.C.P. 704.010(b).)

To determine the amount of equity, the fair market value of the motor vehicle must be determined by reference to used car price guides customarily used by California automobile dealers unless the vehicle is not listed in such guides. (C.C.P. 704.010(c).)

If the debtor has *only one* motor vehicle and it is sold at an execution sale, the proceeds of the sale are exempt in the amount of $1,200 without making a claim. The levying officer may rely upon the records of the Department of Motor Vehicles to determine whether the debtor has only one vehicle. The exemption provided in C.C.P. 704.010(a) is not available in this situation. (C.C.P. 704.010(d); see Legislative Com. Comment—Assembly, Pamphlet, p. 1398.)

See 14 Pacific L.J. 415.

(2) [§307A] (New) Household Furnishings and Personal Effects.

Household furnishings, appliances, provisions, wearing apparel and other personal effects are exempt if ordinarily and reasonably necessary to, and personally used or procured for use by, (a) the debtor and members of his family at his principal place of residence or (b) if the debtor and his spouse live separate and apart, the spouse and members of the spouse's family at the spouse's principal place of residence. (C.C.P. 704.020(a); see Legislative Com. Comment—Assembly, Pamphlet, p. 1400.)

To determine whether an item of property is "ordinarily and reasonably necessary," the court must take into account both (1) the extent to which the item is ordinarily found in a household and (2) whether the item in the debtor's household has extraordinary value compared to the value of similar items found in other households. (C.C.P. 704.020(b).)

If an item is determined to be of the type ordinarily found in a household but not exempt because it has extraordinary value, the proceeds from an execution sale of the item are exempt in an amount determined by the court to be reasonable to purchase a replacement of ordinary value, if a replacement is deemed reasonably necessary. Proceeds determined to be exempt are exempt for a period of 90 days after they are actually received by the debtor. (C.C.P. 704.020(c).)

See 14 Pacific L.J. 415.

(3) [§308A] (New) Materials for Repair or Improvement of Dwelling.

"Material that in good faith is about to be applied to the repair or improvement of a residence is exempt if the equity in the material does not exceed one thousand dollars." The residence may be either the debtor's principal place of residence or, where the debtor and his spouse live separate and apart, the spouse's principal place of residence. (C.C.P. 704.030.)

(4) [§309A] (New) Jewelry, Heirlooms and Works of Art.

Jewelry, heirlooms and works of art are exempt to the extent of $2,500 in aggregate equity. (C.C.P. 704.040.)

(5) [§310A] (New) Health Aids.

Health aids reasonably necessary to enable the debtor or the spouse or a dependent of the debtor to work or sustain health, and prosthetic and orthopedic appliances, are exempt. (C.C.P. 704.050; see Law Rev. Com. Comment, Pamphlet, p. 1401 [the exemption applies to such items as a wheelchair for a person unable to walk to work or an air conditioner needed by a person afflicted with asthma; the exemption does not apply to a swimming pool, sauna, bicycle or golf clubs merely because their use is necessary to sustain good health].)

(6) [§311A] (New) Personal Property Used in Trade, Business or Profession.

"Tools, implements, instruments, materials, uniforms, furnishings, books, equipment, one commercial motor vehicle, one vessel, and other personal property" are exempt to the extent that the aggregate equity therein does not exceed $2,500. To qualify for the exemption the property must be *reasonably necessary to* and *actually used* by either the debtor or his spouse in the exercise of the trade, business or profession by which the debtor or his spouse earns a livelihood. (C.C.P. 704.060(a)(1)(2).)

An exemption of up to $5,000 may be claimed by the debtor and his spouse if they are engaged in the same trade, business or profession and earn their livelihood therein. If the joint exemption is claimed, the debtor or his spouse may not claim the individual exemptions of $2,500. (C.C.P. 704.060(a)(3).)

The proceeds from an execution sale of the property or of insurance or other indemnification obtained due to the loss, damage or destruction of the property are exempt for 90 days after the proceeds are actually received by the debtor or the spouse. The exempt amount is that applied to the particular case less the aggregate equity of any other property to which the exemption has been applied. (C.C.P. 704.060(b).)

This exemption does not apply to a motor vehicle if there is another motor vehicle which is reasonably adequate for use in the trade, business or profession of the debtor or the spouse and the other motor vehicle has been exempted under C.C.P. 704.010 (see Supp., supra, §306A). (C.C.P. 704.060(c).)

See 14 Pacific L.J. 416.

(7) [§312A] (New) Paid Earnings.

All paid earnings traceable into deposit accounts or in cash or its equivalent as provided in C.C.P. 703.080 (see Supp., supra, §295A) are exempt if, prior to payment to the employee, they were subject to an earnings withholding order (see C.C.P. 706.010 et seq., Supp., infra, §338A,344A) or a wage assignment for support (see C.C.P. 706.011, Supp., infra, §338A,345A). (C.C.P. 704.070(b)(1); see Legislative Com. Comment—Assembly, Pamphlet, p. 1403.)

Paid earnings traceable into deposit accounts or in cash or its equivalent are exempt in the amount of 75% if, prior to payment to the employee, they were not subject to an earnings withholding order or a wage assignment for support. (C.C.P. 704.070(b)(2).)

"Paid earnings" are earnings as defined in C.C.P. 706.011 (see Supp., infra, §338A) paid to the employee during the 30-day period ending on the date of the levy. Where paid earnings are subjected to the enforcement of a money judgment other than by a levy, the date of levy is deemed to be the date the earnings were otherwise subjected to the enforcement of the judgment. (C.C.P. 704.070(a)(2).)

(8) [§313A] (New) Deposit Account for Social Security.

(a) *Nature of Account.* The statute applies to deposit accounts in which the United States government directly deposits authorized Social Security payments in the form of regular retirement and survivors' benefits, supplemental security income benefits, coal miners' health benefits and disability insurance benefits. (C.C.P. 704.080(a).)

(b) *Amount of Exemption.* The amount of the exemption *without making a claim* is $500 for deposit accounts in which one depositor is the designated payee of the Social Security payments. (C.C.P. 704.080(b)(1).) The amount is $750 if two or more depositors are the designated payees of the directly deposited payments. However, if the depositors are joint payees of the directly deposited payments and the payments represent a benefit to only one of them, the exempt amount is $500. (C.C.P. 704.080(b)(2).)

The balance of the account is exempt to the extent that it consists of payments authorized by the Social Security Administration. (C.C.P. 704.080(c).)

(c) *Prohibiting Withdrawal of Balance.* Notwithstanding C.C.P. 701.010 et seq. (see Supp., supra, §278A et seq.), the financial institution holding the deposit account which is levied upon or subject to enforcement of a judgment must either place the balance in a suspense account or otherwise prohibit its withdrawal pending notification of the creditor's failure to file the required affidavit (see infra, this section) or the judicial determination of the status of the balance.

Within 10 *business* days after the levy, the financial institution must provide the levying officer with a written notice stating (1) that the account is a deposit account (see supra) and (2) the amount of the balance in excess of the statutory exemption. Promptly upon receipt of the notice, the levying officer must serve the notice on the creditor, either personally or by mail. (C.C.P. 704.080(d).)

(d) *Determination of Exempt Balance.* Notwithstanding the procedure prescribed in C.C.P. 703.510 (see Supp., supra, §300A), the status of the balance of the account must be determined as follows:

(1) Within five days after service of the notice, a creditor desiring to claim that the balance is not exempt must file with the court and with the levying officer an affidavit so alleging. The affidavit must be in the form of the notice of opposition provided by C.C.P. 703.560 (see Supp., supra, §303A). A hearing must be set and held, and notice given, as provided in C.C.P. 703.570, 703.580 (see Supp., supra, §304A). (C.C.P. 704.080(e)(1); see Legislative Com. Comment—Assembly, Pamphlet, p. 1406 [the 5-day period of limitation is extended if the service is made by mail].)

(2) If the creditor fails to file the affidavit with the levying officer and fails to give notice of the hearing within the time provided (10 days prior to hearing date; see Supp., supra, §304A), the levying officer must release the deposit account and notify the financial institution. (C.C.P. 704.080(e)(2).)

(3) The affidavit constitutes the pleading of the creditor, subject to the court's power to permit amendments in the interest of justice. No counteraffidavit is required. (C.C.P. 704.080(e)(3).)

(4) At the hearing the debtor has the burden of proving that the balance is exempt. (C.C.P. 704.080(e)(4).)

(5) The court by order must determine at the conclusion of the hearing whether the balance of the deposit account is totally or partially exempt, and must make an appropriate order for its prompt disposition. No findings are required. (C.C.P. 704.080(e)(5).)

(6) The court must *immediately* transmit a certified copy of its order determining the status of the balance to the financial institution and to the levying officer. Within 3 business days of receipt of the order, the institution must release any part of the balance deemed to be exempt. (C.C.P. 704.080(e)(6).)

(e) *Exemption Based on Other Grounds.* A claim by the debtor that a portion of the balance is exempt on other grounds must be made pursuant to C.C.P. 703.510 et seq. (see Supp., supra, §300A et seq). Such claim of exemption must be determined at the hearing (see supra), provided the debtor has complied with C.C.P. 703.510 et seq. (C.C.P. 704.080(f).)

(9)   [§314A]   (New) Inmate's Trust Account.

The funds of a debtor-inmate, held in trust for him or to his credit, in an inmate's trust account or similar account by the state, a county or city, or any agency thereof, are exempt without making a claim in the amount of $1,000. The exemption applies to debtor-inmates confined in a prison or facility under the jurisdiction of the Department of Corrections or the Department of the Youth Authority, or in any county or city jail, road camp, industrial farm or other local correctional facility. The spouse of the debtor-inmate is entitled to a separate exemption or the spouses may combine their exemptions. (C.C.P. 704.090.)

(10)   [§315A]   (New) Life Insurance, Endowment, Annuity Policies.

Unmatured life insurance policies (including endowment and annuity policies) are exempt *without making a claim,* except as to their loan value. (C.C.P. 704.100(a); see Legislative Com. Comment—Assembly, Pamphlet, p. 1408.)

The aggregate loan value of such policies is exempt in the amount of $4,000. If the debtor is married, each spouse is entitled to a separate exemption of $4,000 or the exemptions may be added together, regardless of whether the policies belong to either or both spouses or whether the debtor's spouse is also a debtor under the judgment. The exemption must first be applied to policies other than that before the court and then, if the exemption is not exhausted, to the policy before the court. (C.C.P. 704.100(b).)

Benefits from *matured* policies are exempt to the extent reasonably necessary to support the debtor and his spouse and dependents. (C.C.P. 704.100(c).)

See 14 Pacific L.J. 417.

(11) [§316A] (New) Public Retirement Benefits.

(a) *Unpaid Benefits.* All amounts held, controlled or in the process of being distributed by a public entity (defined infra, this section), and derived from contributions by the public entity or by its officers or employees for public retirement benefit purposes, are exempt without making a claim. Also exempt without a claim are all rights and benefits accrued or accruing to any person under a public retirement system (defined infra, this section). (C.C.P. 704.110(b).)

(b) *Definitions.* C.C.P. 704.110 defines the following terms:

(1) "Public entity" is "the state, or a city, city and county, county, or other political subdivision of the state, or a public trust, public corporation, or public board, or the governing body of any of them." The definition does not include the United States unless expressly provided in the statute. (C.C.P. 704.110(a)(1).)

(2) "Public retirement benefit" refers to "a pension or an annuity, or a retirement, disability, death, or other benefit, paid or payable by a public retirement system." (C.C.P. 704.110(a)(2).)

(3) "Public retirement system" is defined as a statutory system established by a public entity for "retirment, annuity, or other pension purposes or payment of disability or death benefits." (C.C.P. 704.110(a)(3).)

(c) *Judgment for Child or Spousal Support.* Where amounts described in C.C.P. 704.110(b) become payable and are sought to be applied to the satisfaction of a judgment for child or spousal support, they are generally exempt only to the extent that the court determines under C.C.P. 703.070 (see Supp., supra, §294A). (C.C.P. 704.110(c)(1).)

However, if the amount in question is payable *periodically,* it is subject to a wage assignment for support (see Supp., infra, §338A, 345A) or any other applicable enforcement procedure, except that the amount to be withheld must not exceed that permitted to be withheld on an earnings withholding order for support (see Supp., infra, §344A). A maximum fee of $2 for actual administrative costs may be deducted by the paying entity from each payment made pursuant to a wage assignment under this statute. (C.C.P. 704.110(c)(2).)

(d) *Paid Benefits.* All amounts received by a resident of the state as a public retirement benefit or as a return of contributions and interest thereon are exempt upon making a claim, whether they are from the United States, a public entity or a public retirement system.

(C.C.P. 704.110(d); see Law Rev. Com. Recommendation, Pamphlet, p. 1087.)

(12) [§317A] (New) Public Employee Vacation Credits.

Vacation credits accumulated by a state employee pursuant to Govt.C. 18050 or by any other public employee pursuant to applicable law are exempt without making a claim. (C.C.P. 704.113(a)(b).)

Amounts representing vacation credits which are paid periodically or as a lump sum are exempt to the same extent as earnings of a debtor. Such amounts are subject to any earnings withholding order (see Supp., infra, §338A et seq.) or any wage assignment for support (see Supp., infra, §345A). (C.C.P. 704.113(c).)

(13) [§318A] (New) Private Retirement Benefits.

(a) *Unpaid Benefits.* "All amounts held, controlled, or in process of distribution by a private retirement plan (defined infra, this section), for the payment of benefits as an annuity, pension, retirement allowance, disability payment, or death benefit from a private retirement plan are exempt." (C.C.P. 704.115(b).)

(b) *Definitions.* A "private retirement plan" includes, but is not limited to, union retirement plans; profit-sharing plans designed and used for retirement purposes; and self-employed retirement plans and individual retirement annuities or accounts provided for in the Internal Revenue Code, to the extent the amounts held therein do not exceed the maximum amounts exempt from federal income taxation under the Code. (C.C.P. 704.115(a).)

(c) *Judgment for Child or Spousal Support.* An amount described in C.C.P. 704.115(b) (see supra) which becomes payable and is sought to be applied to the satisfaction of a judgment for child or spousal support is generally exempt only to the extent that the court determines under C.C.P. 703.070 (see Supp., supra, §____). (C.C.P. 704.115(c)(1).)

However, if the amount sought to be applied to the satisfaction of the judgment for child or spousal support is payable *periodically,* that amount is subject to a wage assignment for support (see Supp., infra §____), except that the amount to be withheld must not exceed the amount permitted to be withheld on an earnings withholding order for support (see Supp., infra, §____). (C.C.P. 704.115(c)(2).)

(d) *Paid Benefits.* After payment, the amounts from a private retirement plan and all contributions and interest thereon returned to any member of such plan are exempt. (C.C.P. 704.115(d).)

(e) *Self-Employed and Individual Retirement Benefits.* Except for amounts payable periodically (see infra, this section), the amounts obtained from self-employed retirement plans and individual retirement annuities or accounts are exempt only to the extent necessary to provide for the support of the debtor upon retirement and for the support of his spouse and dependents, taking into account all resources that are likely to be available for such support. In determining the amount of the exemption, the court must allow the debtor such additional amount as is necessary to pay any federal and state income taxes payable as a result of the application of self-employed and individual retirement benefits to the satisfaction of a money judgment. (C.C.P. 704.115(e); see Legislative Com. Comment—Assembly, Pamphlet, p. 1413.)

Where the self-employed and individual retirement benefits are payable *periodically,* the amount of such payment that may be applied to the satisfaction of a money judgment is the same as that which may be withheld from a like amount of earnings under the Wage Garnishment Law (see C.C.P. 706.010 et seq., Supp., infra, §338A et seq.). (C.C.P. 704.115(f).)

(14) [§319A] (New) Unemployment Benefits and Strike Benefits.

(a) *Unemployment Contributions.* Contributions by workers to the Unemployment Compensation Disability Fund and by employers to the Unemployment Fund are exempt without making a claim. (C.C.P. 704.120(a).)

(b) *Unpaid Benefits.* Amounts held for payment of the following benefits are exempt without making a claim: (1) Unemployment compensation benefits payable under Unemp.Ins.C. 100 et seq.; (2) unemployment compensation disability benefits payable under Unemp.Ins.C. 2601 et seq.; (3) extended duration benefits payable under Unemp.Ins.C. 3501 et seq.; (4) federal-state extended benefits payable under Unemp.Ins.C. 4001 et seq.; (5) incentive payments payable under Unemp.Ins.C. 5000 et seq.; (6) benefits under an employer's plan or system that makes provision for employees generally or for a class or group of employees to supplement unemployment compensation benefits; (7) unemployment benefits paid to bona fide members by a fraternal organization; (8) union benefits payable due to a labor dispute. (C.C.P. 704.120(b); on unemployment compensation, see 1 *Summary, Agency and Employment,* §60 et seq.)

See 14 Pacific L.J. 417.

(c) *Paid Benefits.* After payment, the benefits listed in C.C.P. 704.120(b) are exempt upon making a claim. (C.C.P. 704.120(c); see Law Rev. Com. Recommendation, Pamphlet, p. 1089.)

(d) *Judgment for Child Support.* If benefits exempt under C.C.P.

704.120(b) become payable and are sought to be applied to the satisfaction of a judgment for child support, the benefits are generally exempt only to the extent that the court determines under C.C.P. 703.070(c) (see Supp., supra, §294A). (C.C.P. 704.120(d)(1).)

However, if the amount to be applied to the satisfaction of the judgment is payable *periodically,* that amount is subject to a wage assignment for support (see Supp., infra, §338A, 345A) or any other applicable enforcement procedure, except that the amount to be withheld must not exceed the amount permitted to be withheld on an earnings withholding order for support (see Supp., infra, §344A). A maximum fee of $2 for actual administration costs may be deducted by the paying entity from each payment made pursuant to a wage assignment. (C.C.P. 704.120(d)(1); see Legislative Com. Comment— Senate, Pamphlet, p. 1415.)

(15) [§320A] (New) Disability and Health Benefits.

Unpaid benefits from a disability or health insurance policy or program are exempt without making a claim. Paid benefits are exempt upon making a claim of exemption. (C.C.P. 704.130(a); see Law Rev. Com. Recommendation, Pamphlet, p. 1089.) However, these exemptions do not apply to benefits that are paid or payable to cover the cost of health care if the creditor is a provider of health care whose claim is the basis on which the benefits are paid or payable. (C.C.P. 704.130(b).)

(16) [§321A] (New) Damages For Personal Injury.

A cause of action for personal injury is exempt without making a claim, unless otherwise provided in C.C.P. 708.410 et seq. (see Supp., infra, §379A et seq.). (C.C.P. 704.140(a); see Law Rev. Com. Comment, Pamphlet, p. 1416.)

An award of damages or a settlement in a personal injury action is exempt to the extent necessary for the support of the debtor and his spouse and dependents. (C.C.P. 704.140(b).) However, this exemption does not apply if the creditor is a provider of health care whose claim of exemption is based on the providing of health care for the personal injury for which the award or settlement was made. (C.C.P. 704.140(c).) And if the award of damages or settlement is payable *periodically,* the amount of such payment that may be applied to the satisfaction of a money judgment is the amount that may be withheld from a similar amount of earnings under the Wage Garnishment Law (see Supp., infra, §338A et seq.). (C.C.P. 704.140(d).)

[211]

(17) [§322A] (New) Damages For Wrongful Death.

A cause of action for wrongful death is exempt without making a claim, unless otherwise provided in C.C.P. 708.410 et seq. (see Supp., infra, §379A et seq.). (C.C.P. 704.150(a).)

An award of damages or a settlement arising out of the wrongful death of the debtor's spouse or a person on whom the debtor or his spouse was dependent is exempt to the extent reasonably necessary for support of the debtor and his spouse and dependents. (C.C.P. 704.150(b).) However, if such award of damages or settlement is payable *periodically,* the amount of such payment that may be applied to the satisfaction of a money judgment is the same as the amount that may be withheld from a like amount of earnings under the Wage Garnishment Law (see Supp., infra, §338A et seq.). (C.C.P. 704.150(c).)

(18) [§323A] (New) Workers' Compensation.

Unless otherwise provided by the Labor Code statutes on compensation claims (Lab.C. 4900 et seq; see 2 *Summary, Workmen's Compensation,* §219 et seq.), a claim for workers' compensation or workers' compensation awarded or adjudged is exempt before payment without making a claim. After payment, a claim of exemption must be made. (C.C.P. 704.160.)

(19) [§324A] (New) Aid to Needy Persons.

Social service benefits provided pursuant to Welf.C. 10000 et seq. or similar aid provided by a charitable organization or a fraternal benefit society (see Ins.C. 10990) is exempt before payment without making a claim. After payment, a claim of exemption must be made. (C.C.P. 704.170; see Law Rev. Com. Recommendation, Pamphlet, p. 1090.)

(20) [§325A] (New) Relocation Benefits.

Relocation benefits for displacement from a dwelling, to be paid pursuant to Govt.C. 7260 et seq. or the federal Uniform Relocation Assistance and Real Property Acquisition Policies Act of 1970 (42 U.S.C., §4601 et seq.), are exempt before payment without making a claim. After payment, a claim of exemption for the benefits must be made. (C.C.P. 704.180; see Law Rev. Com. Recommendation, Pamphlet, p. 1090.)

(21) [§326A] (New) Financial Aid to Student.

Financial aid for expenses while attending school provided to a student by an institution of higher education is exempt before payment without making a claim. After payment, a claim of exemption for such aid must be made. (C.C.P. 704.190(b); see Law Rev. Com. Recommendation, Pamphlet, p. 1091.)

The definition of an "institution of higher education" is in 20 U.S.C., §1141(a). (C.C.P. 704.190(a); see Legislative Com. Comment —Senate, Pamphlet, p. 1418 [quoting the federal statute in full].)

(22) [§327A] (New) Cemetery Plot.

A *family plot* as described in Health & Saf.C. 8650 is exempt without making a claim. (C.C.P. 704.200(b).) A plot (as described in Health & Saf.C. 7022) in a cemetery (as described in Health & Saf.C. 7003) for the debtor and his spouse is also exempt. (C.C.P. 704.200(c).) However, "[L] and held for the purpose of sale or disposition as cemetery plots or otherwise is not exempt." (C.C.P. 704.200(d).)

See Law Rev. Com. Comment, Pamphlet, p. 1419.

(d) (New) Homestead Exemption.

(1) [§328A] (New) In General.

(a) *Former Law.* The original homestead exemption applied only to a dwelling which had been declared a homestead by recording such a declaration in the county in which the dwelling was situated (see text, §38). Since most homeowners neglected to declare a homestead on their residences, the Legislature extended the homestead exemption to dwellings which had not been declared homesteads (see Supp., supra, §49A et seq.). C.C.P. 704.710 et seq. now apply the same procedures for obtaining a homestead exemption to declared homesteads, undeclared homesteads and mobile homes or vessels. (Law Rev. Com. Recommendation, Pamphlet, p. 1092.)

(b) *Definitions Under New Law.* C.C.P. 704.710 defines the following important terms:

(a) "Dwelling" means a place where a person actually resides and includes, but is not limited to, (1) a house, its outbuildings and the land upon which they are located; (2) a mobile home, its outbuildings and the land upon which they are located; (3) a boat or other waterborne vessel; (4) a condominium as defined in C.C. 783; (5) a planned development as defined in B. & P.C. 11003; (6) a stock cooperative as defined in B. & P.C. 11003.2; (7) a community apartment project as defined in B. & P.C. 11004. (C.C.P. 704.710(a); see Legislative Com. Comment—Senate, Pamphlet, p. 1421 [definition of "dwelling" is intended to include all property for which an exemption could have been claimed under former law and any other property in which the debtor or his spouse actually resides].)

[213]

(b) "Family unit," as defined in C.C.P. 704.710(b), means any of the following:

(1) The debtor and his spouse if the spouses reside together in the homestead.

(2) The debtor and *at least one* of the following persons whom he cares for or maintains in the homestead: (a) The minor child or minor grandchild of the debtor or his spouse or the minor child or grandchild of his deceased spouse or former spouse; (b) the minor brother or sister of the debtor or his spouse or the minor child of a deceased brother or sister of either spouse; (c) the father, mother, grandfather or grandmother of the debtor or his spouse or of his deceased spouse; (d) an unmarried relative falling within the relationships listed above who has reached his majority but is unable to care for or support himself.

(3) The debtor's spouse and *at least one* of the relatives listed above whom the spouse cares for or maintains in the homestead.

(c) "Homestead" is the principal dwelling (1) in which the debtor or his spouse actually reside on the date the creditor's lien attach to the dwelling, and (2) in which the debtor or his spouse actually resided continuously thereafter until the date of the court's determination that the dwelling was a homestead. (C.C.P. 704.710(c).)

If exempt proceeds from the sale or damage or destruction of a homestead are used toward the acquisition of a dwelling within the 6-month period provided by C.C.P. 704.720 (see infra, this section), that dwelling is also a "homestead" if it is the principal dwelling in which the debtor or his spouse actually resided continuously from the date of acquisition until the date the court determines that the dwelling is a homestead. This rule applies whether or not an abstract or certified copy of a judgment was recorded to create a judgment lien before the dwelling was acquired. (C.C.P. 704.710(c); see Legislative Com. Comment—Senate, Pamphlet, p. 1421.)

(d) "Spouse" does not include a married person following entry of a judgment of legal separation of the parties, or an interlocutory judgment of dissolution, unless such married persons reside together in the same dwelling. (C.C.P. 704.710(d).)

(c) *Homestead Exemption.* A homestead is exempt from sale to the extent provided in C.C.P. 704.800 (see Supp., infra, §333A). (C.C.P. 704.720(a).) If a homestead is sold, damaged or destroyed, or acquired for public use, the proceeds, indemnification or compensation therefrom are exempt, to the extent provided in C.C.P. 704.730 (see Supp., infra, §329A), for 6 months after being *actually* received by the debtor, unless a homestead exemption is applied to other property of the debtor or his spouse during such period. (C.C.P. 704.720(b).)

If the debtor and his spouse reside in *separate* homesteads, only one homestead is exempt, and only the proceeds of the exempt homestead are exempt. (C.C.P. 704.720(c).)

See Legislative Com. Comment—Senate, Pamphlet, p. 1422.

On the homestead exemption under the new law, see 14 Pacific L.J. 418.

(2) [§329A] (New) Amount of Exemption.

The amount of the homestead exemption is $45,000 if the debtor or his spouse who resides in the homestead is either or both (a) 65 or older (C.C.P. 704.730(a)(2)(A)) or (b) a member of a family unit, provided there is at least one member of the unit who owns no interest in the homestead or whose only interest is a community property interest with the debtor (C.C.P. 704.730(a)(2)(B)). (See Leg. Com. Comment—Assembly, Pamphlet, p. 1424.)

The combined homestead exemptions of spouses on the same judgment may not exceed $45,000, regardless of whether they are jointly obligated on the judgment and regardless of whether the homestead consists of community or separate property or both. If both spouses are entitled to the exemption, the exemption of proceeds of the homestead must be apportioned between them on the basis of their proportionate interests in the homestead. (C.C.P. 704.730(b); see Legislative Com. Comment—Assembly, Pamphlet, p. 1424.)

In all other cases, the amount of the exemption is $30,000. (C.C.P. 704.730(a)(1).)

See 14 Pacific L.J. 418.

(3) (New) Court Order for Sale.

(aa) [§330A] (New) When Order Is Required.

A court order for sale is *not* required if the dwelling is personal property or real property in which the debtor has a leasehold estate with an unexpired term of less than 2 years at the time of levy. (C.C.P. 704.740(b)(1).) In such cases an exemption claim must be made as provided in C.C.P. 703.510 et seq. (see Supp., supra, §300A et seq.). (C.C.P. 704.740(b)(2).)

In all other cases a court order for sale is required before a dwelling may be sold to enforce a money judgment. (C.C.P. 704.740(a); see Legislative Com. Comment, Pamphlet, p. 1425.)

(bb) [§331A] (New) Application For Order.

(1) *Dwelling in County of Judgment.* Promptly after a dwelling (other than one described in C.C.P. 704.740(b); see Supp., supra,

§330A) is levied upon, the levying officer must serve notice, either personally or by mail, upon the creditor, that the levy has been made and that the property will be released unless the creditor, within 20 days after service of the notice, applies to the court for an order for sale and files a copy of the application with the levying officer. The levying officer must release the dwelling if the creditor fails to file within the allowed time. (C.C.P. 704.750(a); see Legislative Com. Comment, Pamphlet, p. 1426.)

(2) *Dwelling Outside the County of Judgment.* In this situation C.C.P. 704.750(b) requires the creditor to (a) apply for an order for sale to a court in the dwelling county having jurisdiction similar to the court in the judgment county or, if no court of similar jurisdiction exists, to a court of higher jurisdiction in the dwelling county; (b) file with the application an abstract of judgment or, if the judgment is one described in C.C.P. 697.320 (see Supp., supra, §245A), a certified copy of the judgment; (c) Pay a filing fee of $12 (no law library fee is required).

(3) *Contents of Application.* The creditor's application for an order for sale must be made under oath, must describe the dwelling, and must include all of the following:

(a) A statement whether the records of the county tax assessor indicate a current homeowner's exemption or disabled veteran's exemption for the dwelling and the person or persons claiming the exemption. (C.C.P. 704.760(a).)

(b) A statement whether the dwelling is a homestead and the amount of any homestead exemption. The statement may be based upon information and belief. Also required is a statement whether the records of the county recorder indicate that a homestead declaration (see Supp., infra, §334A) describing the dwelling has been recorded by the debtor or his spouse. (C.C.P. 704.760(b).)

(c) A statement of the amount of any liens or encumbrances on the dwelling, the name of each person holding such lien or encumbrance, and the address of such person as used by the county court for the return of the instrument creating the lien or encumbrance after recording. (C.C.P. 704.760(c).)

See 14 Pacific L.J. 419.

(cc) [§332A] (New) Hearing and Order.

(1) *Time of Hearing.* After the creditor has filed an application for an order for sale of a dwelling, the court must set a time and place for a hearing and order the debtor to show cause why the order for sale should not be made. The hearing must be scheduled no later

than 45 days after the filing of the application, unless time is extended for good cause. (C.C.P. 704.770(a).)

(2) *Service of Documents.* Not later than 30 days before the hearing date, the creditor must do both of the following:

(a) Serve on the debtor, either personally or by mail, copies of the order to show cause, the application and the notice of the hearing in the form prescribed in C.C.P. 693.050 (see Supp., supra, §234A). (C.C.P. 704.770(b)(1); see Legislative Com. Comment—Assembly, Pamphlet, p. 1427.)

(b) Personally serve a copy of each of the documents listed above on an occupant of the dwelling or post a copy of such documents in a conspicuous place at the dwelling if no occupant is present at the time personal service is attempted. (C.C.P. 704.770(b)(2).)

(3) *Burden of Proof at Hearing.* The burden of proof is allocated as follows:

(a) If the records of the county tax assessor indicate that either the debtor or his spouse claims a current homeowner's exemption or disabled veteran's exemption for the dwelling, the burden of proving that the dwelling is not a homestead falls upon the *creditor.* If the assessor's records indicate that neither the debtor nor his spouse claim a current homeowner's exemption, the person claiming that the dwelling is a homestead bears the burden of proving that claim. (C.C.P. 704.780(a)(1).)

(b) If the amount of the homestead exemption is stated in the application, the person claiming the exemption has the burden of proving that the amount of the exemption is other than that stated in the application. (C.C.P. 704.780(a)(2).)

(4) *Determination of Exemption.* The court must determine the amount of any homestead exemption and the fair market value of the dwelling. The court must also make an order for sale of the dwelling and include therein the name and address of each person having a lien or encumbrance on the dwelling and the specific amount of the proceeds of the sale to be distributed to such person. Unless otherwise provided, the sale is governed by C.C.P. 701.510 et seq. (see Supp., supra, §282A et seq.). (C.C.P. 704.780(b).)

The court may appoint a qualified appraiser to assist in determining the dwelling's fair market value, and may fix the compensation of the appraiser in a reasonable amount. (C.C.P. 704.780(d).)

(5) *Transmittal of Order.* The court clerk must transmit a certified copy of the court order to the levying officer, and to the clerk of the court in which the judgment was entered if such court is not the same as that making the order for sale. (C.C.P. 704.780(c).)

See 14 Pacific L.J. 420.

(dd)   [§333A]   (New) Procedure After Order of Sale.

(1) *Where Claimant Defaults.* C.C.P. 704.790 contains procedures to be used in cases in which an order of sale is granted upon default. The statute applies in those instances in which neither the debtor nor his spouse nor their attorneys were present at the hearing on the application for an order for sale. (C.C.P. 704.790(a).)

Not more than 10 days after the date of the order for sale, the creditor must serve a copy of the order and a notice of the order in the form prescribed in C.C.P. 693.060 as follows:

(a) Personally or by mail on the debtor and his spouse. (C.C.P. 704.790(b)(1).)

(b) Personally on an occupant of the dwelling or by posting a copy of the order and notice in a conspicuous place at the dwelling if no occupant is present at the time service is attempted. (C.C.P. 704.790(b)(2).)

The creditor must file proof of service and of any posting with the court and with the levying officer. If the creditor fails to comply with the requirements for service and filing, the dwelling may not be sold under the order for sale. (C.C.P. 704.790(c).)

The debtor or his spouse has 10 days after service of the notice of the order within which to file with the levying officer a declaration seeking relief from the default. The declaration must state (1) that their absence from the hearing was due to mistake, inadvertence, surprise or excusable neglect, and (2) that the debtor or his spouse wishes to assert the homestead exemption. The levying officer must then immediately transmit the declaration to the court, which has 20 days within which to set a time and place for a hearing to consider whether its determinations should be modified. The court clerk must promptly issue notice of the hearing to all parties. (C.C.P. 704.790(d).)

See 14 Pacific L.J. 421.

(2) *Minimum Bid.* If no bid at a sale of a homestead pursuant to an order for sale exceeds the amount of the homestead exemption plus any additional amount necessary to satisfy all liens and encumbrances on the property, the homestead may not be sold and must be released. The homestead is not subject to a court order for sale upon subsequent application *by the same creditor* for a period of one year. (C.C.P. 704.800(a).)

If there is no bid that is 90% or more of the fair market value (see Supp., supra, §332A), the homestead may not be sold unless the court, upon motion of the creditor, either (a) grants permission to accept the highest bid that exceeds the amount of the minimum bid (see supra) or (b) makes a new order for sale. (C.C.P. 704.800(b).)

See 14 Pacific L.J. 421.

(3) *Acceleration Clauses and Prepayment Penalties.* Notwithstanding any provision of an obligation, lien or encumbrance on a homestead levy on such a homestead is not by itself ground for acceleration of the obligation secured by the lien or encumbrance. If a homestead is sold pursuant to court order under this statute, the amount payable to satisfy the lien or encumbrance may not include any penalty for prepayment. (C.C.P. 704.810.)

(4) *Where Judgment Debtor is Co-Owner or Owns Less Than Fee.* If the dwelling at an execution sale is owned by the debtor as a joint tenant or tenant in common or if the debtor's interest is a leasehold or other interest less than a fee, the debtor's interest in the dwelling, and not the dwelling itself, is to be sold. In the case of multiple debtors of the same creditor, the debtors' interest must be sold together. Each debtor entitled to a homestead exemption may apply his exemption to his own interest. (C.C.P. 704.820(a); see Legislative Com. Comment, Pamphlet, p. 1431.)

For purposes of this section, references elsewhere in the Homestead Exemption provisions to "dwelling" or "homestead" are deemed to refer to the debtor's interest in the dwelling or homestead. (C.C.P. 704.820(b).)

(5) *Distribution of Proceeds.* C.C.P. 704.850(a) requires proceeds of a sale of a homestead to be distributed by the levying officer in the following order:

(a) To the discharge of any liens and encumbrances on the property.

(b) To the debtor in the amount of any applicable exemption of proceeds as determined by C.C.P. 704.720 (see Supp., supra, §328A).

(c) To the levying officer for the reimbursement of his costs for which an advance was not made.

(d) To the creditor to satisfy, in the order of priority, (1) costs and interest accruing after issuance of the writ authorizing the sale, and (2) the amount due on the judgment as entered on the writ, together with costs and interest.

(e) The remaining proceeds to the debtor.

The provisions governing the time for distributing proceeds (C.C.P. 701.820; see Supp., supra, §289A) and the resolution of conflicting claims to proceeds (C.C.P. 701.830; see Supp., supra, §290A) apply to the distribution of homestead sale proceeds. (C.C.P. 704.850(b).)

See Legislative Com. Comment—Senate, Pamphlet, p. 1433.

(6) *Extensions of Time and Appeals.* The provisions of C.C.P. 703.590 (see Supp., supra, §300A) and 703.600 (see Supp., supra,

§300A) relating to extensions of time and appeals apply to proceedings after the issuance of an order of sale. (C.C.P. 704.830.)

(7) *Costs.* The creditor is ordinarily entitled to recover reasonable costs incurred in a proceeding for the sale of a homestead. However, if no bid is received at the sale that exceeds the amount of the homestead exemption plus any additional amount necessary to satisfy all liens and encumbrances on the property, costs may *not* be recovered. (C.C.P. 704.840.)

(e)   (New) Declared Homesteads.

(1)   [§334A]   (New) Nature of Homestead.

(a) *In General.* C.C.P. 704.910 et seq. provide for a homestead declaration designed to protect a homestead from the attachment of a judgment lien. (See Legislative Com. Comment—Senate, Pamphlet, p. 1434.) C.C.P. 704.910 lists the following definitions applicable to procedures for the declaration of a homestead:

(1) A "declared homestead" is the dwelling described in the homestead declaration. (C.C.P. 704.910(a).)

(2) The term "declared homestead owner" includes both (a) the owner of an interest in the declared homestead who is named as a declared homestead owner in a recorded declaration, and (b) the declarant named in a homestead declaration recorded prior to July 1, 1983, pursuant to former C.C. 1237 et seq., and the declarant's spouse. (C.C.P. 704.910(b).)

(3) "Dwelling" means any interest in *real property* (present or future, vested or contingent, legal or equitable) that is a "dwelling" as defined in C.C.P. 704.710 (see Supp., supra, §328A). "Dwelling" does not include a leasehold estate with an unexpired term of less than 2 years or the interest of the beneficiary of a trust. (C.C.P. 704.910(c).)

(4) A "homestead declaration" includes both a declaration recorded pursuant to this statute and a declaration recorded prior to July 1, 1983, pursuant to former C.C. 1237 et seq. (C.C.P. 704.910(d).)

(5) "Spouse" is a spouse as defined in C.C.P. 704.710 (see Supp., supra, §328A). (C.C.P. 704.910(e).)

(b) *Selection of Homestead.* A dwelling in which an owner or his spouse resides may be selected as a declared homestead. The selection is made by recording a homestead declaration in the office of the county recorder of the county in which the dwelling is located. The dwelling is a declared homestead from the time of recording. (C.C.P. 704.920.)

See 14 Pacific L.J. 422.

(2) [§335A] (New) Creation.

(a) *Contents of Declaration.* In addition to a statement of the declarant's personal knowledge of the facts (see infra, this section), a homestead declaration must contain (1) the declared homestead owner's name (may be husband *and* wife if each owns an interest in the dwelling selected); (2) a description of the dwelling; (3) a statement that the homestead is the principal dwelling of the owner or his spouse and that the owner or his spouse actually resides in the homestead on the date the declaration is recorded. (C.C.P. 704.930(a).)

(b) *Execution of Declaration.* The declaration must be executed and acknowledged in the manner of an acknowledgement of a conveyance of real property (see 3 *Summary, Real Property,* §100 et seq.). The execution of the declaration may be made by the declared homestead owner, his spouse, the guardian or conservator of the person or estate of either the owner of his spouse, or a person acting under a power of attorney or otherwise authorized to act on behalf of the owner or his spouse. The guardian or conservator need not obtain court authorization to execute, acknowledge or record the declaration. (C.C.P. 704.930(b).)

The declaration must include a statement that the facts stated therein are known to be true to the personal knowledge of the person executing and acknowledging the declaration. If the declaration is executed and acknowledged by a person other than the owner or his spouse, it must also contain a statement that such person has authority to act on behalf of the owner or his spouse, and the source of that authority. (C.C.P. 704.930(c).)

(c) *Effect of Declaration.* A homestead declaration does not restrict or limit any right to convey or encumber the homestead. When properly recorded, the declaration is prima facie evidence of the facts stated therein and is conclusive evidence in favor of a purchaser or encumbrancer in good faith and for a valuable consideration. (C.C.P. 704.940; see Legislative Com. Comment, Pamphlet, p. 1437.)

(3) [§336A] (New) Effect of Creation.

(a) *Right To Convey or Encumber Property.* The right to convey or encumber the declared homestead is not restricted or limited in any way by the declaration. (C.C.P. 704.940; see Supp., supra, §335A.)

(b) *Levy of Execution.* The right of levy pursuant to a writ of execution is not affected by a homestead declaration, whether recorded or not. (C.C.P. 704.970(a); see Legislative Com. Comment— Senate, Pamphlet, p. 1440.)

Any levy and sale pursuant to a writ of execution on a dwelling must be made in compliance with C.C.P. 704.710 et seq. (see Supp., supra, §328A), and the debtor and the creditor have all the rights and benefits provided thereby. (C.C.P. 704.970.)

(c) *When Judgment Lien Does Not Attach.* a judgment lien on real property created pursuant to C.C.P. 697.310 et seq. (see Supp., supra, §245A et seq.) does *not* attach to a declared homestead if (1) a homestead declaration describing the homestead was recorded prior to creation of the lien, *and* (2) the declaration names the debtor or his spouse as a declared homestead owner. (C.C.P. 704.950(a); see Legislative Com. Comment—Senate, Pamphlet, p. 1438.)

The general rule of nonattachment does not apply to a judgment lien created by recording a certified copy of a judgment for child or spousal support (see Supp., supra, §245A). (C.C.P. 704.950(b).) Furthermore, a judgment lien *does attach* to a declared homestead in the amount of *any surplus* over the total of the homestead exemption (see C.C.P. 704.730, Supp., supra, §329A) *and* all liens and encumbrances on the homestead at the time of the creation of the lien. (C.C.P. 704.950(c).)

(d) *Proceeds of Sale Exempt.* The proceeds of *a voluntary sale* of a declared homestead are exempt in the amount provided by C.C.P. 704.730 (see Supp., supra, §329A) for a period of 6 months from the date of sale. (C.C.P. 704.960(a).)

If the proceeds of a declared homestead are invested in a new dwelling within 6 months after either the date of a voluntary sale or the receipt of proceeds from an execution sale or of insurance or other indemnification for damage or destruction, the new dwelling may be selected as a declared homestead by recording a homestead declaration within the applicable 6-month period. Such a homestead declaration has the same effect as if it had been recorded at the time of the recording of the prior declaration. (C.C.P. 704.960(b).)

(4) [§337A] (New) Abandonment.

(a) *Declaration of Abandonment.* A declared homestead may be abandoned by a declaration of abandonment. This rule applies whether the homestead declaration was recorded pursuant to the new or the former (C.C. 1237 et seq) homestead statutes. (C.C.P. 704.980(a).)

The declaration of abandonment is executed and acknowledged in the same way as an acknowledgment of a conveyance of real property (see 3 *Summary, Real Property,* §100 et seq.). It must be executed and acknowledged by a declared homestead owner or by a person authorized to act on his behalf. In the latter situation the declaration must contain a statement that the person has authority to act on behalf of the owner and the source of such authority. (C.C.P. 704.980(b).)

The declaration of abandonment affects only the declared homestead of the person named in the declaration. (C.C.P. 704.980(c); see Legislative Com. Comment—Senate, Pamphlet, p. 1441.)

(b) *Recording Homestead For Different Property.* If a declared homestead owner or a person authorized to act on his behalf executes, acknowledges and records a new homestead declaration on different property, the declared homestead on the original property is deemed abandoned by operation of law. This rule only affects the declared homestead of the declared homestead owner named in the new homestead declaration. (C.C.P. 704.990(a).)

However, the rule does not apply to a homestead declaration which includes property described in a previously recorded declaration. To the extent that the prior declaration is still valid, the new declaration is not considered an abandonment of the prior declared homestead. (C.C.P. 704.990(b).)

5. (New) Wage Garnishment.

(a) (New) In General.

(1) [§338A] (New) Nature of Law.

(a) *Former Law and Revision.* Chapter 5 of the new statute (C.C.P. 706.010 et seq.), to be cited as the "Wage Garnishment Law" (C.C.P. 706.010), continues the provisions of the former "Employee's Earnings Protection Law" (see Supp., supra, §133A et seq.) with some technical changes. (See Law Rev. Com. Recommendation, Pamphlet, p. 1123.) In addition to the new title, these changes include an expansion of the type of state taxes subject to garnishment (see Supp., infra, §347A et seq.). (See Law Rev. Com. Recommendation, Pamphlet, p. 1123, footnote 419.)

(b) *Definitions.* C.C.P. 706.011 defines a number of important terms as follows (see Legislative Com. Comment—Senate, Pamphlet, p. 1442; on definitions under former law, see Supp., supra, §133A): (1) *Earnings:* "compensation payable by an employer to an employee for personal services performed by such employee, whether denominated as wages, salary, commission, or otherwise." (2) *Employee:* "a public officer and any individual who performs services subject to the right of the employer to control both what shall be done and how it shall be done." (3) *Employer:* "a person for whom an individual performs services as an employee." (4) *Judgment creditor as applied to the State:* "the specific state agency seeking to collect a judgment or tax liability." (5) *Judgment debtor:* "includes a person from whom the state is seeking to collect a tax liability under Article 4 (commencing with Section 706.070), whether or not a judgment has been obtained on such tax liability." (See Supp., infra, §347A et seq.) (6) *Person:* "includes an individual, a corporation, a partnership or other unincorporated association, and a public entity." (7) *Wage assignment for support:* "an order, made pursuant to Section 4701 or 4801.6 of the Civil Code or Section 3088 of the Probate Code, which requires an employer to withhold earnings for support."

(c) *Exclusive Procedure.* Except for a wage assignment for support (see Supp., infra, §345A), the Wage Garnishment Law is the exclusive judicial procedure to compel an employer to withhold an employee's earnings for payment of a debt. (C.C.P. 706.020; see Law. Rev. Com. Comment, Pamphlet, p. 1443; see also C.C.P. 706.021 [levy of execution on earnings must be made in accordance with this Chapter, not under C.C.P. 699.010 et seq. (see Supp., supra, §249A et seq.)].)

The Wage Garnishment Law has no effect on (1) matters preempted by federal law, such as bankruptcy proceedings and federal tax collection procedures; (2) an employer's deductions for insurance premiums and payments to health, welfare or pension plans; and (3) procedures for examination of a debtor of the judgment debtor (see Supp., infra, §370A et seq.). (See Law Rev. Com. Comment, Pamphlet, p. 1444.)

(d) *No Findings Required.* "No findings are required in court proceedings under this chapter." (C.C.P. 706.106; see Law Rev. Com. Comment, Pamphlet, p. 1482.)

(2) [§339A] (New) Employer's Duty to Withhold.

Except as otherwise provided by statute (see, Supp., infra, §340A [ineffectiveness of subsequent withholding orders]) "an employer shall withhold the amounts required by an earnings withholding order from all earnings of the employee payable for any pay period of such employee which *ends* during the withholding period." (C.C.P. 706.022(b); see C.C.P. 706.022(c) [employer not liable for amounts withheld and paid over to levying officer prior to service of notice of termination (see infra, this section)]; Supp., supra, §133-I [former C.C.P. 723.022].)

The "withholding period" is defined in C.C.P. 706.022(a) as the period which *commences* on the 10th day after service of the withholding order, and continues until the *earliest* of the following dates: "(1) The 100th day after the order was served. (2) The date the employer has withheld the full amount specified in the order. (3) The date of termination specified in a court order served on the employer. (4) The date of termination specified in a notice of termination served on the employer by the levying officer." (See Legislative Com. Comment—Senate, Pamphlet, p. 1445.)

(3) [§340A] (New) Priority of Withholding Order.

Unless an exception for particular orders applies (see infra, this section), the rules governing the priority to be given withholding orders are as follows:

(a) *First order served:* The employer must comply with the first earnings withholding order served on him. (C.C.P. 706.023(a); see Legislative Com. Comment—Senate, Pamphlet, p. 1447; Supp., supra, §133Z [former C.C.P. 723.023].)

(b) *Order served on same day:* If two or more withholding orders are served on the same day, the employer must comply with the order issued pursuant to the judgment first entered. (C.C.P. 706.023(b); see C.C.P. 706.125(c), Supp., infra, §362A [order gives date of entry].) If the judgments were entered on the same day, the employer has discretion to select the one with which he will comply. (C.C.P. 706.023(b).)

(c) *Effect of subsequent orders:* A withholding order served while an employer is required to comply with another order with respect to the earnings of the same employee is ineffective. (C.C.P. 706.023(c); on requirement that ineffective orders be returned, rather than held and given effect when the prior order expires, see Supp., infra, §356A.)

The aforementioned priority rules do not govern withholding orders for support or for taxes, both of which are given priority over other orders (see Supp., infra, §344A [support orders], §351A [taxes].) (On the priority of wage assignments for support over *all* withholding orders, see Supp., infra, §____.)

(4) [§341A] (New) Employer's Payments to Levying Officer.

The amount withheld pursuant to an earnings withholding order must be paid to the levying officer not later than the 15th day of each month, the initial payment to include all amounts withheld during the preceding calendar month up to the close of the pay period ending closest to the last day of that month. Each subsequent monthly payment must include amounts withheld for services rendered in the interim up to the close of the pay period ending closest to the last day of the preceding calendar month. (C.C.P. 706.025(a); see Law Rev. Com. Comment, Pamphlet, p. 1448; Supp., supra, §133-I [Former C.C.P. 723.025.].)

The employer, however, may elect to make more frequent payments, to be made not later than 10 days after the close of the pay period. (C.C.P. 706.025(b).)

The levying officer must receive and account for the payments and, at least once every 30 days, turn them over to the person entitled thereto. (C.C.P. 706.026; see Law Rev. Com. Comment, Pamphlet, p. 1449.)

(5) [§342A] (New) Satisfaction of Judgment Before Termination of Order.

If the underlying judgment is satisfied before the order terminates (see Supp., supra, §339A), the creditor must promptly notify the levying officer, who must promptly serve a notice of termination on the employer. (C.C.P. 706.027; see Supp., supra, §133N [former C.C.P. 723.027]; Law Rev. Com. Comment, Pamphlet, p. 1449.)

(6) [§343A] (New) Subsequent Withholding Order for Costs and Interest.

Subject to the 10-day waiting period specified in C.C.P. 706.107 (see Supp., infra, §358A), the creditor, after the required amount is paid, may apply for another withholding order to cover costs and interest that may have accrued since the original application. (C.C.P. 706.028; see Supp., supra, §133P [former C.C.P. 723.028]; Law Rev. Com. Comment, Pamphlet, p. 1450.)

(7) [§344A] (New) Withholding Order For Support.

(a) *Definition.* A withholding order for support, which must be so designated on its face, is "an earnings withholding order issued on a writ of execution to collect delinquent amounts payable under a judgment for the support of a child, or spouse or former spouse, of the judgment debtor." (C.C.P. 706.030(a); on former C.C.P. 723.030, see Supp., supra, §§133V, 133X; see also Law Rev. Com. Comment, Pamphlet, p. 1452.)

(b) *Termination.* A withholding order for support does *not* terminate 100 days after service (see Supp., supra, §339A); the employer must continue to withhold earnings until the *earliest* of the times specified in C.C.P. 706.022(a)(2)(3)(4) (see Supp., supra, §339A). However, the order will automatically terminate one year after the employment ceases. (C.C.P. 706.030(b)(1); see Law Rev. Com. Comment, Pamphlet, p. 1452.)

(c) *Priority.* "A withholding order for support has priority over any other earnings withholding order." (C.C.P. 706.030(b)(2); as to the priority of a wage assignment for support, see Supp., infra, §345A.)

Although the support order has priority, it does not preclude another withholding order; the employer must withhold earnings pursuant to both the support order and another earnings withholdings order, deducting from the employee's earnings the amount withheld for support before withholding any amount pursuant to the other order. (C.C.P. 706.030(b)(2)(3); see Law Rev. Com. Comment, Pamphlet, p. 1452.)

(a)   [§345A]   (New) Priority of Wage Assignment for Support.

A wage assignment for support made pursuant to C.C. 4701 (child support), C.C. 4801.6 (spousal support), or Prob. C. 3088 (conservatee support) (see C.C.P. 706.010(g)) has priority over any earnings withholding order, including one for support. An employer served with a wage assignment for support must comply, notwithstanding the requirements of any withholding order. When an employer is required to cease withholding earnings pursuant to a withholding order, he must notify the levying officer of the supervening wage assignment for support. (C.C.P. 706.031(a)(b); see Law Rev. Com. Comment, Pamphlet, pg. 1454.)

Although a wage assignment for support has priority (see supra), an employer must withhold earnings pursuant to *both* a wage assignment and a withholding order. (C.C.P. 706.031(c).) However, the general rule is that the amount withheld under the wage assignment must be deducted from the amount that can be withheld pursuant to the withholding order. (C.C.P. 706.031(d)(e); Law Rev. Com. Comment, Pamphlet, p. 1454.) (On former C.C.P. 723.031, see Supp., supra, §133W.)

(b)   [346A]   (New) Restrictions On Earnings Withholding.

(1) *Amount of Earnings Exempt.* The standard or basic exemption is the amount specified in §1673(a) of the Federal Consumer Credit Protection Act of 1968. (C.C.P. 706.050; see Supp., supra, §133K [former C.C.P. 723.050].) That statute restricts garnishment for any workweek to 25% of disposable earnings or disposable earnings less 30 times the federal minimum hourly wage, whichever amount is less. This standard exemption applies to ordinary earnings withholding orders, but not to orders issued for child or spousal support (see infra, this section) or to *court-issued* withholding orders for taxes (see Supp., infra, §349A). (See Legislative Com. Comment—Assembly, Pamphlet, p. 1455.)

(2) *Earnings Necessary For Support of Debtor or His Family.* With certain exceptions (see infra, this section), the portion of the debtor's earnings which he proves is necessary for the support of himself or

his family supported in whole or in part by him is exempt from levy. (C.C.P. 706.051(b); see Supp., supra, §133K [former C.C.P. 723.051]; Legislative Com. Comment—Assembly, Pamphlet, p. 1456.) (On the procedure for claiming the exemption, see Supp., infra, §357A.) In this context, "family of the judgment debtor" includes his spouse or former spouse. (C.C.P. 706.051(a).)

This exemption does not apply to withholding orders for support (see Supp., supra, §344A) or taxes (see Supp., infra, §347A et seq.), or where the debt was incurred either for the common necessaries of life furnished to the debtor or his family or for personal services rendered by an employee or former employee of the debtor. (C.C.P. 706.051(c).)

(3) *Earnings Withholding Order For Support.* Except where the court makes an equitable division of the debtor's earnings (see infra, this section), the amount of his earnings exempt from levy under a withholding order for support is one half of his disposable earnings, plus any amount withheld pursuant to a wage assignment for support. "Disposable earnings" are defined as those remaining after any deductions required by law (see 15 U.S.C., §1672(b)). (C.C.P. 706.052(a); see Law Rev. Com. Comment, Pamphlet, p. 1457.)

Upon the motion of any interested party, the court must make "an equitable division of the judgment debtor's earnings that takes into account the needs of all the persons the judgment debtor is required to support." (C.C.P. 706.052.) However, the order issued to effectuate such division may not authorize a withholding in excess of that authorized under federal law (see 15 U.S.C., §1673(b)(2); Law Rev. Com. Comment, Pamphlet, p. 1458). (C.C.P. 706.052(c).)

(c) (New) Earnings Withholding Order For Taxes.

(1) [§347A] (New) In General.

Earnings withholding orders for taxes, issued to collect a state tax liability (see Supp., infra, §348A), are treated seperately in Article 4 (C.C.P. 706.070 et seq; on former C.C.P. 723.070 et seq., see Supp., supra, §133Q et seq.) of the Wage Garnishment Law. However, where no express exception is made, the general procedural provisions of the Wage Garnishment Law apply. (C.C.P. 706.073; see Law Rev. Com. Comment, Pamphlet, p. 1462.)

As used in this Article, "State" refers to the "State of California and includes any officer, department, board, or agency thereof" (C.C.P. 706.070(a)); "state tax liability" refers to "an amount for which the state has a state tax lien as defined in Section 7162 of the Government Code excluding a state tax lien created pursuant to the Fish and Game Code" (C.C.P. 706.070(b). (On the specific tax liabilties covered, including additions to and deletions from former

C.C.P. 723.070(b), see Law Rev. Com. Comment, Pamphlet, p. 1459).) The term "levying officer" refers to "the specific state agency seeking to collect a state tax liability under this article." (C.C.P. 706.073.)

A withholding order for taxes, which must be so denoted on its face (C.C.P. 706.072(a)), may be issued whether or not the state tax liability has been reduced to judgment (C.C.P. 706.072(d)); see Legislative Com. Comment—Senate, Pamphlet, p. 1462).

The Wage Garnishment Law does not limit the State's right to collect a state tax liability except to the extent that it provides the exclusive method for imposing a levy on employee earnings and precludes the use of other methods of collection to require an employer to withhold earnings in payment of a state tax liability. (C.C.P. 706.071; see Law Rev. Com. Comment, Pamphlet, p. 1460 [Article 4 does not apply to the collection of either federal taxes or state taxes not within its scope.].)

The taxpayer's liability may not be reviewed in any court proceeding under the Wage Garnishment Law. (C.C.P. 706.082.)

(2) [§348A] (New) Conditions For Issuance.

A withholding order for taxes may be issued only where (1) the existence of the state tax liability appears on the face of the taxpayer's return; or (2) the liability has been assessed or determined in an administrative proceeding in which the taxpayer had notice and an opportunity for administrative review. In the latter case, if a taxpayer makes a timely request for review, the order cannot be issued until the administrative review procedure is completed. (C.C.P. 706.072(b); see Legislative Com. Comment—Senate, Pamphlet, p. 1462; on former C.C.P. 723.072(b), see Supp., supra, §133R.)

If a state tax liability has been assessed or determined prior to July 1, 1983, and the State determines that the requirements of notice and opportunity for review (see supra) may not have been afforded the taxpayer, the State may send him a "Notice of Proposed Issuance of Withholding Order for Taxes" advising him of his right to review. If such right is requested within 30 days from the date the notice was mailed, the State must grant it and may not issue the order until the review procedure is completed. However, if no timely request is made, the State may then issue the order. (C.C.P. 706.072(c).)

(3) [§349A] (New) Issuance of Order.

(a) *By State.* The State may itself issue a withholding order for taxes, which must specify the *total* amount to be withheld, i.e., the unpaid tax liability including any penalties, accrued interest and costs. (C.C.P. 706.074(a); on former C.C.P. 723.074, see Supp., supra,

§133S.) Unless a lesser amount is specified, the amount to be withheld is the same as that which can be withheld on a garnishment by an ordinary creditor (see Supp., supra, §346A). (C.C.P. 706.074(b); Law Rev. Com. Comment, Pamphlet, p. 1463.)

(b) *By Court.* A court may order the issuance of a withholding order for taxes in an amount in excess of that authorized by C.C.P. 706.074 (see supra). (C.C.P. 706.076(a); on former C.C.P. 723.076, see Supp., supra, §133S.) The procedure is as follows:

(1) The State may "at any time" file an application in a court of record in the county of the taxpayer's last known residence. The application must include a statement under oath that the taxpayer has been served with a copy of the application and a notice informing him of its purpose and his right to a hearing. (C.C.P. 706.076(b)(c).)

(2) A hearing is held on notice deposited in the mail at least 10 days before the day set. (C.C.P. 706.076(d).)

(3) After the hearing the court must issue an order requiring withholding of "all earnings of the taxpayer other than that amount which the taxpayer proves is exempt" under C.C.P. 706.051(b) (see Supp., supra, §346A), but not less than that permitted to be withheld under C.C.P. 706.050 (see Supp., supra, §346A). (C.C.P. 706.076(e); see Law Rev. Com. Comment, Pamphlet, p.1466.)

(c) *Temporary Earnings Holding Order.* If the State intends to apply to the court for a withholding order and has determined that collection will be jeopardized during the pendency of the action, the State may issue "a temporary earnings holding order, which shall be denoted as such on its face," requiring the employer to retain earnings then or thereafter due. The original and a copy of this order and a notice informing the taxpayer of his rights are served on the employer, who must deliver copies of each to the taxpayer.

The temporary order expires 15 days from the date it is served on the employer unless extended by the court on an ex parte application for good cause shown. The State may not, for a period of 6 months, serve another temporary order on the same employer for the same employee, unless the court for good cause shown otherwise orders.

Both C.C.P. 706.153 (employer's duty not to defer or accelerate earnings; see Supp., infra, §366A), and C.C.P. 706.154 (remedies of creditor and limitation of employer's liability; see Supp., infra, §366A) apply to temporary orders issued under this section. (C.C.P. 706.076(f).)

(4) [§350A] (New) Service of Order and Notice.

The State must serve the employer with the withholding order for taxes, plus an additional copy of the order and a notice informing the taxpayer of his rights. Within 10 days from the date of service the employer must deliver copies of each to the taxpayer, except that *immediate* delivery must be made where a jeopardy withholding order has been served (see Supp., infra, §352A). (C.C.P. 706.075(b); on former C.C.P. 723.075(b), see Supp., supra, §133T; see also Legislative Com. Comment—Senate, Pamphlet, p. 1464.) (On when service of a warrant, notice of a levy, or notice or order to withhold must be deemed to be a withholding order for taxes, see C.C.P. 706.084.) Failure to comply does not subject the employer to civil liability, but he may be held in contempt of court. (C.C.P. 706.075(d).)

Service of a withholding order for taxes may be made by mail, or by any authorized state employee, and is complete when *received* by the employer or an authorized person (see C.C.P. 706.101(a)(1)(2), Supp., infra, §354A). Service of any other notice or document in connection with a withholding order for taxes may also be made by mail or by any authorized state employee, and is complete when *deposited* in the mail. (C.C.P. 706.080; on former C.C.P. 723.080, see Supp., supra, §133T.)

Except for forms issued in connection with court-issued orders, which are prescribed by the Judicial Council (see Supp., infra, §359A), the State must prescribe the form of any order, notice, or other document issued in connection with a withholding order for taxes. (C.C.P. 706.081.)

At any time after service of the order, the taxpayer may request an administrative hearing to reconsider or modify the amount to be withheld. The matter must be determined within 15 days after the request is received by the State, and determination of the amount is subject to the standard provided in C.C.P. 706.051 (hardship exemption; Supp., supra, §346A). The taxpayer may obtain judicial review of the determination by filing a petition for a writ of mandamus within 90 days after notice of the determination is delivered or mailed to him. (C.C.P. 706.075(c); on former C.C.P. 723.075(c), see Supp., supra, §133U; see also Legislative Com. Comment—Senate, Pamphlet, p. 1464.)

(5) [§351A] (New) Priority.

(a) *Priority Over Other Orders.* A withholding order for taxes has priority over any earnings withholding order except one for support (see Supp., supra, §344A). When served, the employer must cease withholding pursuant to an ordinary earnings withholding order and notify the levying officer that a supervening withholding order for taxes is in effect. (C.C.P. 706.077(a); see Law Rev. Com. Comment, Pamphlet, p. 1467.) (On former C.C.P. 723.077, see Supp., supra, §133Y; on the priority of wage assignment orders, see Supp., supra, §345A.)

(b) *Priority of First Order for Taxes.* If a withholding order for taxes is in effect, a subsequent such order is ineffective (C.C.P. 706.077(b)), and the employer must promptly notify the taxing agency that issued or obtained the second order of the reason for disregarding it (Law Rev. Com. Comment, Pamphlet, p. 1467).

(6)   [§352A]   (New) Pay Periods Subject to Order.

(a) *Ordinary Withholding Order For Taxes.* Earnings payable for a pay period ending prior to the 10th day after service of an ordinary withholding order for taxes may not be withheld. (C.C.P. 706.078(a); see Law Rev. Com. Comment, Pamphlet, p.1469; Supp, supra, §339A [same date of commencement of withholding period for other withholding orders].)

(b) *Jeopardy Withholding Order For Taxes.* This type of order, which must be so denoted on its face, may be issued upon a State determination that delay in withholding will jeopardize the collection of a state tax liability. Such an order requires that withholding commence at the time of service. (C.C.P. 706.078(b); see Law Rev. Com. Comment, Pamphlet, p. 1469.)

(c) *Termination.* Withholding will continue until the amount specified in the order is paid in full, or the order is withdrawn, except that the order automatically terminates one year after cessation of employment. If the relevant state tax liability is satisfied before withholding is completed, the State must serve a notice of termination on the employer. (C.C.P. 706.078(c); see Law Rev. Com. Comment, Pamphlet, p. 1469.)

(d)   (New) Procedure for Withholding Orders and Exemption Claims.

(1)   [§353A]   (New) Judicial Council Rules.

Except for the State's administrative hearings pursuant to withholding orders for taxes (see Supp., supra, §347A et seq.), the Judicial Council "may provide by rule for the practice and procedure in proceedings under this chapter." (C.C.P. 706.100; see Law Rev. Com. Comment, Pamphlet, p. 1471; Supp., supra, §133C [former C.C.P. 723.100].)

(2)   [§354A]   (New) Service of Order, Notices and Documents.

(a) *Who May Serve.* Although C.C.P. 706.101(a) provides that a withholding order "shall be served" by the levying officer, C.C.P. 706.101(e) states that such order also "may be served" by a registered process server.

(b) *Who May Be Served.* Service of a withholding order must be on the employer by delivery to (1) a managing agent or person in charge of the branch or office where the employee works or from which he is paid (this does not include Controller's office unless state employee works directly for it); or (2) any person on whom a summons may be served under C.C.P. 416.10 et seq. (see *Actions,* §649 et seq.). (C.C.P. 706.101(a); see Legislative Com. Comment—Assembly, Pamphlet, p. 1473; Supp., supra, §133F [former C.C.P. 723.101].)

(c) *Method of Service.* Service of the *withholding order* must ordinarily be made by personal delivery or by registered or certified mail, with return receipt requested, but personal service is required if (1) mailed service is ineffective (C.C.P. 706.101(b); see Legislative Com. Comment—Assembly, Pamphlet, p. 1473.), or (2) such service is requested by the judgment creditor (C.C.P. 706.101(d)).

Service of *other notices or documents* may be made by personal delivery or first class mail. If the service is made after the levying officer has received the employer's return receipt (see supra), service must be made on the person designated thereon to receive notices. (C.C.P. 706.101(c).)

(3) [355A] (New) Application For Order.

The creditor must first obtain a writ of execution to the county where the employer is to be served. If the 180-day period specified in C.C.P. 699.530 for levy under the writ has not expired, he may then file an application with a levying officer in that county, who must promptly issue the order. (C.C.P. 706.102(a); see Legislative Com. Comment—Assembly, Pamphlet, p. 1474; Supp., supra, §133D [former C.C.P. 723.102]; on form and content of application, see Supp., infra, §§359A, 360A.)

This section does not apply to withholding orders for taxes. (C.C.P. 706.102(b); see Supp., supra, §347A et seq.)

(4) [§356A] (New) Service on Employer.

(a) *What Must Be Served.* The levying officer must serve the employer with an original and copy of the withholding order, the form for the employer's return (see Supp., infra, §363A), and the notice to the employee of the withholding order. (C.C.P. 706.103(a); see Legislative Com. Comment—Assembly, Pamphlet, p. 1475; Supp., supra, §133F [former C.C.P. 723.103].) He must also provide the employer with a copy of the employer's intstructions (see Supp., infra, §359A), unless a Judicial Council Rule excuses compliance. (C.C.P. 706.103(b).)

(b) *Time of Service.* No withholding order may be served after the time specified in C.C.P. 699.530(b) (180 days from date writ of execution was issued) has expired. (C.C.P. 706.103(c).)

(c) *Employer's Duty After Service.* Within 10 days from the date of service the employer must deliver to the debtor a copy of the withholding order and the notice to the employee of such order, unless the debtor is no longer employed by the employer and owed no earnings. Failure to comply with this requirement does not subject the employer to any civil liability, but he may be held in contempt of court. (C.C.P. 706.104(a); see Law Rev. Com. Comment, Pamphlet, p. 1476 [contempt appropriate where failure to comply is due to malice or willful neglect, rather than mere inadvertence]; Supp., infra, §133G [former C.C.P. 723.104(a)].)

Within 15 days from the date of service, the employer must complete and mail his "return" to the levying officer. If the withholding order is ineffective, the employer must state in his return that he will not comply for this reason, and must return the order. (C.C.P. 706.104(b); see Supp., supra, §133H [former C.C.P. 723.104(b)].)

(d) *Creation of Lien.* Service of the withholding order creates a lien, in the amount required to be withheld pursuant to the order, on (1) the debtor's earnings and (2) the employer's property subject to the enforcement of a money judgment. This lien continues for one year from the date the earnings become payable, unless the amount required to be withheld is paid. (C.C.P. 706.029; see Legislative Com. Comment—Assembly, Pamphlet, p. 1451 [lien will not expire at end of one year if, prior to that time, levying creditor initiates suit against the employer to recover sums the creditor claims should have been paid under the wage garnishment]; Supp., supra, §133F [former C.C.P. 723.029].)

(5) [§357A] (New) Exemption Claim by Debtor.

(a) *In General.* C.C.P. 706.105 establishes the procedure governing the determination of claims of exemption under C.C.P. 706.051 (see Supp., supra, §346A). The section is *inapplicable* to withholding orders for support (see Supp., supra, §344A) and taxes (see Supp., supra, §347A et seq.). (C.C.P. 106.105(k).)

A debtor may claim an exemption under either of the following circumstances: "(1) No prior hearing has been held with respect to the earnings withholding order. (2) There has been a material change in circumstances since the time of the last prior hearing on the earnings withholding order." (C.C.P. 706.105(a); see Legislative Com. Comment—Assembly, Pamphlet, p. 1480; Supp., supra, §133L [former C.C.P. 723.105(a)].)

The claim is made by filing with the levying officer an original and one copy of the debtor's claim of exemption and his financial statement. (C.C.P. 706.105(b); see Supp., supra, §133L [former C.C.P. 723.105(b)]; Supp., infra, §361A [Forms for claim and financial statement].)

(b) *Notice and Hearing.* On the filing of the claim of exemption, the levying officer must promptly mail to the creditor copies of the claim of exemption and financial statement, together with a *notice of claim of exemption.* This notice must state that the claim of exemption has been filed and that the withholding order will be terminated or modified unless a *notice of opposition* (see Supp., infra, §364A) is filed with the levying officer within 10 days after the date of mailing of the notice of claim. (C.C.P. 706.105(c); see Legislative Com. Comment—Assembly, Pamphlet, p. 1480; Supp., supra, §133M [former C.C.P. 723.105(c)].)

Within this 10-day period, if the creditor desires to contest the claim, he must file the *notice of opposition.* (C.C.P. 706.105(d).) If such notice is timely filed, the creditor is entitled to a hearing, which he may obtain by filing with the court within the same 10-day period a *notice of motion* for an order determining the claim. (C.C.P. 706.105(e); see Legislative Com. Comment—Assembly, Pamphlet, p. 1481; Supp., supra, §133M [former C.C.P. 723.105(e)].)

The hearing must be held no later than 20 days from the date the notice of motion was filed unless a continuance is granted for good cause. Not less than 10 days prior to the hearing the creditor must (1) *give written notice* of the hearing to the levying officer, and (2) *serve notice* of the hearing and a copy of the notice of opposition *by mail* on the debtor and, if the claim of exemption so requested, on his attorney. Service is deemed made on proper deposit in the mail, and the creditor must file proof of such service with the court. On receipt of the notice of hearing the levying officer must file the claim of exemption and the notice of opposition with the court. (C.C.P. 706.105(a); see Legislative Com. Comment—Assembly, Pamphlet, p. 1481.)

(c) *Modification or Termination of Order.* If the levying officer does not receive timely notices of opposition and hearing (see supra), he must serve on the employer one of the following: (1) If all of the earnings were claimed to be exempt—a notice that the withholding order has been terminated; (2) if only a portion of the earnings were claimed to be exempt—a modified withholding order reflecting that amount. (C.C.P. 706.105(f); see Legislative Com. Comment—Assembly, Pamphlet, p. 1481; Supp., supra, §133N [former C.C.P. 723.105(f)].)

After a hearing (see supra), the court may order that the withholding order be modified or terminated. If it does, the clerk must promptly transmit a certified copy of the order to the levying officer; and the levying officer must promptly serve on the employer (1) a copy of the modified withholding order, or (2) a notice that the withholding order has been terminated. The court may order that the withholding order be terminated as of "a date which precedes the date of hearing"; and it must order that any amount withheld in excess of the proper amount be promptly paid to the debtor. (C.C.P. 706.105(g); see Legislative Com. Comment—Assembly, Pamphlet, p. 1482; Supp., supra, §133N [former C.C.P. 723.105(g)].)

(d) *Appeal.* Any court order denying a claim of exemption or modifying or terminating a withholding order may be appealed. An appeal by the creditor from a modifying or terminating order does not stay the order which, until set aside or modified, must be given effect as if the appeal had not been taken. (C.C.P. 706.105(j); see Legislative Com. Comment—Assembly, Pamphlet, p. 1482; Supp., supra, §133-O [former C.C.P. 723.105(j)].)

(e) *Debtor's Recovery of Amounts Withheld.* If an employer has withheld and paid over amounts after the date of termination, but prior to receipt of notice of it, the debtor may recover such amounts only from the levying officer or the creditor, depending on which party has possession of the money. If the employer has withheld amounts after termination, but has not paid them over to the levying officer, he must promptly pay them to the debtor. (C.C.P. 706.105(i); see Legislative Com. Comment—Assembly, Pamphlet, p. 1482; Supp., supra, §133N [former C.C.P. 723. 105(i)].)

(f) *New Withholding Orders.* If the withholding order is terminated by the court (see supra), the creditor cannot immediately apply for another order directed to the same employer with respect to the same debtor. Unless the court otherwise orders or there is a material change in circumstances since the time of the last hearing, the creditor is precluded from making such an application for (1) a period of 100 days following the date of service of the withholding order, or (2) 60 days after the date of its termination, whichever is later. (C.C.P. 706.105(h); see Legislative Com. Comment—Assembly, Pamphlet, p. 1480; Supp., supra, §133P [former C.C.P. 723.105(h)].)

(6) [§358A] (New) Service of Another Order.

If the creditor obtains a withholding order, and the employer withholds earnings pursuant thereto, the creditor cannot have another order served during the 10 days following expiration of the prior order. (C.C.P. 706.107; see Law Rev. Com. Comment, Pamphlet, p. 1483; Supp., supra, §133P [former C.C.P. 723.107].) The purpose of this limitation is to give other creditors a 10-day period in which to serve their withholding orders. (Law Rev. Com. Comment, Pamphlet, p. 1483.)

Since each state agency is considered a separate entity for the purposes of the Wage Garnishment Law (see C.C.P. 706.011(d)), a state agency may serve a withholding order within the 10-day period, even though another agency has been making collection. (Law Rev. Com. Comment, Pamphlet, p. 1483.)

(e) (New) Forms.

(1) [§359A] (New) Judicial Council Forms and Instructions.

Except for withholding orders for taxes (prescribed by the State; see C.C.P. 706.081, Supp., supra, §350A), the Judicial Council must prescribe the form of the applications, notices, claims of exemption, orders, and other required documents (see C.C.P. 681.030, Supp., supra, §234A), and only these forms may be used to implement the Wage Garnishment Law. (C.C.P. 706.120; see Law Rev. Com. Comment, Pamphlet, p. 1484; Supp., supra, §133C [former C.C.P. 723.120].) (On the levying officer's duty to supply copies of the forms for the debtor's claim of exemption and financial statement, see Supp., infra, §361A.)

The Council must also prepare "employer's instructions," and revisions or supplements to them, to provide the employer with the information needed to comply with the law and, except to the extent that the instructions are included in the required forms, must provide the levying officer with copies to give to employers. (C.C.P. 706.127; see Law Rev. Com. Comment, Pamphlet, p. 1490; Supp., supra, §133C [former C.C.P. 723.127].)

(2) [§360A] (New) Application and Notice.

(a) *Application for Issuance of Order.* Pursuant to C.C.P. 706.121, the application must be executed under oath and must include all of the following:

(1) The debtor's name, last known address and, if known, social security number.

(2) The creditor's name and address.

(3) The court and date of the judgment.

(4) The date of issuance of the writ of execution.

(5) The total amount to be withheld (not to exceed the amount required to satisfy the writ of execution plus the levying officer's statutory fee).

(6) The employer's name and address.

(7) The name and address of the person to whom the withheld money is to be paid.

See Law Rev. Com. Comment, Pamphlet, p. 1484; Supp., supra, §133D [former C.C.P. 723.121].

(b) *Notice to Employee of Order.* The notice must contain a statement informing the employee "in simple terms" of the nature of a wage garnishment and the right to, and procedure for claiming, an exemption. The Judicial Council may also insert any other information deemed useful or appropriate, but must include the following: (1) The fact that the named employer has been ordered to withhold a specified amount from the employee's earnings and to pay such amount to the levying officer for transmittal to the person specified in the withholding order; (2) the manner of computing the amount to be withheld; (3) the employee's right to keep more or all of his earnings by proving their necessity for the support of himself or his family; and (4) the employee's right to a court hearing to establish such necessity, and the procedure for obtaining it (filing a claim of exemption and financial statement, forms for which may be obtained without charge from the levying officer). (C.C.P. 706.122; see Legislative Com. Comment—Assembly, Pamphlet, p. 1486; Supp., supra, §133G [former C.C.P. 723.122].) (On notice to the employee in the case of a withholding order for taxes, see Supp., supra, §350A.)

(3) [§361A] (New) Debtor's Exemption Claim and Financial Statement.

The claim of exemption must (a) be executed under oath; (b) contain the debtor's present mailing address; and (c) indicate the amount of earnings which the debtor believes should be withheld each pay period. (C.C.P. 706.123; see Law Rev. Com. Comment, Pamphlet, p. 1486.)

The financial statement must be executed as provided in C.C.P. 703.530 (see Supp., supra, §301A) and contain all of the information required by that section, plus information on whether any withholding orders, or wage assignments for support, are in effect with respect to the earnings of the debtor or his spouse or dependents. (C.C.P. 706.124, superseding former C.C.P. 723.124, Supp., supra, §133L; see Legislative Com. Comment—Assembly, Pamphlet, p. 1487.)

Levying officers must provide copies of the forms for the claim of exemption and financial statement without charge. (C.C.P. 706.129; see Supp., supra, §133L [former C.C.P. 723.129].)

(4) [§362A] (New) Withholding Order.

Pursuant to C.C.P. 706.125, the withholding order must include all of the following:

(a) The debtor's name and address and, if known, his social security number.

(b) The employer's name and address.

(c) The levying officer's name and address.

(d) The court, and date of the judgment, and the name of the creditor.

(e) The date of issuance of the writ of execution.

(f) The total amount to be withheld, including the levying officer's statutory fee.

(g) A description of the withholding period.

See Law Rev. Com. Comment, Pamphlet, p. 1488; Supp., supra, §133E [former C.C.P. 723.125].

The withholding order must also include the following orders to the employer: (a) To withhold and pay over to the levying officer the amount required; (b) to fill out, and send to the levying officer by first-class mail within 15 days after service of the withholding order, the "employer's return" (see Supp., infra, §363A); (c) to deliver to the debtor, within 10 days after service, a copy of the withholding order and the notice to employee (see Supp., supra, §360A), unless the debtor is no longer employed and is owed no earnings. (C.C.P. 706.125.)

(5) [§363A] (New) Employer's Return.

The "employer's return" must be executed under oath and include all of the following information: (1) The names and addresses of the levying officer and debtor and, if known, the debtor's social security number, and (2) a direction that the form be mailed to the levying officer no later than 15 days after the date of service of the withholding order. (C.C.P. 706.126(a); see Supp., infra, §133H [former C.C.P. 723.126].)

The return form must also require the employer to supply all of the following information:

(1) The date the withholding order was served on the employer.

(2) Whether the debtor is employed by the employer or otherwise owed earnings by him, and, if so, the amount of the debtor's earnings for the last pay period and the length of that period.

(3) Specified information concerning any earlier withholding order (names of creditor and levying officer and dates of issuance, service and expiration) and whether such order has priority.

(4) Whether, on the date of service, the employer was required to comply with a wage assignment for support and, if so, the issuing court and date and any other information the Judicial Council determines is needed to identify it.

(5) The name and address of the person to whom notices to the employer are to be sent. (C.C.P. 706.125(b).)

(6) [§364A] (New) Creditor's Notice of Opposition.

Pursuant to C.C.P. 706.128, the notice of opposition must be executed under oath and include all of the following:

(a) The debtor's name, last known address and, if known, social security number.

(b) The creditor's name and address.

(c) The date that the notice of claim of exemption was mailed.

(d) The amount of the claimed exemption which the creditor disputes.

(e) The factual and legal grounds for opposing the claim of exemption.

See Supp., supra, §133M [former C.C.P. 723.128].

(f) (New) Administration and Enforcement.

(1) [§365A] (New) State Exemption From Earnings Garnishment.

The Judicial Council is authorized to "perform all acts required by the Administrator of the Wage and Hour Division of the United States Department of Labor as conditions to exemption of this state from the earnings garnishment provisions of the Consumer Credit Protection Act of 1968 (15 U.S.C., §1671–1677)." This authorization includes, but is not limited to:

(a) Representing and acting on behalf of the State in relation to the Administrator with regard to matters concerning the application, interpretation and enforcement of state laws regulating withholding of earnings.

(b) Submitting to the Administrator a certified copy of every state statute affecting earnings withholding, and of any state Supreme Court decision involving such statutes.

(c) Submitting to the Administrator any information he may request regarding the enforcement of state earnings withholding laws. (C.C.P. 706.151; see Law Rev. Com. Comment, Pamphlet, p. 1491; Supp., supra, §133C [former C.C.P. 723.151].)

(2) [§366A] (New) Wrongful Acts of Employer.

(a) *Failure To Pay or Withhold Earnings.* It is a *misdemeanor* for an employer to withhold earnings and, with intent to defraud either the creditor or the debtor, fail to pay the earnings over to the levying officer. (C.C.P. 706.152; see Supp., supra, §133C [former C.C.P. 723.152].)

(b) *Deferment or Acceleration of Payment of Earnings.* The

creditor may bring a *civil action* against an employer who defers or accelerates a payment of earnings to an employee with the intent to defeat or diminish the creditor's rights under a withholding order (C.C.P. 706.153(a).) The amount that should have been withheld and paid over may be recovered. This remedy is not exclusive. (C.C.P. 706.153(b); see Supp., supra, §133C [former C.C.P. 723.153].)

(c) *Failure To Withhold or Pay Over Amount Withheld.* The creditor *may sue* an employer who fails to perform such acts and may recover the amount that should have been withheld or paid over. Such remedy is not exclusive. (C.C.P. 706.154(a); see Supp., supra, §133C [former C.C.P. 723.154].) However, "an employer who complies with any written order or written notice which purports to be given or served in accordance with the provisions of this chapter is not subject to any civil or criminal liability for such compliance unless the employer has actively participated in a fraud." (C.C.P. 706.154(b); see Law Rev. Com. Comment, Pamphlet, p. 1493.)

6.   (New) Miscellaneous Creditors' Remedies.

(a)   [§367A]   (New) Written Interrogatories to Judgment Debtor.

The creditor may propound written interrogatories to the debtor in the manner provided in C.C.P. 2030 (see *Cal. Evidence,* 2d, §978 et seq.) requesting information to aid in enforcement of the money judgment. The debtor must respond in the manner and within the time provided by C.C.P. 2030. (C.C.P. 708.020(a); see Law Rev. Com. Comment, Pamphlet, p. 1494 [requirement of former C.C.P. 714.5 that debtor be represented by counsel (see Supp., supra, §124A) was omitted].)

Interrogatories may not be served within 120 days after the debtor has responded to previously served interrogatories, or within 120 days after the debtor has been examined (see Supp., infra, §368A et seq.). (C.C.P. 708.020(b) [debtor not required to respond to any interrogatories served within these periods].) And if enforcement of the judgment is stayed on appeal by the giving of a sufficient undertaking (see C.C.P. 916 et seq.; *Appeal,* §155 et seq.), the stay applies to interrogatories. All other stays also apply to interrogatories unless the court makes an order to the contrary. (C.C.P. 708.010(b); see Legislative Com. Comment—Assembly, Pamphlet, p. 1494.) Otherwise, written interrogatories may be used at any time a money judgment is enforceable. (C.C.P. 708.010(a).)

Interrogatories may be enforced, "to the extent practicable," in the same manner as interrogatories in a civil action. (C.C.P. 708.020(c); see Law Rev. Com. Comment, Pamphlet, p. 1495 [sanctions include being required to pay attorney's fees (see *Cal. Evidence,*

2d, §1020) and being held in contempt (see *Cal. Evidence,* 2d, §1018)].)

See 14 Pacific L.J. 426.

(b) (New) Examination Proceeding.

(1) [§368A] (New) In General.

(a) *Proper Court.* The general rule is that the proper court for examination of a person is the court in which the money judgment is entered. (C.C.P. 708.160(a); see Law Rev. Com. Comment, Pamphlet, p. 1504.) However, no person may be required to attend an examination outside his county of residence or place of business unless the distance is less than 150 miles. (C.C.P. 708.160(b); see text, §123 [former C.C.P. 717.1].) If the prospective examinee's place of residence and business are not in the county where judgment is entered, a court of similar jurisdiction (or higher, if none similar) in his county of residence or business is a proper court for examination. (C.C.P. 708.160(c); on the procedure for obtaining an examination in a court other than the court in which judgment is entered, see C.C.P. 708.160(d) [abstract of the judgment, required affidavits, filing fee of $12].)

(b) *Referee.* The examination may be conducted by a court-appointed referee (C.C.P. 708.140(a)), who must be a member of the State Bar (C.C.P. 708.140(b)). This requirement does not limit a court's power to appoint a temporary judge pursuant to Cal. Const., Art. VI, §21. (C.C.P. 708.140(c).)

In conducting the examination the referee generally has the same powers as a court, except the powers to (1) punish for contempt; (2) award attorney's fees (see Supp., infra, §371A); and (3) determine a contested claim of exemption or a third-party claim (see Supp., infra, §370A). (C.C.P. 708.140(b); see Law Rev. Com. Comment, Pamphlet, p. 1502.)

(c) *Witnesses.* "Witnesses may be required to appear and testify before the court or referee in an examination proceeding . . . in the same manner as upon the trial of an issue." (C.C.P. 708.130(a); see Law Rev. Com. Comment, Pamphlet, p. 1501.)

The privilege not to testify against one's spouse (see Ev.C. 970 et seq., *Cal. Evidence,* 2d, §828 et seq.) is not applicable in examination proceedings. (C.C.P. 708.130(b).) "This is to prevent the privilege from being used as a collusive device for the spouse to conceal assets liable for the satisfaction of the judgment." (Law Rev. Com. Recommendation, Pamphlet, p. 1128.)

(d) *Appearance by Representatives of Organizations.* If an organization is served with an order to appear for an examination, it must designate to represent it one or more officers, directors, managing agents or other persons familiar with its property and debts. (C.C.P. 708.150(a); see Law Rev. Com. Comment, Pamphlet, p. 1503.) (On requirement that the order advise the organization of its duty to make such designation, see C.C.P. 708.150(c).)

If the order to appear designates a specific individual, he must appear for the examination and may be accompanied by one or more officers, etc., familiar with the property and debts of the organization. (C.C.P. 708.150(b).)

(e) *Protective Orders.* In any examination proceeding, "the court may, on motion of the person to be examined or on its own motion, make such protective orders as justice may require." (C.C.P. 708.200; see Law Rev. Com. Comment, Pamphlet, p. 1507.)

(2) [§369A] (New) Examination of Judgment Debtor.

The creditor may apply to the proper court (see Supp., supra, §368A) for an order requiring the debtor to appear, at a time and place specified, to furnish information to aid in enforcement of the money judgment. (C.C.P. 708.110(a); see Law Rev. Com. Comment, Pamphlet, p. 1496; on the former procedure, see text, §124.) The order must inform the debtor that failure to comply may lead to arrest and punishment for contempt, and the imposition of attorney's fees. (C.C.P. 708.110(e); see Law Rev. Com. Comment, Pamphlet, p. 1497.)

In order to prevent harassment of the debtor (see Law Rev. Com. Recommendation, Pamphlet, p. 1124), a creditor who has caused the debtor to be examined during the preceding 120 days may not obtain another order unless he shows good cause. (C.C.P. 708.110(c); see Law Rev. Com. Comment, Pamphlet, p. 1496.)

The court must make the order upon an ex parte application if there has been no examination within the 120-day period. (C.C.P. 708.110(b).) If there has been an examination within this period, an ex parte application is still sufficient, unless the court directs, or a court rule requires, that it be made on noticed motion. (C.C.P. 708.110(c).)

The creditor must personally serve a copy of the order on the debtor not less than 10 days before the date of examination. Service creates a lien on the debtor's personal property. (C.C.P. 708.110(d); see Law Rev. Com. Comment, Pamphlet, p. 1496.)

See 14 Pacific L.J. 426.

(3) [§370A] (New) Examination of Third Person.

(a) *Issuance of Order.* Upon ex parte application by a creditor who has a money judgment, and satisfactory proof by the creditor (by affidavit or otherwise) that a third person either has possession or control of property in which the debtor has an interest or is indebted to the debtor for more than $250, the court must make an order directing the third person to appear, at a specified time and place, to answer concerning such property or debt. (C.C.P. 708.120(a); see Legislative Com. Comment—Assembly, Pamphlet, p. 1499 [requirement of former C.C.P. 717 that a writ of execution be first issued is not continued]; on the former procedure, see text, §126 et seq.)

The order must inform the third person that failure to comply may result in arrest and punishment for contempt, and the imposition of attorney's fees. It must also inform the debtor of his right to file an exemption claim (see infra, this section), and the procedure for so doing. (C.C.P. 708.120(e); see Legislative Com. Comment—Assembly, Pamphlet, p. 1500.)

See 14 Pacific L.J. 427.

(b) *Service of Order.* A copy of the order must be served *personally* on the third person, and *personally or by mail* on the debtor, not less than 10 days prior to the date of examination. (C.C.P. 708.120(b); see Legislative Com. Comment—Assembly, Pamphlet, p. 1499; Law Rev. Com. Recommendation, Pamphlet, p. 1125 [judgment debtor is served because he is an interested party]; 14 Pacific L.J. 428.)

(c) *Mileage Fees.* At the time an order is served on the third person, the person serving it must tender fees for the mileage necessary to be traveled from the third person's residence to the place of examination. The fees must be the same as those generally provided for witnesses in civil proceedings in the examining court. (C.C.P. 708.120(f); see Legislative Com. Comment—Assembly, Pamphlet, p. 1500.) An order is *not effective* unless this requirement is complied with. (C.C.P. 708.120(f).)

(d) *Creation of Lien.* If the property or debt is sufficiently described in the affidavit or application so that it can be identified, service of the order on the third person creates a lien on the debtor's interest in the property, or on the debt, for one year from the date of the order (unless extended or terminated by the court). (C.C.P. 708.120(c); see Legislative Com. Comment—Assembly, p. 1499.)

(e) *Debtor's Claim of Exemption.* By application on noticed motion, filed with the court and served on the creditor not later than 3 days before the examination date, the debtor may claim an exemption for all or any portion of the property or debt. No notice of opposition to the claim is required. (C.C.P. 708.120(d); see Legislative Com. Comment—Assembly, Pamphlet, p. 1499.)

The debtor must execute an affidavit in support of the application (for contents, see Supp., supra, §301A), and the issue must be determined by the *court.* (C.C.P. 708.120(d); on referee's inability to decide such matters, see Supp., supra, §368A).

Failure to make a claim of exemption precludes a later claim *only* if the property or debt is identifiable and the debtor receives at least 10 days notice of the examination. (C.C.P. 708.120(d).)

(f) *Determination of Third Person's Adverse Claim.* With certain exceptions (see infra, this section), if a third person claims an interest in the property adverse to the debtor or denies the debt, the court may, at the creditor's request, determine the matter. The court may grant a continuance for a reasonable time to allow the parties to prepare for the hearing. The determination is conclusive, but may be appealed. (C.C.P. 708.180(a); see Legislative Com. Comment—Assembly, Pamphlet, p. 1506.)

Upon an ex parte application of the creditor, the court may forbid transfer of the property, or payment of the debt, *to the debtor* until the matter is decided pursuant to C.C.P. 708.180(a) (see supra) or until a creditor's suit is commenced and settled (see Supp., infra, §373A et seq.). The court may require an undertaking and modify or vacate the order *with or without a hearing.* (C.C.P. 708.180(c); see Legislative Com. Comment—Assembly, Pamphlet, p. 1507.)

The court may also forbid the transfer or other disposition of the property *to any person* or forbid payment of the debt, but only upon a noticed motion application, and after determining that the debtor probably owns an interest in the property or that the debt is probably owed to the debtor. In this situation the court *must* require an undertaking, and may modify or vacate the order *after notice and hearing.* (C.C.P. 708.180(d).)

Provided that the third person's claim is made in good faith, the court may *not* determine the claim if *any* of the following conditions is satisfied: (1) The court is an improper court for the trial of an independent civil action (including a creditor's suit) for the determination of the matter; (2) at the time of service of an order of examination on the third person, a civil action) (including a creditor's suit) is pending on the matter; (3) the court determines that the matter should be decided in a creditor's suit. (C.C.P. 708.180(b); see Legislative Com. Comment—Assembly, Pamphlet, p. 1506; 14 Pacific L.J. 428.)

(g) *Intervention.* A person claiming an interest in the property or debt may be permitted to intervene. The intervenor's rights are determined pursuant to C.C.P. 708.180 (see supra). (C.C.P. 708.190; see Law Rev. Com. Comment, Pamphlet, p. 1507.)

(4) [§371A] (New) Failure To Appear for Examination.

If an examination order was served by a "sheriff, marshal,

constable, a person specially appointed by the court in the order, or a registered process server," and the person served fails to appear, the court may have him arrested and punished for contempt. If the failure is without good cause, attorney's fees must be awarded to the creditor. Any fees awarded against the debtor become part of the principal amount of the judgment. (C.C.P. 708.170(a); see Law Rev. Com. Comment, Pamphlet, p. 1505.)

Improper service of an order, which subsequently results in an arrest, is a misdemeanor. (C.C.P. 708.170(b).)

(5) [§372A] (New) Order Applying Property to Satisfaction of Judgment.

At the conclusion of the examination proceeding the court may order the debtor's interest in nonexempt property possessed or controlled by the debtor or a third person, or a debt owed by the third person to the debtor, to be applied toward the satisfaction of the judgment. Such order creates a lien on the property or debt. (C.C.P. 708.205(a); see Law Rev. Com. Comment, Pamphlet, p. 1508 [court may order execution to collect amount due, or may direct the person examined to deliver the property or funds to the levying officer, to pay the creditor directly, or to make any necessary assignments or deliveries to a court-appointed receiver].)

The court may *not* make such an order if a third person claims an interest adverse to the debtor, or denies the debt, and the court has not determined the matter pursuant to C.C.P. 708.180(a) (see Supp., supra, §370A). However, the court may forbid transfer of the property or payment of the debt pursuant to C.C.P. 708.180(c)(d) (see Supp., supra, §370A). (C.C.P. 708.205(b).)

(c) (New) Creditor's Suit.

(1) [§373A] (New) Nature of Action.

The creditor may bring an action against a third person who possesses or controls property in which the debtor has an interest, or who is indebted to the debtor, to have the interest or debt applied to the satisfaction of the judgment. (C.C.P. 708.210.) This action may be brought without first levying under a writ of execution (see Supp., supra, §249A et seq.), examining the third person (see Supp., supra, §370A), or utilizing any other procedure for the satisfaction of the judgment. (Law Rev. Com. Comment, Pamphlet, p. 1509 [comment to C.C.P. 708.210].) However, it is anticipated that the creditor's suit, being more expensive and cumbersome, will be reserved for situations in which the creditor believes that the third person will not cooperate, such as where he has failed to perform the duties of a garnishee (see Supp., supra, §278A), or there has been no court determination of disputed ownership of the property (see Supp., supra, §370A). (Law Rev. Com. Comment, Pamphlet, p. 1509 [comment to Article 3].) (On the former procedure, see text, §§143, 144.)

The debtor must be joined in the action, but is not an indispensable party. And his residence may not be considered in determining venue, unless otherwise provided by contract between the debtor and the third person. (C.C.P. 708.220; see Law Rev. Com. Comment, Pamphlet, p. 1510.)

Service of summons on the third person creates a lien on the debtor's interest in the property or on the debt owed to him. (C.C.P. 708.250; see Law Rev. Com. Comment, Pamphlet, p. 1512.)

The parties to a creditor's suit have no right to a jury trial. (C.C.P. 708.270; see Law Rev. Com. Comment, Pamphlet, p. 1513.)

See 14 Pacific L.J. 429.

(2) [§374A] (New) Time For Bringing Suit.

A creditor's suit must be commenced before the expiration of the *later* of the following times: (1) The time when the debtor may bring an action against the third person concerning the property or debt; (2) one year after creation of a lien on the property or debt, if such lien is created within the time when the debtor may bring an action against the third person concerning the property or debt. (C.C.P. 708.230(a); see Law Rev. Com. Comment, Pamphlet, p. 1511.) The latter time extends the liability of the third person for up to an additional year after the debtor's time to sue has expired, and thus prevents the third person from avoiding liability by delaying tactics. (Law Rev. Com. Recommendation, Pamphlet, p. 1131.)

A creditor's suit may not be commenced after the period for enforcement of the judgment has expired. (C.C.P. 708.230(b).) However, if the action is commenced within the allowable time period, it may be prosecuted to judgment (C.C.P. 708.230(c)), even though the period for enforcement of the judgment (see C.C.P. 683.020, Supp., supra, §237A-1) has expired (Law Rev. Com. Comment, Pamphlet, p. 1511).

See 14 Pacific L.J. 429.

(3) [§375A] (New) Order Forbidding Transfer or Payment.

Upon an ex parte application of the creditor, or a noticed motion if the court directs or a court rule so requires, the creditor may obtain an order restraining the third person from either transferring to *the debtor* the property in which the debtor allegedly has an interest or paying the alleged debt to the debtor. The order must remain in effect until judgment is entered in the creditor's suit, or until such earlier time as the court may provide, and may be modified or vacated at any time with or without a hearing. The court has the discretion to require an undertaking. (C.C.P. 708.240(a); see Law Rev. Com. Comment, Pamphlet, p. 1512.)

In lieu of, or in addition to, the aforementioned order the creditor may, pursuant to C.C.P. 525 et seq. (see *Provisional Remedies,* §39 et seq.), apply for a temporary restraining order or a preliminary injunction, or both, restraining the third person from transferring the property *to any person,* or otherwise disposing of it. (C.C.P. 708.240(b); see Law Rev. Com. Comment, Pamphlet, p. 1512.)

(4) [§376A] (New) Debtor's Claim of Exemption.

(a) *Filing of Claim.* Upon application on noticed motion, the debtor may claim that all or any part of the property or debt is exempt. The claim must be served, personally or by mail, on the creditor not later than 30 days before the trial date. The debtor must execute an affidavit in support of his application (for contents, see Supp., supra, §301A), but no notice of opposition to the claim is required. (C.C.P. 708.260(a); see Legislative Com. Comment—Assembly, Pamphlet, p. 1513.)

(b) *Waiver of Right.* Failure to make a claim of exemption is a waiver of the exemption unless *both* of the following conditions are satisfied: (1) The debtor has not been served with process satisfactorily identifying the property or debt; and (2) the debtor lacks actual notice of the pendency of the action and the identity of the property or the nature of the debt. (C.C.P. 708.260(b).)

(5) [§377A] (New) Judgment.

(a) *Court Orders.* Except where an exemption is established (see infra, this section), the court must render judgment accordingly if the creditor establishes that the third person has property in which the debtor has an interest or is indebted to the debtor. The property or debt may be applied to the satisfaction of the creditor's judgment. (C.C.P. 708.280(b); see Law Rev. Com. Comment, Pamphlet, p. 1514.)

The court may order the third person not to transfer property in which the debtor has an interest until it can be levied upon, or otherwise applied to the satisfaction of the judgment. (C.C.P. 708.280(c).) If the third person, in *knowing* violation of a court order, has paid the debt to the debtor or transferred the property, or if he has transferred property that was subject to a lien in favor of the creditor, the court must render judgment against the third person for the lesser of (1) the debtor's interest in the property or the amount of the debt, or (2) the amount of the creditor's judgment remaining unsatisfied. (C.C.P. 708.280(d).)

(b) *Where Exemption Established.* The aforementioned orders may not be made if the debtor establishes to the court's satisfaction that the property or debt is exempt from enforcement of a money judgment. (C.C.P. 708.280(a); see Law Rev. Com. Comment, Pamphlet, p. 1514.)

(c) *Costs.* The costs incurred by, or taxed against, the creditor in a creditor's suit may not be recovered from the debtor as a cost of enforcing the judgment. (C.C.P. 708.290; see Legislative Com. Comment—Assembly, Pamphlet, p. 1515.)

(d)   [§378A]   (New) Charging Orders.

"If a money judgment is rendered against a partner but *not against the partnership,* the judgment debtor's interest in the partnership may be applied toward the satisfaction of the judgment by an order charging the judgment debtor's interest" pursuant to Corp. C. 15028 or 15573 (see 6 *Summary, Partnership,* §39). (C.C.P. 708.310; see Legislative Com. Comment—Assembly, Pamphlet, p. 1515.) (On the former law, see text, §142.)

Service of a notice of motion for the charging order on the debtor or the partnership creates a lien on the debtor's partnership interest (C.C.P. 708.320(a); see Law Rev. Com. Comment, Pamphlet, p. 1516) which, if the order is subsequently issued, continues under the terms of the order (C.C.P. 708.320(b)). Denial of the order extinguishes the lien. (C.C.P. 708.320(b).)

See 14 Pacific L.J. 430.

(e)   (New) Lien in Pending Action or Proceeding.

(1)   [§379A]   (New) Nature and Scope of Remedy.

(a) *In General.* A creditor with a money judgment against a debtor who is a party to a pending action or special proceeding may obtain a lien, to the extent necessary to satisfy his judgment, on (1) any cause of action for money or property involved in the action or proceeding, and (2) the debtor's rights under any judgment subsequently procured. (C.C.P. 708.410(a); see Legislative Com. Comment —Assembly, Pamphlet, p. 1517 [the requirement of a court hearing under former C.C.P. 688.1 (see text, §§140, 141) is not continued].) "[A]n action or special proceeding is *pending* until the time for appeal from the judgment has expired or, if an appeal is filed, until the appeal has been finally determined." (C.C.P. 708.410(d).)

To obtain the lien the creditor must file in the pending action or proceeding a *notice of claim* and an abstract or certified copy of his money judgment. (C.C.P. 708.410(b).) The fact and time of the lien's creation must be entered by the court clerk on any judgment subsequently recovered (C.C.P. 708.460(a); see Law Rev. Com. Comment, Pamphlet, p. 1522), and any abstract issued upon the judgment must include a statement of the creditor's lien (C.C.P. 708.460(b)).

See 14 Pacific L.J. 430.

(b) *Service.* At the time of the filing (see supra), or "promptly thereafter," the creditor must, personally or by mail, serve on all existing parties to the action or special proceeding a copy of the notice of lien and a statement of its filing date. Failure to make such service does not affect the lien, but the rights of a party cannot be affected by the lien until he has notice. (C.C.P. 708.410(c); see Legislative Com. Comment—Assembly, Pamphlet, p. 1517.)

(c) *Intervention.* The court in which the action or special proceeding is pending may permit a creditor who has obtained a lien to intervene. (C.C.P. 708.430(a); see Law Rev. Com. Comment, Pamphlet, p. 1520.) However, even without intervention, a creditor is deemed to be a party to the action or special proceeding for the purposes of seeking an order applying the property to the satisfaction of his judgment (see Supp., infra, §383A) or opposing a claim of exemption (see Supp., infra, §382A). (C.C.P. 708.430(b).)

(2) [§380A] (New) Notice of Lien.

Pursuant to C.C.P. 708.420, the notice of lien must contain all of the following:

(a) A statement of the lien's creation and the title of the court and the cause and number of the pending action or proceeding.

(b) The debtor's name and last known address.

(c) The creditor's name and address.

(d) The title of the court where the creditor's judgment is entered and the cause and number of the action, date of entry, date of subsequent renewals, and where entered in the court records.

(e) The amount required to satisfy the creditor's judgment as of the time of the filing of the notice of lien.

(f) A statement that the lien attaches to both the debtor's cause of action and any subsequent judgment (see Supp., supra, §379A).

(g) A statement of the requirements for compromise, dismissal, settlement or satisfaction of the pending action or of the debtor's rights under any judgment secured therein (see Supp., infra, §381A).

(h) A statement of the debtor's right to claim an exemption for all or any portion of the money or property (see Supp., infra, §382A).

See Law Rev. Com. Comment, Pamphlet, p. 1519.

(3) [§381A] (New) Enforcement, Compromise, Dismissal, Settlement, Satisfaction.

Unless the creditor's money judgment is first satisfied or the lien is released, the creditor's consent or court authorization is required before (a) a judgment for the debtor in the action or proceeding may be enforced by writ or otherwise, or (b) there can be, by or on behalf of the debtor, any compromise, dismissal, settlement or satisfaction of the action or proceeding or the judgment procured therein. However, notwithstanding this provision, the rights of a party who compromises, etc. a claim without notice of the lien are unaffected by the lien (see Supp., supra, §379A). (C.C.P. 708.440(a).)

Upon the debtor's application on noticed motion the court may order compromise, etc., on such terms and conditions as it deems necessary. The notice of motion must be served on the creditor personally or by mail. (C.C.P. 708.440(b); see Law Rev. Com. Comment, Pamphlet, p. 1521 [provision permitting compromise, etc., despite creditor's opposition, was added to prevent, e.g., a creditor from forcing the debtor to proceed where the court concludes that settlement is in the parties' best interests].)

(4) [§382A] (New) Debtor's Claim of Exemption.

(a) *Right to Claim.* "If a lien is created under this article, the judgment debtor may claim that all or any portion of the money or property that the judgment debtor may recover in the action or special proceeding is exempt from enforcement of a money judgment." (C.C.P. 708.450(a); see Law Rev. Com. Comment, Pamphlet, p. 1522.)

(b) *Procedure.* The claim must be made by application on noticed motion, supported by affidavit (on contents, see Supp., supra, §301A), and filed and served, personally or by mail, on the creditor not later than 30 days after the debtor has received notice of the creation of the lien. The creditor need not file a notice of opposition. (C.C.P. 708.450(a); see C.C.P. 708.430(b), Supp., supra, §379A [with respect to the claim of exemption, creditor deemed a party to the action or special proceeding].)

Unless continued for good cause, the court must determine the exemption claim at any time prior to the entry of judgment, and may consolidate the exemption hearing with the hearing for an order to enforce the lien (see Supp., infra, §383A). (C.C.P. 708.450(b).)

(c) *Waiver of Right.* The debtor's failure to make a claim of exemption constitutes a waiver of the exemption. (C.C.P. 708.450(a).)

(d) *Termination of Lien.* The court must order the termination of the lien on that portion of the money or property recovered in the action or proceeding that the debtor establishes is completely or partially exempt. (C.C.P. 708.450(c).)

(5) [§383A] (New) Orders in Action To Enforce Lien.

(a) *Order For Application of Recovery To Satisfy Lien.* If the debtor is entitled to money or property under the judgment in the action or proceeding, and a lien thereon has been created, the court may, upon application on noticed motion of any party, order that the debtor's rights to such money or property be applied to the satisfaction of the lien. The notice of motion must be served, personally or by mail, on all other parties. (C.C.P. 708.470(a); see C.C.P. 708.430(b) [creditor deemed to be a party for purposes of applying for order to enforce lien]; Law Rev. Com. Comment, Pamphlet, p. 1523 [C.C.P. 708.470 is drawn from C.C.P. 708.280(b)–(d) (see Supp., supra, §377A)].)

(b) *Order Prohibiting Transfer of Property.* If the judgment determines that the debtor has an interest in property, the court may issue an order prohibiting its transfer until it can be levied upon or otherwise applied to the satisfaction of the lien. (C.C.P. 708.470(b).)

(c) *Judgment Against Party Making Transfer.* If a party (other than the debtor) having notice of the lien has transferred property subject thereto, or has paid an amount subject to the lien to the debtor, the court must render judgment against the party in an amount equal to the lesser of (1) the value of the debtor's interest in the property or the amount paid to him, or (2) the amount of the creditor's lien. (C.C.P. 708.470(c).)

(6) [§384A] (New) Enforcement of Lien After Final Judgment.

A lien created in a pending action or proceeding may be enforced "by any applicable procedure" either after entry of the judgment and expiration of the time for appeal (C.C.P. 708.480(a)) or, if an appeal is filed, after final determination (C.C.P. 708.480(b)).

The remedies for the enforcement of the lien include levy on the judgment under a writ of execution and sale or collection pursuant to such levy (see Supp., supra, §249A et seq.), appointment of a receiver to collect the judgment (see Supp., infra, §389A), application for an assignment order (see Supp., infra, §385A et seq.), and collection from a public entity owing money to the debtor (see Supp., infra, §390A et seq.). (Legislative Com. Comment—Assembly, Pamphlet, p. 1523 [former law restricted creditor to action for foreclosure of the lien, where judgment debtor of the creditor's debtor did not voluntarily pay the creditor to discharge the lien and the creditor's debtor took no steps to enforce the judgment].)

(f) (New) Assignment Order.

(1) [§385A] (New) Nature of Remedy.

(a) *In General.* On noticed motion by the creditor, served personally or by mail on the debtor (C.C.P. 708.510(b)), the court may order the debtor to assign to the creditor, or to a receiver (see Supp., infra, §389A), "all or part of a right to payment due or to become due, whether or not the right is conditioned on future developments" (C.C.P. 708.510(a)). (For limitations on the right to make, and the amount of, the assignment, see infra, this section.)

The assignment order is a new procedure for reaching certain forms of property unreachable by levy under a writ of execution, such as the nonexempt loan value of an unmatured life insurance policy (see Supp., supra, §315A), as well as an optional procedure for reaching assignable forms of property that are subject to levy. (Legislative Com. Comment—Assembly, Pamphlet, p. 1525.)

See 14 Pacific L.J. 431.

(b) *Types of Payment Assignable.* These include, but are not limited to: (1) wages due from the federal government not subject to withholding under a withholding order, (2) rents, (3) commissions, (4) royalties, (5) payments due from a patent or copyright, (6) loan value of an insurance policy. (C.C.P. 708.510(a).)

(c) *Factors Considered.* The court may consider all relevant factors in determining whether an assignment is an appropriate remedy. Such factors include (1) the reasonable requirements of a debtor who is a natural person and of persons supported by him, (2) payments the debtor is required to make or that are deducted for other judgments and wage assignments, (3) the amount remaining due on the money judgment, (4) the amount being or to be received in satisfaction of the right to payment that may be assigned. (C.C.P. 708.510(c).)

(d) *Limitations.* The court may not order an assignment that is otherwise prohibited by law. (C.C.P. 708.510(a); see Legislative Com. Comment—Assembly, Pamphlet, p. 1526 [examples of nonassignable rights include federal employees' retirement benefits (5 U.S.C., §8346) and railroad employees' annuities (45 U.S.C., §231m)].)

An assignment of a right to payment may not be in an amount in excess of that necessary to satisfy the creditor's judgment. (C.C.P. 708.510(d); see Legislative Com. Comment—Assembly, Pamphlet, p. 1526.)

If the assignment involves earnings or periodic payments pursuant to a pension or retirement plan, the amount assigned must not exceed that which may be withheld from a like amount of earnings under the Wage Garnishment Law (see Supp., supra, §338A et seq.). (C.C.P. 705.510(e).)

Where a specific amount of the payment to be assigned is exempt by another statutory provision, the amount of the exemption must be deducted from the amount assigned. (C.C.P. 708.510(f).)

(e) *Restraining Order.* At the time the motion for an assignment order is made, or thereafter, the creditor may apply for an order restraining the debtor from assigning, or otherwise disposing of, the right to payment sought to be assigned. The application may be made ex parte unless the court directs, or a court rule requires, that it be made on noticed motion. (C.C.P. 708.520(a); see Law Rev. Com. Comment, Pamphlet, p. 1527.)

The court may (1) issue the restraining order upon a showing of need; (2) require the creditor to provide an undertaking (C.C.P. 708.520(b)); and (3) modify or vacate the order at any time with or without a hearing on such terms as are just (C.C.P. 708.520(c)).

The order must be personally served on the debtor and contain notice that failure to comply may subject him to being held in contempt. (C.C.P. 708.520(d).)

(2)   [§386A]   (New) Effect of Assignment Ordered.

The effect and priority of an assignment order is governed by C.C. 955.1, which provides that (1) the transfer of general intangibles and other rights to payment is perfected against third persons upon delivery of a written assignment thereof to the transferee, and (2) as between bona fide assignees of the same right for value without notice, priority is given to the assignee first giving notice thereof to the obligor. (C.C.P. 708.530.)

A creditor (or receiver) who is assigned a right to payment is a bona fide assignee for value under C.C. 955.1 (C.C.P. 708.530), but will have priority over another assignee of the same right for value and without notice *only* if he first gives notice to the obligor (Law Rev. Com. Comment, Pamphlet, p. 1527).

The obligor's rights are not affected by an assignment order until he receives notice of it. The term "obligor" refers to both the person obligated to make payment to the debtor, as well as one who may become obligated to make such payments in the future. (C.C.P. 708.540; see Law Rev. Com. Comment, Pamphlet, p. 1528.)

(3)   [§387A]   (New) Exemption Procedure.

By noticed motion filed not later than 3 days before the hearing date on the creditor's motion for an assignment order, the debtor may claim that all or a portion of the right to payment is exempt. Failure to make such claim is a waiver of the exemption. (C.C.P. 708.550(a); see Law Rev. Com. Comment, Pamphlet, p. 1528.)

The notice of motion must be personally served on the creditor not later than 3 days before the date set for the hearing (C.C.P. 708.550(b)), at which the court must determine any claim of exemption (C.C.P. 708.550(c)).

(4) [§388A] (New) Modification or Setting Aside of Order.

Either the creditor or the debtor, on noticed motion served on the other party personally or by mail, may apply for an order to modify or set aside the assignment order. (C.C.P. 708.560(a).) The court must grant such order upon a showing of a material change in circumstances since the time of the previous hearing on the assignment order, and may order a reassignment of the right to payments. The order must state whether and to what extent it applies to payments already made. (C.C.P. 708.560(b); see Law Rev. Com. Comment, Pamphlet, p. 1529.)

(g) [§389A] (New) Receiver To Enforce Judgment.

(1) *In General.* "The court may appoint a receiver to enforce the judgment where the judgment creditor shows that, considering the interests of both the judgment creditor and the judgment debtor, the appointment of a receiver is a reasonable method to obtain the fair and orderly satisfaction of the judgment." (C.C.P. 708.620.) This provision eliminates the former requirements that a writ of execution be returned unsatisfied or that the debtor refuse to apply property in satisfaction of the judgment. (Legislative Com. Comment—Assembly, Pamphlet, p. 1530; see Law Rev. Com. Recommendation, Pamphlet, p. 1138 [requirement of an unsatisfied writ of execution is "an empty formality which results in a delay of at least 10 days in the attempt to reach the judgment debtor's assets and merely increases the costs of collection"].) (On the former law, see text, §179 et seq.)

General receiver provisions (C.C.P. 564 et seq., 571 et seq.; see *Provisional Remedies,* §236 et seq.) govern the appointment, qualifications, powers, rights and duties of a receiver appointed to enforce a judgment. (C.C.P. 708.610; see Law Rev. Com. Comment, Pamphlet, p. 1529.)

See 14 Pacific L.J. 432.

(2) *Transfer of Alcoholic Beverage License.* The court may appoint a receiver to transfer the debtor's interest in a transferable alcoholic beverage license (see B. & P.C. 24070 et seq.), *unless* the debtor establishes that the amount of delinquent taxes and claims of creditors

having priority over the judgment creditor exceed the *probable* sale price of the license. (C.C.P. 708.630(a)(b); see Legislative Com. Comment—Assembly, Pamphlet, p. 1531 [under former C.C.P. 688(f), alcoholic beverage licenses not reachable by any state enforcement process].)

The receiver may exercise the powers of the licensee, and must comply with the transfer provisions of the Alcoholic Beverage Control Act (B. & P.C. 23000 et seq.) and the applicable regulations of the Department of Alcoholic Beverage Control. An application must be filed to transfer the license to the receiver, and a temporary retail permit must be obtained during the pendency of the transfer. (C.C.P. 708.630(c); see Legislative Com. Comment—Assembly, Pamphlet, p. 1531.)

See 14 Pacific L.J. 432.

(h)   (New) Where Judgment Debtor Is Creditor of Public Entity.

(1)   [§390A]   (New) In General.

(a) *Nature of Remedy.* C.C.P. 708.710 et seq. continue the exclusive procedure under former law for reaching money owed to the debtor by a public entity (see text, §134 et seq.), namely, filing with the entity an abstract or transcript of the judgment and an affidavit stating the amount owing thereon (on the §6 filing fee, see C.C.P. 708.785(a)), payment by the entity of the required amount into court, and transfer by the court of the nonexempt portion of this amount to the creditor. (Law. Rev. Com. Recommendation, Pamphlet, p. 1139.) Although this procedure generally governs all obligations of public entities to be applied to the satisfaction of a money judgment, it is not applicable to earnings of public officers and employees (governed by C.C.P. 706.010 et seq.; see Supp., supra, §338A et seq.) and obligations that are the subject of a pending action or special proceeding (governed by C.C.P. 708.410 et seq.; see Supp., supra, §379A et seq.) (C.C.P. 708.720.) Nor does it authorize the filing against an overpayment of tax, penalty or interest, or interest allowable with respect to an overpayment, under Rev.C. 23001 or Unemp. Ins.C. 13000. (C.C.P. 708.795; see Legislative Com. Comment—Senate, Pamphlet, p. 1540.)

The special procedure for application of a *condemnation award* due the debtor to satisfaction of a judgment (see former C.C.P. 710(d), text, §138) was eliminated as unnecessary. (Law Rev. Com. Comment, Pamphlet, p. 1534 [depending on whether the judgment in the condemnation proceeding is pending or final, the creditor may either obtain a lien in the pending proceeding (C.C.P. 708.410 et seq.) or file an abstract or certified copy of a final judgment with the public entity (C.C.P. 708.710); where the public entity has deposited the award with the court holding the condemnation proceeding and the creditor has not obtained a lien, the creditor may use such procedure as garnishment or motion].)

See 14 Pacific L.J. 432.

(b) *Definitions.* C.C.P. 708.710 defines the following terms: (1) *Local public entity:* "any public entity other than the state;" (2) *Public entity:* "the state, a county, city, district, public authority, public agency, and any other political subdivision in the state;" (3) *State:* "the State of California;" (4) *State agency:* "a state office, officer, department, division, bureau, board, commission or agency claims against which are paid by warrants drawn by the Controller". (See Law Rev. Com. Comment, Pamphlet, p. 1532.)

(c) *Filing.* If money is owing and unpaid to the debtor by a public entity, the creditor may file with the appropriate entity (see Supp., infra, §391A et seq.) an abstract or certified copy of the judgment, plus an affidavit stating the creditor's desire to apply the obligation to the satisfaction of the judgment and the exact amount required for such satisfaction. (C.C.P. 708.730(a); see Law Rev. Com. Comment, Pamphlet, p. 1533 [phrase "owing and unpaid" refers to "an existing and unsatisfied legal liability on the part of the public entity"].)

(d) *Notice to Debtor.* Promptly after the filing (see supra) the creditor must serve, personally or by mail, notice thereof on the debtor. (C.C.P. 708.730(b); see Law Rev. Com. Comment, Pamphlet, p. 1534 [former C.C.P. 710 (see text, §139) did not require notice to the debtor].)

(e) *Liability of Public Officer.* The creditor may include in the affidavit any facts tending to establish the debtor's identity (C.C.P. 708.730(a)); and no public officer or employee may be held liable for failure to comply with C.C.P. 708.710 et seq. unless there is sufficient information in the abstract or certified copy of the judgment together with the affidavit, or in the papers and records on file in the office where the officer or employee works, to enable him, in the exercise of reasonable diligence, to ascertain the debtor's identity. The term "office" does not include a branch or subordinate office located in a different city. (C.C.P. 708.790.)

(2) [§391A] (New) Where Debtor Is Creditor of State Agency.

(a) *Time of Filing.* The abstract or certified copy of the judgment and the affidavit (see Supp., supra, §390A) must be filed by the creditor with the state agency owing the money to the debtor prior to the time the agency presents the debtor's claim to the Controller. (C.C.P. 708.740(a); on former procedure, see text, §137 et seq.)

(b) *Presentation of Debtor's Claim to Controller.* In making such presentation the state agency must note the fact of the filing (see supra), and specify the amount required to satisfy the judgment and any amounts advanced to, or owed by, the debtor for any purpose. (C.C.P. 708.740(b).)

(c) *Discharge of Debtor's Claim.* This is accomplished by the Controller's (1) depositing with the court the amount due the debtor (after deductions for amounts advanced to, or owed by, the debtor) required to satisfy the judgment "in full or to the greatest extent," and (2) paying any balance to the debtor. (C.C.P. 708.740(c).)

(3) [§392A] (New) Where Debtor Is Creditor of Other Public Entity.

The abstract or certified copy of the judgment and the affidavit (see Supp., supra, §390A) must be filed by the creditor with the auditor of the public entity or, if there is no auditor, with the official whose duty corresponds to that of auditor. (C.C.P. 708.750.)

To discharge the debtor's claim the auditor or other official must follow the same procedure prescribed for the Controller for situations where the debtor is the creditor of a state agency (see Supp., supra, §391A). (C.C.P. 708.750.)

(4) [§393A] (New) Where Debtor is Contractor on Public Works.

To determine the amount of the contract price "owing and unpaid" (see Supp., supra, §390A et seq.) to a debtor who is a contractor on a public work, it is necessary to deduct therefrom sums owed to persons described in C.C. 3181 (mechanics, materialmen, subcontractors, etc.), but only to the extent that claims for such sums are made in accordance with the provisions governing filings of stop notices on public works (C.C. 3179 et seq.; see *Actions*, §139). (C.C.P. 708.760(a).)

The Controller, auditor or other public disbursing officer may not deposit with the court the amount due the debtor until after the contract is completed. However, such deposit can be made prior to the time the payments to materialmen, etc (see supra) are made, so long as a sufficient amount to cover them is retained. (C.C.P. 708.760(b)); see Law Rev. Com. Comment, Pamphlet, p. 1537 [C.C.P. 708.760(b) is intended to permit payment to the creditor without the necessity of awaiting the resolution of disputes among other contractors].)

(5) [§394A] (New) Procedure.

(a) *Notice of Deposit.* The court clerk must cause this notice to be served, personally or by mail, on the debtor promptly after the public entity has made the required deposit with the court (see Supp., supra, §390A et seq.). (C.C.P. 708.770(a); see Legislative Com. Comment— Assembly, Pamphlet, p. 1538 [notice of deposit enables debtor to make claim of exemption before the money is paid over to the creditor].)

(b) *Exemption Claim.* To make such claim the debtor, within 10 days after service of the notice of deposit, must (1) file a claim of exemption (on contents, see Supp., supra, §301A) and a notice of motion for an order determining the claim of exemption, and (2) serve on the creditor, personally or by mail, copies of the notice of motion and claim of exemption, and a notice of hearing on the motion. (C.C.P. 708.770(b).)

To oppose the motion the creditor, within 10 days after being served, must file a *notice of opposition* executed under oath (on contents, see Supp., supra, §303A), and serve a copy of it on the debtor, personally or by mail. (C.C.P. 708.770(d).)

Unless continued for good cause, the hearing on the motion must be held not later than 30 days after the notice of motion was filed. (C.C.P. 708.770(c).) The following sections applicable to exemption claims under a writ of execution are applicable to such claims when made by a debtor of a public entity: C.C.P. 703.580(a)–(d) (hearing and order; see Supp., supra, §304A); C.C.P. 703.590 (extension of time; see Supp., infra, §300A) and C.C.P. 703.600 (appeals; see Supp., supra, §300A). (C.C.P. 708.770(e).)

Failure of the debtor to make a claim of exemption constitutes a waiver of the exemption. (C.C.P. 708.770(f).)

(c) *Distribution of Money.* After the period for making a claim of exemption (see supra) has expired and no claim has been made, or after determination of any claim made within this period, the court must pay to the creditor the nonexempt portion of the money deposited to which he is entitled, and any balance to the debtor, unless other disposition is required by law. (C.C.P. 708.775; see Law Rev. Com. Comment, Pamphlet, p. 1538.)

(d) *Lien.* Filing of the abstract or certified copy of the judgment and the affidavit (see Supp., supra, §390A) creates a lien on the money owing and unpaid to the debtor equal to that which may properly be applied to satisfaction of the judgment. (C.C.P. 708.780; see Law Rev. Com. Comment, Pamphlet, p. 1538.)

(i) **[§395A]** **(New) Enforcement Against Franchise.**

Former law permitted a levy of execution on, and sale of, a franchise to satisfy a money judgment (former C.C.P. 724a et seq.), a procedure which was inadequate due to the impracticality of levy on a franchise, the inadequacy of sale as a means of reaching the value of the franchise, and problems involving transfer. (Law Rev. Com. Recommendation, Pamphlet, p. 1143.)

The new law, applicable to franchises "granted by a *public entity* and all the rights and privileges thereof, other than the franchise of being a corporation" (C.C.P. 708.910), permits the court to order a franchise to be applied in satisfaction of the judgment in the manner most satisfactory under the circumstances (see infra, this section). The order of application is subject to all applicable laws governing sale, transfer or other actions concerning the franchise, such as Public Utilities Commission approval and compliance with statutory or administrative regulations. (C.C.P. 708.930.)

The court's power to issue an order applying a franchise to satisfaction of a money judgment is discretionary (C.C.P. 708.920(a)) and is governed by the following procedure:

(1) *Application for order and notice:* The creditor's application for the order must be on noticed motion, which must be served, personally or by mail, on both the debtor and the public entity that granted the franchise. (C.C.P. 708.920(a).)

(2) *Factors considered in issuing order:* The court must consider the nature of the franchise, its transferability, the likelihood that its application to satisfaction of the judgment will yield a substantial amount, and all other circumstances of the case. (C.C.P. 708.920(a).)

(3) *Methods of applying franchise to satisfaction of judgment:* These include sale, assignment, appointment of a receiver, or any other means appearing proper to the court. (C.C.P. 708.920(b).)

(4) *Additional provisions:* The court may also provide for such matters as the place of sale, possession of the debtor's property necessary for exercise of the franchise, receipt of franchise proceeds, recovery of penalties recoverable for injury to the franchise or for damages or other cause, and the debtor's powers and duties and liability for penalties and forfeitures. (C.C.P. 708.920(b).)

See 14 Pacific L.J. 433.

(j) [§396A] (New) Other Enforcement Procedures.

(1) *Trusts.* C.C.P. 709.010 establishes an exclusive procedure for applying the debtor's interest as a beneficiary of a trust to the satisfaction of a money judgment. The term "trust" has the meaning provided in Prob.C. 1138 (see 7 *Summary,* Trusts, §8), except that it includes a trust subject to court supervision under Prob.C. 1120 (see 7 *Summary, Wills and Probate,* §245 et seq.). (C.C.P. 709.010(a); see Law Rev. Com. Comment, Pamphlet, p. 1542 [section applicable to written, voluntary express trusts (testamentary or inter vivos), but not

to such trust as Totten trusts, investment trusts and deeds of trust].) Spendthrift trusts are excluded from the statute's coverage, except for surplus amounts liable pursuant to C.C. 859 (see 7 *Summary, Trusts,* §98). (C.C.P. 709.010(c).)

On the creditor's petition to the probate court, the debtor's interest in the trust may be applied to the satisfaction of a judgment by such means as the court determines are proper, such as imposition of a lien on, or sale of, the debtor's interest, collection of trust income, and liquidation and transfer of trust assets by the trustee. (C.C.P. 709.010(b); see Law Rev. Com. Comment, Pamphlet, p. 1542.)

(2) *Contingent Interest.* The creditor may apply on noticed motion for an order applying to the satisfaction of a money judgment a contingent remainder, executory interest, or other nonvested property interest of the debtor. In applying these interests to the satisfaction of the judgment, the court may use such means as it deems proper to protect the interest of the debtor and creditor, such as imposition of a lien on, or sale of, the debtor's interest. (C.C.P. 709.020; see Law Rev. Com. Comment, Pamphlet, p. 1543; on former law exempting contingent interests from enforcement of a money judgment, see text, §16.)

(3) *Guardianship or Conservatorship Estates.* Property in a guardianship or conservatorship estate is not subject to enforcement of a money judgment. However, the creditor may apply to the court in which the guardianship or conservatorship proceeding is pending for an order requiring payment of the judgment. (C.C.P. 709.030; see text, §16; Law Rev. Com. Recommendation, Pamphlet, p. 1142 [such property is not subject to normal enforcement remedies, even if held in the name of the guardian or conservator].)

C.   (New) Enforcement of Nonmoney Judgments.

1.   (New) In General.

(a)   [§397A]   (New) Nature and Scope of Remedies.

Division 3 of the Enforcement of Judgments Law consolidates the provisions governing the enforcement of nonmoney judgments, such as judgments for the sale (see Supp., infra, §405A) or possession (see Supp., infra, §401A et seq.) of property. (Law Rev. Com. Recommendation, Pamphlet, p. 1155.) Such judgments are enforceable against public entities (C.C.P. 712.070), and by a court-appointed receiver (C.C.P. 712.060; see Supp., supra, §389A; on former law, see text, §179 et seq.).

Division 3 also replaces writs formerly used to enforce nonmoney judgments, i.e., writs of possession, restitution, execution, assistance or enforcement (see text, §183 et seq.) with the *writ of possession* and the *writ of sale.* (On issuance of these writs, see Supp., infra, §398A.) The writ of execution is now reserved for the enforcement of *money* judgments. (Law Rev. Com. Recommendation, Pamphlet, p. 1155.)

(b) [§398A] (New) Issuance of Writ of Possession or Sale.

(1) *In General.* After entry of a judgment for possession or sale of property the court clerk, upon application of the creditor, must issue a writ of possession or sale directed to the levying officer in the county of enforcement (separate writ required for each such county). Successive writs may be issued until the judgment is satisfied, except that a new writ may not be issued for a county within 180 days after the issuance of a prior writ for that county, unless the prior writ is first returned. (C.C.P. 712.010; see Law Rev. Com. Comment, Pamphlet, p. 1544.)

(2) *Contents.* C.C.P. 712.020, in addition to requiring the levying officer to enforce the judgment, provides that the writ must include the following information:

(a) The date of issuance.

(b) The title of the court where the judgment is entered and the cause and number of the action.

(c) The creditor's name and address, and the debtor's name and last known address.

(d) The date of judgment, and of any subsequent renewals, and where entered in the court records.

(e) The amount required to satisfy any money judgment included in the judgment for possession or sale, as of the date the writ was issued, and the amount of interest accruing daily as of that date.

(f) The name and address of any person requesting notice of sale under the judgment.

(g) Any other information required to be included (see Supp., infra, §401A et seq.).

See Law Rev. Com. Comment, Pamphlet, p. 1545.

(c) [§399A] (New) Delivery and Execution of Writ.

Upon delivery of the writ of possession or sale to the levying officer, together with the creditor's written instructions, the levying officer must execute the writ in the manner prescribed by law. (C.C.P. 712.030; on similar provision for writ of execution, see Supp., supra, §258A.) The return of the writ is governed by C.C.P. 699.560, covering return of writs of execution (see Supp., supra, §260A). (C.C.P. 712.050; see Law Rev. Com. Comment, Pamphlet, p. 1547 [former law (see text, §183 et seq.) did not provide for the return of a writ of possession or sale].)

The levying officer may not levy upon or otherwise seize property under the writ after the expiration of 180 days from its date of issuance. (C.C.P. 712.030(b).)

(d) [§400A] (New) Collection of Money Amounts.

If so ordered in a judgment for sale, a *money judgment* included therein may *only* be enforced as ordered by the court. (C.C.P. 712.040(c); see Legislative Com. Comment—Senate, Pamphlet, p. 1546.) Otherwise, to satisfy a money judgment included in a judgment for possession or sale, a writ of possession or sale may be enforced as a writ of execution. And, if the writ of possession or sale is no longer leviable as a writ of execution (after it has been returned or 180 days have elapsed since its issuance), or if the creditor, for any reason, does not desire issuance of a writ of possession or sale, a writ of execution may be issued to satisfy a money judgment included in the judgment of possession or sale. (C.C.P. 712.040(a); Legislative Com. Comment—Senate, Pamphlet, p. 1546.)

Regardless of whether a writ of possession or sale has been issued, enforced or returned, the creditor may use any of the appropriate remedies available for enforcement of money judgments (see Supp., supra, §338A et seq. [wage garnishment]; Supp., supra, §367A et seq. [miscellaneous creditors' remedies]) to satisfy a money judgment included in the judgment. (C.C.P. 712.040(b).)

2. [§401A] (New) Judgment For Possession of Personal Property.

(a) *Writ of Possession.* "A judgment for possession of personal property may be enforced by a writ of possession of personal property." (C.C.P. 714.010(a); on former law, see text, §184.) In addition to the information required by C.C.P. 712.020 (see Supp., supra, §398A), the writ must contain a description of the relevant property and its value (if specified in the judgment or a supplemental order). (C.C.P. 714.010(b); see Law Rev. Com. Comment, Pamphlet, p. 1548; on the form for the writ, see C.C.P. 693.010, Supp., supra, §234A.)

(b) *Execution.* To execute the writ of possession the levying officer must (1) search for the property specified therein; (2) take custody of it in the same manner as for a levy under a writ of execution (if the property is in the possession of the debtor or his agent); and (3) deliver the property to the creditor in satisfaction of the judgment. (C.C.P. 714.020(a); on seizing personal property used as a dwelling, see Supp., supra, §267A; on seizing property in a private place, see Supp., supra, §250A.)

(c) *Where Property Cannot Be Taken Into Custody.* In this event the levying officer must demand the property from the debtor (if he can be located), and if custody is not then obtained, must so state in his return. (C.C.P. 714.020(b); see Law Rev. Com. Comment, Pamphlet, p. 1549.) Thereafter, the judgment for the possession of the property may be enforced in the same manner as a money judgment for the *value of the property* (C.C.P. 714.020(b)); and, under these circumstances, the writ of possession may be treated as a writ of execution (C.C.P. 714.020(c)).

(d) *Turnover Order.* After entry of a judgment for possession of personal property, and whether or not a writ of possession of personal property has been issued, the creditor may apply for an order directing the debtor to transfer to the creditor possession of the property or documentary evidence of title thereto, or both. The application may be made ex parte unless the court directs, or a court rule requires, that it be made upon noticed motion. (C.C.P. 714.030(a); see Law Rev. Com. Comment, Pamphlet, p. 1550.) The court may issue the order upon a showing of need. (C.C.P. 714.030(b).)

The order must be personally served on the debtor and contain a notice that failure to comply may subject him to being held in contempt. (C.C.P. 714.030(c).)

3.   (New) Judgment For Possession of Real Property.

(a)   [§402A]   (New) Writ of Possession.

"A judgment for possession of real property may be enforced by a writ of possession of real property." (C.C.P. 715.010(a); on former law, see text, §184.)

In addition to the information required by C.C.P. 712.020 (see Supp., supra, §398A), the writ must contain (1) a description of the real property; (2) a statement of the time in which the property must be vacated and the consequences of noncompliance (see Supp., infra, §403A); and (3) a statement that any personal property remaining after the creditor has been placed in possession of the real property will be disposed of in accordance with C.C.P. 1174 (see 3 *Summary, Real Property,* §524 et seq.), unless the debtor or other owner pays the creditor reasonable storage costs and takes possession within 15 days after the creditor has taken possession of the real property. (C.C.P. 715.010(b); see Law Rev. Com. Comment, Pamphlet, p. 1551; on the form for the writ, see C.C.P. 693.010, Supp., supra, §234A.)

The writ of possession must be accompanied by a notice giving the address and telephone number of the levying officer's office and directing the occupant to contact such office if he is not named in the writ of possession and claims either a right to possession accruing prior to the commencement of the unlawful detainer action or to have been in possession of the property on the date such action was filed (on the occupant's rights in this situation, see Supp., infra, §403A). (C.C.P. 715.010(c).)

(b) [§403A] (New) Execution of Writ.

(1) *By Levying Officer.* The levying officer must either (a) serve a copy of the writ on *one* occupant of the property (C.C.P. 715.020(a)), or (b) if unable to serve an occupant, post a copy of the writ in a conspicuous place on the property and serve another copy, personally or by mail, on the debtor (copy may be mailed to the property if the debtor's address is unknown). (C.C.P. 715.020(b)). Service on an occupant may be made by leaving a copy of the writ with the occupant personally or, if the occupant is absent, with a person of "suitable age and discretion" on the property at the time of service who is either the occupant's employee or agent or a member of his household. (C.C.P. 715.020(a).)

(2) *By Registered Process Server.* If a proper writ of possession is delivered to the sheriff, marshal or constable and that officer fails to execute it within 3 days (excluding weekends and legal holidays), a registered process server may execute the writ in either of the aforementioned methods (see supra). (C.C.P. 715.040(a); see Legislative Com. Comment—Assembly, Pamphlet, p. 1554 [process servers do not have the authority to remove occupants from the property (see infra, this section)]; C.C.P. 715.040(d) [process server's fee may be allowed as a recoverable cost].)

Within 5 days after execution all of the following papers must be filed with the levying officer: (1) The writ itself; (2) the process server's affidavit stating the manner of execution; (3) proof of service; (4) written instructions to the levying officer (see Supp., supra, §236A). (C.C.P. 715.040(b).)

All other duties under the writ (including returning it to the court) must be performed by the levying officer upon receipt of his $14 fee (see Govt.C. 26733). (C.C.P. 715.040(c).)

(3) *Failure To Vacate Property.* Upon a failure to vacate within 5 days from the date of service by either of the allowable methods (see supra), the levying officer must remove the occupants and place the creditor in possession. The 5-day period is not subject to the extensions provided by C.C.P. 684.120 (see Supp., supra, §235A). (C.C.P. 715.020(c).) However, unless the person is named in the writ, the levying officer is precluded from removing any person claiming a right to possession accruing prior to the commencement of the unlawful detainer action, or to have been in possession on the date of the filing of such action. (C.C.P. 715.020(d).)

[265]

(c) [§404A]   (New) Disposition of Personal Property.

Personal property remaining on the real property after the creditor is placed in possession (see Supp., supra, §403A) must be disposed of in accordance with C.C.P. 1174(e)–(m) (see 3 *Summary, Real Property,* §532, Supp., §538A). (C.C.P. 715.030; see Law Rev. Com. Comment, Pamphlet, p. 1533.) References in C.C.P. 1174 to the "landlord" and "tenant" are to be treated as references to the creditor and to the debtor or other occupant, respectively. (C.C.P. 715.030.)

4. [§405A]   (New) Judgment For Sale of Property.

(a) *Writ of Sale.* A judgment for sale of real or personal property may be enforced by a writ of sale issued to the levying officer (C.C.P. 716.010(a); see Supp., supra, §398A), and accompanied by a certified copy of the judgment (C.C.P. 716.010(c); see Law Rev. Com. Comment, Pamphlet, p. 1554). (On former law, allowing enforcement through an order of sale or writ of enforcement without resort to a writ of sale, see text, §183.) In addition to the information required by C.C.P. 712.020 (see Supp., supra, §398A), the writ must contain a description of the property. (C.C.P. 716.010(b).)

To execute the writ the levying officer must (1) levy upon the property in the manner prescribed for levy under a writ of execution (see Supp., supra, §261A-2 et seq.); (2) except as otherwise ordered by the court, give notice of sale and sell the property in the manner prescribed for such acts under a writ of execution (see Supp., supra, §282A et seq.); and (3) apply the proceeds of sale in conformity with the judgment for sale. (C.C.P. 716.020; see Legislative Com. Comment—Assembly, Pamphlet, p. 1555.)

(b) *Turnover Order.* If a writ of sale is issued, the creditor may apply ex parte or on noticed motion (if the court directs or a court rule requires) for an order directing the debtor to transfer to the levying officer possession of the property and any documentary evidence of title. (C.C.P. 716.030(a).) The court may issue the order upon a showing of need. (C.C.P. 716.030(b).) It must be personally served on the debtor and contain notice that failure to comply may subject him to being held in contempt. (C.C.P. 716.030(c).)

(c) *Receiver.* A judgment for sale of real or personal property may also be enforced by a receiver appointed for that purpose. (Law Rev. Com. Recommendation, Pamphlet, p. 1160; see Supp., supra, §389A.)

5. [§406A]   (New) Other Judgments.

"A judgment not otherwise enforceable pursuant to this title may be enforced by personally serving a certified copy of the judgment on the person required to obey it and invoking the power of the court to punish for contempt." (C.C.P. 717.010.)

The person against whom a judgment has been rendered may be held in contempt where he has notice or knowledge of the judgment, and the ability to comply, but *wilfully* refuses to do so. (Law Rev. Com. Recommendation, Pamphlet, p. 1160.)

D. (New) Third-Party Claims and Related Procedures.

1. [§407A] (New) In General.

Under the new law the third-party claims procedure is applicable regardless of whether the property is levied upon under a writ of execution, a writ of attachment or a prejudgment writ of possession. (See Law Rev. Com. Recommendation, Pamphlet, p. 1152 ["from the standpoint of the third person, it is irrelevant whether the interfering levy takes place under a writ of attachment or a writ of execution"]; C.C.P. 720.020, 720.030.) Hence, for purposes of this procedure (C.C.P. 720.010), "creditor" refers not only to the judgment creditor, but also to the plaintiff in the case of a levy under a writ of attachment or prejudgment writ of possession of personal property (C.C.P. 720.020), while "debtor" refers to the defendant in such cases, as well as to the judgment debtor (C.C.P. 720.030). (On the former third-party claims procedure in attachment cases, see *Provisional Remedies,* §215, Supp., §342A.)

See 14 Pacific L.J. 434.

New C.C. 1861.25, added in conforming legislation in 1982, makes the third-party claims procedures applicable to proceedings for enforcement of an innkeeper's lien (see 3 *Summary, Personal Property,* text and Supp., §152 et seq.).

2. (New) Third-Party Claims of Ownership and Possession.

(a) [§408A] (New) Right To Claim.

If a third person has a claim of ownership or right to possession in property and such claim is superior to the creditor's lien, he may file a third-party claim (1) "[w]here *real property* has been levied upon under a writ of attachment or a writ of execution"; or (2) "[w]here *personal property* has been levied upon where a writ of attachment, a writ of execution, a prejudgment or postjudgment writ of possession, or a writ of sale." (C.C.P. 720.110; see Law Rev. Com. Comment, Pamphlet, p. 1558 [third-party claims procedure does not preclude use of quiet title action]; Law Rev. Com. Recommendation, Pamphlet, p. 1145 [existing remedies do not provide adequate protection to the third person; an action to enjoin sale of the property under a writ of execution requires that he provide an undertaking, and an action to quiet title after the property has been sold involves considerable delay and expense].)

(b)   [§409A]   (New) Time and Manner of Making Claim.

(1) *In General.* A third-party claim is made by filing with the levying officer the claim and two copies. The claim must be made *after* the levy on the property, but *before* any of the following: (a) Sale of the property; (b) delivery of possession to the creditor; (c) payment of proceeds of collection to the creditor. (C.C.P. 720.120; see Law Rev. Com. Comment, Pamphlet, p. 1559.)

(2) *Contents.* The claim, which must be executed under oath, must contain (a) the third person's name and an address in the State where he can be served by mail; (b) a description of the property involved and of the interest claimed, including the facts on which the claim is based; and (c) an estimate of the claimed interest's market value. (C.C.P. 720.130(a).)

The third person must attach to the claim a copy of any writing on which the claim is based. The court has the discretion to exclude the writing from if a copy has not been attached to the claim. (C.C.P. 720.130(b).)

(3) *Service on Creditor.* Not later than 5 days after the filing of the claim, the levying officer must serve on the creditor, personally or by mail, (a) a copy of the claim; (b) a statement whether the third person has filed an undertaking to release the property (see Supp., infra, §424A); and (c) notices that, in order to avoid release of the property, the creditor must, within 10 days after having been served, either object to the third person's undertaking or, if none was filed, file his own undertaking (see Supp., infra, §411A). (C.C.P. 720.140(a)(b); see Law Rev. Com. Comment, Pamphlet, p. 1560.)

Service of the aforementioned papers may be made notwithstanding any defect, informality or insufficiency of the claim. (C.C.P. 720.140(d).)

(4) *Service on Debtor.* Not later than 5 days after the filing of the third-party claim, a copy of the papers required to be served on the creditor (see supra) must be served, personally or by mail, on the debtor. (C.C.P. 720.140(c).)

(c)   [§410A]   (New) Effect of Filing or Not Filing Claim.

Except as otherwise provided by statute (see, e.g., Supp., supra, §253A [disposition of perishable property]; Supp., infra, §411A [effect of filing undertaking]; Supp., infra, §421A [satisfaction from released property after hearing]), the timely filing of a third-party claim precludes the levying officer from (1) selling the property; (2) delivering possession thereof to the creditor; or (3) paying the proceeds of collection to the creditor. (C.C.P. 720.150(a); see Law Rev. Com. Comment, Pamphlet, p. 1561.)

A third person's interest in property is not affected by his failure to file a third-party claim. (C.C.P. 720.150(b).)

(d) [§411A] (New) Creditor's Undertaking.

(1) *Effect.* A timely (see Supp., supra, §409A) and satisfactory (see infra, this section) creditor's undertaking (a) requires the levying officer to execute the writ unless the third person files an undertaking (see Supp., infra, §424A), and (b) after sale, payment or delivery of the property pursuant to the writ, frees the property of all third-party claims for which the creditor has given the undertaking. (C.C.P. 720.160(a); see Law Rev. Com. Comment, Pamphlet, p. 1562.) (On creditor's undertaking where third person claims a *security interest* or *lien* in the property, see Supp., infra, §415A.)

(2) *Amount.* The basic amounts required for a creditor's undertaking are (a) for superior court pending actions or judgments—the *lesser* of $7,500 or twice the amount of the execution or other enforcement lien; (b) for municipal or justice court pending actions or judgments—the *lesser* of $2,500 or twice the amount of the execution or other enforcement lien. The creditor, however, may elect to file an undertaking in a larger amount. (C.C.P. 720.160(b); see Law Rev. Com. Recommendation, Pamphlet, p. 1148 [creditor's filing of a larger undertaking than required forces third person to file a larger undertaking to obtain the release of the property].)

The court may *decrease* the amount of the undertaking below the aforementioned limits if, after a third-person's motion to *increase* the undertaking to an amount sufficient to indemnify him (see Supp., infra, §426A), the court determines that the amount of the undertaking is *more than sufficient* to cover the third person's probable recovery if he ultimately prevails. (C.C.P. 720.160(b); see Law Rev. Com. Recommendation, Pamphlet, p. 1148.)

(3) *Contents.* The creditor's undertaking must (a) be made in favor of the third person; (b) indemnify the third person against losses caused by the enforcement proceedings; and (c) be conditioned on a final judgment affirming the third person's ownership or right to possession of the property. (C.C.P. 720.160(c).)

(4) *Public Entity's Notice of Opposition.* If the creditor is a public entity exempt from giving an undertaking, it must file with the levying officer a notice of its opposition to the third-party claim. When filed, such notice satisfies the requirement of an undertaking.

(C.C.P. 720.160(d); see Law Rev. Com. Comment, Pamphlet, p. 1563.)

(5) *Release of Property.* In cases where the third person has not filed an undertaking to release the property (see Supp., infra, §424A), the creditor's failure to file a timely (see Supp., infra, §409A) and satisfactory (see supra) undertaking (or notice of opposition for a public entity) requires the levying officer to release the property "unless it is to be held under another lien or unless otherwise ordered by the court." (C.C.P. 720.170(a); see Law Rev. Com. Comment, Pamphlet, p. 1563.)

The release is governed by C.C.P. 699.060 (see Supp., supra, §252A), except that if personal property which has been taken into custody is to be released to the debtor and the debtor has not claimed the property within 30 days after being given notice of its location, the levying officer must release it to the *third person* (rather than selling it and depositing the proceeds for the debtor). (C.C.P. 720.170(b)(c).)

A release of the property does not preclude a hearing (see Supp., infra, §417 et seq.) on the third-party claim. (C.C.P. 720.170(d); see Law Rev. Com. Comment, Pamphlet, p. 1564 [upon creditor's prevailing at hearing, released property may again be levied upon].)

3.   (New) Third-Party Claim of Security Interest or Lien.

(a)   [§412A]   (New) Right To Claim.

If a third person's claimed security interest in, or lien on, personal property is *superior* to the creditor's lien, he may file a third-party claim where the property has been levied upon under a writ of attachment, a writ of execution, a prejudgment or postjudgment writ of possession or a writ of sale. (C.C.P. 720.210(a); see Legislative Com. Comment—Assembly, Pamphlet, p. 1565.)

A secured party whose claimed security interest in *fixtures* is superior to the creditor's lien on the property may also file a third-party claim. For this purpose references in the provisions governing third-party claims are deemed to be references to fixtures. (C.C.P. 720.210(b).)

(b)   [§413A]   (New) Time and Manner of Making Claim.

(1) *In General.* A third-party claimant must file his claim and two copies with the levying officer *after* levy on the personal property, but *before* (a) sale of the property; (b) delivery of possession to the creditor; or (c) payment of the proceeds of collection to the creditor. (C.C.P. 720.220; see Law Rev. Com. Comment, Pamphlet, p. 1565.)

(2) *Contents.* The claim must be executed under oath and contain (a) the name of the secured party or lienholder and an address in the State where service by mail may be made; (b) a description of the property involved and of the security interest or lien claimed, including the facts upon which it is based; and (c) a statement of the total amount due, or to accrue, under the security interest or lien and the applicable rate of interest. (C.C.P. 720.230(a).)

A copy of the security interest and any financing statement or, in case of a lien, a copy of any writing upon which the claim is based, must be attached to the claim. The court may exclude from evidence any writing a copy of which was not so attached. (C.C.P. 720.230(b).)

(3) *Service on Creditor.* Not later than 5 days after the claim is filed, the levying officer must serve on the creditor, personally or by mail, (a) a copy of the claim; (b) a statement whether the third person has filed an undertaking to release the property (see Supp., infra, §424A); and (c) notice that the property will be released unless, within 10 days after being served with the claim, the creditor objects to any undertaking filed by the third person or, if no such undertaking is filed, *either* files his own undertaking and statement attacking the validity or priority of the security interest or the amount claimed (see Supp., infra, §415A) *or* deposits with the levying officer the amount due plus interest. (C.C.P. 720.240(a)(b); see Law Rev. Com. Comment, Pamphlet, p. 1567.)

The levying officer may serve the aforementioned papers notwithstanding any defect, informality or insufficiency of the claim. (C.C.P. 720.240(d).)

(4) *Service on Debtor.* Not later than 5 days after the claim is filed, the levying officer must also serve on the debtor, personally or by mail, a *copy* of the papers required to be served on the creditor (see supra). (C.C.P. 720.240(c).)

(c) [§414A] (New) Effect of Filing or Not Filing Claim.

Except as otherwise provided by statute (see Law Rev. Com. Comment, Pamphlet, p. 1561), the timely (see Supp., supra, §413A) filing of a third-party claim precludes the levying officer, with respect to the personal property in which the security interest or lien is claimed, from (1) selling the property; (2) delivering possession to the creditor; or (3) paying the proceeds of collection to the creditor. (C.C.P. 720.250(a).)

The intrest of a secured party or lienholder in the property is not affected by such party's failure to file a third-party claim. (C.C.P. 720.250(b); see Law Rev. Com. Comment, Pamphlet, p. 1568.)

(d) [§415A] (New) Creditor's Undertaking.

(1) *Effect.* The creditor's act of (a) filing an undertaking and a statement challenging the security interest (see infra, this section), or (b) making a deposit of the amount claimed, (1) requires the levying officer to execute the writ unless the secured party or lienholder, in response to the creditor's undertaking, files an undertaking to release the property (see Supp., infra, §424A), and (2) after sale, payment or delivery of the property, frees the property of all claims or liens for which the creditor has given the undertaking or made the deposit. (C.C.P. 720.260(a); see Legislative Com. Comment—Assembly, Pamphlet, p. 1569.)

(2) *Amount.* Generally, the amount of the undertaking must be: (a) For actions pending or judgments entered in superior court—the *lesser* of $7,500 or twice the amount of the execution or other enforcement lien; (b) for actions pending or judgments entered in municipal or justice court—the *lesser* of $2,500 or twice the amount of the execution or other enforcement lien. However, the creditor may elect to file an undertaking in a larger amount. And the court, where the sufficiency of the undertaking is challenged, may order it decreased to an amount sufficient to cover the probable recovery of the secured party or lineholder, even though such amount is lower than the aforementioned limits. (C.C.P. 720.260(b).)

(3) *Contents.* The undertaking must be made in favor of the secured party or lienholder, must indemnify such party against losses caused by the enforcement proceedings and must be conditioned on a final judgment affirming the priority of the third person's security interest or lien over the creditor's lien. (C.C.P. 720.260(c).)

(4) *Creditor's Statement Challenging Security Interest.* Upon filing of his undertaking, the creditor must also file with the levying officer a statement under oath that, for the reasons specified, the security interest is invalid or not entitled to priority over his lien, or that the amount demanded in the third-party claim exceeds the amount to which the secured party is entitled. (C.C.P. 720.280(a); see Law Rev. Com. Comment, Pamphlet, p. 1571.) A copy of the statement must be served personally or by mail on both the secured party and the debtor. (C.C.P. 720.280(b)(c).)

(5) *Public Entity's Notice of Opposition.* If the creditor is a public entity exempt from giving an undertaking, it must file with the levying officer a notice of its opposition to the third-party claim. When filed, the notice satisfies the requirement of an undertaking. (C.C.P. 720.260(d).)

(6) *Release of Property.* When a third person has not filed an undertaking to release the property (see Supp., infra, §424A), the creditor's failure to file an undertaking and statement or to deposit

the amount claimed (see supra) requires the levying officer to release the property "unless it is to be held under another lien or unless otherwise ordered by the court." (C.C.P. 720.270(a); see Law Rev. Com. Comment, Pamphlet, p. 1570.)

The release is governed by C.C.P. 699.060 (see Supp., supra, §252A), except that if the property taken into custody is to be released to the debtor and the debtor has not claimed the property within 30 days after being given notice of its location, the levying officer must release it to the *secured party* or *lienholder* (rather than selling it and depositing the proceeds for the debtor). (C.C.P. 720.270(c).)

A hearing on the third-party claim (see Supp., infra, §417A et seq.) may be held notwithstanding the release of the property. (C.C.P. 720.270(d).)

(e) [§416A] (New) Payment to Secured Party or Lienholder.

Upon receiving a sufficient deposit from the creditor, the levying officer must *promptly* tender or pay the deposit to the secured party or lienholder. Reasonable time for a check to clear is permitted. (C.C.P. 720.290(a); see Law Rev. Com. Comment, Pamphlet, p. 1572.)

If the tender is accepted, the interest of the secured party or lienholder passes to the creditor. On distribution of any proceeds (see Supp., supra, §288A), the creditor is entitled to the proceeds "to the extent of the deposit in the priority of the interest for which the deposit is made." (C.C.P. 720.290(b).) If tender is refused, the deposit must be placed with the court treasurer payable to the order of the secured party or lienholder. (C.C.P. 720.290(c).)

4. (New) Hearing on Third-Party Claim.

(a) [§417A] (New) Application and Notice.

Not later than 15 days after the third-party claim is filed, *either* the creditor or third person may petition for a hearing to determine the validity of the claim and the proper disposition of the property. (C.C.P. 720.310(a); on the former procedure, see text, §107.)

Unless continued for good cause, the hearing must be held within 20 days after the petition is filed. (C.C.P. 720.310(c).) The hearing may occur regardless of whether an undertaking has been filed, but not if a deposit of the amount of the claim has been made (see Supp., supra, §415A). (C.C.P. 720.310(b).)

Not less than 10 days prior to the hearing the petitioner must, personally or by mail, serve notice of the time and place of the hearing on the creditor or third person (whichever is not the petitioner) and on the *debtor,* and file a copy of the notice with the levying officer. (C.C.P. 720.320(a); see Law Rev. Com. Recommendation, Pamphlet, p. 1149 [former procedure did not require notice to the debtor].) The notice must include a statement of the purpose for the hearing (see supra). (C.C.P. 720.320(b).)

See 14 Pacific L.J. 436.

(b)   [§418A]   (New)   Papers Filed by Levying Officer.

Promptly after receiving the notice of hearing, the levying officer must file with the court the third-party claim and, if relevant, the following papers: (1) The creditor's statement in opposition to the claim of a secured party (see Supp., supra, §415A); (2) the creditor's undertaking (see Supp., supra, §§411A, 415A); (3) the third person's undertaking to release (see Supp., infra, §424A); (4) a public entity's notice of opposition (see Supp., supra, §§411A, 415A). (C.C.P. 720.330; see Law Rev. Com. Comment, Pamphlet, p. 1573.)

(c)   [§419A]   (New)   Creditor's Statement in Opposition.

If a notice of opposition to a third-party claim by a secured party (see Supp., supra, §415A) has not been filed, the creditor must file such statement (1) at the time he files for a petition for a hearing, or (2) where the petition for a hearing was filed by the secured party, not later than 5 days before the hearing date. A copy of the statement of opposition must be served, personally or by mail, on the secured party (1) along with the notice of hearing (where petition for hearing filed by creditor), or (2) not later than 5 days before the hearing date (where petition for hearing filed by secured party). (C.C.P. 720.340; see 14 Pacific L.J. 436.)

(d)   [§420A]   (New)   Hearing and Determination.

(1) *Pleadings.* The third-party claim constitutes the third person's pleading. The creditor's statement of opposition to a third-party claim by a secured party (see Supp., supra, §415A) constitutes the creditor's pleading. The court may amend such pleadings in the interest of justice. (C.C.P. 720.350(a); see Law Rev. Com. Comment, Pamphlet, p. 1574.)

A third-party claim of ownership, right to possession, or a lien, is deemed controverted by the creditor. (C.C.P. 720.350(b); see Law Rev. Com. Comment, Pamphlet, p. 1574.)

(2) *Conduct of Hearing.* At the hearing the burden of proof is on the third person. (C.C.P. 720.360.) The parties have no right to a jury trial. (C.C.P. 720.410.)

Neither the petition for hearing nor the proceedings pursuant thereto may be dismissed without the consent of the party (creditor or third person) who did *not* file the petition. (C.C.P. 720.370.)

The court may make an order staying the sale of the property under a writ, or enjoining any transfer or other disposition of the property levied upon, until the hearing has been concluded. (C.C.P. 720.280(a); see Law Rev. Com. Comment, Pamphlet, p. 1576.) After the filing of a third-party claim the creditor, debtor or third person may apply for such an order, even if the creditor has previously filed an undertaking requiring the levying officer to execute the writ (see Supp., supra, §§411A, 415A). (C.C.P. 720.380(b).)

The court may modify or vacate its order prior to the termination of the proceedings upon such terms as are just. (C.C.P. 720.380(c).)

(3) *Determination of Claim and Disposition of Property.* At the conclusion of the hearing the court must determine the validity of the third-party claim. It may also order the disposition of the property or proceeds in accordance with the parties' interest. Subject to the right to appeal (see infra, this section), the court's judgment is conclusive between the parties. (C.C.P. 720.390.)

No findings are required. (C.C.P. 720.400.)

(4) *Appeal.* The court's judgment (see supra) may be appealed in the manner governing appeals from such court. (C.C.P. 720.420.)

(e) [§421A] (New) Satisfaction From Released Property.

If property has been released pursuant to the third person's filing of an undertaking (see Supp., infra, §424A) or the creditor's failure to do so (see Supp., supra, §§411A, 415A), it may only be levied upon or otherwise applied to the satisfaction of the judgment if it is determined that the *debtor* has an interest therein that permits such action. (C.C.P. 720.430; see Law Rev. Com. Comment, Pamphlet, p. 1577.)

5. (New) Creditor's Demand That Third-Party File Claim.

(a) [§422A] (New) Filing and Service of Demand.

(1) *In General.* "A creditor may make a demand . . . that a *secured party* or *lienholder* file a third-party claim to personal property that has been levied upon under a writ of attachment or a writ of execution." (C.C.P. 720.510.) The demand and a copy must be filed with the levying officer *after* levy on the property, but *before* sale of the property or payment of the proceeds of collection to the creditor. (C.C.P. 720.520(a).)

(2) *Service.* *Promptly* after the filing of the demand, the levying officer who levied on the property (or other officer whose office is

closer to the place of service) must personally serve the demand on the secured party or lienholder. Such service must be attested by the levying officer's certificate, which must be filed in the action promptly after service. (C.C.P. 720.520(b)(c).)

(3) *Contents.* The demand must contain (a) the name and address of the secured party or lienholder; (b) the creditor's name and address; (c) a detailed description of the property levied upon and the date of levy; (d) a statement of the effect of failure to comply with the demand (see Supp., infra, §423A); and (e) a statement of the right of the secured party or lienholder to share in any excess proceeds of an execution sale, even if the priority of the security interest or lien is waived (due to such parties' failure to comply with the demand; see Supp., infra, §423A). (C.C.P. 720.530.)

(4) *Prohibition of Release, Sale or Other Disposition.* The levying officer may not release, etc., the property described in the demand before the expiration of 30 days after service of the demand on the secured party or lienholder, unless otherwise provided by statute. (C.C.P. 720.540; see Law Rev. Com. Comment, Pamphlet, p. 1579 [perishable property (see Supp., supra, §253A) is an example of property that may be sold or released before the expiration of the 30-day period].)

(b) [§423A] (New) Effect of Failure To Make Third-Party Claim.

If there is no third-party claim within 30 days after service of the demand, the secured party or lienholder is deemed to have waived *any priority* the security interest or lien may have had over the creditor's lien, and the property may be applied toward satisfaction of the judgment free of the security interest or lien. (C.C.P. 720.550(a).) However, if the creditor's lien on the property is released, the security interest or lien is restored to its former position of priority. (C.C.P. 720.550(b); see Law Rev. Com. Comment, Pamphlet, p. 1579.)

6. [§424A] (New) Third-Party Undertaking To Release Property.

(a) *Right To File.* A third person may give an undertaking to release property where he claims (1) ownership or the right to possession of *real property* levied upon under a writ of attachment or a writ of execution, or (2) ownership or the right to possession of, or a security interest in or a lien on, *personal property* levied upon under a writ of attachment, a writ of execution or a writ of sale. (C.C.P. 720.610; see Law Rev. Com. Comment, Pamphlet, p. 1580; on former law, see text, §114.)

(b) *When and With Whom To File.* The undertaking and two

copies must be filed with the levying officer (1) at the time a third-party claim is filed (see Supp., supra, §§408A, 412A), or (2) if such a claim has previously been filed, at any time *before* the levying officer sells the property, delivers possession to the creditor, or pays the proceeds of collection to the creditor. (C.C.P. 720.620; see Legislative Com. Comment—Assembly, Pamphlet, p. 1581.)

(c) *Contents.* The undertaking must be made in favor of the creditor (C.C.P. 720.620(b)) and contain a description of the property to be released and the third person's interest (C.C.P. 720.630(a)). It must also provide that if the debtor is finally adjudged to have an interest in the property, the third person must pay the creditor the *lesser* of (1) the amount required to satisfy the creditor's judgment against the debtor, or (2) the market value of the debtor's interest in the property. (C.C.P. 720.630(b); see Law Rev. Com. Comment, Pamphlet, p. 1582.)

(d) *Amount.* If the creditor has given an undertaking (see Supp., supra, §§411A, 415A), the third person's undertaking must be for an equal amount. (C.C.P. 720.630(d).) Otherwise, unless the third person elects to file a larger undertaking, the amount must be the *lesser* of (1) twice the property's market value, or (2) twice the amount of the creditor's lien on the property. (C.C.P. 720.630(c).)

(e) *Service.* If the undertaking is filed *when* the third-party claim is filed, the levying officer must serve a copy of the undertaking on both the creditor and debtor, together with the notice of the filing of the third-party claim (see Supp., supra, §§409A, 413A). (C.C.P. 720.640(a); see Law Rev. Com. Comment, Pamphlet, p. 1582.)

If the undertaking is filed *after* the third-party claim, the levying officer has 5 days to serve, personally or by mail, a copy of the undertaking on the creditor and debtor, together with a notice that unless the creditor objects to the undertaking within the time specified in the notice, the property will be released. (C.C.P. 720.640(b).)

(f) *Release of Property.* The levying officer must release the property as prescribed by C.C.P. 720.170 (see Supp., supra, §411A) *promptly* after the expiration of the time allowed for objecting to the undertaking (10 days after service of undertaking on creditor; see Supp., infra, §426A), unless within such time the creditor has objected to the undertaking and filed with the levying officer a copy of the notice of motion (see Supp., infra, §426A). (C.C.P. 720.660.)

(g) *Effective Date.* The undertaking becomes effective upon *release* of the property described therein. (C.C.P. 720.650; see Law Rev. Com. Comment, Pamphlet, p. 158 [when the property has been released, the undertaking will have achieved its purpose and the period for making an objection will have expired (see Supp., infra, 426A)].)

See 14 Pacific L.J. 437.

7. (New) Undertakings.

(a) [§425A] (New) In General.

The general provisions governing undertakings given in connection with third-party claims and related procedures are contained in C.C.P. 710.710 et seq. (C.C.P. 720.710; see Law Rev. Com. Comment, Pamphlet, p. 1583.) As used in these provisions, "beneficiary" refers to "the person to be benefitted by an undertaking" (C.C.P. 720.720(a)), and "principal" refers to "the person who files an undertaking" (C.C.P. 720.720(b)).

An undertaking must be executed by two or more *personal* sureties or by one *corporate* surety possessing a certificate of authority to write surety insurance (see Ins.C. 105). (C.C.P. 720.730; Law Rev. Com. Comment, Pamphlet, p. 1584.)

Except for a third person's undertaking to release property, which is effective when the property is released (see Supp., supra, §424A), an undertaking becomes effective upon filing. (C.C.P. 720.750; see Law Rev. Com. Comment, Pamphlet, p. 1584.)

If the amount of an undertaking is dependent on the value of property or an interest therein, the undertaking must include the principal's estimate of the *market value* of such property or interest. (C.C.P. 720.740.)

An undertaking filed with the levying officer and remaining in his possession when the writ is to be returned must be filed by him with the court when the writ is returned. (C.C.P. 720.800; see Legislative Com. Comment—Assembly, Pamphlet, p. 1587.)

(b) [§426A] (New) Beneficiary's Objection to Undertaking.

(1) *Grounds.* The beneficiary's objection may be based on *either or both* of the following grounds: (a) insufficiency of the sureties; (b) insufficiency of the amount of the undertaking. (C.C.P. 720.760(a).)

(2) *Noticed Motion.* The objection must be made on noticed motion within 10 days after service of a copy of the undertaking on the beneficiary. The notice of motion must specify the *precise ground* for the objection. (C.C.P. 720.760(b).) If such ground is that the market value of the property on which the undertaking depends exceeds the value estimated in the undertaking, the notice must state the beneficiary's estimate of such value. (C.C.P. 720.760(c).)

One copy of the notice of motion must be served personally or by mail on the principal, and another filed with the levying officer. (C.C.P. 720.760(b).)

(3) *Hearing.* "Unless the parties otherwise agree, the hearing on an objection shall be held not less than 10 nor more than 15 days after service of the notice of motion." (C.C.P. 720.770(a).) The hearing must be conducted in such manner as the court determines is proper. The attendance of witnesses and procurement and introduction of evidence may be regulated in the same manner as in the trial of a civil case. The court may appoint one or more disinterested persons to appraise the property. (C.C.P. 720.770(b).)

A determination that the undertaking is insufficient requires the court to specify the reason for the insufficiency and to order the filing, within 5 days, of an undertaking sufficient with respect to both the sureties and the amount. (C.C.P. 720.770(c).) Failure to comply with such order terminates all rights obtained by the filing of the original undertaking (C.C.P. 720.770(c)), but such undertaking remains in effect until a sufficient one is filed in its place (C.C.P. 720.770(d)).

A determination that an undertaking is sufficient precludes future objections except upon a showing of changed circumstances. (C.C.P. 720.770(e).)

If the objection is on the ground that the amount is insufficient to indemnify the beneficiary, the court must order the amount adjusted to the level of the probable recovery of the beneficiary if he prevails in proceedings to enforce the undertaking. The amount may be decreased below the limits prescribed by C.C.P. 720.160 (see Supp., supra, §411A) or 720.260 (see Supp., supra, §415A). (C.C.P. 720.770(f); see Law Rev. Com. Comment, Pamphlet, p. 1586 [undertaking may not be decreased on the *principal's initiative,* but only after the beneficiary's objection to the amount and the court's determination that it is more than adequate].)

(4) *Acceptance of Beneficiary's Estimate of Value.* No hearing is required on an objection made on the ground that the market value of the relevant property exceeds the value estimated in the undertaking, if the principal accepts the beneficiary's estimate and immediately files an increased undertaking based thereon. The beneficiary is then bound by his estimate in any hearing on the sufficiency of the undertaking. (C.C.P. 720.780.)

(5) *Waiver.* If no objection is made within 10 days after service of a copy of the undertaking on the beneficiary (see supra), the beneficiary is deemed to have waived any objections. (C.C.P. 720.760(b).)

(c) [§427A] (New) Liability of Surety.

Notwithstanding C.C. 2845, allowing a surety to require the creditor to proceed against the principal (see *Actions,* §135), a judgment of liability on an undertaking must be for the beneficiary and against the sureties, and may be enforced *directly* against the sureties, whose liability is limited to the amount of the undertaking. This provision does not affect the surety's subrogation rights against the principal. (C.C.P. 720.790(a).)

The sureties' liability on the undertaking may be enforced by a motion, pursuant to C.C.P. 1058a, in the court having jurisdiction of the enforcement proceedings without the necessity of an independent action. (C.C.P. 720.790(b); see Law Rev. Com. Comment, Pamphlet, p. 1587.) (C.C.P. 1058a was repealed in 1982 and replaced, in substance, with C.C.P. 996.440.)

E. (New) Satisfaction of Judgment.

1. (New) Satisfaction in Full.

(a) [§428A] (New) Methods of Satisfaction.

"A money judgment may be satisfied by payment of the full amount required to satisfy the judgment or by acceptance by the judgment creditor of a lesser sum in full satisfaction of the judgment." (C.C.P. 724.010(a); see Legislative Com. Comment—Assembly, Pamphlet, p. 1588; on the former law, see text, §425 et seq.) The court clerk must enter satisfaction of the judgment in the register of actions when (a) the court so orders; (b) a writ is returned satisfied for the full amount of a lump-sum judgment; (c) an acknowledgment of satisfaction is filed with the court. (C.C.P. 724.020.)

Where the judgment is satisfied by levy, the creditor must give or file an acknowledgment of satisfaction only after receiving from the levying officer the full amount required to satisfy the judgment. (C.C.P. 724.010(b).) Where the judgment is satisfied by payment to the creditor by check or other form of *noncash* payment, the creditor's obligation to give or file an acknowledgment of satisfaction arises only after such payment has actually been honored. (C.C.P. 724.010(c).)

(b) (New) Acknowledgment of Satisfaction.

(1) [§429A] (New) Creditor's Duty.

(a) *Filing. Immediately* after a money judgment is satisfied, the creditor must file with the court an acknowledgment of satisfaction, unless the judgment is satisfied in full pursuant to a writ (see Supp., supra, §428A). (C.C.P. 724.030; see Legislative Com. Comment—Assembly, Pamphlet, p. 1589.) If an abstract of a money judgment which has been satisfied has been recorded with the recorder of any county, the creditor must *immediately* (1) file an acknowledgment of satisfaction with the court, and (2) serve the acknowledgment, personally or by mail, on the debtor. (C.C.P. 724.040; see Legislative Com.

Comment—Assembly, Pamphlet, p. 1590 [section is applicable whether judgment is satisfied pursuant to a writ or by other means].) (On the former 30-day period for filing and serving the acknowledgment, see text, §225.)

(b) *Liability for Requiring Additional Performance or Payment.* The creditor may agree to deliver an acknowledgment of satisfaction to the debtor prior to full satisfaction of the judgment in consideration for the debtor's agreement either to furnish security or to execute a promissory note, or both, in an amount that does not exceed the amount of the judgment. (C.C.P. 724.070(b).) In all other situations where the creditor *intentionally* conditions delivery of the acknowledgment on (1) the performance of any act or (2) the payment of an amount in excess of the amount of the judgment, he is liable to the debtor for the *greater* of the damages caused by such action or $250. (C.C.P. 724.070(a).)

The damages recoverable pursuant to an action involving the satisfaction of a money judgment are not in derogation of any other damages or penalties to which an aggrieved person may be entitled (C.C.P. 724.090), and the prevailing party may be awarded attorney's fees (C.C.P. 724.080).

(2) [§430A] (New) Demand For Acknowledgment.

Once a money judgment has been satisfied, a written demand for acknowledgment thereof, served personally or by mail on the creditor, may be made by (a) the debtor; (b) the owner of real or personal property subject to a lien created under the judgment; or (c) a person having a security interest in, or a lien on, personal property subject to a lien created under the judgment. The demand may require the creditor to do one or both of the following: (1) File an acknowledgment of satisfaction with the court; (2) execute and deliver an acknowledgment of satisfaction to the person making the demand. (C.C.P. 724.050(a); see Legislative Com. Comment—Assembly, Pamphlet, p. 1592 [creditor can be compelled to file an acknowledgment of satisfaction in any case where a money judgment has been satisfied, regardless of the means of satisfaction].)

The creditor must comply with the demand not later than 15 days after actual receipt. (C.C.P. 724.050(c).) Noncompliance permits the person making the demand to apply on noticed motion, served personally or by mail on the creditor, for an order requiring compliance. Upon determining that the judgment has been satisfied and that the creditor has not complied with the demand, the court must either (1) order compliance, or (2) order the clerk to enter satisfaction of judgment. (C.C.P. 724.050(d).)

Where the creditor's noncompliance is *without just cause,* he is liable to the person making the demand for all damages caused thereby, and must also forfeit $100. (C.C.P. 724.050(e).)

The demand must inform the creditor of the 15 days allowed for complying and of the damages and penalties that may be imposed for noncompliance. (C.C.P. 724.050(b).)

See 14 Pacific L.J. 438.

(c) [§431A] (New) Content and Manner of Execution.

An acknowledgment of satisfaction of judgment must contain the following information:

(1) The title of the court.

(2) The cause and number of the action.

(3) The names and addresses of the creditor, the debtor (as it appears on any recorded abstract of judgment), and the assignee of record, if any.

(4) The date of entry of judgment, and of any renewals, and where entered in the court records.

(5) A statement either that the judgment is satisfied in full or that the creditor has accepted other payment or performance in full satisfaction.

(6) A statement of each county, and book and page of the county records, where an abstract of the judgment has been recorded, plus a notice that the acknowledgment of satisfaction (or a court clerk's certificate of satisfaction) will have to be recorded with the county recorder of each such county in order to release the judgment lien on real property therein.

(7) A statement of the file number of each notice of judgment lien filed with the Secretary of State, plus a notice that the acknowledgment of satisfaction (or a termination statement or a court clerk's certificate of satisfaction) must be filed in that office to terminate the judgment lien on personal property. (C.C.P. 724.060(a); see Law Rev. Com. Comment, Pamphlet, p. 1594.)

The acknowledgment of satisfaction must be made in the manner of an acknowledgment of a conveyance of real property (C.C.P. 724.060(b)), and must be executed and acknowledged by the creditor, assignee of record, or the attorney for the creditor or assignee, unless his authority has been revoked (C.C.P. 724.060(c)).

(d) [§432A] (New) Certificate of Satisfaction.

If satisfaction of a judgment has been entered in the register of actions, the court clerk must issue a certificate of satisfaction of judgment upon application and payment of a $3 fee. (C.C.P. 724.100(a); see Law Rev. Com. Comment, Pamphlet, p. 1596 [certificate of satisfaction serves same function as an acknowledgment of satisfaction and can be used where the latter cannot be easily obtained].)

The certificate must contain (1) the title of the court; (2) the cause and number of the action; (3) the names of the creditor and debtor; (4) the date of entry of judgment, and of any renewals, and where entered in the court records; (5) the date of entry of satisfaction of judgment, and where entered in the register of actions. (C.C.P. 724.100(b).)

See 14 Pacific L.J. 439.

2. [§433A] (New) Acknowledgment of Partial Satisfaction.

(a) *Demand for Delivery.* The debtor or the owner of real or personal property subject to a judgment lien created under a money judgment may serve on the creditor, personally or by mail, a written demand that the creditor execute, acknowledge and deliver an acknowledgment of partial satisfaction of judgment to the person making the demand. If there has been partial satisfaction, the creditor must comply not later than 15 days after actual receipt of the demand. (C.C.P. 724.110(a); see Law Rev. Com. Comment, Pamphlet, p. 1596 [there is neither a sanction for failure to comply with the demand nor a provision for awarding attorney's fees to the prevailing party].)

(b) *Failure To Comply With Demand.* The debtor or owner of the property may apply on noticed motion, served personally or by mail on the creditor, for an order requiring compliance. Upon determining that the judgment has been partially satisfied and that the creditor has not complied with the demand, the court must determine the amount of the partial satisfaction and order the creditor to comply with the demand. (C.C.P. 724.110(b).)

(c) *Execution and Contents of Acknowledgment.* In addition to the information specified in C.C.P. 724.060(a)(1)–(4), pertaining to acknowledgments of full satisfaction of judgment (see Supp., supra, §431A), an acknowledgment of partial satisfaction must contain statements (1) of the amount received by the creditor in partial satisfaction; (2) of each county, and the book and page of the county records, where any abstract of judgment has been recorded; (3) of the file number of any notice of judgment lien filed with the Secretary of State. (C.C.P. 724.120.)

The acknowledgment of partial satisfaction must be made in the same manner and by the same person as an acknowledgment of full satisfaction of judgment (see C.C.P. 724.060(b)(c), Supp., supra, §431A). (C.C.P. 724.120.)

See 14 Pacific L.J. 439.

3.   (New) Acknowledgment of Satisfaction of Installments.

(a)   [§434A]   (New) Demand For Delivery of Acknowledgment.

(1) *Definitions.* "Installment judgment" refers to the following money judgments under which a lien may be created on an interest in *real property:* (1) judgments for spousal or child support payable in installments; (2) judgments against a health care provider requiring periodic payments; (3) workers' compensation award judgments payable in installments. (C.C.P. 724.210(a), 697.320, 697.330; see Law Rev. Com. Comment, Pamphlet, p. 1598.)

"Matured installments" means the sum, as of the date specified in the demand (see infra, this section), of the matured amounts and installments, the accrued interest, and the added costs (see Supp., supra, §§240A, 240A-1). (C.C.P. 724.210(b).)

(2) *Delivery, Contents, Time For Compliance.* If real property is subject to a judgment lien created under an installment judgment, the debtor or the owner of the property may serve on the creditor, personally or by mail, a written demand for delivery of an acknowledgment of satisfaction of matured installments. (C.C.P. 724.220(a).) If the matured installments have been satisfied as of the date specified in the demand, the creditor must comply not later than 15 days after actual receipt of the demand. (724.220(c); see Law Rev. Com. Comment, Pamphlet, p. 1599.)

The demand must inform the creditor of the time for compliance (see supra) and the penalties for noncompliance (see Supp., infra, §430A). (C.C.P. 724.220(b).)

(3) *Proceeding To Compel Compliance.* If the creditor fails to comply with the demand, the debtor or owner of the real property may apply on noticed motion, served personally or by mail on the creditor, for an order requiring compliance. Upon determining that the matured installments have been satisfied as of the date specified in the demand and that the creditor has failed to comply, the court must either (a) order compliance or (b) determine that the matured installments as of the date specified in the demand have been satisfied. (C.C.P. 724.230.)

See 14 Pacific L.J. 439.

(b)   [§435A]   (New) Content and Manner of Execution.

An acknowledgment of satisfaction of matured installments must contain the following information: (1) The title of the court; (2) the cause and number of the action; (3) the names and addresses of the creditor, the debtor (as appearing on the certified copy of judgment recorded to create the lien), and the assignee of record, if any; (4) the date of entry of the judgment, and of any renewals, and where entered in the court record; (5) a statement that the matured installments had been satisfied as of a specified date; (6) a statement of each county, and book and page of the county records, where any certified copy of the judgment has been recorded. (C.C.P. 724.250(a).)

An acknowledgment of satisfaction of matured installments must be made in the same manner and by the same person as an acknowledgment of judgment (see Supp., supra, §431A). (C.C.P. 724.250(a).) However, if any amount of child or spousal support has been directed to be made to an officer designated by the court, and such directive is set forth in the certified copy of the judgment (or amended or supplemental order) that was recorded to create the lien, the acknowledgment of satisfaction is ineffective unless executed, or approved in writing, by the designated officer. (C.C.P. 724.250(b).)

(c) [§436A] (New) Liability For Failure To Comply.

If the matured installments have been satisfied as of the date specified in the demand and the creditor fails *without just cause* to make a timely compliance with the demand, he is liable to the person making the demand for all damages caused by such failure, and must also forfeit to such person $100. (C.C.P. 724.240(a).) These damages are not in derogation of any other damages or penalties to which an aggrieved person is entitled. (C.C.P. 724.240(b).)

Reasonable attorney's fees must be awarded to the prevailing party. (C.C.P. 724.260.)

Chapter XI

ATTACK ON JUDGMENT IN TRIAL COURT

Sections added in this Supplement:

p. 3580:

Error: Outline, "(aa) Issue of Damages in Tort, 3676" should be "(aa) [§96] Issue of Damages in Tort, 3676."

1. [§1] Nature and Significance of Concept.

See *Gonzales v. California* (1977) 68 C.A.3d 621, 632, 137 C.R. 681, quoting the text; Rest.2d, Judgments §78 et seq.; 6 (Part 2) Cal. Practice (Rev. ed.) 477; C.J.E.R., Judges Benchbook, Civil, Chap. 17.

2. [§2] Methods of Direct Attack.

(a) *In Trial Court by Motion.*

(6) Writ of error *coram nobis.* See Supp., infra, §2A.

(7) Setting aside condemnation award for nonpayment.

That portion of former C.C.P. 1252 cited in the text has been superseded by C.C.P. 1268.020(b). (See 5 *Summary, Constitutional Law,* Supp., §741A.)

[§2A] (New) Coram Nobis.

The use of the writ of error coram nobis in a civil case was the subject of two conflicting decisions of the Court of Appeal.

In *Rollins v. San Francisco* (1974) 37 C.A.3d 145, 112 C.R. 168, plaintiff sued defendants for wrongful death of his wife. Jury verdicts were for defendants, the trial judge denied a motion for new trial and plaintiff appealed. Plaintiff's theories of malpractice in erroneous medical decisions and delay in taking essential steps had apparently been rejected by the jury for lack of expert supporting evidence. However, while the appeal was pending, an addendum to the autopsy was found in the hospital records, and this expert evidence, significantly contradicting the defense experts, would have been a sufficient basis for granting a motion for new trial on the ground of newly discovered evidence. Since the time for such a motion had long expired, plaintiff sought to bring the evidence before the appellate court by a motion to augment the record under Rule 12 (see *Appeal*, §412). *Held*, neither augmentation of the record nor factfinding on appeal was proper (see *Appeal*, §§413, 569), but, treating the motion to augment as a petition for a writ of error coram vobis, relief could be obtained in the trial court.

(a) The dicta in the *Dyer* and *Page* cases (text, §2) recognize the availability of the writ "following a judgment in a civil proceeding where the error to be corrected does not appear in the record and no other remedy is available." (37 C.A.3d 149, citing the text, *Actions*, §22.)

(b) Since the petition is addressed to an appellate court it is technically *coram vobis*. (37 C.A.3d 150, footnote 5, citing the text, *Actions*, §22.) But the proper relief is to reverse the judgment and remand the matter to the trial court for reconsideration of its order denying a new trial. (37 C.A.3d 150.)

The court added: "Further authority for this disposition lies in our rarely exercised inherent discretionary powers in the interests of justice . . . and Code of Civil Procedure section 43." (37 C.A.3d 150; see *Appeal*, §§526, 554.)

In *Los Angeles Airways v. Hughes Tool Co.* (1979) 95 C.A.3d 1, 156 C.R. 805, plaintiff entered into negotiations to sell its assets to defendant (controlled by Howard Hughes). An oral agreement was reached with Robert Mahue, representing Hughes, but no written agreement was ever executed. Plaintiff sued for damages for breach of contract. The trial judge found that neither party intended to be bound by the agreement until a final written contract was prepared and approved by the appropriate corporate officers. Judgment was accordingly entered for defendant, and plaintiff appealed. While the appeal was pending, Mr. Hughes died, and in probate proceedings documents were found which, plaintiff claimed, were intentionally suppressed and would show that Mahue had authority to make a final binding agreement. The time for a statutory new trial motion had expired, but plaintiff, relying on *Rollins,* filed a petition in the appellate court for a writ of error coram vobis, in order to obtain a new trial. In considering the petition the court assumed the sufficiency of the factual showing—plaintiff's diligence, and the materiality of the evidence sought—and stated the legal issue as follows: "whether the fact that fraudulently concealed evidence, material to the plaintiff's case, was discovered while the judgment was on appeal and after the time for a new trial motion had lapsed, is grounds for any relief in the appellate court." (95 C.A.3d 6.) *Held,* the appellate court had no power to grant relief.

(a) *General rule on finality of judgment despite newly discovered evidence.* "[A]fter a judgment has become final, newly discovered evidence generally is not a ground for reopening that judgment unless the concealment of that evidence prevented a fair adversary hearing, kept the claimant out of court entirely or utterly deprived him of a claim or defense, or precipitated a grave miscarriage of justice such as the conviction of an innocent person." (95 C.A.3d 6.) Thus, whatever the technical form of the relief sought—independent direct attack by action or motion, or collateral attack by offense or defense in a separate action—"it is crucial to be able to demonstrate what amounts to due process deprivation: that the issue in question was really never litigated in any meaningful fashion." (95 C.A.3d 7.)

(b) *The extrinsic fraud exception.* Fraud internal to the adversary proceeding, such as perjury, is not a basis for relief; but fraud which prevents the defrauded party from having the issue tried is extrinsic and a basis for relief: "Obviously, where there has been little or no judicial time invested in trial of a cause or an issue, the factor of judicial economy which otherwise weighs in favor of finality is less strong, and the equitable considerations of fair hearing and of penalizing fraud weigh more compellingly." (95 C.A.3d 7, citing the text, §183 et seq., for full discussion of extrinsic fraud, and Rest., Judgments §§118, 121.) Here the fraud—deliberate concealment of evidence during discovery proceedings—is, like perjury, intrinsic; i.e., evidence was offered, and the contract issue was litigated; plaintiff was not totally deprived of an opportunity to present its claim, but was only prevented from making a stronger showing. (95 C.A.3d 8.)

(c) *Coram nobis or coram vobis not available.* These writs have chiefly been invoked in criminal cases, but in *Rollins v. San Francisco* the court held that they could be used in a civil case where newly discovered material evidence was sought. *Rollins* was "an abrupt departure from precedent" and this court declines to follow it: "A rule permitting the criteria for a new trial to govern a case where the evidence is discovered later, has no basis in the statutes or in any other case. It would extend the time for a motion for a new trial by pure judicial fiat." (95 C.A.3d 9.) And there is good reason to limit the time for a new trial motion: Many of the considerations depend on actual perceptions throughout the trial which are not preserved on the cold record; and "the fresher in memory are the events of the trial, the more rationally may the trial court exercise the broad discretion it has." (95 C.A.3d 9.) The Legislature has set the time limit, and when that time has expired the stricter test of extrinsic fraud must be met. (95 C.A.3d 9, 10.)

3. [§3] Presumption of Jurisdiction.

See Rest.2d, Judgments §77.

1. [§4] Nature and Grounds.

See Rest.2d, Judgments §79.

(a) [§5] Subsequent Action.

See *Estate of Wemyss* (1975) 49 C.A.3d 53, 58, 122 C.R. 134, quoting the text.

In *Kachig v. Boothe* (1971) 22 C.A.3d 626, 99 C.R. 393, a judgment had been obtained in favor of agents against a principal, by use of a false document and perjured testimony. In this action he relied on loose language in *Jorgensen v. Jorgensen* (text, §186) supporting relief where the adversary was a fiduciary, even though the fraud occurred during a judicial proceeding. The court observed that neither *Jorgensen* nor the authorities cited therein applied the supposed rule to a case in which there was a full adversary trial; and in *Pico v. Cohn* (text, §197) and *Robinson v. Robinson* (1961) 198 C.A.2d 193, 196, 17 C.R. 786, following *Pico,* equitable relief was denied despite the fact that the perjury was committed by persons in a fiduciary relationship. (22 C.A.3d 635.) The rule should, therefore, remain undisturbed:

"The policy considerations underlying the doctrine of finality of judgments are today at least as important as, if not more important than, ever. In view of that fact and in view of *Pico, Robinson* and the other cases uniformly denying equitable relief on allegations of perjured testimony and false documents, and in the absence of a more definite imperative from our high court, we do not deem it appropriate to apply the quoted language of *Jorgensen* to a case in which there was a full, adversary trial in the prior action. Were we to do so, a precedent would be established opening the door to multiplicity of litigation in every case involving a fiduciary in which the fiduciary prevailed." (22 C.A.3d 636.)

In *Rios v. Allstate Ins. Co.* (1977) 68 C.A.3d 811, 137 C.R. 441, plaintiff made a claim against defendant insurer under the uninsured motorist coverage of his policy, and an arbitration award was made against plaintiff. Plaintiff contended that the unfavorable award was based on false testimony produced by defendant; but, instead of seeking to set the award aside for fraud under C.C.P. 1286.2, he brought this action for damages for the tort of bad faith of defendant insurer in dealing with his claim. *Held,* judgment for defendant on demurrer affirmed.

(a) The complaint stated a cause of action for violation by the insurer of the implied covenant of good faith. (68 C.A.3d 817.)

(b) This action was technically not a collateral attack on the final arbitration award; i.e., plaintiff did not challenge the award or demand payment under the uninsured motorist provision of the policy, but sought damages on a cause of action different from that adjudicated in the arbitration proceeding. (68 C.A.3d 818.)

(c) However, in bringing the action without first availing himself of the statutory procedure for setting aside the award he was attempting to circumvent the rule that equitable relief will not be granted against a final judgment where the fraud is intrinsic (see text, §197). *Kachig v. Boothe,* supra, is in point. (68 C.A.3d 819, 820.)

(b) [§6] Subsequent Motion.

See *Jones v. World Life Research Institute* (1976) 60 C.A.3d 836, 839, 844, 131 C.R. 674, *Jurisdiction,* Supp., §207A; *Becker v. S. P. V. Const. Co.* (1980) 27 C.3d 489, 494, 165 C.R. 825, 612 P.2d 915, *Proceedings Without Trial,* Supp., §156A.

Cross-Reference: 6 *Summary, Husband and Wife,* §107.

(b) [§10] Lack of Jurisdiction Shown by Record.

See *Estate of Buckley* (1982) 132 C.A.3d 434, 450, 183 C.R. 281 [issuance of letters of administration without appellant having published notice or having filed affidavit required by Prob.C. 333].

Cross-Reference: 6 *Summary, Husband and Wife,* §107.

(1) [§11] California Judgment: Inadmissible.

See Rest.2d, Judgments §12, Comments c, d; §77, Comment b.

(2) [§12] Foreign Judgment.

See Rest.2d, Judgments §77, Comment b; §81, Comment b.

On registration of sister state money judgments and foreign support orders as a means of enforcement, see *Enforcement of Judgment,* Supp., §195A et seq., and §195F et seq., respectively.

Cross-References: 6 *Summary, Husband and Wife,* §71 et seq.; 6 *Summary, Parent and Child,* §11; 6 *Summary, Husband and Wife,* §82 et seq.; 6 *Summary, Parent and Child,* §46 et seq.

1. [§16] Nature and Object of Motion.

See 6 (Part 2) Cal Practice (Rev. ed.) 337, 415; C.J.E.R., Judges Benchbook, Civil, §17.3 et seq.; 58 Am.Jur.2d 175 et seq.; 18 Am.Jur. P.P. Forms (Rev. ed.) 567 et seq.

2. [§17] Statutory Grounds Exclusive.

See *Chevalier v. Dubin* (1980) 104 C.A.3d 975, 978, 164 C.R. 118 [alleged incompetency of counsel not a ground in civil case].

(a) [§19] In General.

p. 3598:

Former C.C.P. 1257, insofar as it incorporated the general procedures for new trial, has been superseded by C.C.P. 1230.040. (See 5 *Summary, Constitutional Law,* Supp., §675A.)

(New) No new trial after small claims court appeal: In a case appealed from the small claims court the judgment of the superior court after a trial de novo is final. No further appeal lies, and for the same policy reasons there is no right to move for a new trial. (*Eloby v. Superior Court* (1978) 78 C.A.3d 972, 975, 144 C.R. 597, *Courts,* Supp., §204A.)

(2) [§21] Expanded Scope of Statute.

See *In re Marriage of Beilock* (1978) 81 C.A.3d 713, 719, 146 C.R. 675.

p. 3600:

(c) *Judgment by default.* See *Don v. Cruz* (1982) 131 C.A.3d 695, 706, 182 C.R. 581, Supp., infra, §43.

(g) *(New) Order granting motion to quash writ of execution. In re Marriage of Beilock,* supra, involved the following proceedings: (1) The wife filed a petition for a writ of execution for arrearages in child and spousal support payments (analogous to a complaint) and obtained the writ; (2) the husband filed a motion to quash the execution and set aside the levy (analogous to an answer) and the motion was granted; (3) the wife moved for a new trial on the grounds of insufficiency of the evidence and order against the law, and the motion was granted. *Held,* affirmed. There was a "trial" in the broad sense of the term, in which the court considered issues of fact and law raised by "pleadings." (81 C.A.3d 721.)

(c) [§22] Exception: Complete Statutory Plan Excluding Motion.

Cross-Reference: 6 *Summary, Parent and Child,* §106 et seq.

(a) [§23] Nature and Scope of Ground.

See 58 Am.Jur.2d 222 et seq.

(b) [§24] Misconduct of Court, Counsel or Adverse Party.

(1) *Misconduct of Court.* See 58 Am.Jur.2d 241; 18 Am.Jur. P.P. Forms (Rev. ed.) 578; *Jacoby v. Feldman* (1978) 81 C.A.3d 432, 446, 146 C.R. 334, quoting the text.

(2) *Misconduct of Adverse Party or Counsel.* See 58 Am.Jur.2d 245, 301; 18 Am.Jur. P.P. Forms (Rev. ed.) 583. On Rules 7–105, 7–106, and 7–107 of the new Rules of Professional Conduct, see *Attorneys,* Supp., §§205, 239, 241.

On argument misleading jury, see *Los Angeles v. Decker* (1977) 18 C.3d 860, 871, 135 C.R. 647, 558 P.2d 545, *Trial,* Supp., §176A.

(c) [§25] Irregularities in Formation of Jury.

See 58 Am.Jur.2d 227.

2. [§26] Misconduct of Jury.

See 58 Am.Jur.2d 266; 18 Am.Jur. P.P. Forms (Rev. ed.) 581.

On juror's nondisclosure of acquaintance or relationship with attorney or partner or associate of attorney, see 64 A.L.R.3d 126.

(a) [§27] Nature of Ground.

See 58 Am.Jur.2d 367; 18 Am.Jur. P.P. Forms (Rev. ed.) 588.

(a) [§30] Nature of Ground.

See 58 Am.Jur.2d 374; 18 Am.Jur. P.P. Forms (Rev. ed.) 589; 55 A.L.R.3d 696 [evidence going to amount of recovery].

(a) [§34] Nature of Ground.

See 58 Am.Jur.2d 342.

(b) [§35] Power and Duty To Weigh Evidence.

See *Widener v. Pac. Gas & Elec. Co.* (1977) 75 C.A.3d 415, 440, 142 C.R. 304.

(a) [§38] In General: Matters Not Covered.

p. 3615:

Evidence without conflict and insufficient as matter of law: See *In re Marriage of Beilock* (1978) 81 C.A.3d 713, 728, 733, 146 C.R. 675, Supp., infra, §90, upholding an order granting new trial on this ground.

Error: Line 7 of §38, citation of *O'Malley v. Carrick* should be 60 C.A. 48.

(b) [§39] Improper Verdict.

See 58 Am.Jur.2d 341.

7. [§41] Error in Law Excepted To.

See 58 Am.Jur.2d 323; 18 Am.Jur. P.P. Forms (Rev. ed.) 583.

(b) Erroneous ruling on evidence: See *Richard v. Scott* (1978) 79 C.A.3d 57, 63, 144 C.R. 672, Supp., infra, §96.

(a) [§42] Former Law.

(1) *Excessive Damages: Passion and Prejudice.* See *Kolar v. Los Angeles* (1976) 54 C.A.3d 873, 878, 127 C.R. 15, citing the text.

(b) [§43] New Statutory Grounds.

See 18 Am.Jur. P.P. Forms (Rev. ed.) 582.

(New) Construction of old language: In *Stevens v. Parke, Davis & Co.* (1973) 9 C.3d 51, 107 C.R. 45, 507 P.2d 653, the judge granted a conditional new trial order on the ground that "the verdict is excessive, that it is not sustained by the evidence, and that it is based upon prejudice and passion on the part of the jury." The Supreme Court pointed out that the reference to "passion and prejudice," though no longer appropriate, indicated that the ground was excessive damages; hence, despite the use of the words "not sustained by the evidence" the order should be construed as based solely on the ground of excessiveness of damages. (9 C.3d 59, 50.) The court added that the same rule on specification of reasons applies to both grounds. (See Supp., infra, §86A.)

(New) After default judgment: "[A] trial court has authority to grant a new trial after a default judgment on the ground that damages are excessive as a matter of law." (*Don v. Cruz* (1982) 131 C.A.3d 695, 706, 182 C.R. 581.)

Cross-References: 4 *Summary, Torts,* §§931 et seq., 937.

(c) [§44] Appellate Review Contrasted.

See *Schroeder v. Auto Driveaway Co.* (1974) 11 C.3d 908, 918, 114 C.R. 622, 523 P.2d 662, citing the text.

(a) [§45] No New Trial on Court's Own Motion.

In *Smith v. Superior Court* (1976) 64 C.A.3d 434, 134 C.R. 531, plaintiff sued for damages for personal injuries. She received judgment for $2,100, and neither party moved for a new trial within the 15-day period allowed. Defendant then made a motion to tax costs under C.C.P. 998, because she had offered before trial to allow judgment for $4,000 to be taken against her. At the hearing of the motion the judge announced, without notice, that he intended to grant a new trial, and he entered an order accordingly. *Held,* mandamus granted to compel vacation of the order.

(1) A court can grant a new trial only by following the statutory procedure on timely filing of a motion. (64 C.A.3d 436, citing the text.)

(2) *Jacuzzi v. Jacuzzi Bros.* (text, §46) "did not go so far as Witkin in interpreting its holding." The court there declared that the judge could properly review his own order for sanctions, and in doing so he could vacate the judgment which itself was dependent on that order. Here the trial judge was not reviewing a previous order or motion, but was hearing arguments on the unrelated cost bill. (64 C.A.3d 437.)

(b) [§46] Inherent Power: Jacuzzi Case.

The *Jacuzzi* case was distinguished, and the rule that the trial court has no inherent power was reaffirmed, in *Smith v. Superior Court* (1976) 64 C.A.3d 434, 437, 134 C.R. 531, Supp., supra, §45.

(1) [§47] Statutory Requirements.

See 6 (Part 2) Cal Practice (Rev. ed.) 398 et seq.; C.E.B., Civ. Lit. Forms, §2.1; C.E.B., Judicial Council Forms, SC-135(79); 18 Am.Jur. P.P. Forms (Rev. ed.) 572, 573.

The motion can be granted only on a ground specified in the notice of intention to move for a new trial. (See *Wagner v. Singleton* (1982) 133 C.A.3d 69, 72, 183 C.R. 631 [notice specified ground of "insufficiency of the evidence" while order granting the motion indicated it was granted on basis of "prejudicial misconduct of counsel"].)

On amendment of motion after expiration of time for filing, see 69 A.L.R.3d 845.

(aa) [§52] Meaning: After Decision Rendered.

See *Ehrler v. Ehrler* (1981) 126 C.A.3d 147, 152, 178 C.R. 642, quoting the text.

p. 3629:

Separate trial of issue: For the 1977 amendment of C.C.P. 598, see *Trial,* Supp., §128A.

[§52A] (New) After Bifurcated Trial.

Rule 232.5, effective January 1, 1975, and as amended in 1982, outlines the procedure for bifurcated trials. (See *Trial,* Supp., §349-I.)

With respect to a motion for new trial, it provides that the motion "shall be made after all the issues are tried." This is necessarily subject to the exception stated in the earlier part of the Rule: "when an interlocutory judgment or a separate judgment may otherwise be properly entered" after trial of a separate issue. (See *Trial*, Supp., §349-I.)

(bb) [§53] Premature Notice Ineffectual.

See *Ruiz v. Ruiz* (1980) 104 C.A.3d 374, 378, 163 C.R. 708; *Ehrler v. Ehrler* (1981) 126 C.A.3d 147, 152, 178 C.R. 642.

(aa) [§55] Notice of Entry by Clerk.

(New) Notice of entry of order: In re Marriage of Beilock (1978) 81 C.A.3d 713, 146 C.R. 675, involved a motion for new trial after an order quashing a writ of execution. (See Supp., supra, §21.) The issue of timeliness of the motion was new: Since there was no "judgment" there no notice of entry given under C.C.P. 664.5; however, the clerk, pursuant to Rule 204 (see *Proceedings Without Trial*, Supp., §26) did send both parties a copy of the minute order on January 4, and a formal written order was signed and filed on February 1. The notice of intention to move for new trial was filed on February 8, too late if the time ran from the clerk's mailing of the copy of the minute order, but timely if the time ran from the filing of the formal written order. *Held,* the motion for new trial was timely. In order to be effective in releasing property levied upon, there had to be "a separate piece of paper" signed by the court, quashing the execution and authorizing the levying officer to release the seized property. Hence the filing of this formal written order was the judicial act which started the time running. (81 C.A.3d 723.)

(bb) [§56] Notice of Entry by Party.

(2) *Form of Notice.* See 6 (Part 2) Cal Practice (Rev. ed.) 51; C.E.B., Civ. Lit. Forms, §2.1; 15 Am.Jur. P.P. Forms (Rev. ed.) 361, 362.

(cc) [§57] Commencement and Running of Periods.

(1-A) *(New) Computation of Period.* The general rule of C.C.P. 12 applies; i.e., the first day is excluded and the last day is included. (*LaBorne v. Mulvany* (1974) 43 C.A.3d 905, 909, 119 C.R. 596.)

(dd) [§58] Late Filing Void.

See *Douglas v. Janis* (1974) 43 C.A.3d 931, 936, 118 C.R. 280.

3. [§61]   Affidavits and Counteraffidavits.

(a) *Necessity.* See *Linhart v. Nelson* (1976) 18 C.3d 641, 134 C.R. 813, 557 P.2d 104, Supp., infra, §65.

(b) *Form.* See 6 (Part 2) Cal Practice (Rev. ed.) 419, 421; 18 Am.Jur. P.P. Forms (Rev. ed.) 590.

(c) *Procedure.* See 6 (Part 2) Cal Practice (Rev. ed.) 417, 420.

4. [§62]   Points and Authorities.

See C.E.B., Civ. Lit. Forms, §2.2.

(a)   [§63]   Notice of Hearing.

See C.J.E.R., Judges Benchbook, Civil, §17.17 et seq.

(c)   [§65]   Evidence and Argument.

(2) *No Oral Testimony.* The express language of C.C.P. 657, limiting the showing on the first four grounds to affidavits, was applied in *Linhart v. Nelson* (1976) 18 C.3d 641, 134 C.R. 813, 557 P.2d 104.

After plaintiff received verdict and judgment for damages for personal injuries, defendants' investigator interviewed the jurors. His affidavit in support of the motion contained averments of jury misconduct (discussion of liability insurance and attorney fees); but affidavits that he had prepared for five jurors who had indicated a willingness to sign were rejected by them when plaintiff's attorney cautioned them against signing, and only the foreman signed the prepared affidavit. Plaintiff filed affidavits in opposition—a second affidavit by the foreman and an affidavit of another juror—stating that the improper discussion had ended after other jurors pointed out that there was no evidence on these subjects, and that the verdict was based solely on the issues of compensation for injury, disability, and medical expense. Defendants subpenaed three jurors to testify at the hearing on the motion, but the trial judge refused to permit them to testify and denied the motion. *Held,* affirmed.

The opinion cited *Cembrook v. Sterling Drug* (text, p. 3639) with approval, and disapproved contrary implications in *Saltzman v. Sunset Tel. etc. Co.* (text, §26). The court pointed out that to allow witnesses to testify for one party would make it necessary for opposing parties —without the time to undertake discovery—to subpena all jurors and other witnesses, and could result in a virtual retrial of the case. (18 C.3d 644.) Moreover, to permit interrogation of unwilling trial jurors "touches the integrity" of the process: "First, once aware that after sitting through a lengthy trial he himself may be placed on trial, only the most courageous prospective juror will not seek excuse from service. Secondly, if jury deliberations are subject to compulsory disclosure, independent thought and debate will surely be stifled." (18 C.3d 644.)

p. 3640:

(4) *Hearing in Chambers.* C.C.P. 166 was subdivided in 1982, and C.C.P. 166(2) became C.C.P. 166(a)(3).

(1) [§66] Trial Judge.

Under new Rule 232.5 (see Supp., supra, §52A), if issues tried separately in a bifurcated trial "were tried by different judges, each judge shall hear and determine the motion as to the issues tried by that judge." If a judge is unable to act on the motion, the provisions of C.C.P. 661 (see text, p. 3640) apply.

(1) [§68] Commencement and Running of Period.

p. 3643:

Entry in permanent minutes: See *LaBorne v. Mulvany* (1974) 43 C.A.3d 905, 119 C.R. 596, Supp., infra, §114.

(2) [§69] Time Jurisdictional.

See *Worth v. Asiatic Transpacific* (1979) 93 C.A.3d 849, 853, 854, 156 C.R. 110.

(1) [§70] In General.

See 58 Am.Jur.2d 437; 18 Am.Jur. P.P. Forms (Rev. ed.) 600.

(a) *Minute Entry or Filed Order.*

Entry in permanent minutes: See *LaBorne v. Mulvany* (1974) 43 C.A.3d 905, 119 C.R. 596, Supp., infra, §114.

(bb) [§72] Method of Entry.

See *Kolar v. Los Angeles* (1976) 54 C.A.3d 873, 877, 127 C.R. 15 [entry in minutes sufficient; no need for judge's signature].

(i) [§73] In General.

(New) Ground implied in stated reasons: In *Jones v. Citrus Motors Ontario* (1973) 8 C.3d 706, 106 C.R. 28, 505 P.2d 220, plaintiffs sued defendant car dealer for damages for injuries suffered in a collision as a result of his allegedly negligent repair of the car before its sale. The verdict was for defendant, and plaintiffs moved for a new trial on several grounds, including insufficiency of the evidence. The judge granted the motion in an elaborate order three pages long (see 8 C.3d 708, footnote 2), carefully and clearly setting forth the precise respects in which the evidence was insufficient. Thus, the specification of *reasons* (see text, §80 et seq.) was adequate, but nowhere in the order

did the judge explicitly state the *ground* of insufficiency of the evidence. *Held,* order affirmed.

(a) Inclusion of the statutory language is preferable, and "we do not condone failure to state explicitly the grounds." (8 C.3d 711.)

(b) However, the ground is adequately specified if the intention of the judge is clear. And here, his final statement, "it would appear that the jury was somehow misled into an area of speculation not supported by the evidence," and the lengthy analysis of the evidence, were "undeniably addressed to the issue of insufficiency." (8 C.3d 710.) This analysis constituted the "reason" (see text, §80), and: "It is difficult to conceive of a court specifying a reason without simultaneously revealing an intention as to the ground. Because a reason must be directed to explaining and supporting a particular ground . . ., it would seem that the reason necessarily reflects that ground." (8 C.3d 710.)

(iv) [§76] Other Variant Forms.

(b) Where sole ground of motion is insufficiency of evidence: See *La Manna v. Stewart* (1975) 13 C.3d 413, 418, 118 C.R. 761, 530 P.2d 1073 [following *Mercer,* but reiterating warning, text, p. 3650]; 64 Cal. L. Rev. 286.

(i) [§80] Nature and Purpose of Requirement.

p. 3655:

(b) *Dual Purposes.* See 64 Cal. L. Rev. 288.

p. 3656:

(d) *(New) Oral Statement Ineffective.* The statute contemplates a written specification of reasons in one of two places: the order itself or a separate document filed. Oral statements by the judge at the hearing of the motion for new trial do not satisfy the requirement. (*Stevens v. Parke, Davis & Co.* (1973) 9 C.3d 51, 62, 63, 107 C.R. 45, 507 P.2d 653; *La Manna v. Stewart* (1975) 13 C.3d 413, 419, 118 C.R. 761, 530 P.2d 1073; *Worden v. Gentry* (1975) 50 C.A.3d 600, 604, 123 C.R. 496.)

(e) *(New) Strict Compliance With Requirement.* In *La Manna v. Stewart,* supra, the court emphatically rejected the notion that "substantial compliance" may be acceptable (in this case an oral statement of reasons, and an attempt by counsel to furnish a draft of the specifications, which the court did not use; see Supp., infra, §87). The statement in *Mercer* that the statute "should be given a reasonable and practical construction" (see text, §82) was made in reference to the *content* of the specification. "We did not mean, however, that there is any room for such 'construction' of the detailed statutory requirements of the *form* of the specification of reasons. On that point our position was categorical: noting the needless administrative burden that would arise from litigating and relitigating such questions of form, we declared (at p. 124) that 'The only solution is to insist, as we do, upon *full and timely* compliance with this remedial legislation.' . . . We reaffirm that position today." (13 C.3d 423.)

See 64 Cal. L. Rev. 286.

[§80A] (New) Applies to Conditional Order.

In *Neal v. Farmers Insurance Exchange* (1978) 21 C.3d 910, 148 C.R. 389, 582 P.2d 980, the jury brought in a large verdict for compensatory and punitive damages, the judge granted a conditional new trial order, plaintiff accepted the remittitur, and the new trial was denied. *Held,* although an order *denying* a motion for new trial is not subject to the specification requirement, an order *conditionally granting* it is an order *granting,* as much as an unconditional order, and the same reasons for specification are present. "We therefore hold that the requirements of section 657 are applicable to conditional new trial orders entered pursuant to the provisions of section 662.5 of the Code of Civil Procedure, even when subsequent actions of a party fulfilling a condition stated therein have the effect of negating that order for new trial." (21 C.3d 931.)

(ii) [§81] No Nunc Pro Tunc Correction.

(New) Specification timely if within 60 plus 10 days: In *Fortenberry v. Weber* (1971) 18 C.A.3d 213, 221, 95 C.R. 834, the order granting a new trial was made on the 60th day. Within 10 days thereafter the memorandum specifying reasons was filed. *Held,* this was timely. The specification of reasons must be made within 10 days after the order, but need not be made within the jurisdictional 60-day period for the order (text, §§68, 69). Hence, if the judge takes the full 60 days for the order, he has an additional 10-day period to specify reasons.

See also *Widener v. Pac. Gas & Elec. Co.* (1977) 75 C.A.3d 415, 439, 142 C.R. 304 ["Amplification" of order filed within period, setting forth adequate specification of reasons].

Late specification ineffective: See *Smith v. Moffat* (1977) 73 C.A.3d 86, 91, 140 C.R. 566 [minute order granting motion entered; superfluous signed order filed 14 days later and specification filed 6 days after that].

(iii) [§81A] (New) Remedy of Aggrieved Party.

In *LaBorne v. Mulvany* (1974) 43 C.A.3d 905, 917, 119 C.R. 596, the court suggested that the successful moving party who was concerned about the lack of a statement of reasons could seek mandamus within the 10-day period to compel the judge to specify. In *Zhadan v. Downtown L. A. Motors* (1976) 66 C.A.3d 481, 494, 136 C.R. 132, defendant, whose new trial motion had been granted without an adequate statement of reasons, contended that plaintiff could not challenge the order on appeal unless he first sought mandamus to compel specification. In rejecting this contention the court pointed out that *LaBorne* dealt solely with the party *in whose favor* the motion was granted, and that nothing in the case suggested that the party *against whom* it was granted had a duty to take steps to bring about an adequate specification for the purpose of sustaining the very order he was attacking. The court also pointed out that the judge has 10 days to cure his failure to specify, and until that period has elapsed it cannot be known whether the order will be defective in its final form.

(i) [§82] General Principles.

See *Meiner v. Ford Motor Co.* (1971) 17 C.A.3d 127, 135, 94 C.R. 702, Supp., infra, §85.

Where there are two or more issues upon which there is evidence to support the jury verdict, the order must specify the reasons why the evidence on each is insufficient. (*Previte v. Lincolnwood* (1975) 48 C.A.3d 976, 987, 122 C.R. 194 [several issues of fraud, proper specification only as to one]; *Devine v. Murrietta* (1975) 49 C.A.3d 855, 861, 122 C.R. 847 [issues of negligence and proximate cause, no specification on latter issue].)

(iii) [§84] Rejection of Ultimate Facts Theory.

p. 3660:

Scala case: See *Dorsic v. Kurtin* (1971) 19 C.A.3d 226, 232, 96 C.R. 528 [applying *Scala* test and holding specification insufficient]; *Aronowicz v. Nalley's* (1972) 30 C.A.3d 27, 39, 106 C.R. 424 [same; statements of ultimate fact without identification of any portion or record or reference to any evidence]; *Miller v. Los Angeles County Flood Control Dist.* (1973) 8 C.3d 689, 106 C.R. 1, 505 P.2d 193, Supp., infra, §85; *Stevens v. Parke, Davis & Co.* (1973) 9 C.3d 51, 60, 61, 62, 107 C.R. 45, 507 P.2d 653, Supp., infra, §86A; *LaBorne v. Mulvany* (1974) 43 C.A.3d 905, 916, 119 C.R. 596 [applying *Scala* test and holding specification insufficient].

(iv) [§85] Proper Specifications.

In *San Francisco B.A.R.T. Dist. v. Fremont Meadows* (1971) 20 C.A.3d 797, 97 C.R. 898, plaintiff sued to condemn property, and the jury verdict evaluated the property at 90¢ per square foot. In his order granting a new trial to defendant owner the judge stated that the verdict ignored the highest and best use, that the jury gave too great a consideration to one comparable sale, improperly excluding other comparable sales, and that the evidence of unique location and highest and best use demonstrated gross inadequacy of the award. *Held,* this was sufficient. (20 C.A.3d 801.)

In *Miller v. Los Angeles County Flood Control Dist.* (1973) 8 C.3d 689, 106 C.R. 1, 505 P.2d 193, the court, as in *Scala* (text, p. 3662) compared the inadequate specification with suggested statements which would have been sufficient. Plaintiffs' home was destroyed by flood, and a death and personal injuries also resulted. A verdict was returned against defendant District, and the judge granted its motion for a new trial, with the following specification: "the only basis on which the District could be held liable to the plaintiffs under the facts of this case would relate to some condition of danger in the debris basin or dam creating it; the District is immune from any liability having to do with its design; the District completely and adequately discharged any obligation it had in the maintenance of the basin and dam as demonstrated by the overwhelming preponderance of the evidence." *Held,* this was insufficient.

(a) The first part merely echoed the instructions on design immunity, and the last part failed to identify the aspects of the evidence which convinced the judge that the District had properly discharged its duty. (8 C.3d 698.)

(b) There were several ways in which a good specification might have been made:

"For example, the trial judge may have believed the testimony of the District's employees that the debris basin had been cleaned out by the date of the accident. If so, review could have focused on the adequacy of that testimony. Alternately, the judge may have disbelieved plaintiffs' witnesses, a pair of young boys who allegedly viewed the basin two days before the accident and found it filled with mud. If that was the basis for the judge's reasoning, then it should have been stated, along with the reasons for disbelieving or otherwise rejecting the boys' testimony. Finally, the trial court may have determined that the District, by sending a crew of men to clean out the basin, had done all that was reasonably necessary to maintain it, and that the fact that such work was not completed by the date of the accident did not negate the reasonableness of the District's action. . . . A statement to this effect would have drawn attention to the testimony relating to the efforts of the District's maintenance crew and the notice to the District of the imminent danger of flood." (8 C.3d 699.)

(New) Where judge disbelieves witness or testimony. How is the trial judge to specify his reasons when they are based on his determination from observation of a witness, that his testimony is not worthy of credence? This question was explored by the majority and dissenting opinions in *Meiner v. Ford Motor Co.* (1971) 17 C.A.3d 127, 94 C.R. 702.

Plaintiff, driving a Ford, was injured in a collision with another car. He sued defendant manufacturer and defendant dealer on the theory of strict products liability, alleging that the accident was caused by a defect in the steering wheel of his car. The jury gave him a verdict of $300,000, and the trial judge granted a new trial on the ground of insufficiency of the evidence. The specification was that "The plaintiff's expert testimony, when weighed against the overwhelming expert testimony introduced by defendant, is completely lacking in probative force to establish the proposition of fact to which it is addressed; namely, that there was a temporary failure of the steering mechanism or that said steering mechanism or any other portion of the vehicle was defective." He added that, weighing the evidence, that of defendants was "overwhelmingly more persuasive and probable" than that of plaintiff. (17 C.A.3d 135.) *Held,* order affirmed.

(a) The test of *Mercer* and *Scala* was met. Like the reference in *Scala* to tiles not delivered, the reference here to the cause of the accident as not being a failure of the steering mechanism but rather plaintiff's negligence in turning at excessive speed onto the wrong side of the intersecting street, was sufficient. (17 C.A.3d 139.)

(b) The dissenting justice argued that the judge who disbelieves a witness ought to say *why,* and if his belief is based on the witness' demeanor, *what it was* about that demeanor which cast doubt on his veracity. (17 C.A.3d 151; see *Klinger v. Henderson,* text, p. 3662.) The majority conceded that this kind of statement might be desirable (citing *Klinger,* supra), but held that it is not required by the statute or controlling decisions. Since the court in *Scala* declared that the judge need not discuss the testimony of particular witnesses (3 C.3d 370), "*a fortiori,* he is not required to state why he disbelieved the testimony of a particular witness." (17 C.A.3d 139.)

(c) There is no way of knowing how much of the determination of unreliability is based on the grounds of impeachment, demonstrated on the record, and how much on the purely subjective reaction of the trier of facts:

"On the cold record a witness may be clear, concise, direct, unimpeached, uncontradicted—but on a face to face evaluation, so exude insincerity as to render his credibility factor nil. Another witness may fumble, bumble, be unsure, uncertain, contradict himself, and on the basis of a written transcript be hardly worthy of belief. But one who sees, hears and observes him may be convinced of his honesty, his integrity, his reliability." (17 C.A.3d 140.)

Thus, the judge who disbelieves a witness because of his demeanor and manner of testifying should say so, but that statement should be enough; he should not be required to attempt a description of extra-record matters such as intonations, movements, bearing or expression. (17 C.A.3d 141.)

See also *Kramer v. Gaddis* (1976) 56 C.A.3d 837, 841, 128 C.R. 860; *O'Kelly v. Willig Freight Lines* (1977) 66 C.A.3d 578, 582, 136 C.R. 171; *Clemmer v. Hartford Ins. Co.* (1978) 22 C.3d 865, 888, 151 C.R. 285, 587 P.2d 1098.

[§86A]   (New) Excessive Damages.

The tests laid down for specification of the ground of insufficiency of the evidence (text, §82 et seq.) are also applicable to the ground of excessive damages, for a finding that damages are excessive necessarily implies that the evidence did not justify the award (see text, §43), and C.C.P. 657 places both grounds in its conclusive presumption on review (see text, §88). "In light of the parallel treatment of the two grounds in the statute, we are of the opinion that what we have said as to the required content of the specification where 'insufficiency of the evidence' is relied upon should apply where 'excessive or inadequate damages' is the designated ground." (*Stevens v. Parke, Davis & Co.* (1973) 9 C.3d 51, 61, 107 C.R. 45, 507 P.2d 653.)

In the *Stevens* case the judge merely made a statement of ultimate fact that did not go beyond the ground of the order; and his reference to "prejudice and passion" (the language of the superseded statute, see text, §42) was not a "reason" providing an insight into the record. (9 C.3d 62.)

See also *Dizon v. Pope* (1974) 44 C.A.3d 146, 149, 118 C.R. 465 ["The plaintiff sustained special damages of $1536.00. The injury was to soft tissue and does not appear to be permanent"; no statement of how judge arrived at total of special damages or significance of mention of soft tissue].

Sufficient specification: See *Kolar v. Los Angeles* (1976) 54 C.A.3d 873, 877, 879, 127 C.R. 15.

[§86B]   (New) Inadequate Damages.

The *Stevens* approach and text (Supp., supra, §86A) were applied to hold insufficient an order granting a new trial on the issue of damages which merely recited that "inadequate damages were awarded to plaintiff." (*Krueger v. Meyer* (1975) 48 C.A.3d 760, 764, 121 C.R. 814.)

See also *Wilson v. R. D. Werner Co.* (1980) 108 C.A.3d 878, 881, 882, 166 C.R. 797 [specification left it open to speculation whether court believed that jury improperly omitted to compensate for pain and suffering or for loss of ability to work].

For a sufficient specification, see *Sanchez v. Hasencamp* (1980) 107 C.A.3d 935, 939, 941, 166 C.R. 118; *Truhitte v. French Hospital* (1982) 128 C.A.3d 332, 352, 180 C.R. 152.

[§86C] (New) Excessive Punitive Damages.

In *Zhadan v. Downtown L. A. Motors* (1976) 66 C.A.3d 481, 493, 136 C.R. 132, the court applied the tests of the *Stevens* case (Supp., supra, §86A) to a statement of reasons why a punitive damage award was excessive. The only reason stated—that the verdict was based on prejudice and passion—was obviously insufficient.

But in *Neal v. Farmers Insurance Exchange* (1978) 21 C.3d 910, 148 C.R. 389, 582 P.2d 980, Supp., supra, §80A, the court declared that the *Stevens* case requirement that the order "indicate the respects in which the evidence dictated a less sizeable verdict" does not apply where the challenge is to the amount of punitive damages award. "In such a case we think that the specification is adequate when, as here, it makes reference to those aspects of the trial proceedings which, in the trial court's view, improperly led the jury to inflate its award." Here the judge pointed to instances of misconduct of plaintiff's counsel and referred to the guidelines for awarding punitive damages, and the statement was adequate. (21 C.3d 932.)

(dd) [§87] Judge Must Personally Prepare Specification.

Recent cases take a strict and inflexible approach to the requirement that the judge must personally prepare the specification, and hold invalid any order which discloses the hand of counsel in that preparation.

(1) A direction that counsel prepare the order is no compliance at all; and the fact that counsel made a timely attempt to obtain compliance, by submitting a memorandum with proposed specifications for the judge's consideration, is immaterial where the judge took no action thereon. (*Worden v. Gentry* (1975) 50 C.A.3d 600, 606, 123 C.R. 496.)

(2) An order incorporating by reference a written argument of counsel for the moving party is insufficient. "The adoption of the attorney's argument no more serves the statutory purpose than does

the adoption of an attorney's post-argument specifications." (*Devine v. Murrieta* (1975) 49 C.A.3d 855, 860, 122 C.R. 847.)

(3) An order adopting the specification of reasons voluntarily drafted by counsel is likewise insufficient. In *Oberstein v. Bisset* (1976) 55 C.A.3d 184, 189, 190, 127 C.R. 413, the court thought that the language of *La Manna* (see Supp., supra, §80) rendered impermissible the suggestion in the text that the judge can accept the benefits of counsel's efforts:

"We cannot agree with the rationale that if the attorney can point out deficiencies in the judge's specification it must follow that he should be authorized to prepare and submit a specification of reasons which he, the attorney deems adequate. It is one thing to point out legal deficiencies in the judge's statement of reasons by citing pertinent case law and another thing to draft what the attorney feels are adequate specifications. The specification of reasons must be the product of the judge's mental processes and not that of the attorney for the moving party." (55 C.A.3d 190.)

See also *Estate of Sheldon* (1977) 75 C.A.3d 364, 370, 142 C.R. 119, citing the text [order prepared by counsel "is jurisdictionally defective"].

(cc) [§90] Other Grounds.

In re Marriage of Beilock (1978) 81 C.A.3d 713, 146 C.R. 675, Supp., supra, §21, follows the *Treber* analysis. The motion for new trial was made on two grounds: insufficiency of evidence and decision against law. The judge's order granting the motion did not specify any ground or reasons. (81 C.A.3d 724.) After an extended discussion of *Le Manna v. Stewart* (Supp., supra, §80) and *Treber,* the court declared that it was its duty to search the record to determine whether the decision was "against the law" (81 C.A.3d 728); and, after such search, it concluded that the order was contrary to law, and affirmed the order granting a new trial (81 C.A.3d 733).

(1) [§91] Nature of Power.

Insubstantial changes in the language of C.C.P. 662 were made in 1981.

(1) [§95] Nature of Power.

Improper where issue of liability inseparable from that of damages: See *Liodas v. Sahadi* (1977) 19 C.3d 278, 286, 137 C.R. 635, 562 P.2d 316.

(aa) [§96] Issue of Damages in Tort.

(New) Interpretation of order not expressly limited: In *O'Kelly v.*

Willig Freight Lines (1977) 66 C.A.3d 578, 136 C.R. 171, the verdict for plaintiff included a special verdict apportioning damages under the comparative negligence doctrine, and the order granting a new trial was construed as limited to the issue of proper apportionment. The court said: "It is clear from the order . . ., and from the specification of reasons, that the trial court did not intend a total retrial, nor a retrial concerning the total amount of damage." (66 C.A.3d 583.)

In *Richard v. Scott* (1978) 79 C.A.3d 57, 144 C.R. 672, the court refused to interpret the unambiguous order in this manner. The dissenting justice thought *O'Kelly* was precisely in point (79 C.A.3d 71), but the majority opinion states: "[W]e think the majority in *O'Kelly* strained mightily to divine the trial judge's intention from his order and specification of reasons. . . . We, therefore, decline to extend *O'Kelly* beyond the particular facts presented there." (79 C.A.3d 68.) The court added: "The request for a limited new trial . . . should be addressed to the trial judge; it should not be made to a reviewing court for the first time on an appeal from an order granting a new trial." (79 C.A.3d 69.)

(aa) [§98] Theory of Limitation.

See *Wilson v. R. D. Werner Co.* (1980) 108 C.A.3d 878, 883, 166 C.R. 797.

(aa) [§102] Nature and Forms.

See 58 Am.Jur.2d 443; 18 Am.Jur. P.P. Forms (Rev. ed.) 603, 604.

(aa) [§105] Nature of Remittitur.

(1) *Judicially Developed Rule.*

On the plaintiff's right to challenge the accepted reduced award when the defendant appeals, see *Miller v. National American Life Ins. Co.* (1976) 54 C.A.3d 331, 343, 126 C.R. 731, *Appeal,* Supp., §141A.

(ee) [§112] Procedure.

(2) *Order:* A minute order which does not state the ground of additur or the amount is not fatally defective. (*San Francisco B.A.R.T. Dist. v. Fremont Meadows* (1971) 20 C.A.3d 797, 802, 97 C.R. 898 [pointing out that the oral statement in court made these clear, and that plaintiff failed to seek clarification].)

(a) [§113] Minute Entry or Signed Order.

Minute entry effective, later signed order superfluous: See *Smith v. Moffat* (1977) 73 C.A.3d 86, 91, 140 C.R. 566.

(b) [§114] Permanent Minutes: Substantial Compliance.

Error: The 60-day period does not run from the date of entry of the order (text, p. 3691); the period continues to run until the order is entered. Since the motion is not determined until the order ruling on it is entered in the permanent minutes of the court (C.C.P. 660, text, §113), this must be done within the 60-day period.

Substantial compliance: In *LaBorne v. Mulvany* (1974) 43 C.A.3d 905, 119 C.R. 596, the judge's order, entered in the permanent minutes, bore the timely date of January 19. However, it was subsequently stamped by a deputy clerk with the additional date of January 23, which was one day late. *Held,* the order was valid, under the principles of *Desherow v. Rhodes* (text, p. 3691): "[W]here the trial judge's order was (1) timely reduced to writing (Jan. 19, 1973); (2) timely recorded in a permanent record; and (3) as evidenced by the notation of entry in a specified book at a definite page, timely delivered to the custodian of records, the essentials for processing an order into the permanent minutes of the court are present and the subsequent stamping of an entry date by the deputy clerk is an additional step not required for the order to substantially comply with the requirements of section 660." (43 C.A.3d 913.)

(1) [§117] In General.

(a) *Appeal and Cross-Appeal.* The respondent should take a precautionary cross-appeal from the judgment: See *Miller v. Los Angeles C. F. C. District* (1973) 8 C.3d 689, 696, 106 C.R. 1, 505 P.2d 193, footnote 7, citing the text; *Worth v. Asiatic Transpacific* (1979) 93 C.A.3d 849, 857, 156 C.R. 110, quoting the text.

(i) [§119] Reversible Error.

(b) *Prejudicial Effect.* Harmless error: See *Osborne v. Cal-Am Financial Corp.* (1978) 80 C.A.3d 259, 266, 145 C.R. 584, Supp., infra, §121.

(c) *Waiver or Estoppel.*

p. 3697:

Where motion granted: See *Miller v. National American Life Ins. Co.* (1976) 54 C.A.3d 331, 346, 126 C.R. 731, quoting the text.

Misconduct of counsel: In an appeal by a defendant from a judgment after denial of a motion for new trial, the failure of defendant's counsel to object or except may be treated as a waiver of the error. But where the trial judge determines that the misconduct was serious and grants a new trial, the reviewing court is not concerned with the failure to object or except; i.e., the technical waiver by defendant's counsel cannot deprive the trial judge of the power to correct a miscarriage of justice. "Thus the question is not whether the challenged acts by opposing counsel were prejudicially erroneous, but whether they were sufficiently opprobrious so that the trial court *could* conclude that they were improper." (*Seimon v. Southern Pac. Transp. Co.* (1977) 67 C.A.3d 600, 605, 136 C.R. 787.)

(ii) [§120] Discretion Upheld.

See *Richard v. Scott* (1978) 79 C.A.3d 57, 64, 144 C.R. 672, quoting the text; *Jacoby v. Feldman* (1978) 81 C.A.3d 432, 446, 146 C.R. 334, quoting the text.

Review of order denying motion: See *Los Angeles v. Decker* (1977) 18 C.3d 860, 872, 135 C.R. 647, 558 P.2d 545, *Appeal,* Supp., §294 [independent review of order].

(iii) [§121] Discretion Abused.

(a) *Order Granting Reversed.* In *Osborne v. Cal-Am Financial Corp.* (1978) 80 C.A.3d 259, 145 C.R. 584, plaintiff seller sued defendant purchaser for damages for refusal to purchase real property. The jury returned a verdict for defendant purchaser, on evidence of timely rescission by the purchaser. The judge granted plaintiff a new trial on the ground that he, the judge, had admonished plaintiff and his counsel in front of the jury, and had refused to allow plaintiff to call an expert witness in rebuttal. In a memorandum opinion the judge indicated that he was convinced the plaintiff's case had no merit, that plaintiff's own conduct had produced the admonitions, and that there was no excuse for not calling the witness on the case in chief. His reason for granting the new trial was that, to ensure justice for all, it must be afforded to "the worst." *Held,* order reversed. "[T]he trial judge appears to be saying he does not think his conduct could have been prejudicial; but he grants a new trial because he believes such grant is required as a matter of form to foster the appearance of justice. If that is the basis for his order, it is unsound, because it is clear that new trials may not be granted except for prejudicial error. The grant of a new trial for harmless error violates the constitutional provision and wastes judicial time and resources to no purpose." (80 C.A.3d 266.)

(b) *Order Denying Held Error and Judgment Reversed.* See *Los Angeles v. Decker* (1977) 18 C.3d 860, 872, 135 C.R. 647, 558 P.2d 545, *Appeal,* Supp., §294 [independent review of order].

A. [§122] Nature and Purpose of Statute.

Insubstantial changes in the language of C.C.P. 663 were made in 1981 to conform to statutes eliminating findings of fact (see *Trial,* Supp., §349A et seq.). The statute now reads: "A judgment or decree, when based upon *a decision* by the court, or the special verdict of a jury, may, upon motion of the party aggrieved, be set aside and vacated by the same court, and another and different judgment entered, for either of the following causes, materially affecting *the* substantial rights of the party and entitling *the party* to a different judgment: (1) Incorrect or erroneous *legal basis for the decision,* not consistent with or not supported by the *facts;* and in such case when the judgment is set aside, the *statement of decision* shall be amended and corrected. (2) A judgment or decree not consistent with or not supported by the special verdict."

See 6 (Part 1) Cal Practice (Rev. ed.) 565 et seq.; Federal Procedure, Lawyers Edition §51:17 et seq.

B. [§123] Motion for New Trial Distinguished.

(2) *Evidence Sufficient: Motion To Vacate.* See *Alameda v. Carleson* (1971) 5 C.3d 730, 738, 97 C.R. 385, 488 P.2d 953, citing the text.

1. [§124] Notice of Motion.

(a) *Form and Content.* See 15 Am.Jur. P.P. Forms (Rev. ed.) 471, 472; C.E.B., Civ. Lit. Forms, §2.1; 6 (Part 1) Cal Practice (Rev. ed.) 567.

2. [§125] Hearing and Determination.

(c) *Form of Order.* See 6 (Part 1) Cal Practice (Rev. ed.) 568.

1. [§126] Nature of Relief.

See 5 (Part 1) Cal Practice (Rev. ed.) 328 et seq.; 6 (Part 2) Cal Practice (Rev. ed.) 482 et seq.; 2 C.E.B., Civ. Proc. Before Trial (1978 ed.), §30.62 et seq.

Federal Rule 60: See 50 So. Cal. L. Rev. 1207 [Negligent Litigation and Relief from Judgments]; 30 Hastings L. J. 41 [A Morass Unrelieved by a Rule]; Federal Procedure, Lawyers Edition, §51.17 et seq.

(a) [§127] Actions and Proceedings.

(New) Small claims court: The motion may be made in the small claims court. (*Burley v. Stein* (1974) 40 C.A.3d 752, 115 C.R. 279, *Courts,* Supp., §199A.)

(New) Reviewing court: C.C.P. 418.10(c), providing for review by mandamus of an order denying a motion to quash summons (see *Jurisdiction,* §133), requires filing of the petition within 10 days after service of notice of the order, unless time is extended for good cause. In *Cornell University Med. College v. Superior Court* (1974) 38 C.A.3d

311, 113 C.R. 291, petitioner, through a mistake of counsel's messenger, deposited the petition in the wrong court. On discovery of the mistake petitioner moved for an extension, the superior court granted it, and petitioner filed the petition in the Court of Appeal. *Held*, the petition was properly filed and the writ could issue: Where a trial court would have been authorized to grant relief under C.C.P. 473, a reviewing court may grant similar relief. (38 C.A.3d 315.)

3. [§129] Persons Entitled to Relief.

(a) *Party or Representative of Party.*

Trustee in bankruptcy: See *Clemmer v. Hartford Ins. Co.* (1978) 22 C.3d 865, 885, 886, 151 C.R. 285, 587 P.2d 1098.

p. 3705:

Nonparty cannot make motion: See *Roski v. Superior Court* (1971) 17 C.A.3d 841, 846, 95 C.R. 312.

1. [§130] Fraud.

See *In re Marriage of Jacobs* (1982) 128 C.A.3d 273, 284, 180 C.R. 234; *Don v. Cruz* (1982) 131 C.A.3d 695, 702, 182 C.R. 581, footnote 2, citing the text; Rest.2d, Judgments §68.

(a) [§131] Mistake of Fact.

See *In re Marriage of Jacobs* (1982) 128 C.A.3d 273, 284, 180 C.R. 234; *Don v. Cruz* (1982) 131 C.A.3d 695, 702, 182 C.R. 581 [C.C.P.473 does not apply to judicial mistakes]; Rest.2d, Judgments §68.

(cc) [§135] Cases Denying Relief.

See *Martin v. Johnson* (1979) 88 C.A.3d 595, 606, 151 C.R. 816.

(1) [§136] Nature of Ground.

See Rest.2d, Judgments §68.

(1) [§139] Office Practice or Press of Business.

"Whether we characterize the conduct of defendant's counsel as reasonable or the conduct of plaintiff's counsel as unreasonable—the result is the same under the peculiar factual context of this case. Given the short period of time in which an answer had to be filed, and the press of business at defense counsel's office arising from the illness of the chief trial attorney, the limited office hours during Christmas week, and defense counsel's preoccupation with other litigated matters, it might be found that the failure to file a timely

answer or a request for an extension to file an answer was excusable."
(*Robinson v. Varela* (1977) 67 C.A.3d 611, 616, 136 C.R. 783, citing
the text [order vacating default affirmed].)

(2) [§140] Reliance on Opposing Counsel.

See *Robinson v. Varela* (1977) 67 C.A.3d 611, 616, 136 C.R. 783,
citing the text ["the quiet taking of default on the beginning of the
first day on which defendant's answer was delinquent was the sort of
professional discourtesy which, under *Smith,* justified vacating the
default"].

(4) [§142] Reliance on Other Persons.

Insurance carrier: A defendant seeking to vacate a default under
C.C.P. 473 or by appeal to the court's equitable powers, who alleges
reasonable reliance on his insurance carrier, must also establish
justification for the carrier's inaction. Hence, reliance on an insurance
carrier is legally equivalent to reliance on an attorney. (*Don v. Cruz*
(1982) 131 C.A.3d 695, 701, 702, 182 C.R. 581.)

On reliance on third person as ground for equitable relief against
judgment, see text, §189.

(a) [§149] Form and Content.

See 15 Am.Jur. P.P. Forms (Rev. ed.) 469; 5 (Part 1) Cal
Practice (Rev. ed.) 337; 6 (Part 2) Cal Practice (Rev. ed.) 485; 2
C.E.B., Civ. Proc. Before Trial (1978 ed.), §30.64; C.E.B., Civ. Lit.
Forms, §38.4.

(1) [§150] Period: 6 Months.

(a) *The Two Limitations.*

Jurisdictional limitation: See *Marianos v. Tutunjian* (1977) 70
C.A.3d 61, 65, 138 C.R. 529, *Courts,* Supp., §172.

Renewed motion: See *Northridge Financial Corp. v. Hamblin*
(1975) 48 C.A.3d 819, 825, 122 C.R. 109, citing the text [original
motion made within period, denied; motion to reconsider (treated as
renewal) made after period expired, properly denied].

(2) [§151] When Time Begins To Run.

(a) Time runs from rendition of judgment: See *In re Marriage of
Jacobs* (1982) 128 C.A.3d 273, 182, 180 C.R. 234 [stipulated interlocutory judgment].

(b) Time runs from entry of default: See *Weiss v. Blumencranc*
(1976) 61 C.A.3d 536, 541, 131 C.R. 298.

(c)   [§153]   Reasonable Time.

Lack of diligence: "Defendant has not cited, nor has independent research disclosed, any case in which a court has set aside a default where, in making application therefor, there has been an unexplained delay of anything approaching three months after full knowledge of the entry of the default." (*Ludka v. Memor Magnetics Int.* (1972) 25 C.A.3d 316, 322, 101 C.R. 615 [upholding order denying relief].)

See *In re Marriage of Jacobs* (1982) 128 C.A.3d 273, 280, 180 C.R. 234 [motion to set aside interlocutory judgment filed 1 day less than 6 months after entry was within reasonable time].

(a)   [§154]   Proof of Excuse and Diligence.

See 15 Am.Jur. P.P. Forms (Rev. ed.) 487; 5 (Part 1) Cal Practice (Rev. ed.) 338; 6 (Part 2) Cal Practice (Rev. ed.) 486; 2 C.E.B., Civ. Proc. Before Trial (1978 ed.), §30.65; C.E.B., Civ. Lit. Forms, §38.5.

(2)   [§156]   Affidavits.

See 15 Am.Jur. P.P. Forms (Rev. ed.) 487; 5 (Part 1) Cal Practice (Rev. ed.) 339, 340; 6 (Part 2) Cal Practice (Rev. ed.) 486; 2 C.E.B., Civ. Proc. Before Trial (1978 ed.), §30.66, C.E.B., Civ. Proc. Forms, pp. 417, 418 became C.E.B., Civ. Lit. Forms, §38.6, but was subsequently withdrawn.

C.C.P. 473, as amended in 1981, specifically provides that no affidavit or declaration of merits is required by the moving party.

(a)   [§159]   Entry and Effect.

See 15 Am.Jur. P.P. Forms (Rev. ed.) 505; 5 (Part 1) Cal Practice (Rev. ed.) 349; 6 (Part 2) Cal Practice (Rev. ed.) 487; 2 C.E.B., Civ. Proc. Before Trial (1978 ed.), §30.71; C.E.B., Civ. Lit. Forms, §38.8.

(2)   [§163]   Reversal of Order.

See *Martin v. Cook* (1977) 68 C.A.3d 799, 810, 137 C.R. 434, *Proceedings Without Trial,* Supp., §96.

(c)   [§164]   Order Denying Relief.

(1) *Policy Influencing Reversal.* In *Nicholson v. Rose* (1980) 106 C.A.3d 457, 165 C.R. 156, defendants engaged in dilatory tactics, and failed to appear at pretrial hearings and at the trial. The judge gave plaintiff a default judgment for compensatory and punitive damages ($32,000 plus $10,000), and denied defendants' motion to vacate. The

appellate court found adequate evidentiary support for the judgment and no abuse of discretion in denying the motion to vacate. The judgment was nevertheless reversed with directions to grant a new trial, on the grounds that (a) a default judgment for punitive damages is disfavored, and (b) the record was uncertain on whether plaintiff's counsel had attempted to contact defendant's counsel when the latter failed to appear at the trial. (106 C.A.3d 462.) However, the reversal was conditioned on defendants' payment to plaintiff of $5,000 as compensation for wasted time, unnecessary expense, and aggravation caused by dilatoriness. (106 C.A.3d 463.)

(2) *Affirmance.* See *Ford v. Herndon* (1976) 62 C.A.3d 492, 497, 133 C.R.111; *Border v. Kuznetz* (1980) 103 C.A.3d Supp. 14, 18, 162 C.R. 881.

1. [§165] In General.

(a) Time limitations of C.C.P. 473 do not apply: See *Becker v. S. P. V. Const. Co.* (1980) 27 C.3d 489, 492, 165 C.R. 825, 612 P.2d 915, *Proceedings Without Trial,* Supp., §156A.

(a) [§166] Judgment Void on Its Face.

See *Young v. Young* (1970) 14 C.A.3d 1, 4, 92 C.R. 148, citing the text [support order modified without notice to party or appearance]; *Westport Oil Co. v. Garrison* (1971) 19 C.A.3d 974, 978, 97 C.R. 287, citing the text [default judgment beyond power of clerk].

(1) [§169] Former Statute.

See 5 (Part 1) Cal Practice (Rev. ed.) 342; 2 C.E.B., Civ. Proc. Before Trial (1978 ed.), §30.75; 15 Am.Jur. P.P. Forms (Rev. ed.) 486.

(2) [§170] New Statute.

See *Goya v. P. E. R. U. Enterprises* (1978) 87 C.A.3d 886, 890, 151 C.R. 258; Rest.2d, Judgments §65; 5 (Part 1) Cal Practice (Rev. ed.) 342; 1 C.E.B., Civ. Proc. Before Trial (1977 ed.), §8.30 et seq.; 2 C.E.B., Civ. Proc. Before Trial (1978 ed.), §30.75.

(2) [§172] Notice of Motion.

(a) *Service and Filing.* See 5 (Part 1) Cal Practice (Rev. ed.) 343.

(3) [§173] Order.

See 5 (Part 1) Cal Practice (Rev. ed.) 349; 15 Am.Jur. P.P. Forms (Rev. ed.) 507; *Goya v. P. E. R. U. Enterprises* (1978) 87 C.A.3d 886, 893, 151 C.R. 258.

(a) [§175] In General.

See Rest. 2d, Judgments §79 et seq.; 6 (Part 2) Cal Practice (Rev. ed.) 530 et seq.; Federal Procedure, Lawyers Edition §51:115 et seq.; 15 Am.Jur. P.P. Forms (Rev. ed.) 518; *In re Marriage of Guardino* (1979) 95 C.A.3d 77, 88, 156 C.R. 883, citing the text.

(b) [§176] Scope of Relief.

See Rest. 2d, Judgments §64, Comment d; §79 et seq.

(c) [§177] Jurisdiction of Courts.

p. 3747:

(c) Reconciliation of *Charters, Auslender* and *Security Bank:* See *Steiner v. Flournoy* (1972) 23 C.A.3d 1051, 1057, 100 C.R. 680, quoting the text.

Cross-References: 7 Summary, Wills and Probate, §§234, 236.

(d) [§178] Parties Entitled to Relief.

See Rest. 2d, Judgments §64.

Third person adversely affected: See *Villarruel v. Arreola* (1977) 66 C.A.3d 309, 318, 136 C.R. 19.

Cross-Reference: 5 Summary, Constitutional Law, §523.

(a) [§179] Propriety of Remedy.

See *Estate of Edwards* (1972) 25 C.A.3d 906, 911, 102 C.R. 216, citing *Cowan* (text, p. 3749) and the text, and suggesting that independent action is preferable where one party is deceased; 6 (Part 2) Cal Practice (Rev. ed) 488 et seq.

Motion proper: See *Villarruel v. Arreola* (1977) 66 C.A.3d 309, 318, 136 C.R. 19; *Gregory v. Hamilton* (1978) 77 C.A.3d 213, 220, 142 C.R. 563, citing the text; *Baske v. Burke* (1981) 125 C.A.3d 38, 45, 177 C.R. 794.

(b) [§180] Not Prerequisite to Action.

See Rest.2d, Judgments §78.

(c) [§181] Effect of Denial of Motion.

See *Flood v. Simpson* (1975) 45 C.A.3d 644, 650, 119 C.R. 675, citing the text.

1. [§182] Void Judgment.

See Rest.2d, Judgments §§65, 69; 6 (Part 2) Cal Practice (Rev. ed.) 498 et seq., 504 et seq.

Where a judgment is obtained by a false return of service, the court has inherent power to set it aside. In such case the action is not brought under C.C.P. 473.5, which refers only to persons upon whom service was made or attempted and who did not have actual notice of the action. (*In re Marriage of Smith* (1982) 135 C.A.3d 543, 555, 185 C.R. 411, following *Sullivan v. Sullivan* 256 C.A.2d 301, footnote 1.)

(a) [§183] Rule and Test.

See 78 A.L.R.3d 150; Rest. 2d, Judgments §70; 6 (Part 2) Cal Practice (Rev. ed.) 488 et seq.

For an argument that the extrinsic-intrinsic distinction should be abolished, see 12 Pacific L. J. 1013.

(b) [§184] Fraud Preventing Appearance or Contest.

See *In re Marriage of Park* (1980) 27 C.3d 337, 343, 165 C.R. 792, 612 P.2d 882 [husband, with knowledge of wife's deportation, concealed facts from court]; Rest. 2d, Judgments §70.

(1) [§185] In General.

See *Pentz v. Kuppinger* (1973) 31 C.A.3d 590, 596, 107 C.R. 540, citing the text [judgment of Mexican court]; *Granzella v. Jargoyhen* (1974) 43 C.A.3d 551, 555, 117 C.R. 710, quoting the text [complaint alleged reliance on defendant's representation that forged will was genuine]; 84 A.L.R.3d 1119 [*Granzella* case]; *Morales v. Field etc.* (1979) 99 C.A.3d 307, 313, 160 C.R. 239 [attorney's dual representation of trustee and third party, without disclosure to beneficiary of trust].

(2) [§186] Husband and Wife Cases.

Extrinsic fraud may be found even though the party actually appears at conferences and a hearing. *In re Marriage of Brennan* (1981) 124 C.A.3d 598, 177 C.R. 520, is an extreme illustration: the husband represented to the wife that he was bankrupt, and that she did not need an attorney but should discuss the dissolution arrangements with C, his attorney. She did so and he repeated that stock in her husband's corporation was worthless, and that provisions of the agreement for property and support were all that she would receive from the Court. She appeared in court without counsel; later the proposed judgment was sent to her and she signed on her husband's assurance that "The whole matter will be dropped." Shortly afterwards she received notice of entry of judgment, and later discovered that the husband's stock was worth $250,000. *Held,* the motion to set aside the decree should have been granted. "It is true Susan appeared in court but not to engage in battle. . . . She was in court merely to

put her stamp of approval on the representations made to her. . . .
Clearly these statements by Joseph and his attorney to Susan were
designed primarily to prevent a trial of the issues normally contested
in a dissolution proceeding." (124 C.A.3d 606.)

Cross-References: 6 *Summary, Husband and Wife,* §§121, 107.

(a) [§187] In General.

See *Baske v. Burke* (1981) 125 C.A.3d 38, 43, 177 C.R. 794;
Rest.2d, Judgments §§70, 71; 6 (Part 2) Cal Practice (Rev. ed.) 488 et
seq.

Cross-Reference: 1 *Summary, Contracts,* §295 et seq.

(b) [§188] Incapacity of Attorney or Party.

See Rest.2d, Judgments §72.

(c) [§189] Reliance on Third Person.

Insurance carrier: See *Don v. Cruz* (1982) 131 C.A.3d 695, 700,
182 C.R. 581, Supp., supra, §142.

(a) [§192] Extrinsic Fraud or Mistake.

See *New York Higher Ed. Assn. Corp. v. Siegel* (1979) 91 C.A.3d
684, 688, 154 C.R. 200, quoting the text; *Baske v. Burke* (1981) 125
C.A.3d 38, 46, 177 C.R. 794; Rest.2d, Judgments §74.

(a) [§194] In General.

See Rest.2d, Judgments §74.

(b) [§195] Diligence Shown.

See *In re Marriage of Park* (1980) 27 C.3d 337, 345, 165 C.R.
729, 612 P.2d 882.

(c) [§196] Diligence Not Shown.

See *In re Marriage of Guardino* (1979) 95 C.A.3d 77, 93, 156
C.R. 883; *Alexander v. Abbey of the Chimes* (1980) 104 C.A.3d 39, 48,
163 C.R. 377.

1. [§197] Rule and Theory.

See *Kachig v. Boothe* (1971) 22 C.A.3d 626, 632, 99 C.R. 393,
Supp., supra, §5, citing the text; *Beresh v. Sovereign Life Ins. Co.*
(1979) 92 C.A.3d 547, 553, 155 C.R. 74; *In re Marriage of Guardino*
(1979) 95 C.A.3d 77, 89, 156 C.R. 883.

For an argument that the extrinsic-intrinsic distinction should be
abolished, see 12 Pacific L. J. 1013.

Chapter XII

EXTRAORDINARY WRITS

1. [§1] In General.

See 86 Harv. L. Rev. 595 [federal supervisory and advisory mandamus under All Writs Act]; 2 Federal Procedure, Lawyers Edition § 3:367 et seq.

p. 3781:

Audita querela: See 7 Am.Jur.2d 423.

Cross-References: 6 *Summary, Parent and Child,* §§95, 96.

2. [§2] Certiorari: Review of Judicial Action.

See *Ratchford v. Sonoma* (1972) 22 C.A.3d 1056, 1065, 99 C.R. 887, citing the text.

3. [§3] Prohibition: Restraint of Judicial Action.

See 63 Am.Jur.2d 225 et seq.; 20 Am.Jur. P.P. Forms (Rev. ed.) 443.

Cross-Reference: 5 *Summary, Constitutional Law,* §609.

4. [§4] Mandamus: Compulsion of Ministerial Duty.

See 86 Harv. L. Rev. 595 [federal supervisory and advisory mandamus under All Writs Act]; 17 Am.Jur. P.P. Forms (Rev. ed.) 180.

On the distinction between traditional mandamus and administrative mandamus (text, §210), see *Vernon Fire Fighters v. Vernon* (1980) 107 C.A.3d 802, 808, 810, 165 C.R. 908.

5. [§5] Constitutional Revision of 1966.

Art. VI, §10, gives individual superior court *judges* jurisdiction only to issue writs of habeas corpus.

On "proceedings for extraordinary relief in the nature of mandamus, certiorari, and prohibition," see Supp., infra, §11A.

(a) [§6] Nature of Proceeding.

See 65 Am.Jur.2d 230; 21 Am.Jur. P.P. Forms (Rev. ed.) 5 et seq.; *Citizens Utilities Co. v. Superior Court* (1976) 56 C.A.3d 399, 405, 128 C.R. 582 [privately owned public utility water franchise].

Challenge to defective city charter: See *Oakland Mun. Imp. League v. Oakland* (1972) 23 C.A.3d 165, 169, 100 C.R. 29.

(b) [§7] Action by Attorney General.

See 21 Am.Jur. P.P. Forms (Rev. ed.) 18.

p. 3786:

C.C.P. 804: The arrest statutes were repealed and this section was amended in 1973 to eliminate reference to arrest and bail. (See *Provisional Remedies,* Supp., §7A.)

(c) [§8] Action on Relation of Private Person.

See 21 Am.Jur. P.P. Forms (Rev. ed.) 8.

(b) [§11] Special Types of Review.

Rule 57 was amended, effective January 1, 1980, to refer to the Workers' Compensation Appeals Board.

On review of decisions of the Agricultural Labor Relations Board, see Supp., infra, §11A.

[§11A] (New) Review of Decisions of California A.L.R.B.

Lab.C. 1160.8 provides that a person aggrieved by a "final order" of the Agricultural Labor Relations Board (see 1 *Summary, Agency and Employment,* Supp., §37A) "may obtain a *review* of such order in the *court of appeal* having jurisdiction over the county wherein the unfair labor practice in question was alleged to have been engaged in." The statutory language was taken from the National Labor Relations Act, and the task of harmonizing the language of Lab.C. 1160.8 with the limitations on Court of Appeal jurisdiction under Cal. Const., Art. VI, §§10 and 11 was recently undertaken by the Supreme Court. In *Tex-Cal Land Management v. Agricultural Lab. Rel. Bd.* (1979) 24 C.3d 335, 156 C.R. 1, 595 P.2d 579, the constitutionality of the Labor Code section was upheld and the nature of the review was determined: "[T]he functions assigned a Court of Appeal by section 1160.8 are within its original jurisdiction over a proceeding 'for extraordinary relief in the nature of mandamus.," (24 C.3d 350.) (For a full discussion of the facts and holding in *Tex-Cal* see 4 *Summary, Torts,* Supp., §411P; 68 Cal. L. Rev. 618.)

(e) [§14] Habeas Corpus.

(1-A) *(New) Both writs available:* Where the punishment is only a fine, habeas corpus will not lie; but where both fines and imprisonment are ordered, the reviewing court may treat the petition for habeas corpus as also a petition for certiorari. (*In re Coleman* (1974) 12 C.3d 568, 572, 116 C.R. 381, 526 P.2d 533, footnote 2, citing the text, *Provisional Remedies,* §111.)

(a) [§15] Mandamus.

See 63 Am.Jur.2d 228.

(d) [§18] Prohibitory Injunction.

See 63 Am.Jur.2d 228.
Cross-Reference: 5 *Summary, Constitutional Law,* §58.

C. [§22] Discretionary Issuance of Prohibition or Mandamus.
p. 3797:

(4) Question of public importance: See *Hogya v. Superior Court* (1977) 75 C.A.3d 122, 129, 142 C.R. 325.

(2) [§25] Nonappealable Judgments or Orders.

See 7 Cal Practice (Rev. ed.) 584.
p. 3800:

(d) *Superior Court Judgment on Appeal From Small Claims Court.* See *Davis v. Superior Court* (1980) 102 C.A.3d 164, 168, 162 C.R. 167, *Courts,* Supp., §200.

(b) [§26] Legislative and Ministerial Acts Not Reviewable.

Although abandonment of a highway by a county board of supervisors has been considered a legislative act, issuance of the writ to determine whether the board had jurisdiction to proceed was approved in *Ratchford v. Sonoma* (1972) 22 C.A.3d 1056, 1070, 99 C.R. 887.

B. [§28] Lack of or Excess of Jurisdiction.

See *People v. Cimarusti* (1978) 81 C.A.3d 314, 319, 146 C.R. 421, *Jurisdiction*, Supp., §194A, citing the text.

1. [§35] Act Must Be Judicial.

See 63 Am.Jur.2d 240.

(b) [§38] Exception: Partially Completed or Continuing Act.

See *People v. Superior Court (Douglas)* (1979) 24 C.3d 428, 431, 155 C.R. 704, 595 P.2d 139, footnote 2: "Issuance of a writ of prohibition to restrain further proceedings in an ongoing criminal jury trial is unusual. Although we do not question the court's power to have done so, we do question the appropriateness of such action. Considerations of orderly procedure, in our view, require that such power be exercised sparingly and only in the most compelling of circumstances once a criminal jury trial is underway and jeopardy has attached."

B. [§39] Lack of or Excess of Jurisdiction.

See 63 Am.Jur.2d 248 et seq; *Allstate Ins. Co. v. Superior Court* (1982) 132 C.A.3d 670, 676, 183 C.R. 330, citing the text.

(a) [§40] Nature of Condition.

See 63 Am.Jur.2d 234, 258.

p. 3815:

Prohibition lies to challenge a criminal statute or ordinance void on its face. (*Dulaney v. Municipal Court* (1974) 11 C.3d 77, 81, 112 C.R. 777, 520 P.2d 1, citing the text.)

(1) [§44] Alternative Writ.

See *Atlas Plastering v. Superior Court* (1977) 72 C.A.3d 63, 68, 140 C.R. 59, citing the text.

(a) [§46] Existence of Remedy by Appeal.

See 63 Am.Jur.2d 236.

(bb) [§50] No Practical Stay.

See *United Farm Workers Organizing Committee v. Superior Court* (1971) 4 C.3d 556, 563, 94 C.R. 263, 483 P.2d 1215, footnote 7, citing the text [petitioners' unchallenged assertion of inability to post a bond in amount required was sufficient to establish inadequacy of remedy by appeal from injunction].

(1) *Unlawful Detainer.* The holding in *Woods-Drury v. Superior Court* was abrogated in 1980 by an amendment to C.C.P. 1176. (See *Pleading,* Supp., §506.)

(a) [§61] Rule and Theory.

See *People v. El Dorado* (1971) 5 C.3d 480, 491, 96 C.R. 553, 487 P.2d 1193, citing the text.

On a sufficient showing it is an abuse of discretion for the lower court to deny the writ. (*King v. Martin* (1971) 21 C.A.3d 791, 796, 98 C.R. 711, citing the text; *Yamada Bros. v. Ag. Lab. Rel. Bd.* (1979) 99 C.A.3d 112, 124, 159 C.R. 905.)

Test of beneficial interest: "When the duty is sharp and the public need weighty, the courts will grant a mandamus at the behest of an applicant who shows no greater personal interest than that of a citizen who wants the law enforced. . . . When the public need is less pointed, the courts hold the petitioner to a sharper showing of personal need. Decisions of the latter sort declare that the applicant's right to the writ must be 'clear and certain.' " (*McDonald v. Stockton Met. Transit Dist.* (1973) 36 C.A.3d 436, 440, 111 C.R. 637.) (On the loose test where public interest is involved, see text, §69.)

(2) [§63] No Beneficial Interest in Petitioner.

See *McDonald v. Stockton Met. Transit Dist.* (1973) 36 C.A.3d 436, 443, 111 C.R. 637, Supp., supra, §61; *Carsten v. Psychology Examining Com.* (1980) 27 C.3d 793, 796, 166 C.R. 844, 614 P.2d 276, Supp., infra, §63A.

[§63A] (New) Minority Member of Administrative Agency.

In *Carsten v. Psychology Examining Com.* (1980) 27 C.3d 793, 166 C.R. 844, 614 P.2d 276, petitioner, a member of defendant Psychology Examining Committee of the Board of Medical Quality Assurance, sought mandamus to compel defendant to comply with the statutory conditions governing the professional examination. *Held,* in this case of first impression, she lacked standing to sue.

(1) Since she neither sought a license nor was in danger of losing one, she was not a beneficially interested person. (27 C.3d 797.)

(2) She could not assert the right of a state taxpayer because (a) she was seeking an advisory opinion on how the Board should conduct its examinations in the future, and the judgment sought would not affect any person; (b) she was, as a member of the Board, attempting to sue herself, a practice which should not be permitted. (27 C.3d 798.)

(3) Strong considerations of public policy are opposed to permitting such actions by disgruntled governmental agency members: (a) It would be disruptive of the administrative process, for members would be compelled to testify against each other and to reveal internal discussions and deliberations; and frequent suits would severely tax the limited budgetary resources of most public agencies. (b) It would adversely affect the judicial process, by requiring a rerun of the administrative proceedings: "The dissident board member, having failed to persuade her four colleagues to her viewpoint, now has to persuade merely one judge." (27 C.3d 799.)

The opinion concludes that "the California judiciary is ill-equipped to add to its already heavy burden the duty of serving as an ombudsman for the plethora of state administrative agencies and local agencies that exist in every one of our 58 counties." (27 C.3d 801.)

Three justices joined in a strong dissent, citing such cases as *Hollman v. Warren* (text, §69), and arguing that petitioner had standing to sue as a citizen and taxpayer.

(3) [§67] No Present Ability To Perform.

No power to do act requested: See *Franklin v. Municipal Court* (1972) 26 C.A.3d 884, 898, 103 C.R. 354.

(d) [§69] Exception: Public Interest.

See *American Friends Service Committee v. Procunier* (1973) 33 C.A.3d 252, 256, 109 C.R. 22, citing the text [nonprofit corporations interested in prison inmates and prison reform, and citizen taxpayer, had standing to sue defendants, Director of Corrections and members of California Adult Authority, to compel compliance with allegedly applicable statute in making rules and regulations]; *State Bd. of Pharmacy v. Superior Court* (1978) 78 C.A.3d 641, 646, 144 C.R. 320, citing the text; *Green v. Obledo* (1981) 29 C.3d 126, 144, 172 C.R. 206, 624 P.2d 256 [calculation of AFDC benefits].

(1) [§70] Duties of Taxing Officials.

Cross-Reference: 5 *Summary, Taxation*, §200.

(aa) [§71] Local Officials.

See *People v. El Dorado* (1971) 5 C.3d 480, 491, 96 C.R. 553, 487 P.2d 1193; *Jolicoeur v. Mihaly* (1971) 5 C.3d 565, 570, 96 C.R. 697, 488 P.2d 1, footnote 2 [voting registrars]; *Calif. Housing Finance Agency v. Elliott* (1976) 17 C.3d 575, 579, 131 C.R. 361, 551 P.2d 1193 [compel public officer to issue bonds, incidentally determining constitutionality of law authorizing the bonds]; *Holt v. Kelly* (1978) 20 C.3d 560, 564, 143 C.R. 625, 574 P.2d 441, Supp., infra, §74.

On review of resolution of necessity adopted by governing body of public entity prior to commencing eminent domain proceeding, see C.C.P. 1245.255, as amended in 1978, and Law Rev. Com. Comment, pointing out that the remedy is by ordinary mandamus under C.C.P. 1085, not administrative mandamus. (See also 10 Pacific L. J. 548; 5 *Summary, Constitutional Law,* Supp., §702A-1.)

(bb) [§72] State Officials.

See *Schmitz v. Younger* (1978) 21 C.3d 90, 93, 145 C.R. 517, 577 P.2d 652 [compel Attorney General to prepare title and summary for proposed initiative measure].

Govt.C. 65956, as amended in 1982, provides that when a public hearing on a development project has not been held at least 60 days prior to the time limits set by Govt.C. 65950 and 65952, an applicant may file an action for mandamus to compel the agency to hold the hearing, and such action has preference over other matters (see *Trial,* Supp., §47).

(4) [§74] Allowance or Payment of Claim.

The principle stated in this section was applied in *Glendale City Employees' Assn. v. Glendale* (1975) 15 C.3d 328, 124 C.R. 513, 540 P.2d 609. Plaintiff city employee's association reached a binding agreement with defendant city, which provided for a survey of salaries in other cities and stated an intent to place Glendale salaries in "an above average position." The survey was conducted and defendant adopted an ordinance based on a comparison of graphs; plaintiffs objected that an arithmetic average method should have been used. In this action against the city and its councilmen, the trial court agreed with plaintiffs' interpretation, concluded that the ordinance did not meet the criteria of the agreement, and issued mandamus to compel defendants to compute and pay compensation in accordance with the formula set forth in its findings and conclusions. *Held,* affirmed.

(a) Enforcement of the plaintiff's right requires official action—here to implement the formula in the agreement; hence the action on contract is an inadequate remedy and mandamus will lie. (15 C.3d 343, citing *Ross, Tevis* and *Flora Crane Service* cases, text, pp. 3850, 3851.)

(b) The objection that defendants are being compelled to adopt a salary ordinance—a legislative act which is within their discretion—is untenable. The trial judge proceeded on the theory that the council's approval of the agreement was itself the legislative act that fixed the salaries. "The writ, therefore, did not command the enactment of a new salary ordinance, but directed the non-legislative and ministerial acts of computing and paying the salaries as fixed by the memorandum and judgment. The use of mandamus in the present case thus falls within the established principle that mandamus may issue to compel the performance of a ministerial duty or to correct an abuse of discretion." (15 C.3d 344, citing the text.)

One justice, dissenting, took sharp issue with this explanation of the effect of the judgment, and found none of the cited cases in point. Proceeding from the basic assertion that "appellate courts do not order a political subdivision as an entity, or its legislative body, to act or to refrain from acting in any specified manner" (15 C.3d 349), he posed the question whether defendant councilmen would be cited for contempt if they refused to adopt the new salary ordinance commanded by the lower court. This, he said, is one of the pitfalls faced by the judiciary when it attempts to interfere with the legislative process. (15 C.3d 350.)

On *Glendale* case, see 65 Cal. L. Rev. 472.

See also *A.B.C. Federation of Teachers v. A.B.C. U. S. Dist.* (1977) 75 C.A.3d 332, 341, 142 C.R. 111, quoting the text.

Recovery of money ancillary to underlying proceeding: In *Holt v. Kelly* (1978) 20 C.3d 560, 143 C.R. 625, 574 P.2d 441, petitioner was arrested by a sheriff's deputy, and a footlocker trunk was taken from him by the booking officer. The latter filled out an arrest record form, noting the receipt of the trunk and generally designating its contents (clothes, tools, hand tools and rifles). But no inventory was made of the contents, and no receipt was given to petitioner as required by P.C. 4003. Petitioner sought mandamus in the Court of Appeal against respondent sheriff to compel the return of the property or its value. *Held,* writ granted. Most of the property had been lost by negligent practices of respondent, but such misconduct cannot be the basis for denial of mandamus. The writ is available to compel performance of a ministerial duty even if the ultimate goal may be recovery of a sum of money; and it will lie where recovery of money is merely ancillary to an underlying proceeding which seeks performance of a ministerial duty. (20 C.3d 565, footnote 5, citing *Flora Crane, Reed* and *Daugherty* cases, text, p. 3851.)

(1)   [§75]   Mandamus Cannot Control Discretion.

See *Larson v. Redondo Beach* (1972) 27 C.A.3d 332, 337, 103 C.R. 592 [city's management of small craft harbor].

(2) [§76] Compelling Exercise of Discretion.

See *Carmona v. Division of Industrial Safety* (1975) 13 C.3d 303, 309, 118 C.R. 473, 530 P.2d 161, footnote 4, citing the text; *Anderson v. Phillips* (1975) 13 C.3d 733, 737, 119 C.R. 879, 532 P.2d 1247; *Payne v. Superior Court* (1976) 17 C.3d 908, 925, 926, 132 C.R. 405, 553 P.2d 565, *Pleading,* Supp., §91A, citing the text; *South Dakota v. Brown* (1978) 20 C.3d 765, 779, 144 C.R. 758, 576 P.2d 473; *TRIM v. Monterey* (1978) 86 C.A.3d 539, 546, 150 C.R. 351 [following *Knoff v. San Francisco,* text, p. 3852].

(3) [§77] Controlling Abuse of Discretion.

See *Fidelity & Casualty Co. v. Work. Comp. App. Bd.* (1980) 103 C.A.3d 1001, 1009, 163 C.R. 339.

(New) Quasi-legislative action: "If an administrative agency has exceeded its authority in the exercise of its quasi-legislative powers, a court may issue a writ of mandate." (*Clean Air Constituency v. Calif. State Air Resources Bd.* (1974) 11 C.3d 801, 809, 114 C.R. 577, 523 P.2d 617.) (See 20 Santa Clara L. Rev. 351 [criticizing this use of the writ].)

3. [§78] Acts of Officers of Corporations and Associations.

On administrative mandamus to review decisions of a private hospital, see *Anton v. San Antonio Com. Hosp.* (1977) 19 C.3d 802, 815, 140 C.R. 442, 567 P.2d 1162, Supp., infra, §§214A, 219.

p. 3855:

(b) *Labor Unions.* See 48 Am.Jur.2d 367 et seq.

Cross-References: 4 *Summary, Torts,* §§412, 413; 6 *Summary, Corporations,* §42.

(2) [§80] Review of Abuse of Discretion.

Where facts not in dispute (here stipulated) and question is one of law: See *Hurtado v. Superior Court* (1974) 11 C.3d 574, 579, 114 C.R. 106, 522 P.2d 666; *Franchise Tax Bd. v. Municipal Court* (1975) 45 C.A.3d 377, 385, 119 C.R. 552, citing the text; *La Bue v. Superior Court* (1977) 75 C.A.3d 264, 268, 142 C.R. 83.

(4) [§86] Pleadings.

(b) *Compelling Leave To Amend.* In *Beckstead v. Superior Court* (1971) 21 C.A.3d 780, 782, 98 C.R. 779, the lower court sustained a demurrer to a class action without leave to amend, and dismissed the action. The appellate court, in granting mandamus to vacate the judgment and order and permit amendment, apparently regarded the writ remedy as normal and routine, and did not discuss the matter of adequacy of remedy by appeal.

(c) *Compelling Leave To File.* See *Holtz v. Superior Court* (1970) 3 C.3d 296, 301, 90 C.R. 345, 475 P.2d 441, footnote 4.

(d) *Compelling the Striking of Pleading or Sustaining of Demurrer.* See *Los Angeles v. Superior Court* (1977) 73 C.A.3d 509, 511, 142 C.R. 292 [compel sustaining of general demurrer; 21 similar cases pending, prompt determination of issue required]; *Allstate Ins. Co. v. Superior Court* (1982) 132 C.A.3d 670, 676, 183 C.R. 330, citing the text.

The same use of the writ is involved where the lower court erroneously denies a motion for judgment on the pleadings. (*Stencel Aero Engineering v. Superior Court* (1976) 56 C.A.3d 978, 984, 128 C.R. 691, citing *Babb* case, text, p. 3861.)

p. 3861:

Review by writ should be limited to extraordinary circumstances: See *Burrus v. Municipal Court* (1973) 36 C.A.3d 233, 236, 111 C.R. 539, Supp., infra, §178.

Cross-Reference: 4 Summary, Torts, §258.

(5) [§87] Evidence: Discovery and Production.

p. 3862:

(b) *Preventing.* See *Long Beach v. Superior Court* (1976) 64 C.A.3d 65, 70, 134 C.R. 468.

(6) [§88] Trial or Hearing.

(a) *Right to Trial or Hearing.* See *Yoakum v. Small Claims Court* (1975) 53 C.A.3d 398, 403, 125 C.R. 882 [superior court properly issued mandamus to compel small claims court to hear party's motion for relief from default].

p. 3863:

(a-1) *(New) Right to Jury Trial.* Denial of the right to a jury trial is reversible error and may be reviewed on appeal from the judgment. (See *Heim v. Houston* (1976) 60 C.A.3d 770, 131 C.R. 755, *Trial,* Supp., §84.) But there are highly practical reasons for seeking immediate relief by writ: "After a trial to the court it may be difficult for the petitioner to establish that he was prejudiced by the denial of a jury trial. In addition, even if he could establish such prejudice as to warrant reversal of the judgment, such a procedure would be inefficient and time consuming." (*Byram v. Superior Court* (1977) 74 C.A.3d 648, 654, 141 C.R. 604, *Trial,* Supp., §89A.) (See also *Selby Constructors v. McCarthy* (1979) 91 C.A.3d 517, 522, 154 C.R. 164 ["Such a review would normally appear to be the better practice in the interest of saving the time needlessly expended in a court trial if an erroneous jury-trial denial has occurred"].)

(a-2) *(New) Right to Unprejudiced Judge.* Instead of issuing prohibition to restrain a disqualified judge from acting, the reviewing court may issue mandamus to compel the superior court to disqualify the judge from hearing or ruling on any matter related to the cause. (See *Pacific etc. Conference v. Superior Court* (1978) 82 C.A.3d 72, 78, 147 C.R. 44, *Courts,* Supp., §§73, 89.)

(b-1) *(New) Orders in Coordination Proceedings.* (See *Pleading,* Supp., §265P.)

(7) [§89] Judgment.

(b) *Summary Judgment.* Nonappealable order granting partial summary judgment: See *Tauber-Arons Auctioneers Co. v. Superior Court* (1980) 101 C.A.3d 268, 273, 161 C.R. 789.

p. 3866:

(d) *Enforcement of Judgment.* Mandamus is now the specified remedy for enforcement of judgments against *public entities.* (See Govt.C. 965.7 and 965.8, added in 1980, applicable to the state and its entities; and Govt.C. 970.2, applicable to local public entities.)

(e) *Vacating Judgment.* See *Ursino v. Superior Court* (1974) 39 C.A.3d 611, 617, 114 C.R. 404.

(b) [§92] Question of Fact.

See *Malibu West Swimming Club v. Flournoy* (1976) 60 C.A.3d 161, 164, 131 C.R. 279, citing the text.

(d) [§94] Respondent's Acquiescence and Alternative Writ.

p. 3870:

(2) *Issuance of Alternative Writ.* See *Maddern v. Superior Court* (1972) 22 C.A.3d 998, 1002, 99 C.R. 832, citing the text; *Hollister Canning Co. v. Superior Court* (1972) 26 C.A.3d 186, 194, 102 C.R. 713, citing the text; *Huntington Beach v. Superior Court* (1978) 78 C.A.3d 333, 339, 144 C.R. 236; *People v. Superior Court (Douglas)* (1979) 24 C.3d 428, 431, 155 C.R. 704, 595 P.2d 139.

In *Culver City v. State Bd. of Equalization* (1972) 29 C.A.3d 404, 412, 105 C.R. 602, the court observed that nearly all of the decisions on this point (except *Mannheim v. Superior Court*) involved original proceedings in the appellate courts on matters of importance requiring prompt determination. The court concluded that issuance of an alternative writ by the superior court was not a conclusive determination of inadequacy of the appellate remedy.

(3) *(New) Issuance of Order To Show Cause.* The rule first announced in prohibition cases, that an order to show cause has the same effect as an alternative writ in conclusively determining inadequacy of the remedy by appeal, necessarily applies in mandamus cases. (See *Ingram v. Superior Court* (1979) 98 C.A.3d 483, 489, 159 C.R. 557; *Fidelity & Cas. Co. v. Work. Comp. App. Bd.* (1980) 103 C.A.3d 1001, 1009, 163 C.R. 339.)

[§94A] (New) Supreme Court's Direction To Issue Writ.

The Supreme Court, after taking a case over on hearing granted, sometimes retransfers it to the Court of Appeal with directions to reexamine the matter in the light of a controlling decision. (See *Appeal,* §619 and Supp., §§619A, 619B.) The Supreme Court may also direct the Court of Appeal to issue an alternative writ; and such a direction is regarded as an implied determination that the petitioners have no other adequate remedy and that extraordinary relief is appropriate. (See *Dept. of General Services v. Superior Court* (1978) 85 C.A.3d 273, 279, 147 C.R. 422; *O'Connor v. Superior Court* (1979) 90 C.A.3d 107, 110, 153 C.R. 306.)

(1) [§95] Normally Adequate.

See *Culver City v. State Bd. of Equalization* (1972) 29 C.A.3d 404, 409, 105 C.R. 602; *Malibu West Swimming Club v. Flournoy* (1976) 60 C.A.3d 161, 164, 131 C.R. 279 [payment of tax under protest and action for refund].

(3) [§97] Mandamus Prohibited by Statute.

In 1980 Govt.C. 955.5 was repealed and replaced by Govt.C. 965.5 and 965.6. Mandamus is now the specified means of enforcing payment of allowed claims and judgments against public entities. (See Supp., supra, §89.)

(b) [§98] Remedy by Motion.

See *Cartwright v. Swoap* (1974) 40 C.A.3d 567, 571, 115 C.R. 402, citing the text.

That portion of former C.C.P. 1252 cited in the text has been superseded by C.C.P. 1268.020. (See 5 *Summary, Constitutional Law,* Supp., §741A.)

(d) [§100] Remedy by Special Proceeding.

In *Knoll v. Davidson* (1974) 12 C.3d 335, 116 C.R. 97, 525 P.2d 1273, petitioners, seeking to file declarations of candidacy for a county office, filed a petition under Elec.C. 6403. The Court of

Appeal granted the requested relief, and defendant Registrar sought review in the Supreme Court by certiorari. The Supreme Court denied the writ but ordered a hearing of the cause on its own motion, and rendered an opinion clarifying the situation confused by *Donnellan v. Hite* (text, p. 3874) and *Wallace v. Superior Court* (text, p. 711).

(1) *Wallace* held that certiorari would lie because the order under Elec.C. 6403 was nonappealable, but this is erroneous: Unless the statute creating a special proceeding prohibits an appeal the final judgment therein is appealable (see *Appeal,* §55); hence a superior court order under Elec.C. 6403 is appealable to the Court of Appeal, and a Court of Appeal order under that section is reviewable by the Supreme Court on its own motion or on petition for hearing. (12 C.3d 343.)

(2) *Donnellan* held that relief under Elec.C. 6403 was an adequate remedy at law barring mandamus, but this is also erroneous: Procedurally the special proceeding and mandamus are virtually identical, and there is no basis for drawing a distinction between the two remedies. "We conclude that relief sought under section 6403 is a form of relief available in a special proceeding in the nature of mandamus which should proceed through the court system according to the normal procedure prescribed and developed for such a prerogative writ." (12 C.3d 343.)

Donnellan and *Wallace* were disapproved. (12 C.3d 343.)

Elec.C. 6403 was repealed and replaced by Elec.C. 10015 in 1976. Under Elec.C. 10015, any voter can seek a writ of mandamus concerning errors and omissions in ballots, voter pamphlets or other official election matters, and such an action or appeal has priority over all other civil matters.

(1) [§101] In General.

See *Conway v. Municipal Court* (1980) 107 C.A.3d 1009, 1015, 166 C.R. 246.

p. 3876:

The *Schweiger* theory is also applicable where the Appellate Department refuses to certify the case to the court of appeal. (See *Randone v. Appellate Department* (1971) 5 C.3d 536, 542, 96 C.R. 709, 488 P.2d 13.)

(1) [§104] No Direct Appeal.

See *San Diego Wholesale Credit Men's Assn. v. Superior Court* (1973) 35 C.A.3d 458, 462, 110 C.R. 657 [no right of appeal from order denying application for writ of attachment, hence writ may issue to compel lower court to order issuance]; *Running Fence Corp. v. Superior Court* (1975) 51 C.A.3d 400, 409, 124 C.R. 339 [reviewing cases]; *Nazaroff v. Superior Court* (1978) 80 C.A.3d 553, 557, 145 C.R. 657, *Proceedings Without Trial,* Supp., §198B.

In the *Nazaroff* case, supra, plaintiff mother, whose child died from the effects of near drowning in defendant's pool, filed a complaint for wrongful death and emotional distress suffered from witnessing the tragic event. The trial court granted defendant's motion for partial summary judgment on the cause of action for emotional distress. Since the wrongful death cause was unaffected, no final appealable judgment could be entered, but the order barred a hearing on the merits for a substantial part of plaintiff's case. Accordingly mandamus was proper to review the order, and the writ was granted.

(2)   [§105]   Refusal To Assume Jurisdiction.

See *Hollister Canning Co. v. Superior Court* (1972) 26 C.A.3d 186, 193, 102 C.R. 713, citing the text; *Kinder v. Superior Court* (1978) 78 C.A.3d 574, 578, 144 C.R. 291, quoting the text [fact that judgment dismissing order to show cause was appealable does not preclude review by mandamus].

(3)   [§106]   Public Interest in Prompt Decision.

In *Randone v. Appellate Department* (1971) 5 C.3d 536, 96 C.R. 709, 488 P.2d 13, the California statute on attachment in contract actions was held unconstitutional. (See *Provisional Remedies,* Supp., §118A.) The case arose in the municipal court, its decision upholding the statute was affirmed by the Appellate Department without opinion, and the Appellate Department refused certification to the Court of Appeal (see Supp., supra, §101). The Supreme Court said:

"Having exhausted all the available procedural measures on appeal, the Randones petitioned this court for an original writ to review the lower court decision maintaining the attachment. Recognizing that defendants' challenge to the constitutionality of section 537, subdivision 1, involved a question of general importance, over which a considerable conflict had emerged in our lower courts, and that the issue would often arise in municipal court proceedings from which no appeal to our court would be possible without a certification by the superior court, we exercised our discretion and issued an alternative writ of mandamus to determine whether the lower court abused its discretion in refusing to dissolve the attachment at issue." (5 C.3d 542.)

The "abuse of discretion" which is the basis of this review on mandamus is ordinarily an erroneous decision on an issue of jurisdiction, pleading or practice. (See text, §80, and *Treber* and *Vasquez* cases, text, p. 3881.) It may, however, be an error of substantive law, and "abuse of discretion" means only that the decision is wrong in law and would be reversed by the reviewing court if its review power were invoked by the normal process of appeal instead of the more expeditious procedure by writ. (See, e.g., *Lockhart*, text, p. 3880, and *Brown*, text, p. 3881.)

Mannheim v. Superior Court (1970) 3 C.3d 678, 91 C.R. 585, 478 P.2d 17, text, §89, is a particularly instructive example. The Probate Court made a decree in an heirship proceeding allocating only half of former community property to the heirs of the predeceased husband of the testatrix. Petitioner, on behalf of those heirs, moved for an order that the remaining one-half also be distributed to them, rather than to the State by escheat. The issue was one of interpretation of Prob.C. 228, and the Probate Court denied the motion. Petitioner had his remedy by appeal under Prob.C. 1240, since the order denying the motion "probably did constitute a refusal to make an order determining heirship" (3 C.3d 686, footnote 7). But the slow process of appeal was avoided by obtaining an alternative writ in the court of appeal, which conclusively determined the inadequacy of the appellate remedy, and, when the Supreme Court granted a hearing after decision by the court of appeal, it accepted that determination. (See text, §94.)

Thus the Supreme Court on mandamus did exactly what it would have done on appeal: It directed the lower court to make the right decision on the substantive law: "Here there is no dispute concerning the facts. The only issue is whether, as a matter of law, the provisions of section 228, as amended, control the right of succession to Mrs. Nieto's estate. If they do, the probate court is under a legal duty to apply them, and it may be directed to perform that duty by writ of mandate." (3 C.3d 685.)

In *Hogya v. Superior Court* (1977) 75 C.A.3d 122, 142 C.R. 325, *Pleading*, Supp., §185C, plaintiff brought a class action under the Consumers Legal Remedies Act on behalf of about 350,000 consumers who allegedly purchased falsely upgraded beef (good to choice) from Navy commissaries in San Diego County. The lower court held hearings under C.C. 1781 and concluded that, although the statutory criteria were met, certification should be denied on the nonstatutory ground that no substantial benefits would result. *Held*, mandamus granted to compel vacation of the order denying certification.

(a) Although in the case of most interim orders the parties are relegated to a review on appeal from the final judgment, mandamus may issue "to consider instances of a grave nature or of sufficient legal impact, or to review questions of first impression and general importance to the bench and bar where general guidelines can be laid down for future cases." (75 C.A.3d 129, citing the text, §§22, 125.)

(b) Under these principles the writ should be granted: (1) Petitioner will otherwise be forced to bear the burden of the trial and appeal individually; in the context of other facts, appeal does not appear to be a practical remedy. (2) The trial court found that the total claim of a single member of the class would be less than $10, and the total recovery not over $160,000, while the legal fees and costs of the trial would be over that amount. Thus the expense of proceeding through trial is grossly disproportionate to the damages recoverable, and appeal is not an adequate remedy. (3) The facts are not in dispute; hence if the trial court was under a legal duty to certify the class mandamus is appropriate to compel performance. (4) The issue raised is substantial and the case is one of first impression and general interest. (75 C.A.3d 130, 131.)

The opinion concludes with a restatement of the *Oceanside* qualification (see Supp., infra, §125).

See also *Bayless v. Limber* (1972) 26 C.A.3d 463, 467, 102 C.R. 647; *Duran v. Cassidy* (1972) 28 C.A.3d 574, 579, 104 C.R. 793; *San Diego Unified Port Dist. v. Superior Court* (1977) 67 C.A.3d 361, 364, 365, 136 C.R. 557 [significant question of law—federal preemption; if action permitted, substantial discovery and trial expenses would be imposed on plaintiff district and the public]; *Huntington Beach v. Superior Court* (1978) 78 C.A.3d 333, 339, 144 C.R. 236, citing the text [important question of law, relief by mandamus would prevent needless expensive trial].

(b) [§108] When Reviewing Court May Act.

Election controversy: "Cases affecting the right to vote and the method of conducting elections are obviously of great public importance. Moreover, the necessity of adjudicating the controversy before the election renders it moot usually warrants our bypassing normal procedures of trial and appeal." (*Jolicoeur v. Mihaly* (1971) 5 C.3d 565, 570, 96 C.R. 697, 488 P.2d 1, footnote 1.)

Elec.C. 10015, added in 1976 and derived from Elec.C. 6403, provides that any voter can seek a writ of mandamus concerning errors and omissions in ballots, voter pamphlets or other official election matters, and such an action or appeal has priority over all other civil matters.

(b) [§111] Illustrations: Prohibition.

See 63 Am.Jur.2d 270.

(d) [§113] When Reviewing Court Will Act.

See *Civil Service Employees Ins. Co. v. Superior Court* (1978) 22 C.3d 362, 374, 149 C.R. 360, 584 P.2d 497, footnote 6 [citing the text, §§110–112, on the general rule, but also citing *Rescue Army,* text, p. 3888, on relaxation of the rule where an important issue is presented and the case is briefed and argued without objection].

(a) [§114] General Rules.

See *Mexican-American Political Assn. v. Brown* (1973) 8 C.3d 733, 106 C.R. 12, 505 P.2d 204 [mandamus challenging constitutionality of statutory provisions on incumbent's name on ballot; fact question in dispute].

(b) [§115] When Higher Court Will Act.

See *Villa v. Hall* (1971) 6 C.3d 227, 229, 98 C.R. 460, 490 P.2d 1148 [class action to invalidate portion of California Welfare Reform Act of 1971 on ground of incompatibility with federal Social Security Act; unimpaired operation of welfare program of utmost significance and petitioners would be drastically affected by protracted litigation]; *Sacramento v. Superior Court* (1972) 8 C.3d 479, 481, 105 C.R. 374, 503 P.2d 1382 [prohibition to speedily resolve important jurisdictional question raised by defense of sovereign immunity from suit]; *Thompson v. Mellon* (1973) 9 C.3d 96, 98, 107 C.R. 20, 507 P.2d 628 [mandamus to resolve important constitutional issue of residence requirement for candidate for public office]; *Ramirez v. Brown* (1973) 9 C.3d 199, 203, 107 C.R. 137, 507 P.2d 1345 [mandamus to resolve constitutional issue of right of ex-convicts to vote]; *Coan v. California* (1974) 11 C.3d 286, 291, 113 C.R. 187, 520 P.2d 1003 [mandamus to resolve issue of federal-state relationship, affecting all state employees and state's ability to compete in labor market]; *Clean Air Constituency v. Calif. State Air Resources Bd.* (1974) 11 C.3d 801, 808, 114 C.R. 577, 523 P.2d 617 [mandamus to resolve issue whether Air Resources Bd. had authority to delay program for control of atmospheric emissions of oxides of nitrogen]; *Agricultural Lab. Rel. Bd. v. Superior Court* (1976) 16 C.3d 392, 402, 128 C.R. 183, 546 P.2d 687 [validity of regulation of board giving farm labor organizers qualified right of access to growers' premises]; *Calif. Housing Finance Agency v. Elliott* (1976) 17 C.3d 575, 579, 131 C.R. 361, 551 P.2d 1193 [mandamus to determine validity of revenue bonds issued by a public housing authority]; *Aden v. Younger* (1976) 57 C.A.3d 662, 670, 129 C.R. 535 [mandamus to determine constitutionality of state-wide law involving rights of mental patients]; *Industrial Welfare Com. v. Superior Court* (1980) 27 C.3d 690, 699, 166 C.R. 331, 613 P.2d 579 [challenge of industry-wide "wage orders"].

(New) Jurisdiction accepted despite insufficient showing: In *Adams v. Dept. of Motor Vehicles* (1974) 11 C.3d 146, 113 C.R. 145, 520 P.2d 961, petitioner brought a mandamus proceeding on behalf of himself and a class of persons whose automobiles were held under the garageman's lien statute and sold for charges without a hearing

afforded the owners. The sole basis for seeking the writ in the Supreme Court was that the statute worked great hardship on poor persons. This, said the court, was insufficient to justify bypassing the lower courts, and "As a consequence of petitioners' impatience, this court is denied the record which it would otherwise have had." Then, having pointed out why the petition should have been *denied,* the court explained why it was *granted:* "If the case had not already been briefed and argued here and if the issues presented were not so clearly destined to come before this court . . . , it would not be inappropriate to deny a peremptory writ for procedural reasons. In any event, precipitate resort to the appellate courts will not be encouraged in the future." (11 C.3d 150, footnote 7.)

p. 3892:

Error: The full citation of *People v. El Dorado* is *People v. El Dorado* (1971) 5 C.3d 480, 492, 96 C.R. 553, 487 P.2d 1193.

C. [§117] Moot Case.

p. 3894:

Public interest exception: "[I]f a pending case poses an issue of broad public interest that is likely to recur, the court may exercise an inherent discretion to resolve that issue even though an event occurring during its pendency would normally render the matter moot." (*In re William M.* (1970) 3 C.3d 16, 23, 89 C.R. 33, 473 P.2d 737.)

In the foregoing case the issue was the validity of detention of a minor pending a jurisdictional hearing in the Juvenile Court. The court of appeal denied habeas corpus without opinion, and the Supreme Court granted a hearing and ordered his release to custody of his parents. While the matter was pending in the Supreme Court the minor's jurisdictional hearing was held and he was declared a ward. Thus, the issue of validity of detention was moot and the petitioner did not seek and could not be granted any further relief in the writ proceeding. (3 C.3d 23.) Nevertheless the court thought it advisable to prepare an elaborate advisory opinion on the law: "We doubt that this court will soon be presented with another opportunity to resolve the important questions raised here as to prehearing detention. In the hope that we may provide much-needed guidance for 'the orderly administration of justice' . . . , we explain the grounds which we believe sustain the release of the youth." (3 C.3d 25.)

Zeilenga v. Nelson (1971) 4 C.3d 716, 719, 94 C.R. 602, 484 P.2d 578, is another good illustration. Petitioner, a candidate for election to the Butte County Board of Supervisors, sought mandamus, challenging the 5-year residence requirement; he had been a resident only 1½ years. There was no time before the election for the appeal from the superior court's decision to be decided. Hence the case was moot in the sense that petitioner could not be certified as a candidate for an election already held. But the basic issue of constitutionality of the requirement was of general public interest; it would arise in future elections; if allowed to remain would prevent petitioner from being a candidate in future elections. Hence an opinion, deciding the issue, was proper.

William M. and *Zeilenga* were followed in *Ramirez v. Brown* (1973) 9 C.3d 199, 203, 107 C.R. 137, 507 P.2d 1345. Three petitioners, ex-felons, brought mandamus to challenge the California constitutional prohibition of their right to vote. The three county clerks involved decided not to contest, and advised the court that they would register petitioners. But there were 55 other counties in which petitioners and others might seek to vote. *Held,* the case was not moot: The question was of broad public interest, was likely to recur, and should receive a uniform resolution throughout the state.

United Farm Workers v. Superior Court (1975) 14 C.3d 902, 122 C.R. 877, 537 P.2d 1237, involved a challenge to the constitutionality of ex parte restraining orders against picketing (held unconstitutional; see 5 *Summary, Constitutional Law,* Supp., §171A). The orders had been replaced after a hearing by a preliminary injunction; but the petition for prohibition was considered for the reasons that (1) similar orders were frequently being made, with a critical impact on labor disputes; (2) because of their limited duration such orders elude review on appeal; and (3) the issue is one of broad public interest that is likely to recur. (14 C.3d 906.)

See also *Daly v. Superior Court* (1977) 19 C.3d 122, 141, 137 C.R. 14, 560 P.2d 1193.

1. [§118] In General.

Delay over 60 days: In *Scott v. Municipal Court* (1974) 40 C.A.3d 995, 115 C.R. 620, appellant was held in contempt of the municipal court and sentenced to pay a $100 fine. His petition for review was filed in the superior court nearly 6 months later. *Held,* the superior court acted properly in denying the petition as "not timely filed." The *Glassgold* case (text, p. 3896) and the earlier Supreme Court decision in *Reynolds v. Superior Court* (1883) 64 C. 372, 28 P. 121, were followed. (40 C.A.3d 996.)

Conti v. Board of Civ. Serv. Com. (text, §120) was distinguished: "*Conti* was an action in administrative mandamus to vindicate a private right to public employment. There the plaintiff sought review of the action of an administrative agency and not review of an action of a court. In administrative mandamus, review is essentially a matter of right. In the situation of action of a court, however, review by prerogative writ is a matter of discretion of the reviewing court, albeit a discretion which must be exercised within reasonable bounds and for a proper reason. *Reynolds* teaches that delay in seeking a writ of review beyond the period established for appeal from appealable orders is a significant reason for the higher court to refuse the prerogative writ unless the delay is satisfactorily explained." (40 C.A.3d 997.)

See also *Krueger v. Superior Court* (1979) 89 C.A.3d 934, 938, 152 C.R. 870 [nearly 6 months delay; writ denied]; cf. *Popelka et al. v. Superior Court* (1980) 107 C.A.3d 496, 500, 165 C.R. 748 [petition filed several months after order was untimely, but, since matter fully briefed, case decided on merits].

On laches as a defense in a proceeding brought by the State, see *People v. Dept. of Housing & Community Dev.* (1975) 45 C.A.3d 185, 195, 119 C.R. 266, Supp., infra, §121A.

Cross-Reference: 7 Summary, Equity, §14 et seq.

(b)   [§120]   Prejudice Must Be Shown.

See *Duskin v. San Francisco Redevelopment Agency* (1973) 31 C.A.3d 769, 774, 107 C.R. 667, following *Conti.*

Cross-References: 7 Summary, Equity, §§15, 16.

(d)   [§121A]   (New) Defense Against State.

In *People v. Dept. of Housing & Community Dev.* (1975) 45 C.A.3d 185, 119 C.R. 266, the Department issued a permit to R to build a mobilehome park in Nevada County. R commenced construction and spent about $40,000. About 6 months after the permit had been granted, the district attorney of the county sought mandamus to halt construction and rescind the permit on the ground of failure to comply with CEQA (California Environmental Quality Act). In sustaining R's defense of laches the court examined the policy considerations at some length.

(1) Laches has sometimes been described as "based on estoppel" or as resting on the same principle as estoppel. (45 C.A.3d 195.)

(2) In lawsuits supporting environmental legislation the strong public interest in ecology preservation has prompted some federal and state courts to reject assertions of laches. (45 C.A.3d 196.)

(3) In California, however, estoppel against the government has been upheld on a showing of the same elements that support an estoppel against a private party. (45 C.A.3d 196; see 7 *Summary, Equity,* §138.) The same approach and test may properly be applied to the claim of laches here: The issue is "whether nullification of the developer's permit will cause injustice 'of sufficient dimension' to

warrant judicial refusal to force environmental procedures which should have preceded his project." (45 C.A.3d 197.)

On a review of the facts the court came to the following conclusion:

"Here the state, represented by one agency, received written legal advice describing its environmental responsibilities; the applicant citizen received a permit on the assumption that the agency had met its responsibilities; on the strength of that assumption he commenced his project, incurring substantial expenses and losses over a period of months; only then did the state, acting through another agent, seek judicial action to annul what it had once granted; the citizen's losses are largely irrecoverable; the project is one which conformed with local land use regulations at its inception, hence not recognizable as a gross despoliation of the environment. The state's failure to commence its suit before the citizen incurred heavy loss created an injustice which outweighs any adverse effect of the state's failure to make timely environmental inquiries. We sustain the defense of laches." (45 C.A.3d 200.)

E. [§122] Unclean Hands.

See *San Diego County Dept. v. Superior Court* (1972) 7 C.3d 1, 9, 101 C.R. 541, 496 P.2d 453, citing the text [defense available in writ proceedings generally, but where adoption or guardianship involved such misconduct is less significant, and best interest of child is paramount]; *Pepper v. Superior Court* (1977) 76 C.A.3d 252, 259, 142 C.R. 759, citing the text and 7 *Summary, Equity,* §§10, 13 [inequitable conduct in unconnected transaction not a bar, particularly where policy considerations favor substantive relief].

Cross-Reference: 7 *Summary, Equity,* §8 et seq.

1. [§123] Nature of Problem.

(a) *In General.* See 63 Am.Jur.2d 232 [prohibition].

3. [§125] Prerogative Writ Theory.

In *People v. Medina* (1972) 6 C.3d 484, 491, 99 C.R. 630, 492 P.2d 686, the court said: "We have continued to recognize that the writs of mandate and prohibition are 'extraordinary' and 'prerogative' and that therefore their use for pretrial review may and in some circumstances should be confined to questions of first impression and general importance." The statement was made in support of the proposition that denial of a writ without opinion is not res judicata on the merits. (Supp., infra, §146.)

The meaning and scope of the *Oceanside* doctrine were clarified in *Roberts v. Superior Court* (1973) 9 C.3d 330, 336, 107 C.R. 309,

508 P.2d 309, applying the distinction set forth in the *Pac. Tel. & Tel. Co.* footnote (text, p. 3903). Plaintiff, a personal injury plaintiff, had received psychiatric treatment from Dr. E. Defendants sought discovery of his records, and he refused, claiming privilege (Ev.C. 1014). The trial judge ordered their production and plaintiff sought prohibition. *Held,* it was proper to issue the alternative writ. Objections to discovery on the ground of mere irrelevancy are different from objections based on violation of privilege; in the latter case the need for a writ is obvious. "The person seeking to exercise the privilege must either succumb to the court's order and disclose the privileged information, or subject himself to a charge of contempt for his refusal to obey the court's order pending appeal. The first of these alternatives is hardly an adequate remedy and could lead to disruption of a confidential relationship. The second is clearly inadequate as it would involve the possibility of a jail sentence and additional delay in the principal litigation during review of the contempt order." (9 C.3d 336.)

See also *American Mut. Liab. Ins. Co. v. Superior Court* (1974) 38 C.A.3d 579, 589, 113 C.R. 561, restating *Oceanside* doctrine of restraint, but holding that unusual circumstances (disclosure versus privilege, issue arising during trial) presented a question of general importance and justified issuance of writ; *Sav-On Drugs v. Superior Court* (1975) 15 C.3d 1, 5, 123 C.R. 283, 538 P.2d 739, applying exception of *Pacific Tel. and Roberts*—where to compel an answer would violate a privilege; *Long Beach v. Superior Court* (1976) 64 C.A.3d 65, 69, 134 C.R. 468 [both grounds: violation of privilege and question of first impression]; *Daly v. Superior Court* (1977) 19 C.3d 132, 140, 137 C.R. 14, 560 P.2d 1193 ["The power of a trial court to grant a prospective witness use immunity and derivative use immunity for the purpose of facilitating discovery by a private party is a question meeting these criteria"]; *Britt v. Superior Court* (1978) 20 C.3d 844, 851 143 C.R. 695, 574 P.2d 766; *Hogya v. Superior Court* (1977) 75 C.A.3d 122, 132, 142 C.R. 325, Supp., supra, §106 ["We emphasize, however, that our willingness to consider the denial of class certification before trial in this matter should not be construed as a *right* to review of such an order in every case. The general principles discussed above require an individual determination in each case, upon examination of both facts and issues, whether review by use of prerogative writs should be afforded. . ."]; *South Tahoe Pub. Util. Dist. v. Superior Court* (1979) 90 C.A.3d 135, 137, 154 C.R. 1 [quoting *Oceanside* and *Sav-On Drugs,* but observing that case fell within exception—matter of first impression on scope of attorney's work-product privilege]; *Reuter v. Superior Court* (1979) 93 C.A.3d 332, 336, 155 C.R. 525 [exception where order granting discovery intrudes on constitutional right of privacy]; *Browne v. Superior Court*

(1979) 98 C.A.3d 610, 613, 159 C.R. 669 [exception where question of first impression on protection against unwarranted physical examination of party by nonphysician examiner]; *Woods v. Superior Court* (1981) 28 C.3d 668, 672, 170 C.R. 484, 620 P.2d 1032, Supp., infra, §214B ["we reaffirm our traditional reluctance to interpose prerogative writ review of rulings on pleadings . . . We are persuaded, however, that the procedural validity herein presented is an important and continuing issue in California administrative practice fully meriting our attention"].

1. [§126] Similarities and Differences.

See C.E.B., Civ. Lit. Forms, §33:13 [mandamus]; 7 Cal Practice (Rev. ed.) 589 [certiorari]; 17 Am.Jur. P.P. Forms (Rev. ed.) 182 et seq. [mandamus]; 20 Am.Jur. P.P. Forms (Rev. ed.) 488 et seq. [prohibition].

C.E.B. in text: There are no prohibition forms in the current C.E.B., Civ. Lit. Forms Manual.

2. [§127] Constitution and Statutes.

p. 3905:

Summary judgment statute: C.C.P. 437c was substantially revised in 1973. (See *Proceedings Without Trial,* Supp., §173A.) The definition of "action" was deleted from the first paragraph of that section; it now applies to "any action or proceeding."

4. [§129] Practice.

(d) *Pleading.* See 7 Cal Practice (Rev. ed) 589 [certiorari]; 17 Am.Jur. P.P. Forms (Rev. ed.) 184 et seq. [mandamus]; 20 Am.Jur. P.P. Forms (Rev. ed.) 447 et seq., 451 et seq. [prohibition].

p. 3906:

(e) *Service and filing of petition.* See 17 Am.Jur. P.P. Forms (Rev. ed.) 186 et seq. [mandamus].

(g) *Hearing and determination.* See 17 Am.Jur. P.P. Forms (Rev. ed.) 257 et seq. [mandamus]; 20 Am.Jur. P.P. Forms (Rev. ed.) 469 et seq. [prohibition].

(h) *Procedure after determination.* See 17 Am.Jur. P.P. Forms (Rev. ed.) 264 et seq. [mandamus]; 20 Am.Jur. P.P. Forms (Rev. ed.) 474 et seq. [prohibition].

(k) *Appellate review of superior court judgment.* See 17 Am.Jur. P.P. Forms (Rev. ed.) 282 et seq. [mandamus].

1. [§131] Petitioner.

Party, not attorney, is proper petitioner: In *Mannheim v. Superior*

Court (1970) 3 C.3d 678, 91 C.R. 585, 478 P.2d 17, a petition for mandamus to review the denial of a motion for distribution (see Supp., supra, §106) was filed in the name of M, attorney for the heirs. The court said: "It is inappropriate for an attorney to appear as petitioner in a mandamus proceeding. Nevertheless, we have decided to consider the petition since there is no objection from petitioner's clients or from the real party in interest." (3 C.3d 683, footnote 1.)

(a) [§135] In General.

C.E.B. in text: There are no prohibition forms in the current C.E.B., Civ. Lit. Forms Manual.

(1) *Terminology.* See 7 Cal Practice (Rev. ed.) 589, 592 [certiorari]; 17 Am.Jur. P.P. Forms (Rev. ed.) 179 et seq. [mandamus]; 20 Am.Jur. P.P. Forms (Rev. ed.) 446 et seq. [prohibition].

p. 3911:

(2) *Allegations.* See 7 Cal Practice (Rev. ed.) 585 et seq. [certiorari]; 17 Am.Jur. P.P. Forms (Rev. ed.) 185 et seq. [mandamus]; 20 Am.Jur. P.P. Forms (Rev. ed.) 446 et seq. [prohibition].

(3) *Prayer.* See 7 Cal Practice (Rev. ed.) 589 [certiorari]; 17 Am.Jur. P.P. Forms (Rev. ed.) 185 et seq. [mandamus]; 20 Am.Jur. P.P. Forms (Rev. ed.) 446 et seq. [prohibition].

(4) *Verification.* Amendment to cure defective verification: See *Franchise Tax Bd. v. Municipal Court* (1975) 45 C.A.3d 377, 384, 119 C.R. 552, citing the text.

(New) Insufficient verification on information and belief: C.C.P. 446, permitting verification of a pleading on information and belief (see *Pleading,* §350), "palpably refers to pleadings that *join issues,* such as the common complaint and answer of a lawsuit." Where the paper is to be used as evidence of the facts stated—as is often the case of a petition for mandamus (C.C.P. 1086)—the verification must be positive, i.e., it must state that the matters set forth are true of the petitioner's own knowledge. (*Star Motor Imports v. Superior Court* (1979) 88 C.A.3d 201, 204, 205, 151 C.R. 721 [alternative writ discharged as improvidently granted; see Supp., infra, §171].)

p. 3912:

(5) *(New) Where Appeal Is Pending.* If the petition seeks review of proceedings from which an appeal is pending, (1) the title of the petition must include "Related Appeal Pending," and (2) the first paragraph must set forth the title, superior court docket number, appellate court docket number, if any, and, if brought under P.C. 1238.5, which extends the time for review when the prosecution appeals, the date of filing of the notice of appeal by the prosecution. (Rule 56(a), as amended in 1976.) The new rule implements the

requirement of consolidation in cases under P.C. 1238.5, and will facilitate consolidation in other cases.

(6) *(New) Contents of Cover.* Rule 56 was amended, effective July 1, 1980, to require the cover to contain the following: "the title of the case, the name, address and telephone number of the attorney filing the petition, the name of the trial judge and the number of the case in the trial court, if any."

(b) [§136] Grounds for Relief.

(1) *Certiorari:* See 7 Cal Practice (Rev. ed.) 585 et seq.

(b) [§139] Prohibition.

See *Perlman v. Municipal Court* (1979) 99 C.A.3d 568, 574, 160 C.R. 567, citing the text.

(c) [§140] Mandamus.

Necessity of record: In *Star Motor Imports v. Superior Court* (1979) 88 C.A.3d 201, 151 C.R. 721, the court discharged an alternative writ as improvidently issued on a defective petition alleging the essential factual matter on information and belief. (See Supp., supra, §135; Supp., infra, §171.) The opinion contains the following observations on practice: "Contrary to settled law and what should be settled procedure, the instant writ application was unaccompanied by any record of the superior court's cricitized rulings, or the oral proceedings on which they were based, or any excuse for such a record's nonproduction." (88 C.A.3d 203.) Despite the lack of a record, the court relied on the attorney's averments under oath as indicating his personal knowledge of the matters alleged; later discovery of the defective verification resulted in dismissal. (88 C.A.3d 203.)

See also *Pedlow v. Superior Court* (1980) 112 C.A.3d 368, 370, 169 C.R. 326.

In *Lemelle v. Superior Court* (1978) 77 C.A.3d 148, 156, 143 C.R. 450, involving a petition for mandamus to review denial of a motion for pretrial discovery, the court said: "Just as an appellant must furnish an adequate record on appeal . . ., a petitioner for an extraordinary writ to the trial court must furnish a record sufficient to enable the reviewing court to evaluate the lower court's exercise of discretion." The opinion adds: "The starting point of such a record is a copy of the order to be reviewed.. A proper record should include a copy of all declarations filed in the lower court. It should in most instances also include a transcript of any hearing. In the absence of a transcript the reviewing court will have no way of knowing in many cases what grounds were advanced, what arguments were made and what facts may have been admitted, mutually assumed or judicially noticed at the hearing. In such a case, no abuse of discretion can be found except on the basis of speculation." (77 C.A.3d 156.)

(New) Continuance to permit preparation of written record: In *Darley v. Ward* (1980) 28 C.3d 257, 168 C.R. 481, 617 P.2d 1113, plaintiff, an indigent resident of a low-income neighborhood serviced by a county health clinic, filed a mandamus proceeding to review the board of supervisors' findings and decision to reduce services at the clinic and, possibly, to eliminate the clinic altogether. At the mandamus hearing he produced a certified, but untranscribed tape of the board's 6-hour hearing. The trial court refused to accept the raw tape as a record, or to grant a continuance to permit its transcription, and upheld the challenged findings and decision on the basis of the lack of an adequate record. *Held,* reversed. (1) A tape recording is a "writing" (see *Cal. Evidence,* 2d, §681), and may sometimes be adequate for review of administrative proceedings. (28 C.3d 261, citing *Woodard v. Personnel Commission,* Supp., infra, §229A.) (2) Plaintiff had insufficient time, before the mandamus hearing, to prepare either a written transcript or a settled statement; thus, his production of the certified tape satisfied his initial burden to provide a record. (28 C.2d 261.) (3) While the trial court could properly have refused to review the decision by using the tape, the board should not be allowed to avoid review by demanding a full transcript or stipulated facts without cooperating with plaintiff to provide one or the other form of a record. (28 C.3d 261, 262.) (4) Accordingly, the refusal of a continuance was an abuse of discretion; the court must either accept the raw tape or grant a reasonable continuance to allow preparation of a transcript. (28 C.3d 262, 263.)

1.   [§143]   Service Before Filing.

C.C.P. 1088.5, added in 1982, provides: "Where no alternative writ is sought, proof of service of a copy of the petition need not accompany the application for a writ at the time of filing, but proof of service of a copy of the filed petition must be lodged with the court prior to a hearing or any action by the court."

When a writ of mandamus is sought pursuant to C.C.P. 1088.5, the action may be filed and served in the same manner as an ordinary action under C.C.P. 307 et seq. (P.C. 1107, as amended in 1982.)

(b)   [§146]   Denial Not Res Judicata.

See *Laucirica v. Work. Comp. App. Bd.* (1971) 17 C.A.3d 681, 684, 95 C.R. 219, citing the text [same rule applied to denial of writ of review of decision of Workmen's Compensation Appeals Board]; *People v. Medina* (1972) 6 C.3d 484, 491, 99 C.R. 630, 492 P.2d 686, footnote 6, Supp., supra, §125.

(New) Distinction: Order with stated reasons for decision. See *Richer v. Superior Court* (1976) 63 C.A.3d 748, 755, 134 C.R. 52, *Appeal,* Supp., §634, citing the text [order held to be determination of merits and law of the case].

(New) Distinction: Sole possible ground is on merits. If the sole possible ground of denial was on the merits it will have res judicata effect. (*Consumers Lobby Against Monopolies v. Pub. Util. Com.* (1979) 25 C.3d 891, 901, 160 C.R. 124, 603 P.2d 41, footnote 3, *Judgment,* Supp., §172.)

p. 3918:

Review of Public Utilities Commission decision: See *Consumers Lobby Against Monopolies v. Pub. Util. Com.,* supra, 25 C.3d 900, 901.

(a) [§149] In General.

(1) *Alternative Writ or Order To Show Cause.* See 17 Am.Jur. P.P. Forms (Rev. ed.) 261 et seq. [mandamus]; 20 Am.Jur. P.P. Forms (Rev. ed.) 472 et seq. [prohibition].

(2) *Peremptory Writ.* See 17 Am.Jur. P.P. Forms (Rev. ed.) 278 et seq. [mandamus]; 20 Am.Jur. P.P. Forms (Rev. ed.) 481, 482 [prohibition].

Issuance without alternative writ: See *Goodenough v. Superior Court* (1971) 18 C.A.3d 692, 697, 96 C.R. 165, citing the text; *San Diego Wholesale Credit Men's Assn. v. Superior Court* (1973) 35 C.A.3d 458, 465, 110 C.R. 657, citing the text; *Dept. of Consumer Affairs v. Superior Court* (1977) 71 C.A.3d 97, 99, 139 C.R. 120, citing the text.

Late cases indicate that this procedure is no longer rare, and that no showing of unusual circumstances is necessary. (See *San Francisco v. Superior Court* (1978) 86 C.A.3d 87, 91, 150 C.R. 45 ["The petition and the briefs of the parties fully present the determinative issue. An alternative writ would add nothing to the full presentation already made. A peremptory writ is proper . . . and should issue"]; *Amoroso v. Superior Court* (1979) 89 C.A.3d 240, 243, 152 C.R. 398 [same]; *South Tahoe Pub. Util. Dist. v. Superior Court* (1979) 90 C.A.3d 135, 139, 154 C.R. 1 [application for writ made on notice to respondent and real party in interest, and real party filed a response; peremptory writ issued]; *Tahoe Forest Inn v. Superior Court* (1979) 99 C.A.3d 509, 511, 160 C.R. 314 [petitioners prayed that a peremptory writ issue, respondent filed verified return and answer; peremptory writ issued]; *Blumenthal v. Superior Court* (1980) 103 C.A.3d 317, 320, 163 C.R. 39 ["We have reached our conclusions after full briefing by the parties. The result is clear. The court sees no purpose to be served by issuing an alternative writ"]; *Leach v. Superior Court* (1980) 111

C.A.3d 902, 906, 169 C.R. 42; *United Nuclear Corp. v. Superior Court* (1980) 113 C.A.3d 359, 169 C.R. 827.)

(b) [§150] Prohibition.

See 20 Am.Jur. P.P. Forms (Rev. ed.) 472 et seq., 481, 482.

(c) [§151] Mandamus.

See 17 Am.Jur. P.P. Forms (Rev. ed.) 261 et seq., 278 et seq.

(b) [§154] Prohibition and Mandamus.

(2) *Mandamus.* A new subsection (d) was added to C.C.P. 1094.5 in 1978. (See Supp., infra, §219.) The citation in the text should now be C.C.P. 1094.5(g).

(b) [§156] Return as Answer or Demurrer.

(1) *Return as Answer.* C.C.P. 1069.1, added in 1971, makes applicable to certiorari the provisions of C.C.P. 1089 on return by answer in mandamus proceedings. (See Supp., infra, §158.)

Rule 57 was amended, effective January 1, 1980, to refer to the Workers' Compensation Appeals Board.

(2) *Return by Demurrer.* C.C.P. 1069.1, added in 1971, makes applicable to certiorari the provisions of C.C.P. 1089 on return by demurrer in mandamus proceedings. (See Supp., infra, §159.)

(a) [§158] Answer.

See 17 Am.Jur. P.P. Forms (Rev. ed.) 264 et seq. [mandamus]; 20 Am.Jur. P.P. Forms (Rev. ed.) 475 et seq. [prohibition].

C.C.P. 1089 was amended in 1971 to provide that the court may permit an answer to be filed upon the overruling of a demurrer. The section now reads: "On the date for return of the alternative writ . . . the party upon whom the writ or notice has been served may make a return by demurrer, verified answer or both. If the return is by demurrer alone, the court may allow an answer to be filed within such time as it may designate."

The return must conform to the rules governing an answer in a civil action. (*Dulaney v. Municipal Court* (1974) 11 C.3d 77, 81, 112 C.R. 777, 520 P.2d 1, footnote 3, citing the text.)

Under C.C.P. 1089.5, as added in 1982, the respondent must answer or otherwise respond within 30 days after service of a petition for mandamus where the petition is filed pursuant to C.C.P. 1088.5 (see Supp., supra, §143) and where a record of the proceedings to be reviewed was filed with the petition, or where no record of a proceeding is required. But where a record of the proceeding to be reviewed was requested pursuant to Govt.C. 11523, or otherwise, and was not filed with the petition, the party on whom the petition was served, including real parties in interest, must answer or otherwise respond within 30 days of receipt of a copy of the record.

(b) [§159] Demurrer or Motion To Quash.

Demurrer: C.C.P. 1089 was amended in 1971 to expressly provide for return by demurrer.

See 17 Am.Jur. P.P. Forms (Rev. ed) 268, 269.

p. 3926:

Motion to quash: See *Motors Ins. Corp. v. Div. of Fair Emp. Practices* (1981) 118 C.A.3d 209, 216, 173 C.R. 332; 17 Am.Jur. P.P. Forms (Rev. ed.) 269 et seq.; 20 Am.Jur. P.P. Forms (Rev. ed.) 474, 475.

H. [§161] Replication in Mandamus.

See 17 Am.Jur. P.P. Forms (Rev. ed.) 268 [mandamus]; 20 Am.Jur. P.P. Forms (Rev. ed.) 477 [prohibition].

p. 3927:

C.C.P. 1091 was amended in 1971 to substitute the word "return" for "answer."

(aa) [§164] Hearing on Issues of Law.

C.C.P. 1094 was amended in 1971 to substitute the word "return" for "answer." As further amended in 1982, the statute no longer makes a hearing on the papers mandatory if no return is made. It also now provides that if a petition for mandamus filed pursuant to C.C.P. 1088.5 (see Supp., supra, §143) presents no triable issue of fact or is based solely on an administrative record, the court may determine the matter by *noticed motion of any party* for a judgment on the peremptory writ.

See *Ellerbroek v. Saddleback Valley Unified School Dist. (1981) 125 C.A.3d 348, 359, 177 C.R. 910, quoting the text.*

(bb) [§165] Overruling Without Leave To Answer.

Discretion to allow answer: See C.C.P. 1089, Supp., supra, §158.

(2) [§166] Where Answer Is Filed.

C.C.P. 1090 was amended in 1971 to substitute the word "return" for "answer."

(3) [§167] Proceedings in Reviewing Court.

Third, order a reference: See *Holt v. Kelly* (1978) 20 C.3d 560, 562, 143 C.R. 625, 574 P.2d 441.

(aa) [§168] Issuance and Service.

See 17 Am.Jur. P.P. Forms (Rev. ed.) 278 et seq. [mandamus]; 20 Am.Jur. P.P. Forms (Rev. ed.) 481, 482 [prohibition].

(bb) [§169] Departure From Alternative Writ.

Appellate court may depart: See *Bortin v. Superior Court* (1976) 64 C.A.3d 873, 880, 135 C.R. 30, citing the text; *Barclays Bank of California v. Superior Court* (1977) 69 C.A.3d 593, 602, 137 C.R. 743, citing the text.

(2) [§170] Enforcement of Judgment.

As amended in 1982, C.C.P. 1095 provides that damages and costs may be enforced in the same manner as money judgments generally.

(1) [§171] Procedure.

See 17 Am.Jur. P.P. Forms (Rev. ed.) 274 [mandamus].

Writ discharged and proceeding dismissed: In *Star Motor Imports v. Superior Court* (1979) 88 C.A.3d 201, 151 C.R. 721, the petition for mandamus alleged that the superior court in a trial de novo of a small claims court appeal had permitted the respondent to give testimony consisting of inadmissible hearsay. The Court of Appeal issued an alternative writ in reliance on the attorney's verification of the petition's allegations; he had not attached any record of the trial court's proceedings or shown any excuse for nonproduction of the record. After the alternative writ had issued the Court of Appeal, on a "closer examination" of the petition, discovered that the verification was on information and belief, hence insufficient to constitute evidence of the matter alleged (see Supp., supra, §135). *Held,* the petition was fatally defective, the alternative writ was improvidently issued, and the proceeding should be dismissed. (88 C.A.3d 203, 205.)

(a) [§173] Mandamus and Prohibition.

C.C.P. 1095 was amended in 1982 by (1) substituting "the applicant" for "he" in the first sentence, and (2) deleting specific mention of issuing an execution and providing, instead, for the enforcement of costs and damages in the same manner as money judgments generally.

2. [§175] Costs in Reviewing Court.

Direction in judgment before finality: The rule stated in *Union Trust Co. v. Superior Court* was held inapplicable in *Inyo v. Los Angeles* (1978) 78 C.A.3d 82, 144 C.R. 71. The appellate court had issued a peremptory writ, but the decision was an interim one which did not terminate the proceeding, and continuing jurisdiction was reserved to enforce the writ. Hence the court had jurisdiction to award costs. (78 C.A.3d 85.)

3. [§176] Interest in Mandamus Proceeding.

In *Tripp v. Swoap* (1976) 17 C.3d 671, 131 C.R. 789, 552 P.2d 749, plaintiff's application for disability benefits under the former ATD program was denied. In the present proceeding in administrative mandamus (see text, §213) the superior court issued the writ, ordering defendant Director to set aside his decision and pay benefits with attorneys' fees and interest. *Held,* affirmed. (a) The statute authorizing judicial review of benefit determinations did not specifically authorize interest, but the lack of mention does not preclude an award if another statute allows it. (b) C.C. 3287(a), the general statute, applies: Under the test of *Mass* (text, p. 3938), the state has a legal obligation to furnish benefits to persons who meet the standards of eligibility; benefits are set by fixed payment schedules and are consequently capable of being made certain by calculation; and the right to payment vests on a particular day. (17 C.3d 683.) (c) *Luna v. Carleson* (1975) 45 C.A.3d 670, 119 C.R. 711, taking a contrary view, is disapproved. (17 C.3d 685.)

See also *Ferreira v. Swoap* (1976) 62 C.A.3d 875, 883, 133 C.R. 449 [following *Tripp*].

Cross-Reference: 1 *Summary, Contracts,* §653 et seq.

2. [§178] Appeal.

See *Bloom v. Municipal Court* (1976) 16 C.3d 71, 75, 127 C.R. 317, 545 P.2d 229, citing the text.

p. 3939:

Appeal as normal and adequate remedy: The unrestricted right of appeal from an order denying a petition for mandamus is a "loophole" in our appellate system, according to *Burrus v. Municipal Court* (1973) 36 C.A.3d 233, 111 C.R. 539.

S, assignee of a finance company, sued B in the municipal court for money due ($1,110.24) on a note secured by a chattel mortgage and salary assignment. B filed an answer, and three cross-complaints, all of the latter being found bad on demurrer. His motion for leave to file a fourth amended cross-complaint was denied, and the action was set for trial. He then filed a petition for mandamus in the superior court to compel the municipal court to overrule the demurrer to the third amended cross-complaint or allow filing of the fourth amended cross-complaint. The superior court denied the petition by order stating that no showing had been made of inadequacy of the remedy by appeal. B then filed a request that the superior court certify the action for transfer to the Court of Appeal. The superior court by minute order stated that the application for certification would be deemed a notice of appeal from the order denying the petition for mandamus, and the matter was then handled as an appeal on the merits. *Held,* judgment affirmed, with some strong observations on the bad practice involved.

(a) The superior court did not abuse its discretion in denying mandamus and leaving B to his relatively speedy remedy by appeal from a final judgment on the merits to the Appellate Department of the superior court. The appeal from this obviously correct ruling was "frivolous and vexatious," and a penalty would have been appropriate, except for the fact that the appeal came about by reason of the "gratuitous order" of the superior court that the application for certification be deemed a notice of appeal. (36 C.A.3d 237.)

(b) The policy of the Constitution, statutes and rules is that judgments of the justice or municipal court be reviewed only in the superior court in the absence of unusual circumstances. But the law, contrary to that policy, allows the justice or municipal court litigant to reach the Court of Appeal in any case by petitioning for a writ and appealing from the order of denial: "No matter how frivolous the petition, or how trivial the issue which it raises, the petitioner is entitled, as a matter of right, to go through the entire appellate procedure, with preparation of record, briefs, calendaring and written opinion in the Court of Appeal." (36 C.A.3d 238.)

(c) If the justice or municipal court litigant has an issue "of such gravity or significance as to justify the use of a prerogative writ," but the superior court nevertheless denies the writ, the litigant should not appeal; he should file an original petition in the Court of Appeal or Supreme Court. Such original petitions are less burdensome than appeals, because those obviously without merit can be screened out by summary denial, without going through the effort and expense of a full appellate hearing and decision by opinion. (36 C.A.3d 239.)

The court added this warning:

"So long as the statute allows the use of the appellate process in this kind of situation, it is the responsibility of counsel to use this procedure only when extraordinary circumstances seem to justify it, and it is the duty of the appellate courts to impose sanctions when there is an abuse." (36 C.A.3d 239.)

See also *Gilbert v. Municipal Court* (1977) 73 C.A.3d 723, 728 et seq., 140 C.R. 897, making the same criticism and urging corrective legislative action.

This "loophole" was closed by a 1982 amendment to C.C.P. 904.1. This section now provides that an appeal may *not* be taken from "a judgment granting or denying a petition for issuance of a writ of mandamus or prohibition directed to a municipal court or a justice court or the judge or judges thereof which relates to a matter pending in the municipal or justice court. However, an appellate court may, in its discretion, review a judgment granting or denying a petition for *issuance* of a writ of mandamus or prohibition upon petition for an extraordinary writ."

3. [§179] Stay Pending Appeal.

p. 3940:

A new subsection (d) was added to C.C.P. 1094.5 in 1978. (See Supp., infra, §219.) The citation in the text should now be C.C.P. 1094.5(g).

1. [§183] General Principle.

Complaint or petition in action or special proceeding treated as petition for mandamus: See *Rodriguez v. Superior Court* (1971) 18 C.A.3d 510, 513, 95 C.R. 923 ["Petition for Adoption" of child held sufficient as an imperfectly drawn petition for mandamus to review an administrative order of county adoption agency]; *Mendocino v. California* (1971) 22 C.A.3d 90, 96, 98 C.R. 904 [complaint by county against State, in form of civil action for money, treated as petition for mandamus]; *Scott v. Indian Wells* (1972) 6 C.3d 541, 546, 99 C.R. 745, 492 P.2d 1137 [complaint for declaratory relief challenging administrative order treated as petition for administrative mandamus under C.C.P. 1094.5.].

See also *Calif. Teachers Assn. v. Governing Board* (1977) 70 C.A.3d 833, 844, 139 C.R. 155 [petition for ordinary mandamus where administrative mandamus was correct remedy; after superior court hearing without raising of mislabeling issue, objection not available on appeal]; *Mahdavi v. Fair Emp. Practice Com.* (1977) 67 C.A.3d 326, 336, 136 C.R. 421 [mistaken request for administrative mandamus where ordinary mandamus was correct remedy; ordinary mandamus would have been issued if sufficient showing had been made, but writ was denied for lack of such showing].

p. 3943:

Appeal from nonappealable judgment: The traditional approach set forth in the text is not invariably followed. On stipulation of the parties the reviewing court in its discretion may treat the record on appeal as a petition for an extraordinary writ. (See *Appeal,* Supp., §51A.)

2. [§184] Illustrations.

(a) *Mandamus Issued Though Petition Sought Certiorari.* See *Carmona v. Division of Industrial Safety* (1975) 13 C.3d 303, 309, 118 C.R. 473, 530 P.2d 161, footnote 4, citing the text; *Davis v. Superior Court* (1980) 102 C.A.3d 164, 171, 162 C.R. 167, *Courts,* Supp., §200.

p. 3944:

(e-1) *(New) Relief on Certiorari Granted Though Petition Sought Habeas Corpus.* (See *In re Coleman* (1974) 12 C.3d 568, 572, 116 C.R. 381, 526 P.2d 533, footnote 2, citing the text [union and members violated restraining order against picketing, members sentenced to jail and fined, union fined; petition for habeas corpus, proper as to jailed members, treated as petition for certiorari on behalf of union].)

(4) [§198] Improper Discovery Proceedings.

See *Sav-On Drugs v. Superior Court* (1975) 15 C.3d 1, 5, 123 C.R. 283, 538 P.2d 739 [prohibition to restrain enforcement of order compelling answer to interrogatory which would violate privilege].

(b) [§202] "Prohibitory Mandamus."

"In a number of cases, mandamus has been held to issue to prohibit official conduct where prohibition would not lie because the threatened official act was not judicial but ministerial in nature. (*Sail'er Inn v. Kirby* (1971) 5 C.3d 1, 7, 95 C.R. 329, 485 P.2d 529, citing the text, and concluding with the order (5 C.3d 22): "Let the peremptory writ of mandate issue compelling the Director . . . to cease license revocation proceedings . . . and to cease enforcement of the section".)

See also *Water Users Assn. v. Board of Directors* (1973) 34 C.A.3d 131, 135, 109 C.R. 592, citing the text, but denying the writ.

In *Raley v. Calif. Tahoe Regional Planning Agency* (1977) 68 C.A.3d 965, 137 C.R. 699, the trial judge issued a writ of prohibition, which was technically improper since defendant agency had no judicial powers. The court said: "We view the so-called writ of prohibition as one of 'prohibitory' mandate." (68 C.A.3d 970, footnote 1, citing the text.)

(b) [§204] Development of "Certiorarified Mandamus."

Error: Page 3961, line 15, §204 should be §205.

(a) [§210] Development of Rule.

See 8 Cal. Western L. Rev. 301; dissenting opinion, *Harlow v. Carleson* (1976) 16 C.3d 731, 739, 129 C.R. 298, 548 P.2d 698, listing prior dissents and law review articles criticizing the *Laisne* rule.

In *Anton v. San Antonio Community Hosp.* (1977) 19 C.3d 802, 140 C.R. 442, 567 P.2d 1162, Supp., infra, §§214A, 219, a strong dissenting opinion of one justice reviews the criticisms of the rule and urges its reconsideration so as to allow the Legislature to give greater deference to administrative determinations. (19 C.3d 831 et seq.) The opinion points out that no other state follows the California rule, and quotes Davis' description of the *Strumsky* decision (see Supp., infra, §222A) as an erratic movement "back into medievalism." (19 C.3d 834.)

Cross-Reference: 5 Summary, Constitutional Law, §299 et seq.

(2) [§212] State Constitutional Agencies.

(a) *In General.* See *Washington v. State Personnel Board* (1981) 127 C.A.3d 636, 639, 179 C.R. 637 [State Personnel Board].

p. 3968:

(b) *Alcoholic Beverage Control Board.*

Review by mandamus (B. & P.C. 23090.5): See *Schenley Affiliated Brands Corp. v. Kirby* (1971) 21 C.A.3d 177, 195, 98 C.R. 609.

Review by writ of review: See *Walsh v. Kirby* (1974) 13 C.3d 95, 102, 118 C.R. 1, 529 P.2d 33.

Cross-Reference: 5 Summary, Taxation, §293 et seq.

(a) [§213] Nature and Purpose.

p. 3970:

Not a wholly new system, but a specialized procedure for review of certain types of administrative decisions: See *Anton v. San Antonio Community Hosp.* (1977) 19 C.3d 802, 814, 140 C.R. 442, 567 P.2d 1162, Supp., infra, §§214A, 219; *Woods v. Superior Court* (1981) 28 C.3d 668, 673, 170 C.R. 484, 620 P.2d 1032, citing the text ["mandamus pursuant to section 1094.5, commonly denominated 'administrative' mandamus, is mandamus still. . . . The full panoply of rules applicable to 'ordinary' mandamus applies to 'administrative' mandamus proceedings, except where modified by statute"].

(b) [§214] Scope of Statute.

(1) *In General: Proceedings.*

Final administrative order or decision: See *Board of Medical Quality Assur. v. Superior Court* (1977) 73 C.A.3d 860, 862, 141 C.R. 83 [trial judge exceeded jurisdiction in acting on petition for administrative mandamus while administrative proceeding was still in progress].

Hearing required by law: C.C.P. 1094.5 applies only where the final administrative decision was made in a proceeding in which a hearing is required by law and the agency exercises an adjudicatory function. (*Mahdavi v. Fair Emp. Practice Com.* (1977) 67 C.A.3d 326, 334, 136 C.R. 421 [administrative mandamus not available where statute provided only for discretionary hearing; see 5 *Summary, Constitutional Law,* Supp., §426]; *Royal Convalescent Hosp. v. State Bd. of Control* (1979) 99 C.A.3d 788, 792, 160 C.R. 458 [following *Keeler v. Superior Court*].)

See *Jean v. Civil Service Commission* (1977) 71 C.A.3d 101, 110, 139 C.R. 303 [city charter section construed to entitle probationary employee to a hearing, hence C.C.P. 1094.5 applied].

p. 3971:

(4) *Local Agencies.* See *Topanga Assn. etc. v. Los Angeles* (1974) 11 C.3d 506, 514, 113 C.R. 836, 522 P.2d 12, footnote 12; 10 U.S.F. L. Rev. 361 [Judicial Review of Local Governmental Administrative Decisions in California].

(5) *(New) Nonprofit Corporations and Associations.* (See Supp., infra, §214A.)

Cross-Reference: 5 *Summary, Constitutional Law,* §321 et seq.

[§214A]   (New) Nonprofit Corporations and Associations.

In *Anton v. San Antonio Community Hosp.* (1977) 19 C.3d 802, 140 C.R. 442, 567 P.2d 1162, defendant, a private nonprofit hospital corporation, after extended hearings suspended the hospital privileges of plaintiff doctor. He petitioned for ordinary mandamus (C.C.P. 1085) to compel reinstatement, and the trial judge, applying the substantial evidence test, sustained defendant's action and denied relief. *Held,* reversed; the proper remedy was administrative mandamus under C.C.P. 1094.5, and the independent judgment test should have been applied (see Supp., infra, §219).

(1) *Elements for application of C.C.P. 1094.5.* The three elements —a final order, adjudicatory in nature, and hearing required by law (see text, §214)—were present. Under the case law dealing with a hospital's denial of privileges or explusion from the staff, a doctor has a due process right to a hearing; and this right exists whether the hospital is a public entity or a private corporation. (19 C.3d 815; see 6 *Summary, Corporations,* Supp., §42.)

(2) *C.C.P. 1094.5 applies to nongovernmental agencies.* "It has been widely assumed" that the specialized review under this section

was available only where the administrative decision was by a governmental agency (19 C.3d 815), but this is incorrect:

First, the statutory language is not so limited; and it was drawn directly from C.C.P. 1085, the ordinary mandamus statute, which has been held applicable to private corporations and associations. (19 C.3d 816; see text, §78.) "It would seem to follow, therefore, that section 1094.5, by using substantially identical language in describing the kind of administrative body whose decisions are subject to review under its provisions, was intended to apply to the same spectrum of agencies to which section 1085 has been held applicable *in all cases in which the subject decision is the product of a proceeding in which a hearing and related procedural protections are required by law.*" (19 C.3d 817.)

Second, although the Judicial Council 10th Biennial Report deals exclusively with review of decisions of governmental agencies, and its study was confined to state licensing agencies, the Report adds that "[t]he theories underlying the Council's proposals in this limited field are susceptible, of course, of adaptation to other kinds of administrative action." (19 C.3d 818.)

Third, practical considerations call for administrative mandamus. The Local District Hospital Law makes specific provision for a hearing where public hospitals operated by a hospital district are involved, and the accreditation rules for both public and private hospitals provide for the same kind of hearing. (19 C.3d 818, 819.) The practical necessity of securing accreditation has the effect of insuring that substantially all hospitals in the state, whether public or private, have bylaws governing hearings and appeal procedures. It would be incongruous to use two different kinds of review procedures (19 C.3d 818), and administrative mandamus is the appropriate method (19 C.3d 820).

See also 66 Cal. L. Rev. 201 [*Anton*].

On the standards for review, see Supp., infra, §219.

[§214B]   (New) Decision Applying Invalid Regulation.

In *Woods v. Superior Court* (1981) 28 C.3d 668, 170 C.R. 484, 620 P.2d 1032, applicants, required to vacate apartments unfit for habitation, applied to the County Department of Social Welfare for funds to relocate. At the required "fair hearing" (Welf.C. 10950) their claims were rejected as unauthorized under departmental regulations. The applicants sought administrative mandamus, contending that the regulations violated federal and state law. Petitioner, director of the Department, demurred, contending that the appropriate method of challenging the validity of a department regulation was by petition for ordinary mandamus (C.C.P. 1085) or action for declaratory relief (C.C.P. 1060). The trial judge overruled the demurrer, and petitioner sought an extraordinary writ in the reviewing court to annul the ruling. *Held,* the ruling was correct; administrative mandamus was a proper method of review.

(1) Welf.C. 10950 expressly provides for judicial review of the Director's final decision by petition under C.C.P. 1094.5. (28 C.3d 674.)

(2) Petitioner contended that, because promulgation of a regulation is a "quasi legislative" act, an attack on the validity of the regulation transforms the adjudicatory determination into a quasi-legislative determination, reviewable by ordinary mandamus or declaratory relief. (28 C.3d 676.) This is unsound: "[A]n unsuccessful applicant for welfare benefits may contest the validity of a regulation which mandates the denial of his application both in the 'fair hearing' provided by section 10950 and in the subsequent judicial review under section 1094.5." (28 C.3d 677.)

(3) Proceeding under C.C.P. 1094.5 will not involve the wrong standard of review. The proper scope of review is determined by the task before the court: In reviewing an administrative regulation the court decides only whether the agency reasonably interpreted the legislative mandate; this limited scope of review is not a judicial interference with the administrative discretion in that aspect of the rulemaking function which requires a high degree of technical skill and expertise. "Correspondingly, there is no agency discretion to promulgate a regulation which is inconsistent with the governing statute." (28 C.3d 679.)

(4) An invalid regulation should be subject to attack at the administrative level, to avoid delay and unnecessary expense in vindication of legal rights. "Permitting administrators an opportunity to construe challenged regulations in a manner to avoid their invalidation is preferable to requiring a court challenge. Moreover, in those cases in which the validity of such a regulation must be judicially resolved, the task of a reviewing court is simplified by a narrowing and clarification of the issues in an administrative hearing." (28 C.3d 681.)

(c) [§215] Excluded Agencies and Proceedings.

(2) *Quasi-Legislative Acts.* See *Board of Supervisors v. Calif. Highway Commission* (1976) 57 C.A.3d 952, 960, 961, 129 C.R. 504; *Malibu West Swimming Club v. Flournoy* (1976) 60 C.A.3d 161, 164, 131 C.R. 279; *Lewin v. St. Joseph Hosp.* (1978) 82 C.A.3d 368, 383, 384, 146 C.R. 892, 5 *Summary, Constitutional Law,* Supp., §320A,

citing the text [private association; "the limited judicial review applicable to the quasi-legislative actions of a governmental administrative agency is also appropriately applied to judicial review of rule-making or policy-making actions of a nonprofit hospital corporation"]; *Stauffer Chemical Co. v. Air Resources Board* (1982) 128 C.A.3d 789, 794, 180 C.R. 550.

p. 3972:

(3) *(New) Federal Preemption.* See *San Francisco U. S. Dist. v. California* (1982) 131 C.A.3d 54, 65, 182 C.R. 525 [dictum: 20 U.S.C. 1415(e)(2) should be used to review administrative decision rendered pursuant to Education of All Handicapped Children Act, particularly where state review procedures provide more limited scope of review, as under C.C.P. 1094.5].

(a) [§216] Three Basic Questions.

p. 3973:

(3) *Prejudicial Abuse of Discretion.* See *Guilbert v. Regents of Univ. of Calif.* (1979) 93 C.A.3d 233, 241, 155 C.R. 583 [judge's order denying relief affirmed].

p. 3974:

Penalty: The agency's discretion will ordinarily not be disturbed. (*Cadilla v. Bd. of Med. Examiners* (1972) 26 C.A.3d 961, 966, 103 C.R. 455.)

(b) [§217] Two Rules of Sufficiency of Evidence.

See 8 Cal. Western L. Rev. 311, 313.

(1) *The independent judgment rule.* See *Lacy v. Unemployment Ins. Appeals Bd.* (1971) 17 C.A.3d 1128, 1132, 1134, 95 C.R. 566; *Strumsky v. San Diego County Emp. Retirement Assn.* (1974) 11 C.3d 28, 31, 112 C.R. 805, 520 P.2d 29, Supp., infra, §222A.

(2) *The substantial evidence rule.* See *Bekiaris v. Board of Education* (1972) 6 C.3d 575, 586, 100 C.R. 16, 493 P.2d 480; *Steve P. Rados v. Calif. Occupational S. & H. App. Bd.* (1979) 89 C.A.3d 590, 594, 152 C.R. 510 [test is substantial evidence on the entire record; same test as in review of Workers' Compensation Appeals Board decision].

If the trial court below was limited to the substantial evidence test, the appellate court occupies the same position regarding the administrative record, i.e., the appellate court will review the administrative record to determine if the agency's decision was supported by substantial evidence. (*McCarthy v. Cal. Tahoe Regional Planning Agency* (1982) 129 C.A.3d 222, 228, 180 C.R. 866.)

(a) [§218]   State Agency Without Quasi-Judicial Powers.

See *Lacy v. Unemployment Ins. Appeals Bd.* (1971) 17 C.A.3d 1128, 1132, 95 C.R. 566.

(New) Where credibility of witnesses involved: In *Guymon v. State Bd. of Accountancy* (1976) 55 C.A.3d 1010, 128 C.R. 137, defendant board contended that, even where the independent judgment rule applies, the trial court is nevertheless bound by determinations of credibility of witnesses made by the agency at the administrative hearing. The court held that, although earlier Court of Appeal decisions supported this view, they were no longer persuasive under the *Moran* and *Yakov* line of cases. Hence the trial court, in weighing the evidence at the administrative hearing, must make its own determination of the credibility of witnesses. (55 C.A.3d 1015, 1016.)

(b) [§219]   What Constitutes Vested Right.

See 8 Cal. Western L. Rev. 305; *Strumsky v. San Diego County Emp. Retirement Assn.* (1974) 11 C.3d 28, 112 C.R. 805, 520 P.2d 29, Supp., infra, §222A; *Transcentury Properties v. California* (1974) 41 C.A.3d 835, 844, 116 C.R. 487 [plaintiffs' asserted right to develop seaside property without compliance with Coastal Zone Act]; *Harlow v. Carleson* (1976) 16 C.3d 731, 735, 129 C.R. 298, 548 P.2d 698 [right to welfare benefits under state aid to the permanently and totally disabled program]; *Estes v. Grover City* (1978) 82 C.A.3d 509, 514, 147 C.R. 131 [right of permanent public employee]; *Roccaforte v. San Diego* (1979) 89 C.A.3d 877, 886, 152 C.R. 558 [police officer's rights to injury leave pay, retirement benefits and reemployment]; *Kerrigan v. Fair Emp. Practice Com.* (1979) 91 C.A.3d 43, 51, 154 C.R. 29 [equal employment opportunity; here the statutory right to be free of age discrimination]; *McConville v. Alexis* (1979) 97 C.A.3d 593, 600, 159 C.R. 49 [driver's license; 6-month suspension held a substantial interference with a vested fundamental right; court refuses to follow contrary decision in *McGue v. Sillas* (1978) 82 C.A.3d 799, 804, 147 C.R. 354].

(New) Employee's and Employer's rights in unemployment compensation proceeding. In *Kilpatrick's Bakeries v. Unemp. Ins. App. Bd.* (1978) 77 C.A.3d 539, 143 C.R. 664, the Unemployment Insurance Appeals Board made its decision granting compensation to an employee. The employer sought administrative mandamus, and the trial judge, applying the substantive evidence rule, upheld the Board's decision. *Held,* reversed. Cases prior to *Bixby v. Pierno* (text, §§219, 222) held that both an employee's claim and an employer's petition for review involved property rights and called for review under the independent judgment rule. (77 C.A.3d 542, 543.) Subsequent deci-

sions indicate that the *Bixby* court did not intend to repudiate these decisions by restricting the concept of fundamental right (77 C.A.3d 549). Hence the trial judge should have independently reviewed the Board's determination. (77 C.A.3d 550.)

The same result was reached in *Interstate Brands v. Unemp. Ins. App. Bd.* (1980) 26 C.3d 770, 163 C.R. 619, 608 P.2d 707. The referee, applying the volitional test (see 1 *Summary, Agency and Employment,* §§68, 69), denied benefits to union members locked out after a selective strike. The Board reversed the decision, but the trial judge, on an independent review, ordered reinstatement of the referee's decision denying benefits. The Board appealed, and, relying on language in *Bixby,* contended that independent review was not appropriate unless the right, in addition to being "vested," was "fundamental"; e.g., where it could be shown that an increase in the employer's contribution rate would drive him out of business. (26 C.3d 770.) *Held,* judgment affirmed. The court's concern in *Bixby* was to provide a doctrinal basis for independent review in cases which, although not involving traditional vested property rights, nevertheless had a vital impact on the individual; and in *Bixby* there was neither an economic nor a human dimension of this type. (26 C.3d 779.) Subsequent cases applying the broadened standard in review of other administrative determinations have not cast doubt on the prior holdings in unemployment compensation cases that the employer's right to be free from erroneous charges to his reserve account is a fundamental vested right. (26 C.3d 780.) "It is manifest that any employer—especially in circumstances such as those here before us, where the question of eligibility relates to the entire work force of the employer—has a vital and significant interest at stake in any proceedings concerning the award or denial of benefits. We hold and reaffirm that that interest is sufficient to require independent judicial examination of the factual bases of an administrative determination of eligibility." (26 C.3d 781.)

(New) Doctor's right to hospital privileges. In *Anton v. San Antonio Community Hosp.* (1977) 19 C.3d 802, 140 C.R. 442, 567 P.2d 1162, Supp., supra, §214A, the court first held that C.C.P. 1094.5 applies to decisions of a private nonprofit hospital corporation (see Supp., supra, §214A), and then considered the issue of which standard of review applied. Defendant contended that the *Bixby* and *Strumsky* opinions (text, §222, and Supp., infra, §222A) were grounded on the separation of powers doctrine, which has no application of private entities. *Held,* this is a misconception of the decisions, and the independent judgment rule governs.

First, Bixby makes it clear that the basic consideration is the importance of the affected right to the individual who stands in jeopardy of losing it. Although the *Bixby* decision relied on the separation-of-powers doctrine, *Strumsky* involved a local agency to which that doctrine does not apply. *Strumsky* points out that, although local agencies are not *prevented* from exercising judicial powers by the separation doctrine, they *cannot exercise* such powers because they have no constitutional authority to do so. Similarly, the separation doctrine is irrelevant to nongovernmental agencies which have no judicial powers. Accordingly, the adjudicatory decisions of such agencies are subject to the rule which applies to any administrative agencies lacking judicial powers. (19 C.3d 822.)

Second, applying the *Bixby-Strumsky* rule, the right involved is a property interest which directly relates to the pursuit of the doctor's livelihood, and thus is "fundamental." (19 C.3d 823.)

Third, the contention that the right is not "vested," because staff appointments are made on an annual basis, ignores the realities of the situation. Admission of a doctor to medical staff membership establishes a relationship which, though formally limited in duration, gives rise to rights and obligations different from those in ordinary license and franchise cases. Thus, initial admission is a determination of fitness, and the doctor may not be denied reappointment without an adequate hearing. "In short, the full rights of staff membership *vest* upon appointment, subject to divestment upon periodic review only after a showing of adequate cause for such divestment in a proceeding consistent with minimal due process requirements." (19 C.3d 824.)

See 66 Cal. L. Rev. 201; *Hackethal v. Loma Linda Com. Hosp. Corp.* (1979) 91 C.A.3d 59, 64, 153 C.R. 783 [following *Anton*].

The 1978 Legislature dealt with this situation by amending C.C.P. 1094.5 to add a new subdivision (d) and reletter the remaining subdivisions. New C.C.P. 1094.5 (d) states a general rule and an exception for "cases arising from private hospital boards":

(1) *General rule:* Abuse of discretion is established if the court determines that "the findings are not supported by substantial evidence in the light of the whole record."

(2) *Exception:* In cases in which the petition alleges discriminatory actions prohibited by Health & Saf.C. 1316 (discrimination against podiatrists or osteopaths), and the plaintiff makes a preliminary showing of substantial evidence, "the court shall exercise its independent judgment on the evidence and abuse of discretion shall be established if the court determines that the findings are not supported by the weight of the evidence."

On the substantial evidence rule and independent judgment rule, see text, §217.

For an examination of the constitutional issues raised by C.C.P. 1094.5(d), see 11 Pacific L. J. 1.

See also *Anton v. San Antonio Community Hospital* (1982) 132

C.A.3d 638, 650, 183 C.R. 423 [amendment to C.C.P. 1094.5 was applicable on retrial of *Anton,* supra].

(New) *Applicant's right to welfare benefits.* In *Frink v. Prod* (1982) 31 C.3d 166, 181 C.R. 893, 643 P.2d 476, the trial upheld an administrative decision denying benefits under the Aid to the Totally Disabled program, stating in the judgment that although "the weight of the evidence was in petitioner's favor, there was substantial evidence in the administrative record to support the respondent's decision." On appeal, petitioner claimed that the trial court should have applied the independent judgment rule. *Held,* judgment reversed. Although decisions *terminating* welfare benefits are reviewed by independent judgment, administrative determinations of *applications* have traditionally been reviewed under the substantial evidence rule on the ground that the applicant, unlike persons who have been receiving aid, does not have a vested right to the benefits. (31 C.3d 171.) But "[t]he right of the needy applicant to welfare benefits is as fundamental as the right of a recipient to continued benefits." (31 C.3d 179.) "While the degree to which the right is vested may not be overwhelming, the degree of fundamentalness is. Weighing them together as required by *Bixby* and *Interstate Brands,* we conclude the independent judgment standard should be applied to decisions denying applications for welfare benefits." (30 C.3d 180.)

(a) [§220] Local Agency With Quasi-Judicial Powers.

See *Bekiaris v. Board of Education* (1972) 6 C.3d 575, 586, 100 C.R. 16, 493 P.2d 480, on the rule stated in the text.

As applied to local administrative agencies, the substantial evidence rule was abrogated in *Strumsky v. San Diego County Emp. Retirement Assn.* (1974) 11 C.3d 28, 112 C.R. 805, 520 P.2d 29, Supp., infra, §222A. But it has been held still applicable to tax assessment review boards with constitutional adjudicative powers. (See Supp., infra, §222B.)

(b) [§221] State Agency With Quasi-Judicial Powers.

See *Martin v. State Personnel Bd.* (1972) 26 C.A.3d 573, 577, 103 C.R. 306; *Amluxen v. Regents of U.C.* (1975) 53 C.A.3d 27, 32, 125 C.R. 497, following *Ishimatsu,* text, p. 3978; *Smith v. Regents of U.C.* (1976) 58 C.A.3d 397, 400, 130 C.R. 118; *Millen v. Swoap* (1976) 58 C.A.3d 943, 948, 130 C.R. 387 [denial of application for welfare aid, by Director of State Department of Social Welfare]; *Washington v. State Personnel Board* (1981) 127 C.A.3d 636, 639, 179 C.R. 637; *Chula Vista v. Superior Court* (1982) 133 C.A.3d 472, 488, 183 C.R. 908 [California Coastal Commission].

(c) [§222] No Vested Right.

(1) *In General.* See *Mueller v. MacBan* (1976) 62 C.A.3d 258, 272, 132 C.R. 222.

(2) *Denial of Application for License.* See *Patterson v. Central Coast Etc. Conservation Com.* (1976) 58 C.A.3d 833, 843, 130 C.R. 169; *Housing Development Co. v. Hoschler* (1978) 85 C.A.3d 379, 386, 149 C.R. 400.

(2A) *(New) Denial of Statutory Exemption From Permit Requirement.* See *Alamitos Gen. Hosp. v. Lackner* (1978) 86 C.A.3d 417, 424, 149 C.R. 98.

(4) *Economic Interests or Privileges.* The right of a hospital operated by a public district, to establish employment practices and procedures and to impose conditions of employment, is not a fundamental vested right. Hence, a decision of the Fair Employment Practices Commission, finding discrimination against an employee, was subject to review only under the substantial evidence rule. (*Northern Inyo Hosp. v. Fair Emp. Practice Com.* (1974) 38 C.A.3d 14, 22, 112 C.R. 872.)

See also *Mueller v. MacBan* (1976) 58 C.A.3d 667, 677, 130 C.R. 216, following *Bixby* and *Beverly Hills* cases (text, p. 3978); *Mountain Defense League v. Board of Supervisors* (1977) 65 C.A.3d 723, 730, 135 C.R. 588 [no vested interest in having land kept in natural state instead of being developed by defendants]; *Coldwell Banker & Co. v. Dept. of Insurance* (1980) 102 C.A.3d 381, 406, 162 C.R. 487 [no fundamental or vested right of real estate broker to apply for license to engage in underwritten title company business]; *Standard Oil Co. v. Feldstein* (1980) 105 C.A.3d 590, 603, 605, 164 C.R. 403; *McCarthy v. Cal. Tahoe Regional Planning Agency* (1982) 129 C.A.3d 222, 231, 180 C.R. 866 [vested right for review purposes means preexisting right; direct access to highway was not of such economically essential character as to be of fundamental nature].

On applying the independent judgment standard to decisions denying applications for welfare benefits, see *Frink v. Prod* (1982) 31 C.3d 166, 181 C.R. 893, 643 P.2d 676, disapproving *Contra Costa v. Social Welfare Board* (1962) 199 C.A.2d 468, 18 C.R. 573, cited in the text, p. 3978.

p. 3980:

(5) *(New) Property Interests.* See *Markley v. City Council* (1982) 131 C.A.3d 656, 665, 182 C.R. 659 [neighboring property owner has no fundamentally vested right in neighbor receiving special use permit or receiving or being denied zoning variance].

4. [§222A] (New) Independent Judgment Rule Extended to Local Agencies.

In *Strumsky v. San Diego County Emp. Retirement Assn.* (1974)

11 C.3d 28, 112 C.R. 805, 520 P.2d 29, the Supreme Court abrogated the substantial evidence rule established for local administrative agencies (see text, §220) and held that where a fundamental right is involved the trial court must exercise its independent judgment (see text, §217).

Plaintiff, widow of a county marshal, applied to defendant Board for a service-connected death allowance. The Board, after a hearing on conflicting evidence, denied the application on the ground that the death was not service-connected. Plaintiff petitioned for administrative mandamus, and the trial judge, applying the substantial evidence rule, denied the writ; but he made a supplemental finding that, if the case were one in which an independent judgment on the evidence could be exercised, he would find in the widow's favor. *Held,* reversed for further consideration under the independent judgment rule.

(a) *Origin of substantial evidence rule applied to local agencies.* The theory developed by the courts was that the separation of powers clause of the California Constitution is inapplicable to governmental agencies below the state level. And Article VI, §1, forbidding exercise of judicial powers by legislatively created agencies of statewide jurisdiction, was interpreted as permitting the Legislature to vest such powers in "inferior courts" established at the local level. "Local agencies" were treated as such "inferior courts," and in the exercise of their judicial powers were entitled to have their factual determinations given the same effect as a judicial decision, i.e., affirmed if supported by substantial evidence. (11 C.3d 36; see text, §§211, 220.)

(b) *Criticism of rule.* In the 1950 reorganization of inferior courts the above language of Article VI, §1, was removed, and the section is no longer a basis for the exercise of judicial power by local agencies. Nor do the "home-rule" provisions of Article XI support the judicial powers theory: "In short, although the Legislature retains the authority to grant a multitude of powers to local bodies pursuant to article XI, powers of a *judicial* nature are no longer at its disposal. Moreover, we believe that the amendment to article VI had the effect of withdrawing judicial powers formerly granted pursuant to article XI prior to the amendment, leaving the entire judicial power concentrated in the state court system and some 'constitutional agencies.' " (11 C.3d 42.)

(c) *Abrogation of rule.* At the outset of its opinion (11 C.3d 32) the court said:

"After solemn and extended consideration we have concluded that there no longer exists any rational or legal justification for distinguishing with regard to judicial review between, on the one hand, local agencies and state agencies of local jurisdiction and, on the other, state agencies of legislative origin having statewide jurisdiction. Accordingly, we hold that the scope of judicial review applicable to adjudicatory orders or decisions of the latter class of agencies— which was reaffirmed and explained by us in *Bixby*—is also applicable to adjudicatory orders or decisions of agencies in the former class."

The new rule was restated as follows: "[I]f the order or decision of the agency substantially affects a fundamental vested right, the court, in determining under section 1094.5 of the Code of Civil Procedure whether there has been an abuse of discretion because the findings are not supported by the evidence, must exercise its independent judgment on the evidence and find an abuse of discretion if the findings are not supported by the weight of the evidence. If, on the other hand, the order or decision does not substantially affect a fundamental vested right, the trial court's inquiry will be limited to a determination of whether or not the findings are supported by substantial evidence in light of the whole record." (11 C.3d 44.)

The court concluded with a holding that retirement benefits of this nature are vested and fundamental within the meaning of *Bixby v. Pierno* (text, p. 3979). (11 C.3d 45.)

Three justices dissented, asking "Why has it taken nearly 25 years to make this startling discovery" (of the effect of the 1950 amendment to the Constitution), and adding the disturbing observation that if local agencies cannot exercise quasi-judicial power, the new rule applies whether or not a fundamental right is involved: "The majority can not have it both ways; either local boards have quasi-judicial power or they do not. If, as the majority insist, such power no longer exists, then necessarily *every* agency decision of which someone complains must be independently reviewed by the courts." (11 C.3d 47.)

See 63 Cal. L. Rev. 27; 26 Hastings L. J. 1465; 10 U.S.F. L. Rev. 361 [Judicial Review of Local Governmental Administrative Decisions in California]; 10 U.S.F. L. Rev. 733; 51 Cal. S.B.J. 26; *Valenzuela v. Board of Civ. Service Com.* (1974) 40 C.A.3d 557, 562, 565, 115 C.R. 103 [*Strumsky* rule applied to review of county board's discharge of civil service employee]; *Dickey v. Retirement Board* (1976) 16 C.3d 745, 751, 129 C.R. 289, 548 P.2d 689 [*Strumsky* rule applied to review of city retirement board's decision denying applications by police officers for disability benefits]; but see *Hunt-Wesson Foods v. Alameda* (1974) 41 C.A.3d 163, 116 C.R. 160, Supp., infra, §222B, declaring an exception for tax assessment review board.

5.   [§222B]   (New) Substantial Evidence Rule Retained for Assessment Appeals.

In *Hunt-Wesson Foods v. Alameda* (1974) 41 C.A.3d 163, 116

C.R. 160, plaintiff paid personal property taxes on machinery under protest, and sued to recover alleged overpayments. Its challenge was to the assessor's practice in determining depreciation, which practice had been upheld by the county Assessment Appeals Board. The superior court, applying the independent judgment rule, weighed the evidence and determined that the practice was incorrect and that plaintiff was entitled to a refund. *Held,* reversed; the substantial evidence rule should have been applied.

(a) Prior to *Strumsky* the rule was settled that the determination of a county board of equalization, or its equivalent, a county assessment appeals board, must be upheld if supported by substantial evidence. (41 C.A.3d 169.)

(b) The *Bixby* and *Strumsky* cases (text, §222, and Supp., supra, §222A) must be considered, even though the present proceeding is an action under Rev.C. 5103 rather than an administrative mandamus proceeding under C.C.P. 1094.5. The purpose of this action is the same as that of the writ proceeding: to review a decision of the administrative board. And the holdings of *Bixby* and *Strumsky* "would seem to apply to all reviews of administrative decisions, regardless of how they happen to reach the judicial system." (41 C.A.3d 172.)

(c) *Bixby* is not controlling: The court there noted that it was not dealing with decisions of a constitutionally created agency with adjudicative powers. (41 C.A.3d 173.) *Strumsky* is not controlling: Its reference to "all administrative decisions of an adjudicatory nature" might appear to make it applicable, but other language recognizes that constitutional agencies may have judicial powers and be subject to review only under the substantial evidence rule. (41 C.A.3d 174, 175.)

(d) A board of assessment appeals, though created by local ordinance of the county board of supervisors, derives its power from the Constitution, Art. XIII, §9.5. Hence it is a constitutional agency. (41 C.A.3d 175.)

(e) Not all constitutional agencies have judicial powers; but Art. XIII, §§9 and 9.5, clearly confer adjudicative powers on local boards of equalization and assessment appeals boards. (41 C.A.3d 175.) Hence:

"In performing its adjudicative functions pursuant to the grant of power from the Constitution, the factual determinations of a board of assessment appeals are 'entitled to all the deference and respect due a judicial decision.'" (41 C.A.3d 176, quoting *Strumsky.*) "We thus conclude that the scope of review for a superior court in reviewing the administrative record of a local board of assessment appeals is that of reviewing the entire record to determine if the findings are supported by substantial evidence." (41 C.A.3d 176.)

The provisions of former Art. XIII, §§9 and 9.5, are now in Art. XIII, §16 (see 5 *Summary, Taxation,* Supp., §152).

6. [§222C] (New) Substantial Evidence Rule Retained for Probationary Teachers.

In *Young v. Governing Board* (1974) 40 C.A.3d 769, 775, 780, 115 C.R. 456, the *Strumsky* rule was applied to review of a school district's discharge of a probationary teacher. In *Turner v. Board of Trustees* (1976) 16 C.3d 818, 827, 129 C.R. 443, 548 P.2d 1115, the Supreme Court, in a 4–3 decision, disapproved the *Young* holding. The majority found no legislative intent to give probationary teachers a vested right: "By labelling the position probationary, the Legislature had clearly advised the employee that the position is neither vested nor permanent." (16 C.3d 825.) (See dissent, criticizing the majority for using dictionary definition of "probationary" instead of examining the relevant statutes, and arguing that the statutory provision requiring a showing of "cause" for discharge gives the teacher a vested interest in reemployment.)

7. [§222D] (New) Proof by Preponderance of Evidence.

In *Chamberlain v. Ventura County Civil Service Com.* (1977) 69 C.A.3d 362, 138 C.R. 155, petitioner, a county civil service employee, petitioned for administrative mandamus to compel vacation of a disciplinary order. The trial judge followed the independent judgment rule, as required by *Strumsky* (Supp., supra. §222A), and found that the weight of the evidence supported the agency's decision. Petitioner appealed, contending that in proceedings under C.C.P. 1094.5 to review a disciplinary decision the standard of proof should be *clear and convincing evidence,* not *preponderance of the evidence. Held,* the preponderance standard applies.

(a) The phrase "weight of the evidence" in C.C.P. 1094.5 and in the *Strumsky* opinion had its source in *Drummey v. State Bd. of Funeral Directors* (text, §210), and its meaning is settled by a number of decisions: "The purpose for which a court normally weighs the evidence is to determine which way it preponderates on a given issue. . . . Thus, an unexplained statement that a reviewing court shall weigh the evidence is a statement that it shall determine whether the evidence preponderates in favor of, or against, the administrative decision under review." (69 C.A.3d 368.)

(b) Two Court of Appeal decisions contain statements that in administrative proceedings to discipline public employees their guilt must be established to "a reasonable certainty." (See *Cornell v. Reilly*

(1954) 127 C.A.2d 178, 184, 273 P.2d 572; *Johnstone v. Daly City* (1958) 156 C.A.2d 506, 515, 319 P.2d 756.) These statements are in apparent conflict with *Skelly v. State Personnel Bd.* (1975) 15 C.3d 194, 204, 124 C.R. 14, 539 P.2d 774, footnote 19, but in any event are not controlling: The standard of proof in the original administrative proceedings is irrelevant to the standard on review of such proceedings. The situation is similar to that in criminal proceedings: Proof beyond a reasonable doubt is required in the trial, but on appeal the substantial evidence rule applies. (69 C.A.3d 370.)

8. [§222E] (New) Review of Penalty.

In administrative proceedings to discipline a public employee the *Strumsky* rule (see Supp., supra, §222A) applies only to the issue of guilt or innocence of the charges. Decisions prior to *Strumsky* made it clear that the penalty imposed can be disturbed only for a manifest abuse of discretion, and *Strumsky* did not alter this limitation on the trial court's power. "When the trial court's independent review of the evidence determines that some of the substantive findings of misconduct are unsupported by the evidence, remand to the administrative body is the only means of permitting it to exercise its discretion." (*Zink v. Sausalito* (1977) 70 C.A.3d 662, 666, 139 C.R. 59.)

See also *Matanky v. Board of Med. Examiners* (1978) 79 C.A.3d 293, 304, 144 C.R. 826; *Washington v. State Personnel Board* (1981) 127 C.A.3d 636, 642, 179 C.R. 637; *Dresser v. Board of Medical Quality Assurance* (1982) 130 C.A.3d 506, 518, 181 C.R. 797.

(a) [§224] Agencies Not Under A.P.A.

General statutes of limitation, not the 30-day period of Govt.C. 11523 (text, §225) apply: See *Cameron v. Cozens* (1973) 30 C.A.3d 887, 890, 106 C.R. 537, and footnote 4 [review of order of Department of Motor Vehicles suspending operator's license].

[§224A] (New) Shortened Limitation Period.

(1) *Agency Election.* C.C.P. 1094.6, added in 1976, permits local agencies, except school districts, to shorten the period for review of their decisions, made after hearing, "suspending, demoting, or dismissing an officer or employee, revoking or denying an application for a permit or a license, or denying an application for any retirement benefit or allowance." (C.C.P. 1094.6(e); see 8 Pacific L. J. 247.) The provisions of the new section must be formally adopted by the governing board of the local agency by ordinance or resolution. (C.C.P. 1094.6(g).) And the affected party must be given notice at the time of the decision, that "the time within which judicial review must be sought is governed" by the section. (C.C.P. 1094.6(f).)

(2) *Time Within Which To Petition.* When the new statute applies, review under C.C.P. 1094.5 must be sought "not later than the 90th day following the date on which the decision becomes final." (C.C.P. 1094.6(b).) The decision is final when made if there is no provision for reconsideration. Otherwise it is final when the time for reconsideration expires or an application for reconsideration is denied. (C.C.P. 1094.6(b).) The agency has 90 days after a written request for a record is filed to deliver it to the petitioner. (C.C.P. 1094.6(c).) And, if the request is filed within 10 days after the decision is final, the time for seeking review "shall be extended to not later than the 30th day following the date on which the record is either personally delivered or mailed to the petitioner or his attorney of record, if he has one." (C.C.P. 1094.6(d).)

(b) [§225] Agencies Under A.P.A.

(1) *30-Day Period.*

30 days after last date for reconsideration: See *De Cordoba v. Governing Board* (1977) 71 C.A.3d 155, 158, 139 C.R. 312; *Kupka v. Board of Administration* (1981) 122 C.A.3d 791, 794, 176 C.R. 214 [no motion for relief under C.C.P. 473 can be made].

Extension where record is requested: The extension for filing the petition if a record is requested by the petitioner has been lengthened to 30 days after its delivery to him. (Govt.C. 11523, as amended in 1971.)

See *Liberty v. Calif. Coastal Com.* (1980) 113 C.A.3d 491 497, 170 C.R. 247 [applying extension rule of Govt.C. 11523 to a review of a decision of the California Coastal Commission].

The period does not begin to run until a copy of the Board's decision has been delivered or mailed to the petitioner. (*Koons v. Placer Hills U. S. Dist.* (1976) 61 C.A.3d 484, 490, 139 C.R. 312; *De Cordoba v. Governing Board,* supra, 71 C.A.3d 160.)

(New) No extension where defective record furnished: In *Compton v. Board of Trustees* (1975) 49 C.A.3d 150, 122 C.R. 493, petitioners requested the record, it was delivered, and the petition was filed more than 30 days later. Petitioners contended that the period had not run because the record did not include a copy of the hearing officer's proposed decision. The court emphatically rejected this notion:

"Clearly, if the time for seeking judicial relief starts to run not when the aggrieved party is furnished with an administrative record, but rather when he has received the record to which he is arguably entitled, that time never starts if the courts should ultimately hold that some piece of paper which should have been furnished to the would be petitioner, was not given to him. Yet, necessarily, that is precisely the result we would have to reach, were we to agree with

---

petitioners' contention in this case. For what petitioners claim is nothing less than that their time to file never did start to run because they were never furnished with a copy of the hearing officer's proposed decision—a totally insignificant document as we will show—even though petitioners may technically have been entitled to have it included in the administrative record they requested on June 12." (49 C.A.3d 155.)

Cross-Reference: 5 *Summary, Constitutional Law,* §323 et seq.

Error: In the second paragraph of this section, the cross-reference "infra, §226" should be "infra, §227."

4. [§227] Petition.

(b) *Service.* As amended in 1982, C.C.P. 1107 provides that when a writ of mandamus is sought pursuant to C.C.P. 1088.5 (see Supp., supra, §143), the action may be filed and served in the same manner as an ordinary action under C.C.P. 307 et seq.

(a) [§228] Contents.

Necessity of transcript: See *Ward v. Riverside* (1969) 273 C.A.2d 353, 358, 78 C.R. 46.

(New) Non-A.P.A. Local Agency Proceedings. When a record is requested pursuant to the optional provisions of C.C.P. 1094.6, added in 1976 (see Supp., supra, §224A), the "record shall include the transcript of the proceedings, all pleadings, all notices and orders, any proposed decision by a hearing officer, the final decision, all admitted exhibits, all rejected exhibits *in the possession* of the local agency or its commission, board officer or agent, all written evidence, and any other papers in the case." (C.C.P. 1094.6(c).)

(b) [§229] Obtaining and Filing.

(New) Non-A.P.A. Local Agency Proceedings. When the optional provisions of C.C.P. 1094.6, added in 1976, apply (see Supp., supra, §224A), the agency must prepare and file "the complete record" (see Supp., supra, §228), within 90 days of the filing of "a written request therefor." (C.C.P. 1094.6(c).)

On duty of indigent to furnish record, see supp., infra, §229A.

[§229A] (New) No Free Transcript to Indigent.

In *Civil Service Commission v. Superior Court* (1976) 63 C.A.3d 627, 133 C.R. 825, P, a county employee, pleaded guilty to a charge of felonious assault, and was dismissed from the county civil service. He requested a hearing, and the hearing officer found that he had committed the assault but that there were mitigating circumstances that rendered his discharge inappropriate. The County Civil Service

Commission, without an independent review of the evidence, adopted the finding but rejected the conclusion, and ordered P's dismissal. P sought administrative mandamus, and made a motion, supported by a declaration of indigency, that the Commission be directed to supply him with a free transcript of the proceedings before the hearing officer. The superior judge granted the motion, and the Commission sought mandamus. *Held,* writ granted to compel vacation of the order.

(1) *Question open. Ferguson v. Keays (Appeal,* §408) declared the inherent judicial power to waive filing fees on appeal but expressly left open the question whether indigents were entitled to funds for a transcript; and *Leslie v. Roe (Appeal,* Supp., §373) held that indigency does not entitle a party to a free transcript in a civil appeal. Here, however, the question is whether the *Leslie* holding applies in administrative mandamus where the transcript is necessary to exercise of independent judgment of the evidence under *Strumsky* (Supp., supra, §222A). (63 C.A.3d 629.)

(2) *Controlling authority. I. X. L. Lime Co. v. Superior Court* (text, §157) held that a petitioner seeking certiorari has the burden of paying the fee for a transcript, as does any civil litigant in an appeal. Since administrative mandamus is a codification of "certiorarified mandamus," and the review is the same as that on certiorari, *I. X. L.* is binding on a Court of Appeal. If it is inconsistent with *Strumsky* the Supreme Court alone can so declare. (63 C.A.3d 631.)

(3) *Distinguishable authority. Crespo v. Superior Court (Appeal,* Supp., §373) dealt with the provision (C.C. 237.5) for government-supplied counsel to indigent parents appealing from an order depriving them of custody of children; the court held that this implied a right to a free transcript so that counsel might effectively do his job. Here, however, there is no statute which can justify departure from the *I. X. L.* rule. (63 C.A.3d 631.)

(4) *No constitutional right.* Due process and equal protection do not call for a different rule, where the interest of the indigent is economic. (63 C.A.3d 631, citing *Ortwein v. Schwab* and *United States v. Kras,* 5 Summary, *Constitutional Law,* §§297, 403.)

(5) *No right under C.C.P. 1094.5.* The statute provides that the record may be filed with the petition, with the respondent's points and authorities, "or may be ordered to be filed by the court." Here the court did not order the record filed; it ordered the agency to supply it to P. "We thus do not reach the issue of the extent of power which section 1094.5 vests in the trial court to order that the agency cause the record or proceeding before it to be transcribed and the transcript filed." (63 C.A.3d 632.)

A concurring and dissenting opinion, criticizing the narrow

ground of reversal, argues that there is no constitutional, statutory or common law authority in the superior court to order an agency to supply a free transcript. (63 C.A.3d 638.)

See *Dept. of Consumer Affairs v. Superior Court* (1977) 71 C.A.3d 97, 99, 139 C.R. 120, following *Civil Service Commission,* supra; *Sacramento v. Superior Court* (1980) 113 C.A.3d 715, 717, 170 C.R. 75 [same].

The question left open in *Civil Service Commission,* whether the trial judge has power to order the agency to file a transcript with the court, was answered in *Woodard v. Personnel Commission* (1979) 89 C.A.3d 552, 152 C.R. 658. Petitioner, a school district employee, sought the writ to review his discharge. His attorney offered to proceed with an agreed or settled statement summarizing the evidence; but the agency took the position that the statement prepared by petitioner's counsel was insufficient and that the entire record was necessary for review. Since petitioner had no right to a free transcript, no such record was prepared, and the trial judge denied the writ. *Held,* reversed; the trial judge erroneously refused to exercise his discretion. A tape recording of the proceedings was available; and, since the agency insisted that a full record was necessary for review, either a transcript or production of the tape should have been ordered. "We note the simplicity of either placing the tapes in evidence or comparing the contents of the tapes with the offered statement of facts." (89 C.A.3d 561.)

See also *Darley v. Ward* (1980) 28 C.3d 257, 168 C.R. 481, 617 P.2d 1113, Supp., supra, §140.

The *Woodard* holding, supra, was limited to its particular fact situation in *Sacramento v. Superior Court,* supra, 113 C.A.3d 718: to the extent *Woodard* "implies that in a civil administrative proceeding involving economic interests rather than personal liberties, free transcripts of the administrative hearing must be provided indigents, we consider it to be wrong and in conflict with consistent judicial conclusions to the contrary." (113 C.A.3d 718.)

(c) [§230] Recoverable Costs.

p. 3985:

(New) Record prepared for administrative proceeding: In *Ralph's Chrysler-Plymouth v. New Car Dealers Policy & Appeals Bd.* (1973) 8 C.3d 792, 106 C.R. 169, 505 P.2d 1009, an accusation was filed against Ralph with the Department of Motor Vehicles. The decision was adverse to Ralph, he took an administrative appeal to defendant Board, and, pursuant to the requirement of Veh.C. 3052(c), furnished a copy of the administrative record of the Department at his own cost. The decision of the Board was also adverse, and he sought

administrative mandamus, using the same record. The writ was granted, with an award of costs, including the expense of the record. *Held,* the cost award was proper.

(1) Under Govt.C. 11523 (see 5 *Summary, Constitutional Law,* §328), a petitioner seeking judicial review of an administrative decision must furnish a record of the administrative proceedings; and the administrative agency must prepare it for him after a request and payment of the fee. However, since Veh.C. 3052(c) required such a record for the administrative appeal, no such request was necessary. (8 C.3d 795.)

(2) Under C.C.P. 1094.5(a), if the expense of preparing the record has been borne by the prevailing party, that expense is taxable as costs. Properly interpreted, the statute authorizes a cost award even though the record was not prepared initially for the mandamus proceeding, but was prepared prior thereto. "The section makes absolutely no reference to when the expense must be borne, and there seems to be no reason to penalize a successful petitioner merely because a transcript was prepared during a trial, or prepared in the course of the administrative process so long as the transcript was essential to review and its cost allowable under the language of the applicable statute." (8 C.3d 796.) *Turner v. East Side Canal & Irr. Co.* (1918) 177 C. 570, 171 P. 299, and *Regents of U. C. v. Morris* (1970) 12 C.A.3d 679, 90 C.R. 816, to the extent contrary, were disapproved. (8 C.3d 796.)

(3) No recovery could be had, however, for any evidentiary documents or exhibits which, although used in the administrative proceeding, were not part of the record in the mandamus proceeding. (8 C.3d 797.)

(New) Non-A.P.A. local agency proceedings: When the optional provisions of C.C.P. 1094.6 apply (see Supp., supra, §224A), the agency must prepare the record (see Supp., supra, §229), but the "local agency may recover from the petitioner its actual costs for transcribing or otherwise preparing the record." (C.C.P. 1094.6(c), added in 1976.)

(New) Proceeding in forma pauperis: As amended in 1982, C.C.P. 1094.5(a) provides that where the litigant proceeds in forma pauperis pursuant to Govt.C. 68511.3 and the transcript is necessary to a proper review of the administrative proceedings, the *respondent* must bear the cost of preparing the transcript.

8.   [§233]   Stay of Decision.

C.C.P. 1094.5(f) was amended in 1974 to bar ex parte applications for a stay, by requiring proof of service of the application on the respondent. (See 6 Pacific L. J. 231.) Service may be made under the statutory provisions for service of process (see *Actions,* §610 et seq.) or of motions (see *Proceedings Without Trial,* §13 et seq.). The subsection was relettered C.C.P. 1094.5(g) in 1978. (See Supp., supra, §219.)

(New) Decisions of medical licensing boards and A.P.A. agencies: C.C.P. 1094.5(g), added in 1975, provides that orders and decisions of medical licensing boards regarding licensees may not be stayed unless the court is satisfied that the public interest will not suffer and the board is unlikely to prevail on the merits. In 1978 the subsection was relettered C.C.P. 1094.5(h). (See Supp., supra, §219.) It was amended in 1979 to extend the more stringent standards of C.C.P. 1094.5(h) to all agency decisions under the Administrative Procedure Act when the agency "has adopted the proposed decision of the hearing officer in its entirety or has adopted the proposed decision but reduced the proposed penalty." (See 11 Pacific L. J. 356.)

On power of court to require a bond as a condition of a stay order, see Supp., infra, §233A.

[§233A]   (New) Court's Power To Require Bond.

C.C.P. 1094.5(f), relettered C.C.P. 1094.5(g) in 1978 (see Supp., supra, §219), does not call for a bond as a condition of a stay, but the court has inherent power to require it. (*Venice Canals Resident Home Owners Assn. v. Superior Court* (1977) 72 C.A.3d 675, 140 C.R. 361.)

In the *Venice Canals* case a regional coastal commission granted permits to build 24 single-family dwellings. Petitioners brought an administrative mandamus proceeding to review the decision, and sought a stay. The trial judge issued a stay order on condition that petitioners post a $50,000 bond to protect the rights of permitees who had already commenced construction. Petitioners then sought mandamus in the Court of Appeal to compel vacation of the bond requirement. *Held,* writ denied.

(1) The absence of a bond requirement in C.C.P. 1094.5(f) (now C.C.P. 1094.5(g)) cannot be deemed to give an absolute right to an unconditional stay. The trial court has inherent power to control litigation and prevent misuse of processes lawfully issued. (72 C.A.3d 679, 680, 140 C.R. 361, citing the text, *Courts,* §116.)

(2) The judge gave valid reasons for requiring a bond: The owners would suffer damage to uncompleted houses from the elements, and would also incur losses from delay and rising costs of construction. (72 C.A.3d 680, 683.)

(3) The governing statutes (Coastal Act; see 3 *Summary, Real Property,* Supp., §§39, 39A), in providing for legal remedies of aggrieved parties, make this distinction: (a) In an action to restrain threatened violation of the Act or to enforce affirmative duties

thereunder, a bond cannot be required. (b) In an action for judicial review of permits issued pursuant to the act, no such prohibition is made. (72 C.A.3d 681, 682.) The reason is clear: In the first situation the plaintiffs must promptly produce proof to support their charges. In the second, "plaintiffs can stall proceedings indefinitely until a record is produced from the administrative body which issued the permit." (72 C.A.3d 681.)

The court added that the indigency of one petitioner did not call for a waiver of the bond requirement under *Conover v. Hall (Actions,* Supp., §217A); there were several plaintiffs and no evidence was offered to show that the others could not furnish a bond. (72 C.A.3d 684.)

(b) [§235] Demurrer.

See *Carleson v. Unemp. Ins. App. Bd.* (1976) 64 C.A.3d 145, 150, 134 C.R. 278 [no dispute as to facts; *Sears, Roebuck* case distinguished].

(a) [§237] On Administrative Record.

(1) *In General.*

Hearing ordinarily based on administrative record: See *Transcentury Properties v. California* (1974) 41 C.A.3d 835, 842, 116 C.R. 487.

p. 3988:

(2) *Isolation Approach Discredited.* See *Ferreira v. Swoap* (1976) 62 C.A.3d 875, 882, 133 C.R. 449, citing *Bixby v. Pierno* and the text.

(1) [§238] Where Independent Judgment Rule Applies.

C.C.P. 1094.5(d) was relettered C.C.P. 1094.5(e) in 1978. (See Supp., supra, §219.)

In *California v. Superior Court* (1974) 12 C.3d 237, 257, 115 C.R. 497, 524 P.2d 1281, the court stated that C.C.P. 1094.5(d) (now C.C.P. 1094.5(e)) impliedly recognizes that a case may be *remanded to the agency for reconsideration* whether the independent judgment or the substantial evidence test are employed. This statement was misinterpreted in *Curtin v. Department of Motor Vehicles* (1981) 123 C.A.3d 481, 484, 176 C.R. 690, which cited *California v. Superior Court,* supra, for the statement that the court may admit the evidence *at the hearing on the writ without remanding the case* when either test is employed.

Court may remand to agency for reconsideration: See *Hand v. Board of Examiners* (1977) 66 C.A.3d 605, 614, 616, 136 C.R. 187.

Inadmissible evidence: In *Board of Dental Examiners v. Superior Court* (1976) 55 C.A.3d 811, 127 C.R. 865, the board revoked Dr. K's dental license. In the administrative mandamus proceeding, the trial judge granted Dr. K the right to take depositions of two board members and ordered a third member to answer questions previously put to him on deposition. *Held,* prohibition granted. The showing made by Dr. K's counsel—an information and belief allegation that the board considered evidence outside the administrative record—was based on pure speculation, and was insufficient to overcome the presumption of regularity of the proceeding. (55 C.A.3d 814.)

(New) Limited Discovery. Since C.C.P. 1094.5(d) (now C.C.P. 1094.5(e)) limits the admission of evidence in an administrative mandamus proceeding, it "necessarily restricts the scope of discovery in such [an] action." (*Fairfield v. Superior Court* (1975) 14 C.3d 768, 775, 122 C.R. 543, 537 P.2d 375 [prohibition issued to vacate order requiring councilmen to answer questions concerning their alleged bias and reasons for voting to deny application shopping center use permit].) "In an ordinary civil action, discovery is not limited to questions which may lead to admissible evidence, but includes inquiries relevant to the subject matter of the action which may be helpful in preparation for trial. . . . An administrative mandamus action, on the other hand, reviews the administrative record which should contain all evidence the parties consider necessary to the resolution of contested issues. Consequently posthearing discovery may reasonably be limited to inquiries calculated to yield evidence which through no fault of the offeror does not appear in the administrative record." (*Fairfield v. Superior Court,* supra, 14 C.3d 774, footnote 6.)

(New) Affidavits or declarations: Since presentation of evidence by affidavit is common practice in administrative hearings, C.C.P. 1094.5(e) (formerly 1094.5(d)) is statutory authority for the use of affidavits as direct evidence in administrative mandamus hearings in the superior court, subject to the rules on cross-examination and the prohibition against double hearsay. (*Windigo Mills v. Unemp. Ins. App. Bd.* (1979) 92 C.A.3d 586, 597, 598, 155 C.R. 63.)

(2) [§239] Where Substantial Evidence Rule Applies.

See *Mobil Oil Corp. v. Superior Court* (1976) 59 C.A.3d 293, 305, 306, 130 C.R. 814, where, after determining that the substantial evidence rule applied, the court nevertheless held that it was error for the trial judge to limit discovery.

C.C.P. 1094.5(d) was relettered C.C.P. 1094.5(e) in 1978. (See Supp., supra, §219.)

(a) [§240] Judgment Granting Relief.

C.C.P. 1094.5(e) was relettered C.C.P. 1094.5(f) in 1978. (See Supp., supra, §219.)

(1) *Direction That Decision Be Set Aside.* C.C.P. 1094.5(e) (now C.C.P. 1094.5(f)), authorizing the court to order the respondent to take such further action as is specially enjoined by law, supports an order that welfare benefits wrongfully denied be paid retroactively. (*Tripp v. Swoap* (1976) 17 C.3d 671, 677, 131 C.R. 789, 552 P.2d 749, Supp., supra, §176.)

p. 3990:

(2) *Direction To Reconsider Case.* Cannot control discretion: See *Jaffee v. Psychology Examining Com.* (1979) 92 C.A.3d 160, 169, 154 C.R. 687 [no power to compel board to issue professional license].

(b) [§241] Judgment Denying Relief.

The proceeding is terminated not by a mere minute order but by a judgment; and mandamus will lie to compel rendition and entry of such a judgment. (*Hadley v. Superior Court* (1972) 29 C.A.3d 389, 394, 105 C.R. 500.)

C.C.P. 1094.5(e) was relettered C.C.P. 1094.5(f) in 1978. (See Supp., supra, §219.)

(a) [§242] By Petitioner.

C.C.P. 1094.5(f) was relettered C.C.P. 1094.5(g) in 1978. (See Supp., supra, §219.)

On the more stringent rule for stay orders in some cases, see C.C.P. 1094.5(h), Supp., supra, §233.

(b) [§243] By Agency.

C.C.P. 1094.5(f) was relettered C.C.P. 1094.5(g) in 1978. (See Supp., supra, §219.)